Sex
and
Shopping

The Confessions of a
Nice Jewish Girl

Previous Publications by Judith Krantz

Scruples

Princess Daisy

Mistral's Daughter

I'll Take Manhattan

Till We Meet Again

Dazzle

Scruples Two

Lovers

Spring Collection

The Jewels of Tessa Kent

Sex and Shopping

The Confessions of a Nice Jewish Girl

An Autobiography

Judith Krantz

St. Martin's Press
New York

Design by Heidi Eriksen

ISBN 0-312-25196-3

First Edition: May 2000

10   9   8   7   6   5   4   3   2   1

This book is for the children who are
the future of my family:

*My grandchildren: Kate Mattie Krantz and
Michael Ryan Krantz.*

*Mimi's grandchildren: Adam Michael Guren,
Julie Valerie Guren, Matthew Tarcher Valji, and
Andrea Lauren Valji.*

Jeremy's grandson, James Abraham Tarcher Hood.

Sex
and
Shopping

The Confessions of a
Nice Jewish Girl

Chapter One

I PUSHED, DRAGGED, AND BUMPED MY HEAVY SUITCASE ALONG THE narrow corridor of the night train to Paris. I was so filled with the exhilaration of wild high spirits that I welcomed the challenge of finding a seat. Finally, in triumph, I wedged my luggage into an almost nonexistent slot I'd just noticed with the experienced eye of a veteran of the New York subway.

I was one of the last, amid the overflow crowd of other skiers, to find a place to sit for the long ride back to the Gare du Nord. The slowly moving train started to pick up speed and we were finally well under way, back from Megève, in the French Alps, where I'd just spent two weeks skiing. Twelve hours from now I'd be home, but I had twelve hours to pass with a blessed partition to lean against and a reassuringly bulky sandwich safe in the pocket of my ski parka.

Even if I'd been able to get a ticket in a compartment, I'd have been too blissfully excited to sleep this night anyway, I realized. Right now, at this very minute, it was still January 8, 1949, and I, Judy Tarcher, was only twenty years old. In just two hours, at the very first stroke of midnight, I would turn twenty-one. I would attain my legal majority, I'd be able to vote, I'd be allowed to drink in a bar without false I.D., I could get a driving license—at last, *at last* I'd officially be a grown-up! Tomorrow I was going to be given three birthday parties, and that wonderfully celebratory prospect made me giddy with anticipation as I looked around me, beaming in good humor at the prospect of a night in the packed, lurching corridor.

Dozens of skiers were settling down, already engrossed in newspapers or books. I'd been too busy in the station, struggling to balance my skis on my shoulder and manage my suitcase, to buy a new copy of *Paris Match* or *Elle*. But I'd spent what seemed like most of my lifetime reading, so I welcomed this opportunity to sit back quietly and think about where and whither and what next. I needed this time before I got back to Paris and the bewildering pace of my new existence there. I was living as a "paying guest" in the home of Nicole Bouchet de Fareins, a fascinatingly complicated divorced woman in her late thirties, with three teenaged daughters, and my life held daily surprises.

I knew I was being silly, but I was unable to stop myself as I opened my shoulder bag and fished out a little date book. Once more I checked tomorrow's date. Sunday, January 9, 1949. No, nothing had happened to change it in the two hours since I'd last looked.

As I tucked the book safely away, I realized that a middle-aged, well-nourished Frenchman was looking at me with barely disguised attention as he took a pull on his flask. He was close enough for me to smell the brandy and I imagined, in my heightened sense of self-awareness, that I could read his mind. A fresh young one, he'd probably be thinking, with childishly round pink cheeks, still far too young to be of any real interest yet not totally without a certain appeal. I knew perfectly well that my light brown hair and artless, fluffy bangs framed an ingenuous, innocent face. Petite as I was, this man would never believe I was as good as twenty-one. If he kept on staring, I flattered myself, he might eventually catalog what I considered my only features of distinction, a pouting lower lip that was much fuller than the upper one, and large, light gray-green eyes.

Of course he'd be able to tell with half a glance that there was no possibility that I was French. There was just something about me, I couldn't figure out what, that breathed American-ness. But perhaps, later on, when the train ride had come to seem unbearably long, he'd offer to share some of his brandy with me. Perhaps not. He'd certainly assume that I didn't speak enough French, if any, to offer any amusement.

Losing interest in trying to mind-read, I closed my eyes and returned to my own thoughts of the morrow and Nicole's welcome.

Ah, that Nicole, how she dominated my time in France, I mused. I was still incredulously happy that we'd finally become friends. I hadn't dared to imagine that such a thing could ever happen during those first miserable weeks in September when I'd arrived to live at her house once my family had returned to New York after our summer tour of Europe. For weeks she regarded me with unmistakable suspicion in her brilliantly dark and often frighteningly cold eyes. She'd been so unwelcoming that I realized only dire financial need had made her take me in. But, God almighty, I'd been so lucky to have landed at her house instead of at some proper French lady's.

Fascinating, mysterious undercurrents of intrigue, drama, and inside humor ran among Nicole, her two sisters, and the group of four or five young men in their twenties who dropped by almost every night for a drink and often stayed through a meager dinner that was rolled into the salon on a trolley and carefully served by the three younger girls and me. I was still unable to understand precisely why these eligible fellows came by so often, but I'd learned to accept them with pleasure.

But then every hour in Paris was a major learning experience, I reflected joyously, leaning back against the partition behind me, slumping as comfortably as possible and swaying with the rhythm of the train. I was learning at Nicole's, learning at my relatively new job in public relations, learning even through the laughter I provoked and the criticism I received.

Only a few months earlier, in October, I'd been thoroughly put in my place by Nicole and her sisters. I was just beginning to venture a few quavering, timid words of the language I was learning rapidly through total immersion, which was backed up by my three years of high-school French that consisted of barely remembered written drills in verbs and vocabulary.

After lunch, when Nicole's daughters had gone back to school, I was allowed to join her and her sisters, Francette and Anne, for a demitasse and a single, carefully chosen piece of the brown, roughly hewn lumps of sugar that were the only sweet thing ever offered in these postwar days of strict food rationing. I sat and listened to them chirp at each other, catching words here and there, and sometimes even the meaning of an entire sentence. It seemed to me that Francette, the youngest of the sisters, had said something highly disparaging about love, and in the silence that followed, I'd forced myself to formulate a phrase and finally managed to say that *"l'amour est très agréable."*

They'd turned on me, three enraged harpies, and informed me with vigorous disdain that no little American virgin had so much as the right to *speak* of love, to *dare* to have the slightest opinion, since, silly unformed creature that I was, I could know nothing whatsoever about love and would never know anything as long as I remained in my state of absurd, provincial, ridiculously infantile ignorance.

Oh, they had certainly let me know what they thought about me, I reflected, still a little miffed, but they'd also let the cat out of the bag. Now I realized that virginity, that utterly essential state, that precious condition that must be maintained at whatever price, was, amazingly, not as highly valued in France as it was in the United States.

I couldn't put my finger on when I'd first heard the word "virgin" or known what that meant, but for as long as I could remember, the worst thing you could say about a single girl was that she wasn't one. As far as I knew, the fearsome commandment to be a virgin until marriage cut across all religious lines, as much for Jews like me as for Protestants and Catholics.

A girl who lost her virginity, as far as my Wellesley classmates were concerned, was tarnished in the eyes of everyone who knew of this scandal. She'd severely compromised her chance of marrying the right kind of boy because her reputation was gone, and a girl's reputation . . . well, without a good reputation, what did it matter how popular or cute you were?

I gave up on this particular puzzle, and as the dizzying thought of my birthday returned to my mind, I opened my eyes and searched for my compact. I inspected myself carefully in the compact mirror. You're as good as you're going to get, I silently told my reflection, delighted by my high color, bright eyes, and shining hair. Two weeks of nothing but fresh air and physical effort had been a well-earned tonic after the often difficult months in Paris. I was on the alert every minute of every day, painfully poised at most moments so that I could swim in the unfamiliar waters of a French household and, recently, in a French office as well.

I was more than ready for my thrilling trio of birthday parties, I told myself, my heart beating fast at the thought. Nicole was planning a gala family lunch for me; John Cavanaugh, a couture design assistant and a new friend, was giving me a tea party; and Harrison Elliott, my Californian boss, was having a cocktail party for me, followed by a dinner with some of his former colleagues at Dior, where he'd been head of PR until he'd opened his own firm a year earlier.

I'd told my parents all about these dazzling prospects in the three weekly letters I wrote at their command, but since they rarely wrote back, I had no idea what they thought of my new world—a world that was still so beyond me in its sophistication that I was full of wonder that it had opened up to me at all.

I'd found a job in Paris, I thought with intense gratitude as I bought an orange drink from a vendor who was working his way though the train, and now my parents had to keep their promise to allow me to stay until next summer if I got work. They didn't know it yet, but I knew that I'd never go home. Whenever people asked me how long I was going to stay in Paris, I answered, "Forever!" My passion for the city only grew the more I knew it. As I thought of Paris, I felt that I was able to hold all of it cupped in my hands, a guarantee of constant joy, a discovery I'd been the first in the world to make, a treasure I was determined to possess forever.

I'd never been so happy in all my life! The only disappointment I had was that my birthday had fallen two months too late to vote for Harry Truman in the last election, and that mattered to me, an ardent Democrat. When Truman won, after I'd told everyone I knew to expect Dewey to become president, I'd lost all political credibility. The French blamed the whole upset on my personal lack of political savvy.

They were big on assigning blame, the French, I thought, my cheeks suddenly burning. Like that time, perhaps six or seven weeks earlier, when Hubert, one of the group who came for dinner, had had to spend the night at Nicole's because it was too foggy out to walk safely to the Métro. She'd delegated me to take him sheets and blankets and make up his bed on the big sofa in the salon. So okay, I'd let him kiss me a little, nothing worth speaking of—Hubert was a sweetie—and lo and behold, the next day Nicole all but handed me my walking papers. She was so angry that it took me half an hour to figure out what it was she was screaming about. Hubert had had a wet dream during the night and stained her sofa upholstery, and, of course, it was all my fault! I was, according to her, an *"allumeuse,"* a lighter of fires, as no honest woman would be. Worse, she'd accused me of being a *"demie-vièrge,"* the French expression for the worst kind of sexual tease, as far as I could figure out. All we'd done was a bit of necking, for heaven's sake, absolutely *nothing* compared to what went on during a Princeton football weekend, but try to explain that to a Frenchwoman in a flood of indignation.

Yes, I'd certainly changed worlds when I'd realized I had to live in France, I reflected. If I'd gone home as planned, I'd be dating the kind of Ivy League graduates who knew all the rules as well as I did, eligible boys at the beginning of successful careers in their fathers' businesses, rich, respectful, yearning, courting me like crazy. But here I was, three thousand miles away from my parents, from my native turf, from anyone who knew who Judy Tarcher was or what kind of family she came from—a year of anonymity, a year in which just to be me and find my wings.

I decided it was time to eat my sandwich. Seeing me unwrap my baguette filled with ham and cheese, my curious neighbor pulled out his flask and gestured hospitably at me. *"Voulez-vous en goûter un peu, Madame?"* he asked politely, but I pretended that I didn't speak French. "No, thank you." I smiled as nicely as possible, making a regretful but firmly negative face. Just one drink and I might be in for an all-night conversation, but I was determined to keep myself to myself. All this introspection was putting things into place in a way that hadn't happened since I'd first arrived.

Because I was living at Nicole's, I was meeting a bunch of French aristocrats totally unlike the guys I'd known at college. What exactly had I to expect from them? They were not remotely marriage material for a nice Jewish girl. Not, God forbid, that I wanted to marry! As far as I was concerned, marriage had always loomed as the gateway to slavery and I truly pitied the hordes of my classmates who'd rushed into it right after graduation.

But it was more than odd, I mused, that after four years of fending off men who'd wanted to marry me, here I was, a bare hour or so from turning twenty-one, without even a boyfriend in my life. On those occasions when we ate in a restaurant, we always went en masse, with Nicole as the centerpiece. She was a captivatingly seductive woman when she chose to be, with magnificent long dark hair she refused to cut in the new style, and those gorgeous legs that she knew so well how to display. Was it possible, I asked myself, almost choking on my ham and cheese, that I was too American to even be considered date material by boys who were only a few years older than I was?

No, damn it, that simply was not possible, I assured myself firmly. One of the few areas in which I had definite self-confidence was my ability to ensnare the opposite sex. I could hardly have lost it, could I, because of a difference of three thousand miles? Wasn't I still the girl who had thirteen dates with thirteen different men on thirteen consecutive nights last year at college? Hadn't there been an abortive movement, confined alas to my dorm, to vote me "Most Cuddly" when it came time for the class to vote on "Most Sophisticated," "Most Beautiful," and "Most Intellectual"?

I slumped lower and reflected deeply. Here I was, isolated by an entire ocean from any supervision by my parents or observation by anyone who knew them. Here I was, out of any possibility of contact with the world of eligible Jewish boys who could all find out something about me no matter where they were from, a world that I would most likely enter one day in the far-distant future when I would finally give in and get married. Here I was, free, private, safe from gossip, more independent than I'd ever been or would ever be again in my life. Here I was, old enough to *vote,* for Christ's sake, and I was wasting my evenings on a bunch of guys who didn't take me seriously.

I'd been alone in France four full months and eight days, and during all that time I'd only been kissed by Hubert. It was absurd, ridiculous, insane! I was legally in charge of myself and yet I was still clinging to my state of virginity in a country where being a virgin not only didn't seem crucial but was a sign of being immature, still a kid.

Suddenly I sat up straight on my suitcase, propelled by a conviction that abruptly pierced my mind. *Now that I was old enough to vote, I was old enough to lose my virginity.* I felt liberated from all the old constraints, the old taboos. I didn't understand the connection voting had with virginity, but I didn't need to. I was absolutely certain that one existed, as clearly as I was abruptly but totally liberated from all the old rules and fears that had guaranteed my virginity up until now. The time was right, I told myself, and if ever there was a place that was right, it was Paris. And nobody at home would ever know anything about it! It was the perfect opportunity! Yes, oh yes indeed, *I was going to sleep with the first man who asked me,* and that's a promise, Mr. President!

I felt as stunned as if I were newly born, as if I'd just opened my eyes on an entirely different world from the one I'd entered when I'd clambered onto the train. I was determined, positive, quivering with resolution, decisively aware that I had finally come to my senses, and I could barely wait to get back to Paris to set the wheels in motion. I didn't know how exactly, but now that I'd shed my old constraints, I'd be giving out different vibrations and someone would tune in to them.

Oh, this moment absolutely called for a toast, I thought, looking around at my portly neighbor. He was still awake, but deep in a magazine. I nudged him gently, smiled, and addressed him politely, reminding him of his earlier offer in the most fluent French I'd ever heard myself speak. He looked at me in astonishment, but quickly he smiled back and pulled out his flask, unscrewed a little metal cup, filled it, and handed it to me. I lifted the cup in his direction, but mentally directed the toast at myself. *"Merci mille fois, Monsieur. A votre santé,"* I said, and tossed the spirits down in one fiery, unfaltering gulp.

READER, THAT TRAIN trip took place fifty years ago. I realize that today few, if any, American girls of twenty-one would be so concerned with their virginity, but half a century ago, it had an importance too great to be measured. Looking back at the girl I was, to the girl whose emotions I still remember so vividly, to the girl who was poised on the brink of the happiest time of her life, to the girl whose innocence was intact in so many ways, to the girl who had never wept for a lost love, all I can say is, Weren't you lucky beyond words? And weren't you even luckier to be fully conscious and acutely aware of your luck as it unfolded?

Chapter Two

MANY AUTOBIOGRAPHIES BEGIN WITH A NOSTALGIC LOOK AT CHILD-hood and phrases like "It was always summer as one long blissful, bee-humming day followed another." Or else they start slowly, with a family tree that begins too many generations back from the subject of the autobiography. My childhood summers consisted, by and large, of frequent application of calamine lotion to endless cases of poison ivy, and my family tree is short. More than short, it's a downright twig. I don't even know my father's mother's maiden name, although I do know she was a scarlet woman whose very existence was never to be mentioned in front of him.

I'd rather make my second start at recording my life with the vivid memory of the first time I glimpsed the adult world in all its excitement and glamour. I must have been seven years old when my parents, Jack and Mickey Tarcher, decided that my sister, Mimi, and I were old enough to be taken out for our first evening event, a performance of Les Ballets Russes de Monte Carlo at Carnegie Hall. Mimi would have been five and a half. Our brother, Jeremy, only three, was, of course, left at home with our nurse.

The two of us, Mimi already taller than me, were dressed alike as usual. She wore a coral and white print smocked silk dress and I was in turquoise and white, both of us with patent-leather Mary Janes, white socks, and Buster Brown haircuts with bows in our hair. We were famously delicious-looking children, reader, as you will see for yourself from the pictures in this autobiography, and exceptionally well behaved. Or rather, I was well behaved and Mimi behaved when my mother was watching her.

I don't remember the ballet, but I have a clear-cut vision of the intermission. A friend of the family's, known to everyone simply as Joffe, loomed up as soon as the first half was over and commanded, "Judy and Mimi, come with me, I have a special treat for you." Joffe was Marian Anderson's manager and high in the organization of Sol Hurok, impresario of the Ballets Russes. I thought we might be going backstage, but instead, Joffe, that great, kindly, sweating bulk, escorted us to a box in the center of the first row of the balcony. With alarming formality he presented us to Mrs. Sara Delano Roosevelt, President Roosevelt's mother. No English child meeting the queen could have felt greater awe or a deeper sense of starstruck reverence than I did as I shook hands with this faintly smiling, shawl-draped grande dame who, unimaginably, was the mother of the only president who had ever existed for me, a godlike figure until his death ten years later in the spring of my freshman year at college.

"You're going to have to leave before the next half of the ballet," Mrs. Roosevelt said to us gravely, "and so am I. Do you know why? It's because you're too young and I'm too old."

After the intermission my parents took us next door to the Russian Tea Room, the first time we'd ever been out to a restaurant at night. Every one of the hundreds of times I've been there since has been colored by the rapturous excitement of that first evening.

A New Yorker, a born Democrat, the oldest of three children, the daughter of worldly and cultivated parents—so much at least can be deduced about me from this memory.

I was then in the third grade, but my school days had started long before, at the unusually young age of eighteen months, when my parents had sent me to the wildly experimental City and Country School, during the period when early childhood education was just becoming a subject for intense study.

My primary impressions of school were of block building, and even today I have a book that was published analyzing the various constructions we made, several of them mine. The most elaborate, ambitious, and indeed stunning construction of all I named merely, from lack of imagination or modesty, "A Decoration."

One other memory, however, is surprisingly vivid. One hot June day when I was two and a half, my teachers decided to let the class strip bare and frolic about on the roof of the school in streams of water sprayed from hoses. I immediately ran and hid in the terrifying closet in which the puppets were kept, until a search party discovered me an hour later. No boy was going to see me naked! The mere thought was an outrage from which I've still not entirely recovered. Didn't those teachers have any respect for my modesty?

Family legend has it that when strangers visited the City and Country School, they would spot me tranquilly looking at a picture book, seated on a chair in a world of my own, and comment favorably on my deportment. "She's a problem," my teacher would sigh. "*She's* a problem?" the visitor would ask. "What about all those other kids screaming and tearing out their hair and hitting each other?" "That's the problem, Judy's too well behaved" was the answer.

When I was born, my parents lived in a rented brownstone, 29 Fifth Avenue, a block from Washington Square Park in Greenwich Village. My father was a thriving advertising man who owned his own busy agency, J. D. Tarcher and Co. My mother, a future lawyer, had just received her M.A. in economics from Columbia.

In the fall of 1933, when I was five and a half, we moved uptown, to the St. Urban at 285 Central Park West, a picturesque, late Edwardian building. The massive twelve-story apartment house rejoiced in the possession of a porte cochere through which horses and carriages had been driven when it was built.

The family had left Greenwich Village so that I could start first grade—the youngest and the shortest in the class—at Birch Wathen, a small, private, co-ed school I attended for the next eleven years. I skipped my junior year of high school and graduated in 1944, at sixteen . . . still the youngest and the shortest in the class.

I had been accepted for first grade at Brearley, one of the five fashionably "right" New York schools for future debutantes, but my mother decided that an institution with a tiny Jewish quota might pose problems for me in years to come. Little Birch Wathen, however, had fallen on difficult days because of the Depression and those two Episcopalian maiden ladies, Miss Birch and Miss Wathen, who had formerly educated as few Jews as possible, had been forced to admit as many as they could to keep the school open.

The only Gentiles I remember in all my years there were the teachers and the scholarship kids, most of them boys since this co-ed school was overwhelmingly female. Nevertheless, we had chapel every Friday morning and a much-anticipated Christmas assembly at which Miss Birch would solemnly read us the story of the birth of Christ out of her own family Bible. Afterward we would sing a half dozen Christmas carols, which we'd been practicing for months, and then walk in a dignified manner, one by one, to the rather skimpy Christmas tree and be given a handshake and a candy cane. To this day I know all the words to all the verses of "Good King Wenceslas," and I love to sing "It Came Upon a Midnight Clear" when no one can hear me, since I can't carry a tune. But no sprinkling of spun-sugar Christianity, pretty as it was, had a chance to influence any of us, since we knew perfectly well that we were Jewish.

On the other hand, unlike the other girls in my class, I didn't receive any Jewish education either. My parents were both deeply involved in Jewish philanthropies, often spending four nights a week at various meetings, but, as completely secular Jews, they never felt any need to join a synagogue. One day, when Mimi and I were about seven and nine, my mother told us that she'd enrolled us in the Sunday school at the Spanish and Portuguese Synagogue just down the street. We came home howling with wrath and indignation after one incomprehensible session, during which, to add to our fury, the teachers had insisted on calling us by our full names, Judith and Miriam. "Well, girls, just don't ever complain that I never exposed you to religion," my mother said with a shrug, and that, thank God, was that.

We did go to one or two Passover Seders at the home of Fanny and Leonard Cohen, my parents' closest friends, who had been the only two witnesses at their City Hall wedding. Fanny and Len had been appointed official godparents to all three of us, a position I don't believe exists in Judaism, but my mother wanted to make sure that if she and Daddy died in an accident, they'd bring us up together. I still see the ruby red of the wine in my glass at Fanny's Seder table, I still remember how delicious it was, how I drank as much of it as I could and how I was carried to a bed, where I passed out cold.

I understand the need for religious conviction and I deeply envy those who have that amazing thing called "faith" for the comfort and support it gives them. My exercise teacher and devoted friend for the past twenty years, Diane Severino, was born Catholic and became a born-again Christian more than twenty years ago. She believes every last word in the Old and the New Testaments. Diane assures me that even if I wait until my deathbed to accept Christ as my personal savior, I'll go straight to heaven, as a "completed Jew." Otherwise, unfortunately, I'm doomed to hellfire, deeply fond as she is of me. She doesn't think this is in any way intolerant, merely an ultimate truth that faith has revealed to her.

But my masseuse, Darlene Jamen, is a former secular Jew who had a classic and documented near-death experience when she "drowned" for almost a half hour after a scuba diving accident. She found herself part of a gigantic, glowing, many-colored, marvelously singing crystal. She returned to her body reluctantly, thinking that she'd been expelled from heaven because of her bad spelling. Darlene assures me that I *am*, without question, going to heaven, no matter how little I believe in any religion or an afterlife. Also, she adds, Hitler will go to heaven too, although more slowly than the rest of us. She promises me that in heaven I'll be able to carry a tune. Between Diane and Darlene I can only laugh, throw up my hands, and wish them both the best of luck. If there is a heaven, I'll be there although my spelling too is all but nonexistent. Won't Diane be surprised? Won't *I* be surprised!

I have one more meaningful early memory. My brother, Jeremy, was born on January 2, 1932, almost exactly four years after I was. Soon Mimi and I watched him being diapered. I took one look at his penis and grasped, once and forever, the total conviction that he possessed something *better* than anything I had, something I wanted desperately and something I knew I'd never get. That baroquely curly plump little object was instantly desirable beyond any measure, although I didn't understand why.

Freud was wrong about a number of things, but for little Judy Tarcher, penis envy was as real as the computer I'm writing this on, except that I have a computer . . . two, in fact. Mimi, on the other hand, has no such feeling. Although she also remembers seeing Jeremy being diapered, she thought he was deformed in some way. So there you go . . . another set of different opinions. Maybe I *will* get to heaven and discover that there I have a penis! If I could be sure of this, I'd die happy.

I decided to write this autobiography in July 1998 when it finally occurred to me that I'd been seventy for six months. Good Lord, seventy! What, reader, could sound more definitive? Three score years and ten, that classically biblical age from which to look backward. I can't begin to feel that the number seventy refers to me, but simple math strongly suggests that a baby girl born on January 9, 1928, has a good chance of discovering that she's seventy in 1998. And, unlike Oscar Wilde, I've always been honest about my age, except for a short period right after I wrote my first novel. Wilde said, "I have never admitted that I am more than twenty-nine or thirty at the most. Twenty-nine when there are pink shades, thirty when there are not."

When I was sixty-nine I had no idea how pleased I'd be by seventy. It sounds damn impressive. You can't brush aside seventy until you're eighty. When I give someone advice, I now, albeit foolishly, expect a tiny bit of respect for the years that have supposedly brought me wisdom. However, whatever I've learned, I believe that no one ever fully grows up inside. You can mellow, yes, but total maturity doesn't exist. The great secret is that no adults have ever strode this planet, and neither Eleanor Roosevelt nor Georgia O'Keeffe ever woke up one morning and thought, "Today, right now, this very minute, I'm a one-hundred-percent grown-up."

Reader, try to think of me as going on thirty-six, without pink shades.

Private schools, a nurse, silk dresses, a trip to the ballet . . . it all sounds very privileged. And it was, especially in the depths of the Depression, but this is not the story of a future Marjorie Morningstar, this is the story of a Nice Jewish Girl Who Had Some Amazing Fun and Went Interestingly Askew.

Chapter Three

As American backgrounds go, mine is about as recent as you can get, unless you're an immigrant. My paternal grandfather, Ben, possessed a last name that was pronounced Tatachook, although I don't know how it was spelled. A cabinetmaker, he arrived at Ellis Island in the 1890s from some tiny settlement in Russia. He and his wife, Tilly, gravitated to Mott Street, then a teeming Jewish ghetto on the Lower East Side of Manhattan. There my father, named Jack David, the first of their children, was born in July 1896. Whenever I hear the lighthearted lyric "Oh, tell me what street compares to Mott Street in July," from Rodgers and Hart's ballad "Manhattan," I think of my grandmother giving birth in a mean, low-ceilinged room in a tiny tenement apartment during the tropical heat of a New York summer.

Soon it became evident that there was no future in cabinetmaking for Ben Tatachook, and he moved his family to Bergen County in New Jersey, where he ran a chicken farm as a tenant farmer. Two other children were born, Max and Bess. I have pictures of my father as a young farm boy, in overalls and a straw hat, sucking on a piece of hay. In later life he was never able to so much as look at a dead, unplucked chicken without gagging, and in a moment of self-revelation, so rare as to be astonishing, he told me that one of his farm jobs had been gathering the newly laid chicken eggs.

When my father was thirteen, tragedy and almost unthinkable scandal struck the family. Grandmother Tilly, who obviously had the passion and sense of adventure in the family, ran away with their landlord, one Mr. Janks, himself a married man with five children. She left behind her husband and all three children. At that time, in that particular culture of deeply Orthodox, totally rule-bound Jews, there could have been no worse scandal short of murder.

During my childhood my mother often warned the three of us never to ask my father any questions at all about his life because he had been so traumatized by his mother's abandonment that he didn't remember a single thing that had happened to him before this event. It was The Great Taboo of our life at home, but I've never had much faith in this case of amnesia. (I tend to think amnesia is reserved for shell shock and soap opera.) My father, a man of incredible aloofness, understandably didn't want to discuss his mother, just as he, *not* understandably, never allowed us children to discuss anything personal with him in his role as our father. The taboo of his childhood spread to include any wish for intimacy with his female children during his entire life as an adult. My brother, to my surprise and doubt, tells me that he felt able to talk to Daddy about most things, except baseball, which bored him.

Soon the chicken farm failed and hapless Grandfather Ben returned to Manhattan to open a newsstand, also doomed to fail. At sixteen my father left high school to go to work and support his family, as well as Ben's second wife, Bella, and two half brothers. Clearly dire poverty hadn't prevented Ben from being a marrying man, although there is some strong, unresolvable question about whether he and Tilly ever got a divorce and whether his "remarriage" was legal.

My father started out as an office boy in an advertising agency, emptying wastebaskets and sharpening pencils. In spite of his lack of a higher education, he turned out to be a born copywriter. By the time he was twenty-four, he and a partner had opened their own agency. Their first client was Smith Brothers' Cough Drops—"Trade" and "Mark," as the brothers were known—an American classic now long gone.

Daddy also revised his last name to the more easily pronounced Tarcher and the rest of his family followed suit. As far as I know, outside of our relatives, there is no one else in this entire country named Tarcher. While he was about it, why didn't Daddy, with all his copywriter's cleverness, pick a sturdy, familiar name like Westinghouse, I ask myself as, once again, I have to spell out "Tarcher." Judith Westinghouse? I'd buy a book by a woman with that name.

My mother wasn't born in the United States but in Vilna, in 1900. At that time this much-fought-over city temporarily belonged to Russia, which had seized it from Lithuania. Her father, Joe Brager, a tailor, came to America when she was one and a half, leaving her and his wife, Celia, behind. After he'd saved enough money for their tickets, he sent for them and they arrived when my mother was four. They settled in Williamsburg, Brooklyn, jammed with poor Jews.

Mommy's name, according to my birth certificate, written in my father's handwriting, was Michael, but that must have been an Americanized version of her real name, pronounced something like Mickel, which rhymes with nickel. On her mother's naturalization papers she was identified as Mollie, eleven years of age. But long before that, the Irish Catholic teachers in her public school decided that she looked too Irish to be a Mickel, and called her Mary, which became her legal name, although she was known, all of her life, as Mickey.

Mickey Tarcher was far from thoughtful when she picked my middle name. For many years I kept it well hidden, a deeply embarrassing secret. Reader, I know you understand that no little girl could admit to *Bluma-Gittel!* It means "pretty flower" in Yiddish, and my mother explained it by saying that she'd chosen it to please her own mother, a reason that cuts no ice with me.

When I had to give my middle name for my high-school diploma, I told the school that it was Beryl, although where I discovered this unusual and dated name is as much a mystery to me now as why I liked it then . . . or why I didn't pick Westinghouse. It certainly indicates an early attempt at a glamorous, up-market transformation. Viscountess Beryl sounds just right, very "Happy Valley."

By the time I graduated from college, I opted for plain Judith Tarcher on my diploma. When I needed my birth certificate to get a marriage license, I discovered that my middle name was registered as a simple, blunt Bluma. To me that sounds too much like "bloomer," as in underwear. Why did my mother mislead me until I was twenty-six? Now, after naming hundreds of characters in novels, I've learned to appreciate the quaint charm of Bluma-Gittel, which never fails to win a laugh.

Mickel-Mary-Mollie-Michael-Mickey learned English quickly, a language she spoke with elegant, eloquent, accentless precision, but she continued to speak to her parents in fluent Yiddish, of which my American-born father possessed only a few words. Four other children were born to Celia, of whom three survived, while my grandfather, described by my mother as a man who drank too much and had "unpredictable moods, all bad," struggled to make a living.

My mother, like my father, had to drop out of high school after one year, in her own words, "tearfully and tragically, no go, no shoes, no carfare." She once told me that the only way, in Williamsburg, to tell the *very,* very poor from very poor, was the ability to go to high school. She found out that she was a member of the poorest class when, at fourteen, she had to go to work in a candy factory, dipping cherries in chocolate, in order to contribute to the upkeep of the younger children. As soon as she'd saved enough money, she took a business course at night, and by the time she was sixteen, she was a qualified bookkeeper, stenographer, and typist.

Brilliant, hardworking, indomitable Mickey Brager had huge ambition and she moved, without losing a single day's pay, to half a dozen jobs in the course of the next seven years, eventually earning the sum, amazingly large for 1924, of forty dollars a week. At night she took high-school courses.

For decades I demanded an account of her life. She was a woman who hated to put words on paper, and when I rebelled at never getting any letters from her during four years at college, where, as in Paris, I dutifully wrote home three times a week, she finally sent me a letter that said only, "You know how I dislike writing letters, please don't ask for them." However, I persisted in wanting her history, and eventually she grudgingly wrote four pages of graceful prose.

"I attended lectures," she remembered of this working period of her life. "I stayed up into the morning hours talking, discussing, arguing, criticizing, admiring, and growing. I grew away from Brooklyn, all my waking hours were spent in Manhattan and at twenty-one I moved to Manhattan, where I shared an apartment with another girl." Her parents put up no obstacles to this move, excessively rare for an unmarried girl of that period, because they realized it would do them no good, and in any case, her success so amazed them that they felt no right to meddle in her life.

Not long afterward, my mother met my father and they began to live together sometime in 1923. On October 27, 1924, they went to City Hall and got married. They were such different types that they made an interesting and most attractive couple. My mother was enchanting looking, tiny and graceful, five feet one inch at a generous estimate, a flapper dancing out of a novel by F. Scott Fitzgerald. Her short, fine brown hair was cut close to her beautifully shaped skull in a perfect Vidal Sassoon style, and her bangs reached almost to her carefully plucked and penciled eyebrows. She had a small straight nose, large gray eyes, and a particularly dainty mouth. Daddy was well over five feet ten inches tall, round of face, with a hairline that had already receded as far as it ever would, and big glasses he wore at all times. His look, which never changed as he grew older, was of a wise, thoughtful, benign Buddha. He had a sudden, rare smile that transformed his serene, serious features, although his general aspect was calm and introspective. He had a strong resemblance to the immortal Benny Goodman.

From the minute of her marriage my mother's life was transformed. It was a classic Cinderella story. Daddy's advertising agency was growing quickly, he'd bought out his partner, and he immediately liberated her from all care.

"Do whatever you want to do with your life, Mickey," he told her. Within a month she had entered college at New York University, still shy of one high-school credit. Marriage freed my mother to get a formal education, something my father never had the time to do, although few men were ever more thoroughly self-educated through books. My most familiar image of my father is of him sitting patiently by the front door, coat already on, hat on the console table nearby, engrossed in a book while my mother finished dressing to go out for the evening. If it had taken her two hours longer, he wouldn't have noticed or minded.

In her account of her first four years of marriage, my mother wrote, "I had everything. I had love, comfort, history, economics, and philosophy. My youthful intuitions and emotions were being intellectually validated, my aesthetic expression gratified." At least she put love first.

My mother was to prove a whiz at academics and a genius at family planning. "I never got pregnant when I didn't want to," she told me proudly, "and I always got pregnant when I did."

I was born on an extended Christmas vacation during her senior year in college and was promptly handed over to a German nurse named Mrs. Glentz while the new mother returned to class and graduated that June. My sister, Mimi, was born seventeen months later, the following June, in 1929, during a summer that promised Mommy a few months of leisure for childbearing as she waited impatiently for the next school year to begin so that she could start her graduate studies in economics at Columbia University. My brother, Jeremy, was born in 1932 during yet another Christmas vacation, just before my mother began to write her master's thesis.

In 1934, after ten years of marriage, my energetic mother had garnered two college degrees and three children whose ages ranged from two to six. She chose that presumably idle and unoccupied moment to enter Teachers College, planning to earn a doctorate in education. Soon she decided that she didn't have the patience to become a teacher—an accurate and most fortunate decision for generations of schoolchildren—so she enrolled in NYU Law School instead.

It was too early in history for Mickey Tarcher to have heard of the quaint notion of spending "quality time" with her children. Rather, as she put it, "I would defend the poor, civil liberties, and the right in all things."

My mother stuck to this idealistic creed most of her life. She started her political life as a Young Socialist, and later helped found the Liberal Party in New York with labor leader David Dubinsky, because the Democrats weren't liberal enough for her. She even ran for City Council on the Liberal Party line in the 1940s, and although she lost, she drew more votes than any third-party candidate ever had on the strongly Democratic West Side of Manhattan. However, she cast her last vote for Richard Nixon! This is a family disgrace no one can begin to understand or explain, except that she had become fanatically anti-Communist.

Our family life was dominated by two things: my father's remoteness and my mother's strength. All of his life, the instant Daddy heard a voice raised in anger, or even momentary irritation, he silently got up and left the room, going to his bedroom, where he immediately lost himself in a book. This reaction was particularly impressive and effective during a family dinner.

My father's attitude had the effect of leaving all the power of running the family in my mother's far-from-unwilling hands. It was she who decided which one of us was right or wrong in all disputes, she who meted out punishments and rewards, she who picked our schools, she who decreed if our allowances could be raised from a dime to fifteen cents, she who ran every detail in our daily lives. She was all three branches of our family government. There was no court of appeals.

I HAVE NEVER known a more enigmatic man than my father. This normally silent parent was famous in the world of Jewish philanthropy for his verbal ability and was such an irresistibly effective fund-raiser that he was in demand to speak at charity functions dozens of times a year. He was rarely at home after dinner during the fund-raising season, and my mother was away as well, on her own philanthropic rounds, working particularly hard for HIAS, an organization devoted to helping immigrant Jews get settled in the United States. As they were entirely secular Jews, this unceasing activity was obviously my parents' form of expressing a spiritual feeling they didn't have, and a superb substitute in my opinion.

At any party at our house Daddy would be surrounded by an admiring and devoted circle of women who literally sat at his feet and listened to him discourse for hours on intellectual topics while their husbands huddled together, speaking of worldly matters. Every time he wanted to go to a performance of foreign dance or song—Ravi Shankar, the great Indian master of the sitar, and the Don Cossack Choir were among his favorites—evenings that held no interest for my nonfolkloric mother, he took one of the family's female friends, his "harem," as we called them.

When I worked for him at summer jobs during my years in high school, I was stunned to discover that my father's personality changed entirely at the office. He became a man I hadn't guessed existed, whose voice I'd never heard. J. D. Tarcher was an enormously dynamic, hands-on, effective, and respected tiger of a boss who kept a keen, controlling eye on his many employees, dominated large meetings, commanded every bit of his employees' attention and admiration, and was brimming with original ideas.

Yet at home my father detached himself from the vital life of the family as completely as if he'd been a boarder who paid only for meals and a roof over his head. I remember having only one single private conversation with him during my entire childhood. I was frightened by noises in the night, and Daddy sat by my bed and explained why wood makes sounds as it expands and contracts over a twenty-four-hour period. Scientific truth was the single subject he was willing to broach, one-on-one. The only words of parental advice my father ever gave me were "Nothing is ever lost. Look under things." It's magic. I've found my glasses or keys hundreds of times under absolutely flat sheets of paper. What else might he have told me, what other charms did he know?

Somehow all three of us were resolutely convinced that Daddy loved us a great deal but couldn't possibly, for reasons that were beyond our understanding, express that love. On the other hand, although none of us can remember him getting angry, we all treated him like a barely dormant volcano. We sensed, in the intuitive way of sensitive children, that there was some inexplicable rage simmering inside of him. In fact, my sister was convinced that he was a werewolf when he was out of sight and always made a warning noise to alert him to her approach so that he'd have time to turn back into himself again. I had no such elaborate fantasy. I was simply convinced that if he ever got angry at me, the world would end.

My mother, on the other hand, was angry a great deal of the time, and badly made beds or messy closets would earn us a tirade. We were punished by being denied our favorite radio program—we were only allowed an hour or two of radio on weekends—or being deprived of a week's allowance, nothing worse, but the tongue-lashing that accompanied our crimes left a lasting impression.

However, even though it was often on the level of annoyance, she interacted with us in a way my father never did. We always knew we had a mother who was watching us, ready to jump in and give us direction, and who, when she was feeling especially affectionate, would insist that we sit on her lap, even when we were bigger than she was, something my father never suggested. His only approach to being physically close was to read us the comics before we were old enough to read them ourselves, sitting on the living room sofa, flanked by Mimi and me.

My mother gave us two pieces of direct advice along with the vast amount of indirect influence she exercised. "Never marry a man who smokes a cigar, it's the world's most disgusting habit," she said, adding, "All greens go together in decorating, but never, ever use turquoise anywhere." I dearly love a touch of turquoise in the pottery called majolica that I collect, and all greens do not go together, except in nature. Chartreuse and kelly? But she was not too far wrong about the cigar.

THE HAPPIEST ASPECT of our childhood rested on the fact that Daddy possessed a strong love of art and teaching, which led him to break out of his shell on certain weekends and take us, from time to time, to all of New York's art museums, to the Cloisters, to the planetarium and the aquarium, trips my mother preferred to miss, happy to stay at home and read in peace.

My father was an enthusiastic and patient teacher who enjoyed being with us in that capacity. We went to Jones Beach and Palisades Park and many times to the World's Fair of 1939. There, in the British Pavilion, I flung myself on the deliciously rich-smelling carpet of the backseat of a Rolls-Royce. Home! Home at last! I knew immediately that nothing could be better than this scent and I clung to the carpet, sniffing passionately, refusing to leave the car, until I was bodily removed by my feet.

When we went to visit the shantytown in Central Park where the homeless of the Great Depression had built themselves tiny shelters, I was impressed by the misery, but, frivolous even then, I was captivated by one hut made entirely out of mirrors. I remember circling it and admiring myself in all the glittering fragments. The most memorable of the excursions we all made was down to Mott Street to see the tenement in which Daddy had been born, a trip made permanently marvelous to me by my first, eye-popping taste of a dill pickle out of a barrel. I wrote my English College Board essay on that event, with triumphant results.

My remote and mysterious father was also a dapper man whose expensive, conservative suits were all made to measure by the best tailors in New York. His shirts, pajamas, and underwear were always custom made at Sulka. He never left the house without three hundred dollars in crisp bills in his pocket, a very large sum at that time. Daddy didn't bet on the horses or play cards, nor was he a fabulous tipper, but he always walked around town feeling rich, a pleasure no doubt enjoyed in memory of the boy who had once sharpened pencils at sixteen. The Depression hadn't affected my father's agency, since people always had to advertise or go under. On the other hand, he wasn't interested in making money with his money and he left all investment decisions and art purchases to my mother, with a single startling exception.

One night at dinner, sometime in the mid-1930s, he mentioned calmly that he'd been out all day looking for a country house to buy— we'd always rented in the summer—and had already completed the purchase of a house, called Connemara by its Irish owners. It was on the top of a hill surrounded by fifteen heavily wooded acres on the edge of Fairfield County in North Stamford, Connecticut. My mother knew nothing about this until he spoke, and as soon as he sprang his surprise, she jumped up without a word and left the table.

We children were too young to speculate on what had happened between them to make Daddy act so entirely out of character. In retrospect, obviously my parents must have had a memorable fight and this was his—unforgettable—way of reasserting his authority. For many years Connemara was the center of our family weekends and summers. It was there that my father's large, traditional birthday party was always celebrated, there that he lost himself in making new vistas in the woods by judiciously selecting trees to be cut down, there that he gardened by the hour.

I'm certain that all those years my mother hated and resented the house without anyone knowing it. Only a day or two after my father's death, some twenty-five years later, without a second thought, she sold the large, beautiful house and every last item of its expensive contents to the first person who made an offer, a ridiculously low one, as we all knew. She sent my father's desk, crammed full of albums filled with family photos he'd taken over the years, to Janet Robertson, Fanny and Len's daughter, without bothering to remove a single picture, and she left, at Connemara, all the hundreds of cans of movie film he had taken of us as children. How could this behavior not have meant a long and well-hidden disturbance in their marriage?

My father loved to eat costly and exotic food and never looked at prices in restaurants, which infuriated my mother. However, if she registered an objection, he had only to say "Mickey" in a certain low tone of voice, to shut her up. In his own, totally discreet way, he was the hushed, undemonstrative, effective force who set the tone of the family's emotional climate, permitting my mother total authority until he took it back with a single word.

The more I think about their outwardly unremarkable marriage of thirty-three years, the more fascinatingly complex it seems. Once, when I was about seven, I woke up from a nightmare and sought them out in the living room, where they were still up talking. I padded silently down the hall and stopped outside in my bare feet. Standing there, I heard something about "no divorce" and the phrase "probably better for the children," but that's all I remember hearing before I hurried back to bed, too frightened to cry.

For all I know now, they may have been talking about friends, but it didn't sound that way. I worried, secretly and obsessively, about the possibility of divorce for many years, not daring to tell Mimi what I'd overheard because I was afraid to frighten her. Slowly, as we all got older, I grew out of the idea that it was a possibility and my parents stayed married and seemingly compatible for thirty-three years, until Daddy's early death, from an inoperable brain tumor, in 1962.

In his will he left a quarter of a million dollars to a stranger, in Philadelphia, where he had often spent time because one of his clients, Schenley Distillers, was based there. His half brother Uncle Len, who worked for my father, was executor of his will, and Len refused to reveal a single word about the identity of the stranger. Surely it must have been left to a lady friend, and since it was such a large sum, she must have had a child to support.

After glimpsing the tip of the iceberg in Daddy's will, I've gradually become aware that my father had at least three other long-lasting relationships with other women, all of them "friends of the family," one of them the woman who had introduced him to my mother. After my mother's death, Fanny Cohen, who was exceptionally close to Mimi, revealed that these infidelities first started between the birth of Mimi and Jeremy and deeply embittered my mother.

The women involved, and I knew them all, were lusty, busty, loud, humorous, life-loving, adventurous, and divorced, or between husbands. I had long disliked them all without ever knowing why. They were the opposite of my fastidious, exquisitely groomed, delicate ramrod of a mother, who, for all her good looks, was not a sexy woman.

Why did my mother put up with a situation she was far too smart not to have known about? First, I believe she loved my father deeply and knew, in spite of everything, that he loved her. Also she needed to maintain the status quo to ensure the stability of our lives and her own career, so that she could follow her urgent needs to study and work, lavishly supported by my father. Divorce was not the easy option then that it is now, and I'm sure both of them would have done almost anything to avoid it. For thirty-three years they preserved the facade of a happy marriage.

Obviously Daddy was too intelligent not to know that there was something deeply troubled in his life. He visited twenty-six different psychoanalysts. Once. He never returned to any of them for a second visit, but he read widely in psychoanalytic literature, hoping for a do-it-yourself cure. Alas, it doesn't work that way.

IN ALL FAIRNESS, as much as I suffered from not being able to talk to my father, he was capable of showing me love and pride through an unexpected gesture. For example, when I went on my first trip away from home, sailing overnight on the Hudson River Line to visit a school friend, he came to see the two of us off at the dock, carrying big bouquets of flowers for us. On the night of my first high-school prom he sent me flowers although my date had already sent me a corsage. I wore my date's camellia on my shoulder and my father's flowers on my wrist. Several years later, when I wrote my first published article, called "Love, Life, and Lipstick," for a little magazine published by one of my father's clients, he had it beautifully bound in leather with the check for my first earnings, fifteen dollars, carefully inlaid on the inside cover.

He created other charming and celebratory family occasions. On the first date my parents had, my father took my mother to Voisin, which was then far and away the most elegant and expensive French restaurant in New York. Even Le Pavillon, at its height, never reached the position occupied by Voisin. My mother ordered a chicken sandwich, the most elaborate lunch she could then imagine.

On their twenty-fifth wedding anniversary, the whole family went to Voisin for dinner and, as soon as we were seated, the headwaiter brought out an enormous silver platter covered with a silver dome. Ceremoniously he placed it in front of my mother and raised the dome to reveal a miniature chicken sandwich, after which my father gave us each twenty-five silver dollars to commemorate the occasion.

Daddy had a great feeling for the giving of pleasure, for celebration, which we all three inherited to varying degrees, something we could never have learned from my severely disciplined and deeply thrifty mother.

Yet, in spite of the delightful picture of their twenty-fifth anniversary, in spite of the fact that we all basically believed that our parents were happily married, long before my parents' relationship concerned us, we had been the victims of severe damage done in the name of enlightened child rearing.

The three of us were all born in an era during which a great many educated women, like my mother, had read books by an evil damned devil named Doctor Watson, who conned them into believing that any loving attention given to infants would spoil them for life. He recommended kissing babies only while they were asleep, on the backs of their necks, or better still, giving them a "sturdy handshake." According to Watson, infants, from the very instant of birth, were ultimate masters of manipulation and blackmail, who must be *broken* for their own good, the pediatric equivalent of burning down the village to save it.

We were all put on a strict four-hour feeding schedule, and if we got hungry sooner, too damn bad. If we fussed or screamed for affection or amusement while we lay bored in our cribs, at a period when there wasn't even a Calder mobile overhead, we were checked for open safety pins and wet diapers. If neither was found, we were immediately put back in our cribs and left strictly alone so that we would learn that it didn't do us the slightest good to "act up." I'm intuitively sure we were kissed and hugged more than Dr. Watson would have approved, but the fact remains that my mother leaned on Watson the way a later generation leaned on Spock. It suited her fundamentally Puritan character. From our very earliest moments of existence we were trained to expect a basic climate of emotional dryness and very little contact with our mother. We were not, of course, aware of anything odd about this until we grew much older. For many years I've wondered how it permanently limited our capacity to fully experience emotion. It's ultimately completely unknowable. It was the most horrifyingly *inhuman* and cruel period of child raising in modern times. Better we should have been sent out to live with a wet nurse in the countryside, as the French aristocrats did with their high-born brats! Now when I see my niece, Mallory, and her five-month-old son, Jamie, in complete contact and loving accord whenever he's awake, I realize what a blissfully close, warm, tactile, emotionally fulfilled childhood must be like and how it must lead to a happier child and happier adult.

We even had metal mittens strapped over the thumbs we sucked for solace. I have the most extraordinarily sharp, almost immediate memory of ultimate, elemental fury when I first discovered that the cold metal of a mitten had replaced my warm flesh. I erupted, positively *exploded,* in the greatest madness of my life—I have never been so angry since—until someone just couldn't endure my shrieking and gave me back my thumb. On reflection, this was the very first memory of my life . . . frustration and rage, but, thank God, not helplessness or docility.

Chapter Four

AS WE THREE GREW OLDER, FOR A SHORT PERIOD EACH EVENING, AF-
ter our dinner and our baths, our parents sent for us and played quietly
with us, for all the world as if they were high-born Brits. Soon a
German nurse arrived to put us to bed. In later years, when there were
guests, my mother had only to catch my eye and say, "Good night,
children," for us to immediately go around the room, give everybody
a kiss, and vanish without protest. We were famous in my parents'
circle for our obedience—three heavenly "show-and-tell" children—
but we were, of course, far too well-trained, and each of us has racked
up many years of psychoanalysis to prove it.

While my mother was running amok through the fields of higher
education, the strict German nurses she hired must certainly have approved heartily of our discipline. My mother often told me with pride
that I was entirely toilet-trained by eleven months.

There should have been a warning attached to this accomplishment:
DO NOT TRY THIS AT HOME. I had no choice but to turn out to be
severely controlled in most areas of my life. Reader, I am a control
freak, not of others, but of myself and my surroundings. (Is that a dead
flower in a vase? Can I possibly force myself to ignore it and keep on
with dinner? No, unless I'm a guest at someone else's table.) Being
psychoanalyzed only helps a little with a pattern set so early that it
was hardwired into my personality. To this day, for example, I can't
allow myself to be a single minute late for anything. I've spent a good
part of my life waiting for people who had the lucky freedom of not
being toilet-trained before their first birthday.

Actually I did have a choice, I've just realized. I could have reacted
like Mimi, who rebelled in a multitude of ways. It simply never occurred to me, pathetically good little girl that I was.

However, during the 1930s my mother was widely admired for her
ability to "do everything" and to "have it all," and no one, least of
all she, questioned the fact that her children were brought up by ser-
vants. That was the culture of the times and I don't blame her for it
at all. Working women are always at the mercy of whatever is politically correct during their careers, and my mother was lucky to be guilt-
free.

By the time we moved to the St. Urban, there were five people who enabled my mother to accomplish so much: a live-in nurse, a live-in married couple who worked as cook and butler-driver, a cleaning woman who came in five days a week, and a daily laundress. All of these people together, in those days, cost only a tiny percentage of what they'd be paid today.

Our apartment was very large, a full half of the sixth floor, with an enormous living room. Two bay windows facing Central Park provided splendid views of the reservoir, most of Fifth Avenue, and at least half of Central Park South. My parents each had their own room, which also faced the park. They never shared a room since my father's snoring was so outrageously loud that no one could have slept through it. When they traveled, if by some error there weren't two bedrooms for them in a hotel, my father slept, uncomplainingly, curled up in the tub. He could, and often did, sleep standing up or with his eyes wide open during a dinner party, but in that position he didn't snore.

There was a big pantry and vast kitchen with its own delivery elevator, which would star in hundreds of my worst nightmares. The iceman appeared each day, bearing a huge chunk of ice on his shoulders for the icebox. *Icebox*. Now, there's a good, solid word for you. Often I forget to say "fridge" and say "icebox." It's so deliciously dated it might just come back into style.

At the far end of the apartment lay the vast room that Mimi and I shared, with big windows, from which we had an uninterrupted view of the Hudson River and the Palisades and the sunsets beyond.

The apartment was decorated in a modified, muted Art Deco style by the celebrated book designer Lucien Bernhardt, who had just revamped the jackets of all the Modern Library books. Indirect lighting shone softly through the opaque glass of lowered ceilings; built-in bookcases, cabinets, and closets were everywhere, fashioned from curved and painted wood; the color scheme was subtle, moss greens, beiges, and dull rose, with grass cloth used on many of the walls. There were no printed fabrics or wallpapers anywhere. (I, in reaction, decorate with a multitude of patterns, vivid colors, and details overlaid by details.)

My parents had accumulated a fine collection of Chinese ceramics, a great many rare art books, and a collection of paintings my mother bought for very little money at auction at Parke-Bernet: Renoir, Degas, Soutine, Modigliani, Pasquin, Marie Laurencin, and their favorites, the Mexicans, Diego Rivera and Orozco. (When I asked her once why she hadn't bought more paintings, at the low Depression prices, she shut me up effectively with the excellent question "Why didn't I buy IBM?") A basement laundry and a corps of doormen and elevator men completed the important parts of the St. Urban, where I was to live until I was twenty-four.

Mickey Tarcher, at thirty-one, had come a long way from that desolate but determined fifteen-year-old laboring in a candy factory, but she ran the house perfectly and entertained often and easily.

On New Year's Eve my parents gave such big black-tie parties that they had to use the entire apartment. Mimi and I were allowed to stay up until the party was over, since our bedroom was used for a second buffet and a second bar. Often they entertained their friends with performances by the great folksingers Pete Seeger, Josh White, Burl Ives, and Woody Guthrie. These picturesque and roughly clad men out of another world strummed their guitars and sang of hard times and revolution. I felt distinctly shy and uncomfortable listening from my corner, because I fretted that the performers would feel as if they were being condescended to, when, in reality, they were probably glad for the well-paid bourgeois gig. My father had the greatest, almost wistful, admiration and respect for these legendary figures and helped to support Burl Ives for years. I think I can claim that my parents had an inclination toward Radical Chic before it turned really radical.

The parade of nurses has left surprising few memories. One, whom Mimi and I hated in particular, terrified us by rushing into our bedroom and hysterically shrieking out all the details of the burning of the Hindenburg airship as she had just heard it over the radio. Her name was Clara and she was gone the next day.

Another, the only one we ever liked, was a gentle refugee from Hitler named Irna. She sewed dresses for a tiny doll I owned, giving me the most intense delight. I've always suspected that if there had been a Barbie doll when I was small, and I'd had a lot of them, I'd be a totally different person and might never have felt the need to accomplish anything. Or perhaps I'd have become another Donna Karan? Irna found her reward in marriage to a prosperous dentist. The nurses remained until Jeremy was six and I was ten and my mother decided she could do without them although she'd just passed the Bar. From that time, on, the three of us were allowed to eat dinner with my parents, instead of at the table at one end of our bedroom.

For many years, nurse or no nurse, I was beset by a terror of kidnappers. It was the time of the trial of the kidnapper of the Lindbergh baby, reported in gruesome detail in the newspapers, especially that coveted and forbidden tabloid, the *Daily News,* which the cook secretly saved for me. I was convinced that Mimi and I would be next. It became my self-appointed duty to stay awake to sound the alarm while she slept calmly.

I tried to reason with myself. We lived on the sixth floor of a twelve-story building, and it seemed impossible for the kidnappers to come down from the roof or up from the street. But I had no success. This early notion, which I was too ashamed to mention to anyone, set the stage for insomnia that began seriously after the birth of Nick, my first son, forty-two years ago, when I'd get up often in the middle of the night to make sure he was still breathing. I've only recently semi-conquered it through hypnotherapy.

Once we had been admitted into the dining room, we became the unprotesting subjects of my father's nightly vocabulary tests, for he believed that a large vocabulary was one of the roads to success. He also emerged from his silence to enthrall us with science, another of his deepest interests, particularly the cosmos, the vastness of it, and the amazing smallness of the Milky Way, much less that utterly insignificant planet, Earth. The atom was another of his fascinations, as were extrasensory perception and poltergeists. Daddy may have stopped many interesting arguments, saying that we weren't allowed to fight over something we could look up in a dictionary or book of reference, but he gave us the great gift of intellectual curiosity and, unlike most fathers of that era, he discussed adult subjects.

Although my father knew so much about a variety of things, remembering people's names was almost impossible for him. We were all trained from childhood to pretend that we weren't with him if he met someone he knew and didn't immediately introduce us. Once, in my twenties, riding on a bus with him, he fell into conversation with an acquaintance whose name he'd clearly forgotten. I stared out of the window for blocks and blocks. Finally I risked a peek at my father and noticed that his tie was crooked. I automatically reached over, adjusted it carefully, and returned to my silent contemplation of the passing sidewalks. No one said a word. I still wonder what that man must have thought.

My mother, unwittingly, managed to steer us all away from the legal profession with detailed, always sad stories of the penniless people she'd helped. By that time she had started to work as an unpaid volunteer in the Civil Branch of the Legal Aid Society. Eventually she decided that the only way to be taken seriously was to be on salary. Eventually she rose to the position of attorney in charge, supervising one hundred twenty lawyers. When she reached the mandatory retirement age of seventy, it took two years before they were able to find two men with whom to replace her.

Mickey Tarcher was a magnificent role model in many ways, but as a mother, she was distinctly, even tragically, miscast. She had very little natural maternal instinct, and what she had, she used up on me, a mixed blessing, as I was to find out.

I was the firstborn, I looked very much like her, and she never even tried to make the smallest attempt to hide the fact that I was her undisputed favorite, a much criticized favorite but nevertheless the one she loved best. When Mimi and I were in our forties, she actually tried to explain this to us as logically as she could. "When you've seen one child learn to walk and talk, how interesting can it be to watch another do the same thing?" Yes, those were her very words, and totally unapologetic. She would have agreed with Spiro Agnew about ghettos.

The modern ideal of "unconditional love" would have seemed absurd to my mother. She loved a good child for its goodness, a performing child for its performance. Love was a *reward,* something you earned and had to keep on earning at all times.

Although being loved first and best gave me certain advantages in emotional survival, it had a strong downside. My mother regarded me as an extension of herself, like an arm. There was nothing I could or should be allowed to do or possess unless she could also do it or possess it. In this difficult aspect of her love, she was like an envious older sibling, not a proud mother.

She felt this way all her life and extended it to one of her grandchildren. When Aliza, Mimi's elder daughter, graduated from Harvard Law School, my mother sat watching the ceremony in a raging fury. "If I'd had her advantages," she told Mimi, fiercely, "I'd have been president!"

After I wrote *Scruples* she was puzzled by many things, but in particular by the fact that I had an imagination. "When I was young, I never had any imagination," she complained to me. "Why not?" I asked. "I was too poor" was the serious answer of this otherwise deeply intelligent woman. She had, it should be obvious by now, no sense of humor.

Her common expression, famous in the family, was "The trouble with you, Judy, is . . . ," followed by whatever fault she had just discovered in my character. (Favorite or not, she wasn't blind to my deficiencies.) Once my brother told me, "The trouble with you, Judy, is you're too goolable." "I thought that was pronounced 'gullible,' " I answered, until he began to roar with laughter and I realized the trap I'd fallen into.

She and Mimi lived in a state of constant battle. Mommy insisted that Mimi had bitten her while being breast-fed and caused an abscess, thus announcing her future troublemaking nature. I was the lifelong, self-appointed peacemaker between the two of them, as well as my sister's protector in all things, a veritable Madeleine Albright, running from one of them to the other to get them to agree on terms that would permit them to make up their most recent fight. I pointed out that a newborn doesn't have teeth, but she was never convinced that Mimi's chomping hadn't been deliberate.

Mimi, who had been an adorably pretty child, soon grew into a lovely girl. She looked, for a long time, like a Modigliani without the strangeness. She had a long neck, a long straight nose, an oval face, and fascinating eyes that almost disappeared when she laughed. She was slender, with abundant, shoulder-length brown hair, a gorgeous figure, and great legs, and she was at least five feet six inches tall, almost a goddess compared to my mother and me.

Although she really would have had a miserable life without my good offices, Mimi repaid me with blackmail. For years I was terrorized by her. I'd used an English copy of a French book we were assigned in school for my translation homework and she held the threat of telling our parents about *Emil and the Detectives* over me for at least three years, until I finally threw the incriminating book out of the window and told her to tell and be damned.

Until that moment, I had to make her bed, do her chores, jump to her command, and, worst of all, during dinner, wait until the nurse was out of the room and then throw the food we didn't want out of the window onto the roof of the brownstone below. Mimi squeezed another year of blackmail out of a nurse's tortoiseshell comb I broke by accident and lied about. Later, when I was home for vacation from college, Mimi stole essential items of my wardrobe out of my suitcase and when I'd call home in a fury would never admit to it. Now, at sixty-nine, she's shamelessly delighted with herself for her devilish ways. "I was so powerless," she chuckles, "I had to do something." But to her savior? Apparently.

Her story, which I don't dispute, is that I always knew "in my heart" that she worshiped, adored, and admired me totally in pure "puppy love" and that in addition, in the climate of our family, I needed to have someone to love and protect. She also insists that I knew she wouldn't have followed through on the blackmail. This last is categorically not true. Perhaps she wouldn't, since she says she was too frightened of Mommy to tell on me, but I never guessed it at the time.

I always felt that since I had my mother, it was only fair to leave my father to Mimi, although I doubted she'd get anywhere with him, and she didn't. But that wasn't the reason I let her blackmail me. I put the blame squarely on my abject fear of being found to be guilty of something bad in my mother's eyes and losing the love that was so crucial to me.

In any case, in spite of the distant past, my sister and I are and have always been exceptionally close and we would have been utterly miserable growing up without each other. Today we phone each other at least once a day. There are few greater blessings than a loving and loved sister.

As for Jeremy, rather than greeting him as the long-awaited son every mother is supposed to hope for, Mommy had little emotion invested in him because he was a male. As far as she was concerned, all males, with, I hope but can't be sure, the exception of my father, were a deeply inferior subspecies, to be shown up at all times. She was more convinced on this subject than the most ultrafeminists of recent years, perhaps because of her scorn for her own father.

Because of her verbal agility, none of Mickey Tarcher's children was ever allowed to win an argument, and she sometimes extended this to her social life. As charming as she could often be, and as beloved as she was by her close women friends, she would often tell us with relish how she had engaged her male vis-à-vis at a dinner party in a difference of opinion and then "got him right between the eyes!" We knew that feeling all too well.

Today Jeremy attributes his survival in the face of such maternal indifference to the passion my sister and I had for him. He was an exquisitely beautiful blond boy and we took turns holding him down and kissing him. We also wooed him constantly to "be on my side" during our frequent fights, in which the winner was the one who could sport telltale teeth marks to show my mother, who frowned on biting.

All our friends surrounded Jeremy with admiration and early attempts at flirting. For many childhood years, Jeremy Benjamin Philip Tarcher believed utterly that he was a member of the British royal family who had been stolen away and incarcerated in our home. Who cannot wonder at such a conviction?

We were and remain a family with almost no family ties. Both of my grandfathers were dead before I was old enough to know them, and the scandalous Tilly, although very much alive, was in limbo. Only my mother's mother, Celia, was a link to the older generation.

I remember her as a tiny, gentle woman, always dressed in black, who infrequently came to dinner and gazed wide-eyed with wonder at her grandchildren, with whom she was unable to communicate since she spoke only Yiddish. We loved her visits because she brought a black satchel full of homemade gefilte fish, chopped liver, horseradish, and a challah. The instant we tasted them, we knew immediately that this was the food of life. My grandmother's eyes filled with amazement as she looked in never-ending astonishment at us and our surroundings. To her we had materialized from another universe. We were aliens, two little princesses and a prince, who lived in a palace.

My grandmother died when I was nine, and we three grew up into delicatessen Jews. Without deli and my parents' philanthropy, the existence of anti-Semitism and the State of Israel, perhaps we might have been hard put to feel a strong Jewish identity. But not to worry, anti-Semitisim will outlast even pickled herring or the Americanized bagel. Doesn't anybody out there in the rest of the country between New York and Los Angeles realize that the only right and proper bagel has to be baked by a bagel baker who's learned his trade from another bagel baker, and that basically the only *right* bagel is a plain water bagel?

I sometimes wonder if I'd been adopted at birth by an upper-class Episcopalian couple who lived in a world in which Jews had no place, would I feel like, think like, react like an Episcopalian? Or if I'd been placed in a large, merry, brawling, outgoing Irish family, would I fit in as one of them? In theory I suppose I would, yet somehow I simply cannot imagine it, try as I may. Is this a failure of imagination? Or is there some sort of real genetic "typing" established by many thousands of years of Jews marrying Jews? Is "feeling Jewish" ingrained or learned? Is it nature or nurture or a combination of both? I'll never have the answer, but it's been a far more important part of my life than I realized before I wrote this autobiography.

The only non-born Jew I ever met who seemed utterly Jewish to me was Sammy Davis, Jr., whom I once interviewed at length. From the minute we met, I felt his strong Jewishness; he thought like a Jew, felt like a Jew, reacted to humor like a Jew, possessed every familiar Jewish element and reaction in his personality that I could imagine. He *was* a Jew. Okay, maybe he didn't live exactly like a Jew, but that was incidental. It occurs to me that since he was also a great actor and mimic, perhaps he could also be just as authentically black or Italian . . . I'll never know, except that he would never have made a WASP.

WHEN THEY LEFT school to go to work, my parents had turned away from their siblings, for whom they had been forced to give up their education, although they continued to help them as adults. They turned away as well from the religion that, to them, seemed a part of the narrow lives they were so determined to put behind them. We were brought up in a household without a single trace of religious observance, not even a nod to Hanukkah or High Holy Day temple going.

As the three little Tarchers grew up, we celebrated Christmas. We hung our stockings on the mantel knowing that there would be a dollar bill inside each one in the morning, for years the equivalent for me of ten weeks' allowance. We received piles of wonderful presents, most of them given to us by my father's employees, and we had a traditional turkey dinner.

Only a tree and pine branches were missing from our house, but on Christmas afternoon we always visited close friends, Herb and Grace Mayes, who had a fantastically beautiful tree that almost filled their living room. As long as it wasn't in our house, my mother could accept a tree; somehow she must have equated a display of greenery with worship of Christ. My father's only concession to Judaism was not to go to his office on the High Holy Days, giving as his only reason the fact that it was "a sign of respect." He never said to whom.

I think he stayed away from work so that his employees would know that he identified with and acknowledged his ethnic background, since he always spent the day in the country, enjoying the autumn leaves. The one time I joined him I got a virulent case of poison oak. For years, with my parents' approval, one nurse had us enthusiastically dyeing Easter eggs, which she hid and we found. This may have had a dim connection to religion to her, but to us it was just a wonderfully messy version of the tooth fairy.

My sister and I were precocious snobs about the nuances of the family we knew our parents kept at a deliberate distance, a family that had no social connection to my parents since they had been left behind in my parents' rise to success and status. On a single occasion we were taken to a family wedding in Brooklyn. As we watched the women dancing the hora in a circle, we gazed at each other in astonishment and dismay. We had never witnessed grown-ups doing anything we considered so odd and foreign and hideously embarrassing.

Now life has turned full circle and of my sister's four spectacular grandchildren, the two boys have had their bar mitzvahs and the two girls will have bat mitzvahs. My own two grandchildren are secular half-Jewish, half-Catholic, but celebrate all holidays. And I have danced in a circle of women, although it was after a Lutheran wedding ceremony of two born-again Christians. Go know!

Chapter Five

THE VERY WORST PART OF MY LIFE LASTED FOR EXACTLY EIGHT IN-
tensely formative and never-to-be-underestimated years. They began
when I started first grade. Birch Wathen was then located on Ninety-
third and Ninety-fourth Streets, between Columbus and Amsterdam Avenues, and occupied a number of brownstone houses that surrounded a
large center courtyard, part of which was fenced for athletics and called
"The Silver Cage." It was a beautifully kept school; the mahogany stair-
cases were highly polished, the walls were always freshly painted, gleaming copper bowls of fresh flowers adorned all the landings; but to me it
was a hell on earth and my classmates were fiends.

From the day I entered first grade, I, who had reigned supreme at
the art of block building at City and Country, discovered that I was
unpopular. The instant dislike my classmates took to me has to be
attributed to three reasons. I was far and away the youngest in the
class, I was very small, and, most important of all, I became an immediate teacher's pet, a cute, solemn little target wearing some nurse's
version of Heidi's braids around my head, which didn't help matters.

Instead of sitting in the back of the room and whispering, passing
notes, and making friends, I planted myself in the first row and
watched and listened to the teacher with unwavering attention, raising
my hand quickly whenever I had the right answer, which, unfortunately, was often. I maintained eye contact with my teacher decades
before I had any idea of what eye contact was. There was no possibility
of my being naughty, given my upbringing, and since only the teachers
liked me, I worked ever harder at gaining their approbation, constantly
escalating my unpopularity.

I was annoyingly quick to learn how to read. I remember vividly the
noble thrill of accomplishing this on the first day of school. The book
was *The Gingerbread Man*, and since "gingerbread" was the longest
word in the book, the rest fell into place. It was merely a case of
reading readiness, but it didn't make my classmates like me any better.

Math, beyond multiplication, was to remain a mystery to me. I was
hopelessly bad at athletics. The Silver Cage was where people threw
baseballs *at* me—baseballs that could hurt!—and expected me to actually *hit* them! And I was way beyond bad at singing. We had a
famous choirmaster, Hugh Ross, who taught weekly at the school.

The first day he asked each child to stand up and sing a line for him. This gruff, terrifying man listened to me, put a gentle hand on my shoulder, and said in a voice that was both kind and sad, "You may sit down, my dear. You don't have to try to sing." Oh, the relief! I bless his memory. Oddly enough, I'm not tone-deaf. I can tell in an instant if a note of music is off-key and I have a real ear for learning a foreign language, with almost perfect pronunciation and pitch.

Years later I wasn't allowed to sing the alma mater at high school graduation because I threw off key everyone who heard me. At home, my mother told me to sing if I wanted to, but to go out onto the elevator landing before I started, and close the front door behind me.

As for my ambition for the future, after I gave up on becoming a bareback rider in the circus, I had only one. I yearned for years to become the wife of the United States ambassador to Turkey and to stand at the head of a winding staircase, receiving my guests in a long evening gown. Reader, don't ask.

Grammar school lasted for eight years, from five and a half to thirteen and a half, each year drenched in true suffering and a bitter, bitter sense of inferiority. This suffering was much more *intense than anything I've experienced as an adult,* because I had no life experience or philosophy to help me cope with it, no way to figure out the reasons for it, no weapons with which to combat it, and, worst of all, no one with whom to discuss my situation.

Daddy, no, of course not. Mimi, no, she was too young and wouldn't have understood. A best friend? I didn't have one except for the other two unpopular girls, and our mutual plight was a subject we never admitted to each other. Mommy—she, above all, must *never* know about it.

I had no older person to go to for guidance, so I was thrown for these years into a state of solitude in which I was truly helpless and utterly, mutely alone. Somehow I bore up without being able to share my misery. I used to stare at myself in the mirror for hours, from all angles, looking deeply into my own eyes and trying to see what it was about me that made me so disliked. I looked just like an average girl, I thought, but there must be, I imagined, some good reason I couldn't figure out.

These years marked me for life with feelings of insecurity and shyness with women until I got to know them extremely well. Some of these feelings persist to a minor degree today in spite of the healing existence of a number of closely cherished friends.

I once discussed this with somebody who insisted that "everyone is unpopular in school," but that is total nonsense! I was one of the officially designated "most unpopular" girls in the class. The others were Barbara Bluestein, a great beauty whose crime was to be enormously tall for her age, and sharp-tongued Sally Frowenfeld, who was too sarcastic for her own good.

Perforce, we three outcasts formed a *salon des refusées* and hung out unwillingly together, never invited to birthday parties, never asked to sit with anyone else during lunch, never chosen to be on teams until the last moment, constantly the victims of petty malice and mean, cutting remarks that came from the popular girls as well as the middle range of acceptable girls.

Our standing was as clear-cut as if we were untouchables in India. The others were actually ranked in numerical order. Joan Rosenberger, whose family owned Coro Jewelry, was the "first most popular." I can't think of anything or anyone I wouldn't have sacrificed to be Joan Rosenberger, particularly the year when she presented every girl in the class, even the three of us, with a Charlie McCarthy lapel pin with a movable mouth, the most treasured piece of jewelry I've ever owned.

Who knows if I wouldn't have been better off at Brearley, where I could, at least, have blamed my unpopularity on being Jewish . . . or where it might not have existed at all?

Besides the teachers, my only admirers were most of the small group of little boys in the class. I was indifferent to them, but their undeniable attention saved my tiny sense of self, as well as the fact that once home, I was the unquestioned alpha sibling.

For eight years I experienced unpopularity as *shame,* a shame laid on my shoulders, a shame that must be hidden once I was home. When my mother came home from work, she immediately changed into a dressing gown and lay down in her bedroom, on a strangely narrow Queen Anne sofa covered in green silk, and read the afternoon newspapers, the *Post* and *PM.* I was the only one of the children allowed to knock on her closed door and interrupt her with an account of my day. I stoically confined myself to my scholarly triumphs, putting on an excellent act. I was convinced that if my mother knew the truth about my unpopularity, she would be deeply disappointed by my terrible secret and I would be diminished in her eyes. Since her love and approval were the most important things I possessed in life, I couldn't risk losing a crumb of her favor.

I wasn't wrong. The validity of keeping this agonizing secret was confirmed many times in my adult life when my mother, hearing of a conflict in my life, always—often irrationally—took the side of the other person, however indefensible it might be. "I owe it to you to be the devil's advocate," she'd say. "A mother should tell you the truths your best friend won't tell you."

Mimi, whose age and height were always right for her class, and who was gifted with great, outgoing charm and natural naughtiness, was a rip-roaring success in school. At points she was barely literate, but she was always the president of whatever class she was in . . . it pays to be bad, bad, bad!

Somehow I finally arrived at the face-saving conclusion that the reason none of the girls liked me must be that I didn't have the right clothes. There was good reason to think this. Birch Wathen was a small school full of rich and horrifyingly materialistic kids who knew, to the thread, how thick bobby socks should be, how much better a cashmere sweater was than a Shetland one, what were the right tartan skirts and what were the wrong ones, which brand of penny loafer would do and which wouldn't.

My mother, remembering her own childhood, had vowed that she wasn't going to bring up spoiled children, an aim that she achieved in many ways. One of them was in making sure that we never had the same quantity, or even quality, of clothes worn by our peers. Mimi and I became Cinderellas in our own eyes, particularly since my mother was always beautifully dressed and owned a great many clothes since she had convinced herself that she shouldn't repeat an outfit at the office more than once a month during each of the four seasons. As we grew older, my sister and I spent hours inspecting, admiring, envying, and eventually trying on her wardrobe when she was out for the evening. Once we collaborated on a letter that told her dramatically that she "dressed in satins and silks while we wore rags." This had no effect—in fact, it became a family joke.

In seventh grade my mother gave me her old camel-hair polo coat because she had just bought a new one and we were the same height. I could hardly believe my luck; that coat represented everything that was ultimately desirable and for years I'd mooned at it with the greatest of longing. Every inch of it breathed *total rightness*. I walked to school in it for the first time on my twelfth birthday, bare legs freezing as usual in those days when girls didn't wear pants. I was carrying, along with my schoolbooks, a box of chocolate bars for everyone in the class, traditional for birthday girl to provide. I was giddy with happiness and anticipation, convinced that finally, *finally*, as both the owner of this perfect coat, worn by all the popular girls, and the bearer of candy as well, I would, at last, be treated kindly by kids who'd been vicious to me since first grade.

Of course nothing changed, the coat was never noticed, the candy was routinely accepted. I wish I could say that I learned an important lesson about value systems, but no, this staggering disappointment only convinced me that I had to have better clothes to be accepted, although I wore and loved that coat through high school and college.

My deep and early fixation on clothes, which grew stronger every year, has stood me in good stead during my life, as a fashion editor but even more so as a novelist. I'm able to use clothes inventively as one of the many methods female characters adopt to present themselves to the world, for better or worse. No matter how many other methods I have to use to create a fully believable fictional personality, when it comes to the choice of clothes, I'm in my natural element.

My mother had other methods of keeping us from being spoiled. She often lectured us on the instability of the advertising business. "Never forget, girls, if Daddy lost only one of his biggest clients, which can always happen, we wouldn't be able to live in this apartment and we wouldn't be able to afford to send you to private school." Night after night I lay awake worrying about this possibility. Then I'd worry about kidnappers and the possibility of my parents getting divorced. I had also read *Dracula* and had a violent terror of vampires. For years I even slept with a clove of garlic under my pillow, since, alas, I didn't have a crucifix with which to confront the monster. It's hardly surprising that reading too late, to delay that unwelcome moment of turning off the light, is still one of my worst habits.

I never realized until I was much older that none of my father's clients had ever left him, nor did they in the future. My mother, however, made me profoundly averse to taking financial risks as an adult, and my fear of the stock market has cost my husband and me more money than I ever intend to think about.

Mommy never failed to emphasize the necessity of a career for both her daughters. "When you grow up, the important thing is to get a good job and make your own money" was her battle cry. Not one word was ever spoken about getting married or having children. As a result I worked every summer while I was in high school and college, and I've worked ever since I graduated and married at twenty-six, late for my generation, working part-time until I'd raised my children. I've worked full-time, including most weekends, since I was forty-eight, and I will most certainly be working tomorrow.

My sister, who heard the exact same words, married young. Although she had the always difficult job of bringing up two children, she did volunteer work, never making a penny, until after my mother died at eighty in 1980. *Then* she worked, rebellious to the end.

As my mother would say in irritation, "I can't tell you girls anything." However, she never stopped trying.

WHEN HIGH SCHOOL started at Birch Wathen, the class was enlarged. Now we numbered some ten boys and twenty-six girls. None of the new girls knew that I was historically the lowest of the low, and from the first day of freshman year I found myself part of a clique of three new girls, Barbara Himmel, Elaine Wiener, and Janice Cohen. The four of us immediately became the most popular gang in the class, through the utterly mysterious process by which such things take place. I could hardly believe that this had happened to me. Suddenly popularity with the teachers was a plus, being smart was a plus, and having the boys like you was a plus. The whole school caste system turned upside down and I gloried in every minute of it, although the scars left by grammar school were still raw.

(Finally I've had to admit that those eight long and early years of being a pariah, no matter how distant and no matter how well I understand them intellectually, aren't something I will ever be able to get over entirely, no matter how I grow in years, experience, and success. They've been burned into my psyche. I'll probably feel slightly insecure as I breathe my last, still wondering if I'm wearing exactly the right thing.)

My wonderful new friends and I spent every afternoon of freshman year studying together at each other's apartments, playing big-band records and learning all the words to "Chattanooga Choo-Choo." It seems to me that darling, softhearted, uncomplicated Mrs. Himmel used to come home every day with clothes she'd spent the day buying for Barbara and her sister, Joanne. I've never forgotten her or the weekends I spent at the Himmels' in the country . . . it was such a warm and happy household, where merely existing was more than enough to make your parents adore you. Although Mr. Himmel smoked a cigar, I'd have changed places with Barbara instantly.

In 1942, when the new sensation, Frank Sinatra, was singing at the Paramount, we four cut school to see him perform. Of course, I'd warned my mother of our plan since I was afraid that the school might call to find out what had happened to me and she'd find out how bad I'd been. "You've earned a day off," she said, to my astonishment. My friends and I watched the gasping, screaming, weeping, hysterical teenagers around us with a sense of superiority. We wouldn't have dreamed of behaving like *that*.

During that first year of high school, sex was our main subject of conversation. I had known the facts of life from the age of six. My mother had clearly explained everything to me in medical terms, leaving out only foreplay and the fact that an erection was necessary to put "the Daddy's penis into the Mommy's vagina." I listened quietly, with a carefully hidden but blissful reaction, to all this fascinating information. It sounded MARVELOUS. I could hardly wait to grow up. The next year I told my mother that I'd forgotten how babies were born and she told me the story again. When I tried that a third time, at eight, she said dryly and accurately, "I think you remember," and refused to repeat the delicious details.

My friends, however, had been given less instruction and I felt a mission to try to educate them. They refused to believe me because they thought it was all too disgusting. To each his own.

We spent hours trying to decide on the details of our wedding night. The two major problems were the nightgown and getting into bed. How could a nightgown be properly bridal and still opaque? It occurred to none of us that we could be brazen enough to wear anything transparent, like lace or chiffon. And did you slip into bed by yourself while your husband was in the bathroom brushing his teeth, or did you loll about in a beautifully indifferent pose on a chaise longue, waiting for him to pick you up and carry you to the bed? We speculated wildly but fortunately we never found a satisfactory answer, because no other topic would have fascinated us as intensely.

Chapter Six

AT THE BEGINNING OF MY SOPHOMORE YEAR IN HIGH SCHOOL, IN 1942, a chain of events occurred that changed my innocence forever. A close friend of my mother's phoned me one afternoon to ask if I wanted to go down to Annapolis on a blind date. The young man in question was the son of one of her best friends and the scion of a rich German-Jewish family. The blind date was for a football weekend at the Naval Academy. Until that time, I'd been invited to nothing more exciting than a few afternoon dates with boys who were perhaps a year older than I was. I had never been kissed. I was only fourteen, four months shy of my fifteenth birthday. Stunned and seduced by the glamour of the prospect, I accepted the invitation immediately, already terrified but unable to say no to the irresistibly grown-up proposition.

When my mother came home and heard about it, she groused a bit but didn't object. I had hoped she wouldn't let me go. In fact, I was counting on it, but once she allowed it, I saw no way to get out of my agreement. In hindsight, the fact that my mother permitted such an exceptionally inappropriate date for a girl of fourteen can only be explained by the fact that she didn't know what was right for my level of maturity. She'd been brought up in such deprivation and had been forced to fend for herself so early in her life that she had no idea how much more sheltered I was than she had been.

A few weeks later, when I first went off to Annapolis, I'd reached my full height of five feet two and three-quarter inches. Reader, every quarter of an inch counts! Although I had a round baby face, I looked as old as I would for the next decade. Since this is my life story and there's no one else writing it, I have to say that I was pretty, and even more important, I was cute. Cute was the best possible thing for a girl to be, and what's more, it's something you can keep long after you lose beauty. I had exceptionally good skin that has never known an enlarged pore or a pimple; a funny little nose; and large, wicked, green-blue-gray eyes; and I giggled easily, a perfect audience. Although I've never been close to beautiful, something about me has always attracted the male sex, and my success with men has been usually greater than that of far better-looking girls. So shoot me!

I took the train from Penn Station to Baltimore, wearing my one pair of black suede pumps with a medium heel, and a gray suit and a fur jacket that I'd borrowed from my mother. I had shoulder-length light brown hair with red highlights in it, which I set in pin curls every night to make it curl, and I wore red lipstick so dark that it was almost purple and matching nail polish, both of which I thought were the height of sophistication. I'd coaxed my friendly dentist, a former boyfriend of my mother who enchanted me by calling me "little boy," into taking off all my very visible wire braces the day before I left, chipping away the cement that held a cap on almost every tooth in my mouth. I had exchanged letters with Joe, my blind date, adding more than two years to my age by telling him I was seventeen, which I wouldn't be until almost two years and four months in the future. He was twenty, in his second year of an accelerated three-year wartime course.

In Baltimore I took a taxi across town to another station and caught the little train that wandered out to Annapolis, stopping every five minutes, each stop making me more hideously nervous. Then I took another taxi to the boardinghouse in which Joe had reserved a room for me. Midshipmen were not allowed to have money, so all of this was paid for with cash his mother had sent me, normal practice then. In my room in the boardinghouse, I fussed uselessly with my hair, which was losing its curl in the humid air, wishing I were dead, paralyzed with nerves and stage fright.

"Your drag's here," the landlady called up the stairs. (Dates, both male and female, were always known as "drags.") I finally forced myself to go downstairs where Joe was waiting. The first sight of him shocked me deeply. He was indisputably a *man,* and a truly gorgeous man. The astonishment of his amazing good looks was far more difficult to accept than if he'd been a toad. I would have accepted a toad happily, and relaxed. Joe was blond with very short hair, crinkled like Paul Newman's, splendid features, and a prominent mouth. I had no idea why someone who looked like that would have a blind date, or not reject me for that role. I suddenly realized the full enormity of what I'd done in venturing to Annapolis.

I was too flustered by Joe's maturity and too worried about my hair to remember much about that afternoon or the football game. At the "hop" that night, I wore my girlish high-school-freshman prom dress of pink net. As soon as the hop ended, there was a violent stampede as all the midshipmen and their drags literally ran at top speed back to the boardinghouses, to throw themselves on the floors of the living rooms and make out as fast they could, packed together like sprats in a can, getting in as much sexual satisfaction as they could until one of them would call out the time, uniforms would be adjusted, and they'd run like maniacs back to their barracks. Joe shook my hand and departed. I peeked in curiosity and shock at the squirming, moaning mass activities in the living room—the other girls in the house were all about twenty and most were engaged to their drags—and went upstairs to bed.

The next day I went alone to meet Joe at the "church party," as the Jewish services were called. It was the first time in my life that I'd ever been to a religious service, much less an improvised one. There I sat alone, in an empty church that had been lent to a visiting rabbi, until three hundred midshipmen marched in and sat on the other side of the church. Apparently no other Jewish drags were attending. Eventually I got up the courage to peek at the men in their blue dress uniforms. A number of them were peeking right back at me. Never, ever, in my life have I seen so many magnificent Jewish males in one room.

That afternoon there was a parade, three thousand midshipmen marching in perfect formation, a brave and gallant sight. If all officers in every country were trained and sent off to war wearing tattered, ill-assorted rags, I believe there'd be a slight chance of world peace.

Soon I was back on the train home, weeping uncontrollably the entire way from Annapolis to Manhattan for two reasons: the slackening of the terrible tension I'd been under during the entire weekend and the fact that not one single midshipman in the large stag line had cut in at the hop. It was months before I discovered that unless a formal introduction has been made, cutting in isn't allowed, and before the hop I'd met no one but Joe.

I wrote him a thank-you letter but I didn't hear another word until he phoned a few months later, the evening before New Year's Eve. Clearly he'd been stood up by his date. Did I want to go to the ball that the USO held for all officers, foreign and American, including cadets and midshipmen, the next night? I said yes immediately, although I had no way to get rid of my braces.

It was an evening that should have been drowned in glamour: there were hundreds of Allied officers in their dress uniforms, each, it seemed to me, with a beautiful woman on his arm, dancing in the crowded ballroom of the old Carlton House Hotel. But I was wearing a wristwatch and all I could think of was the approach of midnight. I would be fifteen in nine days and I had never been kissed. One thing was certain: at midnight, kissed I would be. I had had more than twenty-four hours to think about this in dismay and fearful anticipation.

The hour came, I felt Joe's lips, I felt surprise at the stubble of his whiskers, I didn't die or faint—and he only kissed me once. He took me home and soon after he wrote, to my utter amazement, asking me to be his drag for June Week.

It must be understood that June Week was an invitation of major importance, a landmark date in every way. A middie only asked his very best girl to June Week, which lasted for five days and included three formal hops, a number of parades, and all sorts of traditional events, culminating in the graduation of the First Class.

Again my mother agreed that I could go. Most strangely and uncharacteristically, she took me one Saturday to a well-known Madison Avenue shop called Fashions for Girls and, forgetting my clothes allowance, bought me three perfect evening dresses and expensive new cotton day dresses.

Before June Week arrived, my sophomore prom at Birch Wathen took place and Joe managed to get leave that weekend so he could escort me. In that war year of 1943 he was the only date of any girl in the class to be in uniform; the other escorts were high-school boys or 4-F college boys. What a dashing uniform the Annapolis dress whites are and how devastatingly desirable, adult, and heroic Joe, the gorgeous soon-to-be-warrior, looked in them!

All evening long I was the object of totally undiluted, unhidden, sheer gaping envy and disbelieving awe. Since most of my classmates had spent a full eight years treating me as a leper, I had a grand and glorious, fully conscious revenge. It was the most soul-satisfying, Walter Mitty night of my life. I wore my first-ever black dress, off-the-shoulder, spangled here and there with silver, with a wide, many-layered tulle skirt. I was fifteen and a half and brilliantly happy. But not for long.

June Week itself remains a blur in my mind, because of a moment that has wiped out every other memory. One of the hops was called "The Ring Dance." An enormous ring of flowers is built on a platform and a midshipman who intends to give his drag his class crest, a replica of the insignia on his class ring, dances through the ring, stops underneath it, and "pins" his special girl. It was understood that this giving of the crest was almost a proposal of marriage.

Can you believe my horror when, without warning, I found Joe guiding me toward the ring? I was too dumbfounded to protest as he pinned a crest on my evening dress. I didn't want the damn thing, marriage was unthinkable, I was only fifteen, I wasn't in love with him . . . but what could I do? I simply didn't know how to get out of it. I'd lied too convincingly and now my lack of experience left me without savoir faire or poise or presence, and once that crest was on, there was no way I could figure out to give it back. That summer I managed to lose it while weeding our Victory garden, but Mimi, the wretch, found it and gave it back to me.

After June Week, in the summer of 1943, Joe had weeks of leave in New York, where he stayed at his mother's empty apartment, only a few blocks from us. He immediately began to force me into detested sexual activities on the bed in his room. Until then, I had agreed, slow step by slow step, to tongue kissing. Now, resisting all the while, I allowed him to kiss my nipples. I adored the sexual stirrings that this caused in me, but we had certainly gone much farther than I'd ever intended.

However, quickly things changed. Joe was determined to make me masturbate him with my hand until he reached an orgasm into his starched white Navy-issue handkerchief. He was deaf to my anguished protests. If sexual abuse doesn't include rape, I was certainly a victim.

Actually, in many ways rape would have been preferable since only that would finally have caused me to run to my mother instead of maintaining a total silence about what was going on. Rape would have clearly been Joe's fault, nothing I could possibly have permitted even after a struggle. Instead, I fought Joe with all my strength in what developed into a nightly arm-wrestling contest. I stood no chance.

All during those summer weeks of his leave, my mother allowed me to spend each night alone in our apartment. After dinner each night, Joe and I returned to his mother's apartment, where, relentlessly, he achieved his climax with my desperately unwilling assistance. When he left to go back to the academy, I took a bus home after seeing him off at Penn Station. During that trip I was invaded by an almost suicidal feeling of overwhelmingly deep, sad, life-destroying grayness that lasted for weeks. Later in life I realized that it had been a classic depression.

I was so drowned in guilt at the loathsome thing I'd done, over and over again, that I wrote Joe and told him I'd never see him again. He replied, in countless impassioned letters, that unless I continued to keep his crest, he'd be so torn apart that he'd flunk out of the academy. "I'll be sent to sea immediately as an ordinary seaman, the ship will be torpedoed, and I'll drown."

More than thirty years later, in *Princess Daisy,* I was able to recapture some of how I felt in Daisy's reaction to her seduction-rape by Ram, her half brother.

Daisy was filled with her awakened knowledge of physical desire but it was mixed with a kind of shame she had never known before. Her whole mind and body ached with acute conflict and resentment. She wanted to bite, to kick, to shriek to high heaven, to faint, to run away. She wanted to go back to where she had been only an hour ago, but she knew that there was no return. Deep within her something sounded, as if the string of a great

cello had been plucked, a note of remote, mysterious but unmistakable warning. . . . Daisy didn't dare to move or speak. She was
an accomplice. She had *let* him do it to her . . . he left her sickened
with shame, burning, burning.

However, at fifteen, instead of seeing through Joe's cowardly and
disgusting blackmail, I was convinced that he *would* die in the war
and it would be my fault. Through naive stupidity I had permitted
myself to be abused. Like Daisy, I had "let" Joe force me—it takes
two for abuse to happen. I was far too ashamed to tell even Mimi any
details of what he had made me do, although I showed her his letters.
I know now, of course, that there wasn't the slightest chance of Joe's
flunking out; he had too much respect for the safety of his own skin.
Every protected minute of 1942, '43, and '44 that he spent at Annapolis was one minute closer to the end of the war, and, in fact, he
graduated only a year before the war ended, commanded a PT boat,
and survived without a wound.

Of course, as always with anything discreditable, anything that
would put me in a bad light, I never breathed a word to my mother,
who had allowed me, at fifteen, to spend so many nights in Manhattan
that summer with a twenty-one-year-old man. She would have put a
stop to things immediately if I had had the guts to tell her, but even
now I can't imagine that conversation, given the person I was then.

Today, to me, the worst part of the whole business was that I would
never have put up with Joe's sexual demands if I hadn't wanted to
keep shining in my classmates' eyes to maintain the change from my
former unpopular self. A strong part of me absolutely wanted and
needed to continue to wear the Naval Academy crest that gave me
such *vital* status with my classmates. It's hard, now, to realize I was
such a dreadful coward, but everything confirms it. All I had to do
was send that crest back and never answer Joe's letters. Indeed, as far
as the unwanted sexual activity was concerned, I had always been free
to get up and walk away, but I never did it. I was so bewitched by the
power of having a magnificent older boyfriend that I accepted the
heavy, heavy price of my insecurity.

As school began again I managed to spend time with my best friends,
still juniors, who all agreed in hushed voices I can still hear that "the
worst thing a girl could do was touch a boy's thing." As I nodded in
agreement, I could see Joe inexorably unbuttoning his uniform jacket,
taking off his undershirt, and walking toward me as I lay on his bed,
trapped by my own utter confusion and lack of fight. I try to look
back at what was going through my mind then but I find nothing but
fear and a kind of grim resignation.

The gulf between what had happened to me and what my friends regarded as gospel was unbridgeable. I had been pried, step by step, out of the rightful pace of my sexual development and thrust into a life of shame and deception. This may seem an overreaction in these days of easy teenaged sex, but in 1942 and 1943, there was no such thing as teenaged sex, at least in my world.

But I also knew I couldn't continue to allow Joe to do this to me. Eventually, by mail, I convinced him that anything he forced me to do that wasn't "above the waist" would mean the end of our relationship. By the time I'd negotiated this difficult agreement, I had become a high-school senior. A year earlier, my mother, without consulting me beforehand, had decided that three years were enough time "to waste in high school." She'd gone to see Miss Birch and Miss Wathen and arranged for me to skip my junior year of high school by taking extra classes during the school year.

I was desolate. No sooner had I made my three adored friends than I was going to be separated from them and thrust, still fifteen, into a class of relative strangers, several of whom were already eighteen and none of whom was welcoming. Now I really needed the prestige and protection conferred by that Annapolis crest. Some of my new classmates sported engagement rings and planned to marry right after graduation.

During senior year, I was editor of the school magazine and literary editor of the yearbook, and when the school hired an outside coach to produce the senior play, I won the leading part in an audition for which all the girls tried out.

I'd almost always had the lead in all the school plays over the years, although my parents had never taken the time to come to one. In today's child-oriented climate, I'm sure they would have felt forced to leave work and attend the plays, but then they explained calmly how impossible it was to take so much time out of their working days. I simply accepted that as the way things were in our family . . . I don't remember feeling sorry for myself.

The senior play was a grand old chestnut called *Milestones,* which called for me and my husband, Jon Epstein, to age fifty years and celebrate our golden wedding anniversary. We rehearsed at the apartments of various kids, and everybody in the class wanted to coach our kissing scenes. One of the worst of the seniors, a popular, envious, fully developed wench named Patsy March, under the cover of paying attention to me, braided all my long hair in tiny braids during one rehearsal. I was flattered at her attention until I found out what hell it was to undo them.

Since *Milestones* was performed at night, my parents came to see it.

Afterward, backstage, my mother astonished and angered me by declaring, with delighted surprise, that I should go to drama school rather than college. How, with her devotion to education, she could have had such a crazy idea confuses me to this day. She had no knowledge that I could act until that night.

This, it must be understood, was the crucial year of getting into college. In the reading comprehension tests given throughout the city, I came in first, year after year. I was so crazily arrogant that I'd applied only to Wellesley and Smith, without a fallback college. I'd visited Wellesley to be interviewed in the spring after my sixteenth birthday, and I had fallen deeply and uncompromisingly in love with the campus.

In those days there were no SATs but only College Boards, which consisted of three hour-long tests: English, math, and French, all given up at Columbia. I aced the French and the English, writing about that trip to Mott Street in the single essay question.

When I opened the math exam I realized that I knew the answers to only the first two of the hundreds of multiple-choice questions. (To this day I can't even do long division.) I decided it would make far more of a statement not to answer any questions at all. Utter ignorance seemed better than a poor performance. I signed my empty blue book with a flourish and marched up to the front of the room to put it down in front of a proctor. Every head turned as I walked out, feeling a ridiculous, giddy, inexplicable sense of relief and joy and liberty. I'd always thought math was nonsense and I'd resented the mere idea that I should be expected to master it. I had only passed high-school algebra and geometry by ardent cheating, which no teacher ever spotted since cheating was the last thing they expected of me. I was a major academic smart-ass who thumbed my nose at what I, in my teenaged wisdom, decided wasn't important. These days I would never get into a good college.

Then came the long period of waiting to hear. Smith accepted me without an interview, but I hadn't heard a word from Wellesley. The tension mounted. One spring day I was taking part in a senior girls' gymnastic exhibition when my three junior friends entered the balcony of the gym and brought the whole thing to a halt, jumping up and down and screaming at me that they'd gone to my home to find out if I had mail and I'd been accepted at Wellesley. Everything stopped dead as my classmates swarmed around to congratulate me. It was one of the most blissfully promising peak moments of my life.

Perhaps the admissions office had seen my blank blue book in math as the sign of an idiot savant or perhaps it was just my English exam and my interview, but I got into Wellesley in 1944, as far as I know the only Jewish girl from New York to do so in that particular year. (If there was another, how could I have missed her?) This was in the days of a ten percent quota for Catholics and Jews, something that was accepted then as a matter of course, hard as that seems to believe now.

The day after I found out that I was going to Wellesley, I returned to Annapolis for my last June Week. Joe was graduating that year. The night before his graduation he proposed to me, yet again. I'd always managed to fend off his proposals, but this time I said, "I can't *possibly* marry you." Why not? "BECAUSE I'M ONLY SIXTEEN!" I shouted with vicious delight.

Once I'd convinced him of this, he raged, "I suppose you know you've ruined my graduation." I shrugged my shoulders. I'd gotten him safely through the Naval Academy and I didn't care a flying fuck about how he felt. We attended seven hasty postgraduation weddings and returned to New York without saying another word to each other. That night I joined my classmates on the roof of the Hotel Astor, where our class party was held. Harry James was playing his trumpet and Betty Grable was there to listen to her husband. Oh, what heavenly lightness it was to rejoin the kids, to be a kid among kids, to have freed myself from Joe's domination by finally telling him the truth.

In the early 1950s, right after my marriage, someone at a party heard my maiden name. "My God," she screamed, "you're the girl who ruined Joe's life!" "No," I replied, without a second's thought, "he ruined mine." It turned out that her husband was his brother-in-law. She told me that Joe had left the navy right after the war, gone to medical school, married, had four children, and now lived in another city far from New York. "Ruined"? Oh, no, I hardly think so.

In 1978, more than twenty-five years after that party, my memory was still utterly blocked about one aspect of this relationship. I couldn't remember a thing about my own sexual response to Joe once he'd started making me masturbate him repeatedly. I felt certain that I'd never let him touch my body below the waist, but I couldn't swear to it. It was simply a black, blank void in my mind. In the second year of my second round of psychoanalysis, I finally determined to find out exactly what had happened.

I called Information for that city whose name I'd never forgotten, got his phone number, and dialed it. Joe answered the phone on the third ring. I told him who I was. There was almost a two-minute silence while he digested that information. Finally, sounding as if every hair on his head was standing straight up in embarrassment, he asked me how I was.

"I'm fine," I said. "In fact, I've just had my first novel published."

"Congratulations."

"Joe," I demanded, without any more preliminaries, "when we were lying on your bed and doing all that stuff while you were at the academy, did I ever have an orgasm?"

He thought for several more silent minutes. Finally, he answered, "I just don't remember."

"That's simply not possible. You *must* remember. You have to remember, for Christ's sake!"

"No," he said, after another long pause, "I'm sorry, but I don't."

"Shit, shit, shit!" I hung up, absolutely frustrated, knowing that he was lying. On reflection, I realized that if I'd ever had an orgasm, he would have said so, to give himself an excuse for his actions. I'm entirely positive that all he thought about was his own pleasure.

A number of years later one of his classmates sent me a letter from which fluttered Joe's obituary. He had died suddenly, only in his mid-fifties.

"Serves him right, the bastard! *Serves him right!*" I heard myself say out loud in a savage rage as I read the slip of newsprint. Only later did I think of his widow and children, and only because of them have I not used his real name.

As one analyst told me, with memorable understatement, I have "trouble getting in touch with my anger." Joe had to die before I could allow myself to feel the fury I had every right to feel toward him. Or is it against myself, so pathetically vulnerable—and cowardly—at fifteen?

Chapter Seven

I ARRIVED AT WELLESLEY, SHY, APPREHENSIVE, AND BREATHLESS WITH excitement. I had been assigned to a dormitory in the village of Welles-ley called Little House. All freshmen at that time lived in the "Vil" since there wasn't enough housing for us on campus, some of the dorms having been taken over by the Naval Reserve for officers in training.

Little House, which must have once been some family's showplace, was a splendid example of typical New England classical architecture. It stood just off the main street of Wellesley, a two-minute walk from the local drugstore, which I was soon to visit nightly for a chocolate "frappe," New England–speak for "milkshake."

I discovered my ground-floor room, the best in the house, large and graced with a bay window, and at the same time met my roommate. She was named Toddy (born Marilyn) Melvoin. Toddy was from Highland Park, north of Chicago; she'd gone to New Trier, the famous high school of the rich Chicago suburbs; and she was about my height, with blond hair, blue eyes, and an enthusiastic, slightly kooky, totally lovable personality. Toddy is still the only person in the world, outside of my family, who always remembers to phone me on my birthday.

For the first few days, like all the other twenty-one girls in the house, we more or less tiptoed around each other, not exchanging too much personal information. Since Toddy had placed a Bible on her night table, I assumed that she was Christian. It took three days before I found out that she was Jewish and the Bible was a souvenir of her Sunday-school confirmation. I was amazed to find out that Jews owned Bibles. "What about the Old Testament?" she asked. "Oh, yes, of course," I mumbled, reluctant to admit the fathomless depths of my ignorance.

In those days, Sunday school led to something called Confirmation, not a bat mitzvah. The girls at Birch Wathen who had been confirmed often received fur coats. Joan Rosenberger had been given two fur coats, both sheared beaver, one from each set of doting grandparents. When I saw them laid out on the twin beds in her room, I had my single moment of regret for my refusal to go to Sunday school. For graduation from high school my parents gave me a nutria coat, a warm and pretty coat whose short hairs, I discovered, turned into a nasty mat when they got wet.

There was one other Jewish girl in Little House, Marion "Mike" Wise, from Pittsburgh, who'd been assigned a single room. We didn't realize it until years later, but the ten percent Jewish quota applied to dorms also. If there were twenty-three girls in a dorm, as there were in Little House, and three of them were Jewish, two of them would share a room and the third would have to room alone, because no one in the administration would dream of putting a Jew and a Gentile in the same room. Presumably they imagined that the Gentile would never recover from the shock.

Yes, all you Wellesley graduates who never believe me about this, yes, you recent Wellesley presidents who tell me in horror that there couldn't possibly have been such a situation, because you'd never heard of it (you were too young), yes, all you African-Americans and Asians and Hispanics who are at Wellesley now, things were mighty different in the bad old days, before Mildred McAfee Horton, returned from being head of the WAVES, resumed her duties as president of Wellesley and abolished the question about religion on the application form.

Not, as Jerry Seinfeld would say about homosexuality, that we thought there was anything wrong with it. An unraised consciousness on the quota system was universal in 1944. Interestingly enough, I was never aware of any anti-Semitism at college. There were a number of classmates who, at first, flatly refused to believe that Toddy and I were Jewish . . . they'd never seen Jews before and expected the usual caricatures, not our light eyes and small noses. There were even two girls who were so deeply ignorant that they actually expected us to have horns, a story I wouldn't believe unless I'd experienced it myself. But once all that initial flurry of discovery was over, it disappeared.

Wellesley was, for the next four years, a magically wonderful place to be. The ultimately perfect place. My dorm mates gave me the nickname "Torchy," which they call me to this day. I found it a vast improvement on my sister's nickname for me, "Pussy," which it took me many years to convince her was not the best way to attract my attention across a crowded room, and on Jeremy's habit of calling me "Ju," another head-turner.

I possessed something few, if any, other freshmen had, a piece of paper called, oddly, a "Blanket Permission," signed by—who else?—my mother. We were all allowed to spend two nights a week out, until midnight. The Blanket Permission let me stay *overnight anywhere* I wanted to, in a hotel or a private home, as long as I wrote down my destination when signing out. Soon the phone began to ring and blind dates materialized by the dozen.

The explanation for this blizzard of popularity was simple. The *Wellesley Freshman Handbook*, a slim red pamphlet that showed each of our photos as well as our names and our hometowns, quickly found its bootleg way, right off the presses, to every Ivy League men's college. And these schools, from Dartmouth up north to Princeton down south, each had a good share of Jewish boys who had just come home from the war with firm instructions from their mothers to find a nice Jewish girl as quickly as possible.

Those Ivy League boys who hadn't been in the service were looking just as hard as the veterans. But since there were so many more Jewish boys, particularly at Harvard, than there were girls, a true-blue Jewish maiden was a hot ticket. Wellesley was geographically ideal, close to Boston and, unlike Smith or Vassar, easy to reach in those days when few college boys had cars. And my high-school yearbook photo was a good one. Even though Tarcher wasn't a Jewish name, New York was a Jewish city. Someone must have put two and two together and the word quickly got around.

Sometimes a blind date was actually arranged, like the one Fanny Cohen set up for me and Anthony Lewis, the very same Anthony Lewis who has been for long the great political writer for the *New York Times* op-ed page. Never did two people have less in common. It was "Oh, no!" at first sight, for both of us, the only time that's ever happened to me. Tony could tell a frivolous nonintellectual when he saw one and I could tell a sternly dedicated brain. But he took me on a fascinating tour of the inner sanctum of the *Harvard Crimson,* on which he was working already, so that single date wasn't a total loss.

By the third week of freshman year I was booked for a football game every Saturday until Christmas: Harvard–Yale, Yale–Dartmouth, Harvard–Princeton. Only MIT was out of the lineup. Perhaps they didn't have a football team.

Nevertheless, it was at MIT that I had my first and last pair of gin martinis. I threw up neatly in a fraternity-house bathroom, since I'd had an early intimation of what was about to happen. I've never dared to smell gin since. My father, poor innocent, had promised me a hundred dollars if I didn't drink or smoke until I was twenty-one. I had tried a cigarette at thirteen and managed to burn off the eyelashes on one eyelid trying to light it. I finally kept it lit long enough for one disgusting puff and renounced smoking for life. Not only did it taste horrible, but no cigarette could ever make someone who looked like me be mistaken for a sophisticate. Alcohol was another question.

Although gin was out, punch was in. Before every Harvard football game, the big red buckets, with which the boys were supposed to put out fires, were emptied of their sand and refilled with punch made from cheap liquor and enough fruit juice to kill the taste. These were lugged up into the stands and, in the frosty weather, kept us warm and noisy until the end of the game. After the game, couples went from one set of rooms at Harvard to another, sampling the punch at the parties being given everywhere. There is no question that never were so many girls downright stinking drunk on so many weekends as during my four years at college. And so were all the boys. It was a way of life and we didn't question it.

On the other hand, if we'd been found drinking on campus, we'd have been expelled immediately. Sometimes, when I had to sign in on my return to the dorm, I was so smashed that my signature didn't look like mine. I developed two good excuses for that: I'd been laughing so hard that my hand shook, or I'd been rushed because I had to go to the bathroom.

Birch Wathen had given me such a good education that I didn't find freshman year difficult. I took no math, obviously, and no French. I never wanted to have to memorize a foreign language again: all my French in high school had been translation and brute memorization of grammar and verbs, French taught utterly without conversation.

In addition, I had conned my darling pediatrician, who had been my one and only doctor all of my life, and knew how much I hated athletics, into giving me an excuse for gym. ("Judy," Dr. Anderson had said gently as he signed the precious paper, "you know that you can't keep coming here, don't you?" He gestured at the waiting room, in which tiny chairs were gathered around a variety of children's games.) I was assigned to a class with all the girls who had genuine disabilities of one sort or another. We lay down on the gym floor and were trained in relaxation techniques, which soon led to a lovely nap.

Eventually, ashamed of myself, I took folk dancing as my next required sport. It proved far too rigorous, as giant girls flung me around the room from one to another. Crew, even if it had interested me, was out of the question; we'd all heard and believed that rowing made you unable to bear children. Finally, I took canoeing, which, to my disbelief, I *flunked*. The final exam consisted of taking out a canoe and doing all sorts of maneuvers in the middle of Lake Waban. There was such a strong wind that I couldn't handle the canoe and had to be rescued by a motorboat and towed, shivering and humiliated, to shore. The only sport I liked was tennis and I took to wearing my tennis shorts to class, under a raincoat, so I could practice between classes, but I was never more than fair at a sport that required running around in the sun.

However, I took my English courses fairly seriously. In Composition 101, I was assigned an essay that was due on Monday morning. That weekend I spent at Brown and on Saturday night, again at a fraternity house, I discovered the daiquiri. I had three of these sweet, seemingly nonalcoholic drinks and then went back to the hotel where I was staying and, in a visionary state, wrote an essay, in longhand, on the joys of the New York City Yellow Checker taxicab. My professor gave me an A-plus with the notation "Perfect success at sixteen and a half." I've never written drunk again—I'm not sure why—nor did I ever get another A-plus. Perhaps I should have tried longhand again, but I'd learned to touch-type while I was in high school, the most important skill of my life.

Every day we freshmen biked many miles, since the Vil was a great distance from the campus proper. I ate lunch in one of the upper-class dorms because there wasn't enough time to bike home for lunch between my morning and afternoon classes. One day I mentioned to a friendly sophomore that I'd received an invitation to a mixer at a Boston synagogue but I wasn't planning to go.

"You're making a big mistake," she said.

"Oh, please, a mixer in a synagogue—why on earth would I want to go to something like that?" I asked snobbishly. "I know enough boys already."

"More boys than you can imagine in your wildest dreams."

"But what kind of boys?" I asked suspiciously.

"Go and see for yourself. There's no such thing as enough boys."

Reluctantly persuaded, I went and almost immediately met a recent Harvard graduate from Brookline, a suburb of Boston, named Bob Feinberg. He was wonderful looking, dark, with a marvelous aquiline profile and the most beautiful clothes I'd ever seen on any man. Soon I was dating Bob several times a week.

The food at Wellesley was indifferent to horrible, and Bob took me out on weekday nights, feeding me steak and lobster at the local Belmont Country Club and getting me back to my dorm by ten o'clock. I often spent weekends at his family's magnificent house, where his parents and sister were enormously welcoming to me. Parents of my Jewish dates were always marvelously kind. I was, after all, the girl who had all the makings of the perfect daughter-in-law: the right religion, the right speaking voice, the right prosperous and well-regarded parents, the right demure manners, the right Ivy League school. And the right nose.

After religion, the nose was unquestionably the most important detail. The nose I was born with, not a nose-job nose. No plastic surgeon worth his fee would ever have given me my funny but obviously authentic nose, my "marshmallow" nose, as my father called it. For a Jewish girl not to "look like" a Jew, whether anybody would admit it or not—and they wouldn't and probably still won't—was extraordinarily important, equal in importance to light skin in African-American society. A boy could get away with any characteristic of the stereotype of Jewishness that the mind of man has invented, but for a girl the possession of a naturally small, straight nose was inestimable. Any family with an ounce of Jewish self-consciousness or self-hatred could be counted on to adore me. (In my own family, all noses were good and taken for granted.)

Bob and I necked for hours in front of the fire in the Feinbergs' downstairs den. He was the answer to my prayers, a boy who could kiss like an angel and who was too much of a gentleman to even try to touch my breasts. I had come to Wellesley as fiercely armored against the slightest unwelcome sexual attempt as any girl could possibly be. If I knew anything, it was that there would never again be a Joe in my life. Blue balls? Let them suffer, was my motto.

At college, I was living in a wider, freer new world than I could have imagined. I had never known more than a few non-Jews and now I was surrounded by them, ninety percent to be exact, and they were wonderful. Lively, interesting, beautiful, bright, fun-loving girls *who liked me*. They liked me immediately, as a matter of course, without judgment. We were all Wellesley 1948—that was the only thing that mattered. It was the first time in my life I'd been in such a benign and happy atmosphere, liked just because I existed. They even thought I had great clothes!

I had never lived away from my parents' influence before; I had never lived surrounded by nature; I had never been allowed to wear a man's shirt and one pair of navy-issue bell-bottom, cutoff blue jeans day in and day out; I had never made so many new friends, never talked so late into the night. We all must have been just as wild as I was with our newfound freedom, since some of the Little House girls made up a song that began with the immortal line "Shit, fuck, rape, and masturbation." I don't remember the rest—perhaps there was no more to it than that—but it certainly conveys the idea of how liberated we all felt.

The one new aspect of life everyone disliked was "waiting on," as we called our frequent turns at acting as waitresses to the other girls, who dined like ladies at round tables. Most of the college maids were doing war work, never to return, and now everyone shared their tasks, wearing obligatory hair nets. I soon discovered the advantages of waiting on, one of which, since I was constantly hungry, was eating before everyone else. The cooks assumed that no one would want the chicken giblets and livers, and were glad to give all those delicacies to me. I was also able to get an occasional piece of rare meat instead of the overcooked roasts that were reserved for the dining room. My mother, after listening to me complain about the food for months, sent me an occasional whole kosher salami, which I shared with my dorm mates. It was such a delicacy that if it arrived on a Friday, my Catholic friends stayed up till midnight for their share.

Most of my new friends spent their free time smoking, playing bridge, and knitting, usually all three at once. I continued to use every minute I could steal from my homework and my social life to read for pleasure, always including the daily *New York Times,* to which I had a subscription, an exotic source of news, rare at Wellesley. At home I'd read two morning newspapers and two afternoon papers as a matter of course. As for books, I'd been a fanatical bookworm all of my life, the typical kid who reads with a flashlight under the covers at night. Wellesley had a library with stacks crammed with many thousands of books I'd never read or heard of, which I immediately began to explore.

I did make a doomed effort to learn how to knit, I can't imagine why, and actually fashioned a lumpy, lopsided tennis sweater for Jeremy that reached below his knees, before I gave up and went back to novels. Instead, I paid a friend to knit argyle socks in the colors of various colleges that I sent to favored dates, pretending that I'd made them myself. This was major boyfriend voodoo at seven dollars a pair, plus the cost of the wool. I never so much as considered trying to learn bridge, which I assumed involved math or something equally repellent. No, reading was all I wanted, as long as I could also flirt with a large share of the Ivy League, remain a happy-go-lucky prom-trotter, be taken often to Ruby Foo's in Boston's Chinatown for lobster Cantonese, and keep up an only halfway decent grade average, almost always a B.

Chapter Eight

IN APRIL 1945, PRESIDENT ROOSEVELT'S SUDDEN DEATH MADE ME REalize one way in which Toddy, Mike Wise, and I were basically different from our Little House friends. The news had just hit campus and the three of us sat sobbing bitterly in Mike's room while around us we heard several of our friends yelling gleefully, "The old cripple's dead!" Three Jewish Democrats and twenty Gentile Republicans. I was stunned by their horrible words and found it almost impossible to feel at ease with them for a long time. Now, fifty years later, a number of these same girls are Democrats, largely because of Choice.

There was a special assembly given by Wellesley but it was tepid and utterly unsatisfactory. I felt a strong need to go to a proper memorial service. Bob Feinberg took me to one at a large synagogue in Brookline, the first time I'd ever been inside a real temple. I felt slightly comforted by my first experience of a death that was enormously important to me.

When my father died, fifteen years later, when I was thirty-two, I had few tears. Far more than sadness, I felt deep loss for a crucial, irreplaceable relationship that had never been mine to lose. In most of the most basic ways, I'd never had any experience of the father-daughter bond every girl needs in order to grow up normally. I'd been given the financial protection of a comfortable home in which a man lived who was my "father," but that was as far as it went. I'd never known what it was like to have a protective, easily available father who would demonstrate his love openly, who would listen to my troubles, such as they were, and comfort and guide me, as a good father should.

However terrible Jack Tarcher's teenaged trauma at his mother's abandonment had been, he behaved toward me—and Mimi—as an emotional coward and I've never been able to excuse him. Try as I can, I cannot forgive it. I understand that he was a terribly mixed-up human being or he would never have visited twenty-six therapists, but why, oh why, didn't he stick with one of them? No caring, responsible, adult man, however sensitive, should permit himself to hide for a lifetime behind the excuse of his own teenaged pain. Yes, his mother had run off, but was that enough of an excuse for him to withdraw as a parent forever, inflicting damage that no other relationship can repair?

I don't believe so. That saccharine phrase "Daddy's little girl" never fails to make me gasp in the most violent envy when one of my friends uses it to describe herself and her father.

I don't fully understand, even after many years of analysis, just how many ways this affected me, but obviously it was deeply unhealthy. Certainly it forced me to be prematurely stoic and strong . . . but at a great price. I had to learn to repress many of the normal emotions that a little girl feels and give a performance of someone having an absolutely grand old time tap-dancing her way through life. I learned how to ignore my deep emotions and become a people pleaser, which meant keeping a great deal of my inner life hidden, even from myself, until I finally discovered it years later in psychoanalysis. During the early period of analysis I felt as if, unlike other people, my own depth of emotions was no more than a few inches and that I had always lived skating on the surface of them . . . on thin ice. By that time it was too late to experience my emotions; I only had time to recognize that they had probably existed and been stifled at birth. It wasn't until I started writing fiction that I was able to *feel* my emotions as my characters experienced them, but, of course, at one remove. Fictional creation of character isn't actual living, although it often comes amazingly close. When a character goes through a depression, so do I.

After my father's death I suffered a once-in-a-lifetime attack of enormous itching hives that lasted for weeks. I've been told that hives were probably a substitute for unshed tears. But there simply wasn't a fierce emotional connection to my father as there had been to the man who had been president since I was four.

Certain politicians have been the fantasy fathers who substituted for the real one I only knew in a teaching or celebratory mode. I wept in outraged disbelief for hours both times Adlai Stevenson lost; I sobbed for four days for Jack Kennedy, and again for Bobby, but for fewer days and with a less terrible grief. After that I stopped putting my heart into politicians . . . I was too old to try to capture a father in a president or candidate.

IN THE LATE spring of my first year at Wellesley, Bob Feinberg's mother and sister visited New York at a time when I was at college. My mother, a woman who grabbed a simple sandwich at the nearest branch of Schrafft's every single day of her working life, took the entire afternoon off from work to take these two strangers to Voisin, which served the most expensive lunch in the city, something she'd never done for any of her closest friends, not even on their birthdays.

A pattern began to emerge that I would only begin to understand many years later. Joe the midshipman and Bob Feinberg and a number of other boyfriends I had in the future were all sons of rich families. The clothes my mother so amazingly bought me for June Week, breaking every law in her own book, were a way of presenting me at my best, probably subconsciously at that point. If I had become engaged to Joe and married him after the war, I don't believe she would have objected, even though I would have only been seventeen.

My mother never liked or approved of a single one of my dates unless they were going to inherit wealth. As idealistic as she was about her legal work and in spite of all her exhortations to Mimi and me to get a job, at heart she must have wanted her daughters to grab the golden ring of material comfort she'd never had until my father handed it to her, even if it meant an early marriage. She was, after all, only one generation away from arranged marriages and she suffered all her life from the idea that whatever my father had achieved could disappear in a flash.

My sister and I have often asked each other why, if Mommy wanted us to marry rich men, she didn't so much as hint at it. Other mothers had no problem in making such hopes clear to their daughters, but our mother had always disdainfully avoided the mere mention of marriage, much less a "good" one. Unlike her daughters, she would have scorned therapy as sheer weakness; she led an absolutely "unexamined" life and most certainly didn't know enough about herself to realize that she'd never approve of a suitor who wasn't wealthy.

Mickey Tarcher refused to take even such a simple preliminary step as sending me to the dancing class Viola Wolff held for the eligible Jewish kids of Manhattan. "When you need to know how to dance, someone will teach you," she assured me, brushing aside my disappointment. She was too smart not to realize that dancing-school partners weren't old enough to be marriage material.

By the end of the summer of my freshman year I had to break up with Bob Feinberg. He wanted me to marry him and find a place to live near college so that I could continue my education. Over and over for the rest of my college career, this pattern was repeated; the only variations were how my suitors intended to deal with my academic future. As soon as marriage was seriously at issue, I bid each boy goodbye and looked around for the next victim. The turnover rate was fairly rapid. One Valentine's Day, on a whim, I bought valentines that had "Boo!" printed on the first page and "Won't I do?" on the second. I pasted a picture of myself above the "Won't I do?" and mailed twenty-seven of them.

I'll never need to be convinced of the power of direct-mail advertising. Every last one of those poor suckers thought he'd received a valentine created just for him, and I spent the next week on the phone rearranging my social calendar. "Why is the phone always for you, Torchy?" a classmate asked, annoyed. Gleefully, I told pretty, blond Mary-Lou Lindquist, "If you were Jewish, it'd be for you, too."

I've just reread a few pages of *Mistral's Daughter*, by accident, while searching for another reference, and discovered an accurate description of my college sex life, such as it was, in the character of Teddy Lunel, who becomes the mother of Fauve, Mistral's real daughter.

> . . . In that era of the tease, Teddy Lunel was responsible for more aching groins than any other girl in greater Boston . . . A few of her favorite dates were allowed to kiss her for hours, rubbing themselves frantically against her in the back seats of convertibles or on the sofas of darkened rooms in eating clubs or fraternities, striving to gain their orgasms through the thickness of clothes that separated their two bodies, for Teddy would never permit any of them to unzip his fly, to insinuate his hand under her skirt. She triumphed over their desire by refusing it any release except what they could gain without her seeming to notice. None of them was calm enough to guess that Teddy always had an orgasm too, easily, without a sound or a movement that could be detected, produced magically just by the pressure of a rigid penis straining inside a pair of trousers, a secret orgasm that could happen even on a dance floor. She never granted any of them the closeness to her that knowledge of this would have produced, and, for her cruelty to them, she received the tribute of their proposals of marriage.
>
> Teddy was not indifferent to the men who loved her, but somewhere deep within her there was a profound lack of concern with their pain. She was so in love with the idea of her popularity that she never fell in love with any one individual man. This inaccessible, heedless, faraway sensuality was like a few drops of water to men longing to drink their fill: it drove them mad, far more than if she had refused them the kisses she spent so lavishly. . . . "I just hope, Teddy Lunel," one of them had said in a rage, "that someday someone makes you suffer the way you make me."
>
> She looked suitably regretful but she knew it could never happen.

Ah, Teddy, I really regretted it when you had to die so soon after giving birth to Fauve, but your demise had to happen in service of the plot.

At college I played fair. I never encouraged false hopes and none of my former boyfriends ever committed suicide because of my rejection. Reader, call it "heavy necking."

Was I the cock tease Nicole was to accuse me of being during my first months in Paris? My husband assures me that I was the very definition of one, but he adds such a creature was the absolute rule rather than the exception among the "good" girls of his vintage, which is only four and a half years older than mine.

Virginity, as I knew at twenty, was a matter so vital that it reached the level of a mystical commandment, no matter how merely technical it was.

I've recently consulted a few women of my age who went to good colleges and they agree that nothing except actual penetration could destroy your virginity. You could roll around on the floor engaging in every possible form of sexual experimentation, naked or not, and you remained a nice Jewish girl. The important thing was that these fun and games not be conducted with too many boys—perhaps a maximum of a half dozen in a lifetime—and that the boys not know each other.

As I was writing this, I asked my brother what, from a man's point of view, would label a girl "nice." He knew the exact answer. "You could get your hand inside her bra but you could never manage to get the bra off the girl." I expressed astonishment at such a limited horizon. "I thought you meant high-school girls," he explained. "In college you tried to screw 'em."

However, Jeremy was speaking of a period in the 1950s when, in his junior year, girls were admitted to his college, St. John's at Annapolis. In my day, the late forties, actual intercourse was never what my dates had in mind. That would have been going too far, even for the horniest of them. Think of what it could lead to . . . pregnancy, parents' fury, a hasty marriage . . . every sort of unwanted entanglement could stem from penetration. Only one date in four years, a Harvard boy named Tom Langner, actually wanted, even seemed to expect me, good God!, to "go all the way." I was so righteously insulted that I wrote him a letter of vituperative disgust that I read to my friends, to their cheers of approval.

Although I retained my virginity, on the other hand I was as thoroughly lousy, worthless, don't-give-a-damn a member of the Wellesley community as has ever existed. I couldn't possibly find, or want to find, the time to engage in any of the extracurricular activities that were expected of us. I signed up for exactly nothing, zip, nada, no magazine, no newspaper, no plays, no clubs. The major class event of four years at Wellesley was a musical revue called "Junior Show." In early 1947 a committee of all the top class officers came to my room to complain.

"Torchy, you haven't signed up for Junior Show."

"I simply don't have time," I told them.

"Everybody has time. If you can't perform, you can paint scenery or sell tickets, but you must do something."

"Look, after class I need every minute of the afternoon to go to the library or finish my homework, and at night I'm usually out or still studying. I just can't do it."

"You're letting the class down. You're the only one who isn't helping."

"Oh, come on, I'm sorry, but that's the way it is."

They left fuming, but they couldn't force me, and I didn't give a hoot in hell what they thought about me. I had my own close group of accepting friends, and that was enough. I had no desire to be part of the four-hundred-girl class as a unit. My little world was exactly what I wanted. My freshman friends from Little House still lived close by on the same corridor of Claflin, our upper-class dorm, as I did. (And we still have a round-robin letter going.) I had made a number of other pals through sitting next to them in various classes, in particular a congenial group known, for good reason, as the "Lousy Eleven." At Claflin, I'd grown close to three new friends, Audrey Chamberlain, Barbara O'Neill, and Doris Sommer. Senior year, Audrey was voted "Most Sophisticated" and Barbara was voted "Most Beautiful." Doris was from Montreal, a deeply serious philosophy major and also a true beauty. Every late afternoon, the four of us brewed real tea in Audrey's teapot and talked about books. We were considered oddball and intellectual, a decidedly bohemian fringe surrounded by avid bridge players.

Those gung-ho girls who had arrived freshman year, already running hard for class office, the Hillary Rodhams of my day, puzzled me. After my years at Birch Wathen I never had the slightest interest in accumulating any kind of peer power, since it would have been so utterly impossible. I could see no purpose in having power at all—it was friendship that was all-important.

From the beginning of my time at college I was utterly inner-directed, concentrating on having the best of all good times and reading as many of the novels in the stacks as possible: old-fashioned writers like Arnold Bennett and John Galsworthy and G. B. Stern, who would never be assigned in English lit classes, as well as Scott Fitzgerald, Henry James, Edith Wharton, Trollope, Tolstoy, Edna Ferber, Colette, and dozens of others. Trollope, Colette, Virginia Woolf's letters, and eventually Proust would become, over the years, the volumes I read over and over.

Except for one short-story class I took sophomore year, I wrote no fiction at college or at any other time until *Scruples.* My short-story professor, Sylvia Berkman, told me that she was giving me a B instead of an A to teach me "a lesson I'd never forget" because I had "the worst spelling she'd ever encountered on the college level." This put me off fiction from the age of seventeen until the age of forty-eight and a half. A lesson indeed!

I was, and am, almost as dyslexic about spelling as I am about math. If a word looks wrong to me, I look it up in the dictionary. The trouble is that so few words look wrong, and often I don't know what letter to look them up under. I had to actually write my fourth novel, *I'll Take Manhattan,* to learn how to spell "Manhattan." Whenever I send a completed manuscript of a novel off to my publishers, I enclose a note to the unknown freelance copy editor, usually a different one on each book, explaining that I'm not utterly uneducated, I just have a spelling problem.

My favorite place at college was the reading room of the library. It was quiet and furnished with deep easy chairs placed at a good distance from each other. There I spent my happiest hours reading without interruption.

Of all the courses I remember, the best was "Bible," as we called the then-required year of biblical history. For as far back as I can possibly remember, I have been a convinced atheist, and Bible changed nothing. The Bible was all new news to me and infinitely absorbing, as myth, fiction, and history.

Why I made up my mind, at a very young age, that there was no God puzzles me. It's not a small child's typical conclusion, but I always, always knew that for me it was absolutely true and my lack of belief has never wavered. If there were a church where people worshiped the ocean, I might feel inclined to join, or if I had a small household statue of a woman, at whose feet I could lay tribute and make wishes, I'd probably do so. I have a real fondness for rank superstition, and if I have a drink in the garden in the evening, I put a few drops of vodka on the sundial, whose inset metal face was engraved in 1652. But a God conceived by the puny mind of man, and in his fallible image? No. Absolutely not for me. Organized religion has created more murderers and more victims than any other force since the beginning of time. Plague and famine are nothing compared with the devastations of religion.

Recently I saw an astounding color photograph of a view taken by the Hubble Space Telescope during ten days in October 1998. The caption said that it "stared down a corridor of the southern sky, looking twelve billion light-years away. It spied a menagerie of thousands of never-before-seen galaxies, including some colliding or merging." Could "someone up there like me," amid thousands of galaxies? I don't believe so, comforting as it would be. An afterlife seems to me as unlikely as a life before this one. My existence is an accident, the result of one particular tiny, high-powered sperm penetrating one particular egg, a coincidence of place and time and momentum, planned by no guiding intelligence, the result of evolution and uncountable random connections that ended up being lucky for me and unlucky for any alternative candidate for Tarcher firstborn daughter or son.

It seems to me, however, that there must be some sort of "higher power" because otherwise, each of us would be the highest power available, and that is logically impossible as well as a perfectly god-awful idea. But what is this higher power? I'm content to let the higher power define itself, and perfectly content, as well, not to know, as long as it doesn't presume to tell me what to do, what to think, or who to believe. Call it blind faith, for lack of a better term, but not "faith" as most people use that word. I feel that any good deed I do has to be in the here and now, or it doesn't count worth a damn.

IN THE SPRING of my junior year I met Jimmy Kahn, who was at Princeton. If I had been ready to seriously fall in love with any man, it would have been with Jimmy, an utterly adorable boy: tall, blond, and deeply sweet, with blunt, rugged, handsome features. My mother approved totally. Not only was he very rich, but he was so smitten that he joked that he wanted to change his name to Tarcher. He'd been in the navy, so he was a year behind me in school.

Jimmy came up to Wellesley to visit me one early spring weekend a year later, our romance continuing. We went out on the lake in a canoe— I should never put another foot in a canoe—and once away from shore, he revealed that the package he'd been carrying contained a bottle of Haig & Haig Pinch, the favored scotch of the day. We beached the canoe securely, dragging it well up on the beach of the Hunnenwell estate, opposite the college grounds, and had a few slugs out of the bottle. After a while, filled with a love for humanity in general, we invited other couples in canoes to come over and share our scotch.

No good deed goes unpunished. Indeed not. The next day, Babs Butterfield, the president of Claflin, accompanied by all the other dorm officers, showed up in my room looking unusually serious.

"You've been reported drinking out on the lake yesterday, Torchy."

"I wasn't on the lake, I was on the Hunnenwell estate beach."

"That's part of the college."

"How can it be? It's not called Wellesley. It belongs to the Hunnenwells."

"Do you really believe that?"

"Of course I do," I said in genuine indignation, and to this day I'm morally convinced that I was in the right and they were totally wrong. Thirty years later I gave my first heroine, Wilhelmina "Billy" Winthrop, owner of Scruples, the middle name of Hunnenwell in gratitude and commemoration.

The committee retired to discuss my fate. Eventually they decided that since I was less than a semester away from graduation, my punishment would not be expulsion but to be "campused," not allowed to leave Wellesley at night until the end of the year.

That semester I got the only straight A's of my college career. My mother's comment was furious. "I always said you should have been Phi Beta Kappa." "You're wrong about that," I told her. "I know a lot of Phi Betas, and not only are they much smarter than I am, but they're willing to work ten times harder." I was wise enough not to add that they dated far, far less than I did. Why add to her ammunition?

I lectured at Wellesley sometime in the 1980s, and my husband and I were invited to the president's house. I recoiled in shock when she offered me a drink from a well-stocked bar. "Drink? On campus!" I said, "Oh no, I couldn't possibly!" Laughing, she explained that the only rule left was that everybody had to leave their rooms when there was a fire drill, boys included. "Boys?" I squeaked. "Oh yes, they can sleep over, but after three nights they have to leave for a night before they can come back." No, daughters of Wellesley, say it isn't so! "Sleep over," for heaven's sake! Nothing could have made me so aware how times have changed.

Senior year there was a final exam, no longer given, the dreaded "General," a four-hour test during which we wrote a single essay in our major field of study. I received a most unusual letter from the head of the English Department congratulating me and telling me that my paper had reassured the department on the value of making us endure the General, a problem they'd often debated.

The question I'd chosen to tackle was "What is the role of the hero in English literature?" Of course, in those days, they never dreamed of asking the role of the heroine. It occurs to me now that I learned a lot about writing at Wellesley after all, between my major in lit and all my extra reading. I just didn't realize it at the time because it sank in so painlessly.

I believe that fifty percent of basic training for writers is to read and read and read until the building blocks and bones of fiction become part of the way they think. The other fifty percent is divided into twenty-five percent storytelling talent and twenty-five percent the priceless and fairly rare ability to sit down in a chair and keep writing and rewriting and rewriting some more, until you reach the end of the story. All the talent in the world won't produce a novel unless you can make yourself write straight through to the *last* page, keeping the final chapters just as rich and interesting as the first chapters, preferably richer. A novelist has to be a dead-ender, endurance is essential, and I'm far from sure that the bulldog quality can possibly be taught. It has certainly been of enormous value to me to be an obsessive-compulsive. Maybe it was all that early toilet training after all?

However, all the reading and sitting in the world won't produce one novel, much less ten, without the ability to tell a story. I can tell a story, thanks perhaps to a higher power?

JIMMY KAHN, MEANWHILE, couldn't be kept dangling forever. He wanted to get married right after my graduation and live at Princeton while he finished his senior year. I had to stop seeing this darling, sexy boy with whom I had gladly and most enjoyably finally abandoned myself to everything but actual sexual intercourse, my solid-gold virginity technically intact. I invited Larry Goodman, a relatively platonic Yale friend, to my senior prom.

It was impossible for me to think about marriage seriously at that time. In fact, I never gave it one positive thought until five more years had passed. Almost all of my classmates were engaged, and as I said the right things and admired their rings, I marveled to myself that they could be making such wrong decisions. Get married? Stop having fun? Settle down with just one man? Life was just starting, for heaven's sake, how could they not be aching to taste it?

The night before my graduation from Wellesley I didn't sleep. I knew, unreservedly, that I would never again find myself in a place where I could be so thoroughly, constantly happy in such a complete way. Whatever happened, I'd never have the grand, complex experience of these four years again. I was right about my college years. But I was wrong about happiness.

Chapter Nine

ONE WEEK AFTER GRADUATION, IN JUNE 1948, THE TARCHER FAMILY boarded the *Queen Mary* en route to Europe. My father had been planning this trip since the end of World War II, and at last European countries had started luring tourist dollars with the promise of enough gas for driving. He and my mother had traveled widely before the war and he wanted to show his children all the places they loved.

I'd been too busy mourning Wellesley to look forward to it at all. Mimi, just nineteen, was "pinned" to a prince of the fur business. She'd spent her first two college years at Finch Junior College and was finishing up at NYU, still living at home and hoping without success, as she tells me now, that while I was away at college, she'd become the center of my mother's attention.

Once the great ship sailed, our memory of former lives disappeared. Our staterooms were all in first class, but third class was jammed with college boys and we made immediate contact through Larry Goodman, who later became a prominent New York state senator. Mimi and I slipped as many boys as we could up to tea in the first-class lounge until the kindly head steward told us we had to behave ourselves. Older people had noticed this unseemly mingling and complained. After that, we simply moved our daily life down to third class, prompting my mother to cry to the heavens at the injustice of the expense of our wasted passages.

Each evening we mounted abovedecks, changed into long gowns, and joined our parents and Jeremy for dinner, since the food in the first-class dining room was so much better than what was served belowdecks. Right after dinner, without taking the time to change out of our evening dresses, we impatiently rejoined the boys, prefiguring the movie *Titanic* by fifty years. I remember sweeping down the grand staircase one evening, dressed in white, Mimi next to me all in black, and spotting the Duke of Windsor coming up the stairs, walking his little gang of pugs.

"Don't gape!" I hissed at my sister, and the two of us passed him, chattering artificially to each other. As soon as we thought it was safe, we stopped and looked back. The duke, too, had paused and was staring back at us with interest. Overcome with giggles, we fled, thrilled, as we told each other, *to pieces.*

These were the days before rental cars, and my father had shipped over, in the hold of the *Queen Mary,* our 1941 Cadillac, one of the last made before the war. It was an enormous, luxurious gray machine, absolutely cavernous, with plenty of room for six people to sit comfortably, three in front, three in back, with their legs stretched out.

The ship's destination was Southampton, but it made a special stop to let us and the Windsors off at Cherbourg. Everyone on board, it seemed, crowded to the rail to watch our car, held in a heavy sling, being lowered to a barge that was waiting by the side of the ship, which was anchored at quite a distance from the harbor itself.

We five made our way onto the barge followed by our three steamer trunks and many suitcases, which made an impressive pile of luggage. Then we waited, blowing kisses to our boyfriends, until an array of baggage, at least fifteen times as much as we had all together, was deposited on the barge at a small distance from us. Finally the Duke and Duchess of Windsor, who hadn't once made an appearance in the dining room, arrived in all their glory and stood by their Alp of possessions. During the entire trip into port they ignored us as completely as if they'd been alone on the barge, although Mimi and I never took our eyes off them. So much for the duke's decorum when the duchess was watching. In 1980, thirty-two years later, I used an embellished version of this scene in *Princess Daisy,* my second novel.

While my father cleared customs, Mimi and I were supposed to find a young Frenchman named Gérard Tournauer, who was to drive the Cadillac for the next two months. My father, who had the good sense to know he was a terrible driver, had made arrangements through his great friend Roger Falk, an English advertising man, to have Roger's young second cousin, Gérard, a student in architecture at the Ecole des Beaux-Arts, live as a member of our family and be our chauffeur-guide at the same time.

After we'd timidly approached a half dozen likely suspects and asked them their names, giggling nervously, I grew irritated. "How many American girls could there be roaming around the customs shed today?" I asked. "Why doesn't he recognize us? We're standing out like complete goons."

Perhaps Gérard was simply too shy, because eventually we unearthed him, leaning calmly against a pillar. It was immediately evident that we'd never met a man like him before, a man with that particular brand of foreign good looks, pointy, witty, keenly intelligent, and distinctly sardonic, that screams "Frenchman" at a hundred paces. On top of this he was tall and lean, with the most magnificent head of hair, carefully coiffed, dark, and exceptionally wavy. We couldn't believe our luck. This outstandingly gorgeous example of a genuine native was going to belong to us for eight weeks.

Mimi and I had never before competed for a man. We'd gone on countless dates together and never had a problem because we didn't like the same types. Gérard was to prove altogether another matter.

Meanwhile, we drove through Normandy toward Paris, stopping only for dinner, where I spoke my first words of halting, ungrammatical French: *"Toilet, si vous plaisir?"*—the only words I could summon forth.

We arrived well after dark at the Hôtel George V and fell into bed, deeply impressed by the magnificence of our room and bath. Mommy, Daddy, and Jeremy had their own rooms, and my father was furious that knowledgeable Gérard, to whom he had left the making of our French itinerary and reservations, hadn't found something smaller, quainter, and more distinctively French than this, the most typical and grandest of all grand hotels.

I had almost no impression of Paris from the night before. There was little street lighting and I'd been too tired. But the next morning I opened the windows overlooking the avenue George V onto an experience of Paris that I still remember with all my senses. I was plunged instantly into a perfect summer morning in Paris at its peak. The smell of the air, a smell you could taste, the hooting symphony of street noises, the light filtering through the trees, the view across the avenue . . . Imagine everything romantic and foreign and legendary you have ever read or seen in the movies about Paris, and then think of it concentrated into one single moment, and you can almost begin to understand how opening that window affected me. I didn't guess then that it would change my entire future, but I was mad with excitement.

While my mother shopped and my father went to museums, the three of us spent the next ten days seeing every single important historical monument of Paris. Gérard took his guide duties seriously, although we groaned for relief. Longing to stop at every café and shop window, we were marched through every three-star attraction in the green Michelin guide. At night Gérard relented and took Mimi and me to the nightclubs of the boulevard Saint-Germain. Juliette Greco, that luscious bohemian who later became an actress, was singing at Le Club and the teenaged kids known as "les rats" were dancing crazily and unself-consciously at La Rose Rouge. The only available drink was Pernod, nasty but drinkable, since there was nothing else at hand. We soon learned to use unisex bathrooms where the toilet was a hole in a tiled floor, tilted, for women, in the wrong direction. In a year, all this would pass into legend and people would come to see "les rats" as if they were viewing a paid spectacle, but then, in the summer of 1948, it was frenetic, uninhibited, tantalizing, and utterly authentic.

When the *Paris Review* gang arrived and discovered Paris, writing about it as possessively as if they were the very first postwar newcomers, it was a good three years later.

Paris in 1948 is unimaginable in the Paris of today. There was no traffic except for buses and a few ancient, dark red Renault taxis that looked like Model Ts; there was no pollution darkening the ravishing silver-gray of the stones of the squares and churches; there was no hideous modern construction anywhere; there were no advertising signs. It was Paris as if an art director of a musical comedy had re-created the city that existed in 1938, for Paris had remained intact throughout World War II. The Germans had treated Paris as their very own pleasure park, and even though a brief battle for Paris was fought by the French Resistance just before the Allied armies arrived to liberate the city, it had left no visible traces. Every restaurant was full, every café jammed, and Parisians were enjoying the marvelous June weather in a wave of absolute joy I've never seen them exhibit since, in the total of five years I've spent there.

The women strolling the streets were dressed in versions of Dior's New Look, which had been invented only a year before: the most feminine and dramatic dresses and suits, with tightly fitted jackets, tiny corseted waists, and full skirts held out by petticoats that reached to mid-calf, topped by extraordinary hats and worn with high-heeled, perfectly made shoes. We all felt dowdy; we were pathetic in comparison. Our own skirts hung limp, our waists were belted naturally, our jackets fit loosely, and our low shoes were meant for comfort.

Whenever we returned to the hotel after a day of sightseeing, to reach the elevators, Mimi and I had to walk behind my mother, through the vast lobby of the hotel, which was filled by exquisitely turned-out, middle-aged Parisian women taking tea and pastry at tiny tables. The first two days we had to run this gauntlet, there was no doubt that they were all staring at us in suddenly hushed and disparaging wonder. We slunk quickly past, looking at the floor and wishing we were invisible. Finally I had an inspiration. "Let's just stare right back at them," I suggested to Mimi. "Let's look at them as if they look as unfashionable to us as we do to them. Saunter slowly, make eye contact, shoulders back, heads up, eyebrows lifted, no expression, just stare impassively. Remember, *we're young and they're not.*"

It worked! We paraded brazenly through the lobby, boldly inspecting the women who'd been intimidating us. They dropped their eyes and returned to their gossip.

My father, remembering the past, took us all to lunch at La Tour d'Argent. Blinded—indeed crazed—by nostalgia, he ordered for everybody: blinis with caviar and sour cream, pressed duck, and wild strawberries with whipped cream. Mimi and I spent the entire afternoon throwing up violently. Between bouts we took turns reading *Tropic of Cancer,* which Larry Goodman had kindly given me. My curiosity was as strong as my stomach was weak. It was the first time I'd ever read something considered pornographic. Hell, it was pornographic . . . that's why it was so fascinating.

Far and away the most important thing that happened that week in Paris was the introduction Roger Falk had arranged for all of us to his adored first cousin, Ginette Spanier. Ginette was in the exalted position of *"directrice"* at the great couture house of Pierre Balmain.

She was a supremely dynamic, exciting, and strikingly handsome woman, with dark eyes and dark hair, pulled back and parted in the middle, so utterly sophisticated that she was almost beyond sophistication. Ginette wore, as I learned she invariably did, three strands of pearls, pearl earrings, and the latest Balmain suit, always gray. She reigned grandly at her desk at the top of the stairs, overseeing the reception of clients and the behavior of the saleswomen with a firm hand. As soon as she heard our name, this dream of Parisian elegance literally screamed with joy, jumped up, and hugged all of us, leaping up and down in excitement, the last behavior I'd expected of her.

Roger Falk was one of her favorite people in the world and she'd been expecting our arrival. Ginette was Jewish, half-English, half-French, but brought up in Britain. She'd married a French Jewish doctor, Paul-Emile Seidmann, almost immediately before the Germans had marched into France and the two of them had been on the run from the Germans until the war ended and she got a job with the American army as an interpreter. Almost thirty years later, I would write about Ginette as herself, in *Scruples,* and I dedicated *Mistral's Daughter* to her.

That night, the Tarcher family was invited to Ginette and Paul-Emile's large apartment on the avenue Monceau for a drink. Ginette entertained at drinks every single night, culling her guests, as the day passed, from the many people who flocked to Balmain to see the fashion show that took place every afternoon. She seemed to me to know everybody, and I wasn't really surprised, when I got to know her better, to find out that her four closest friends in the world were Noël Coward, Laurence Olivier, Danny Kaye, and Marlene Dietrich.

Paul-Emile was the doctor to everyone in show business who passed through Paris and he told me, years later, that one night he arrived home from the theater to discover, in his bedroom, Vivien Leigh and

Peter Finch, who were having a passionate romance and had run away together. What made Paul-Emile furious was not the situation itself but the fact that Peter Finch was wearing Paul-Emile's new bathrobe. Ginette packed them both off, back to London, and the Olivier marriage continued.

In the 1960s and '70s Ginette made yearly trips to the United States to lecture to women's clubs all over the country on the subject of running Balmain. Once I traveled with her to a large club near Philadelphia and stayed with her while she changed into a white suit with a white mink collar and matching hat. She took one giant gulp of vodka from a silver flask and dashed out onstage, where for an hour she held her audience in a spell of enchantment. It was one of the greatest performances I've ever seen in my life. No wonder she worshiped show people. She was one.

When she wrote me to thank me for the dedication of *Mistral,* she said that the only thing that had pleased her as much that year was being mentioned fifty-nine times in Noël Coward's autobiography. I'm certain the autobiography was more important than the dedication.

My mother ordered a suit from the Balmain collection and had a first canvas fitting. Soon afterward we left Paris for a tour of almost two months. We planned to come back only to pick up the finished suit before we left for London and our return to New York on the *Queen Elizabeth.* Our steamer trunks were stashed at the George V and each of us, including Gérard, was allowed two medium-sized suitcases, which were lashed together inside a metal rack built on the top of the Cadillac. Just hoisting them up and securing them every morning was the work of more than a half hour. Crowds gathered on the street outside the hotel to watch this event, something that hadn't been seen in Paris for many a long year.

We took the classic route toward the South of France, Lyon, Avignon, and Aix, heading toward a little place on the Côte d'Azur that we'd never heard of, suggested by Gérard. Again the Tarcher family was in advance of the crowds. We arrived eight years before Saint-Tropez was discovered by Brigitte Bardot and company.

On the road southward, my poor mother observed with visible disgust the discreet, or so we believed, ways in which Mimi and I tried to be the one to sit next to Gérard. I couldn't believe that Mimi, who was pinned, for God's sake, to a nice boy she professed to care about, actually dared to have the outright, unfair, utterly outrageous nerve to take aim at Gérard. Clearly, as the oldest and the one who was unattached, I was entitled to him, but Mimi had other ideas. Gérard betrayed no preference at all. I was furious and disbelieving, but she stood her ground. Soon, growing too proud to struggle, I left him to her and let Jeremy have my seat in the front of the car.

My mother, unable to endure the sight of all of us eating five-course meals at lunch and dinner, had soup and bread in her room almost every night. My father, at his celebratory peak, urged us to order everything on the menu. As we drove farther and farther south, making excellent time on the almost empty roads, Mimi and I took to hiding on the floor of the car as we passed, slowly and carefully, through the very narrow streets of small villages, where the sight of our overwide, baggage-burdened car brought out hordes of people. We were, quite rightly, ashamed of sitting in that luxurious car as we drove through towns that still gave so much evidence of unrepaired war damage. In contrast to Paris, everywhere in the countryside we could see evidence of the battles that had been fought.

When we reached Saint-Tropez we stayed at a hotel a few miles outside of the village, since the single hotel in the town didn't have enough room for all of us. Walking around Saint-Tropez, that tumbledown, charming, and absolutely untouched fishing village, with only a few cafés, was almost as much of a revelation as seeing Paris for the first time.

The first night there, after dinner, for some reason Mimi's vigilance relaxed enough to allow me to walk with Gérard out to the car park.

"Enfin seul," he said to me, stopping in the road.

"What does that mean?" I asked. During three years of high-school French, our teacher, Mademoiselle Gaillrand, had never spoken to us in her native tongue.

"Alone at last."

WOW! I'd won! I'd beaten the bitch, as I now thought of my sister. Only after I'd spent a few seconds enjoying my triumph did I realize the time for some very quick kissing had come, before we had to take the car back to the restaurant. From that night on, as we progressed along the Côte d'Azur and made our way into Italy, by way of Florence, down to Rome, and back up to Venice (no sight left unseen), I sneaked out of the room Mimi and I shared and met Gérard for long sessions of necking in the front seat of the car.

In Rome we even managed to go off together to the Catacombs, a necking paradise if you close your eyes, an episode I put to good use in a scene in *Mistral's Daughter*. Every night Mimi, eyes narrowed, watched me leave, and every night she tried to blackmail me, threatening to tell Mommy what was going on, but to my credit, I didn't give in, and to her credit, she never snitched.

Eventually things soured between my first Frenchman and me. He, with the normal attitude of a graduate of the Sorbonne, quite naturally expected more, sexually, than I was willing to give. And I, used to college boys, was amazed to have to field his bitter remarks about American virgins. What else could he possibly imagine I would be, for heaven's sake?

The end came in Switzerland when Jeremy, who'd been sharing a room with Gérard, told me that he wore a hair net to bed every night! So that was the secret of his perfectly maintained waves. In a different decade Gérard would have had a gorgeous Afro, but in 1948, the visual picture of a man wearing a hair net was enough to put me off him forever. Later in life he was to win a Prix de Rome and become a highly distinguished architect.

It was in Rome that I first determined not to return to New York. We were all sitting in a café at night and the shape of the large square with an obelisk in the center reminded me of the place Vendôme. In a moment of pure vision, I suddenly knew, as positively, as absolutely as I've ever known any single fact during the rest of my life, that I *had* to stay in Paris, that no power on earth could make me return to New York with my family, that this was the chance of a lifetime.

I had a most desirable job waiting for me in New York. Herb Mayes, he of the magnificent Christmas tree, was one of my father's best friends and the editor in chief of *Good Housekeeping*. Every summer during college I'd worked as a trainee in various departments of the magazine. Herbert had long since become my mentor. He'd commissioned me to write an article for *Good Housekeeping* called "Most Likely to Succeed," which he published in June of my senior year and for which he paid me the huge sum of five hundred dollars. Also, every month of senior year I'd sent him a no-holds-barred critique of every department of the entire magazine and had been paid the generous amount of twenty-five dollars for each effort, money that handsomely supplemented my allowance.

I'd known the Mayeses since I was four, the age at which I conceived a powerful notion, never really abandoned to this day, years after their deaths, that the then-childless Herb and Grace had *bought me* from my parents, since they not only seemed to be, but genuinely were, far more fascinated by me than were any other friends of the family. They never paid the slightest attention to Mimi and Jeremy, which, naturally, pleased me no end. Their daughter, Alex Mayes Birnbaum, who was born when I was thirteen, is a close part of my life today, although she lives in New York and I in L.A. We spend hours on the phone, often speaking of our mothers, who were so close.

But job or no job, I resolved to persuade my parents to allow me to spend a year in Paris. It took weeks of major effort before I succeeded in wearing them down, using powers of insistence I didn't know I possessed. My mother was finally won over by my promise to learn how to speak French. She and Grace Mayes had been taking French lessons for years, and although Mommy was far from a romantic woman, she was in love with the French language and believed no one could be truly educated without it.

Daddy was a more difficult person to persuade. His argument was, of course, philosophical. He didn't feel he had the "moral right to make a decision that would change my life." Only when I pointed out, in a flash of inspiration, that he would be responsible if he so much as sent me across the street to buy a newspaper and, as a result, I was run over and killed by a truck did he finally relent. "I don't want you hanging around doing nothing," he said as he told me I'd have to go home by Christmas if I didn't have a job. I swore to get work as readily as I promised to learn French, anything, *anything* to stay in Paris.

Of course, today I realize that my father was absolutely right. His decision unquestionably changed my entire life. Without Paris *nothing* would have been the same. Without Paris I would still be me, but a me with an utterly different past and present, a different husband, different children, probably a different career, possibly even a different philosophy of life . . . but, trust me, still an atheist. However, Paris was the path taken, Paris was my destiny and my future, and I'm deeply glad that it was so.

Our trip brought us in a circle back to Paris for a week while my mother's suit was completed, and Ginette again invited us for drinks. She assured my parents that she'd watch out for me and supervise my morals. Paul-Emile would take care of my health.

Slightly relieved, my parents now addressed the question of where I would live. One of my father's clients was Coty, then an up-market cosmetic and perfume company, with a boutique on the place Vendôme. The directrice of the boutique, Rosemarie Aubert, was consulted. She knew a "very good" family, named Bouchet de Fareins, where there might be room for me as a paying guest, since they took one girl every year. They were in their country place in Honfleur, Normandy, at the time, but soon she confirmed their willingness and the deal was set. I went to be photographed for my first passport, since I was still included on my mother's, and received a visitor's visa and a ration card.

Ten days of the trip remained. We left for London, carrying as many cartons of fresh eggs as we could to give to my parents' British friends, who had barely seen an egg in years. London was ghastly: poor, devastated, gloomy, and gray, with strict rationing and, as yet, no rebuilding since the Blitz. It existed in another world from Paris. The British had paid a huge price for fighting the Germans and saving our civilization, and things would not return to normal for many years.

As I waited with the family, staying at the shabby, old-fashioned, very comforting Brown's Hotel, I became more ambivalent day by day. Nothing would have crushed me more than being told that for some reason I couldn't stay on in Paris. But on the other hand, I started to realize that I had painted myself into a very scary corner by taking on the biggest possible challenge I could imagine.

I was about to go and live entirely on my own, among foreigners, with barely a word of their language or any knowledge of their history, manners, and attitudes toward little American strangers. How had I managed to get myself into this foolhardy, fearsome position? How could I have fought so hard for something that I wasn't at all sure I could manage to do?

I bluffed my way through every minute of every day, admitting nothing of my petrified second thoughts to anyone because I knew my parents would jump on them and call the whole thing off. Terrified as I was, I still *had to have Paris.* The only faintly happy moment came when my mother took Mimi and me to Simpson's and bought us each a cashmere sweater set, the same sort of twin set that I had dreamed of since grammar school.

As the days passed, my left eyelid began to swell and swell until it grew into a size between a Ping-Pong ball and a tennis ball. Two Harley Street specialists could find nothing wrong with me. At last the dreaded day came and Daddy took me, monster eyelid and all, to the airport after the rest of the family had said a sad good-bye and returned to packing their steamer trunks for loading onto the *Queen Elizabeth.*

The air trip from London to Paris took a little over one hour. As we were about to arrive at Orly, I looked at myself in the mirror of my compact. My eyelid had returned to its normal size.

Chapter Ten

I COULD HAVE LEFT IMMEDIATELY FOR THE BOUCHET DE FAREINS'S Normandy house, but I'd decided, during the period of my highest bravado, that I first wanted to stay a week in Paris on my own, without my family. Arrangements had been made for me to stay in a tiny hotel hear the place de l'Etoile. There I spent one of the loneliest weeks of my life, armed only with a subway map and a guidebook.

I set out every morning to explore the Paris that wasn't monumental, the intimate Paris of little parks and small museums. The early-autumn weather was perfect, the Métro easy to understand, and the sights exquisite, but my sense of being abruptly on my own without language oppressed me at every street corner. The only living soul I spoke to was the ten-year-old boy who operated the elevator, to whom I muttered "Good morning" and "Good evening," not even daring a *bonjour*. My throat was paralyzed.

Every day I had a ham and cheese sandwich in a café for lunch, since "sandwich" was an international word, and every night I ate Chinese food for dinner, because I could understand the written French that translated the Chinese dishes on the menus. Late each afternoon I tortured myself by going to see a French movie without subtitles. I hoped I would get accustomed to hearing spoken French while I followed the action of the picture, but in reality my ignorance was exposed in all its depth.

To make my life more miserable, Gérard had told me that it was well known that prostitutes walked on one side of the Champs-Elysées and decent women on the other. I couldn't remember which side was which, and so I was forced to try to avoid that essential boulevard as much as possible. How, I now wonder in amazement, could I have imagined that anyone would ever have mistaken me, a typical American college girl, with typical shoes, clothes, and hairdo, for any self-respecting French whore? Yet at the time I actually thought it might happen, so great was my ignorance and lack of judgment.

Eventually I took a train to Deauville and a taxi to "Le Bois Normand," the house the Bouchet de Fareinses owned on a country road called la Côte de Grace, a kilometer above the fishing village of Honfleur. I arrived at a tall gate, set in a taller wall, and, shaking with terror, rang. The gardener opened the door, looked at me suspiciously, and went to get Madame. A figure out of a bad dream materialized, a tall, skinny woman with blazing eyes, thin lips, and a severe expression of annoyance at my interruption of her life, her long black hair flying like a witch's locks in the breeze. She shook my hand briefly.

"I do not understand Americans," she said in a soft, halting, hissing voice in the last English sentences she would ever address to me. I could barely understand her heavily accented English, but her tone was clearly hostile. "How can they send their daughters to live with people they do not know?"

I was stunned at this reception. I was a paying guest, this woman took one paying guest every year, and I knew my parents were being charged heavily for my room and board.

Madame led me to the house through magnificent gardens while the gardener brought up the bags. My room was on the second floor of the house, a small room with a spectacular view of a group of three romantically spreading umbrella pines, behind which lay the entire blue estuary of the Seine, and the port of Le Havre far in the distance. The walls were hung with tattered, faded green damask; there were also a tall bed and bolster covered in the same material; and there was a desk, a chair, and a small cabinet that contained a bidet, a sink, and a mirror. At one end of a long corridor was a cramped room containing a toilet that served everyone who had bedrooms on the second floor.

In *Princess Daisy,* I changed Le Bois Normand to La Marée. I can't improve on what I wrote then.

It was a house which could be described by no other word in the language except *enchanted.* There must be in the world many great houses on top of thickly wooded hills overlooking the sea, but no one who had ever spent any time at La Marée had failed to be marked for life by its strange, poetic, nostalgic, tenderly mysterious atmosphere. . . . La Marée itself proved that magic still existed. It had grown out of an ancient farmhouse, little by little over the centuries, and possessed thirteen different levels of roof, each covered with thatch, from which, in the spring, seeds left in the straw would sprout and send up wildflowers. . . . the various parts of the structure . . . wore a rippling mantle of the big-leaved ivy called *la vigne vièrge,* which turned bright red in the autumn. The enormous house looked more like a growing thing than a building. . . . all day long the tall windows were thrown open to the sun. . . . behind the house was a wide gravel terrace from which tangled, fragrant woods led steeply down to the boundaries of two small farms. These woods were crisscrossed by a maze of hidden paths. Beyond the farms was the sea, and on the sea was a constantly changing, gay armada of fishing and pleasure boats going in and out of port . . . in the evening when . . . the lights of Le Havre became visible, there was an almost unbearable poignancy about the moment which caused people to speak in lowered voices or not at all.

I was to grow to love Nicole Bouchet de Fareins almost as much as I loved Le Bois Normand. I only wish I'd known it then. Her deliberately ungracious welcome had made me feel utterly self-conscious and had taken away my small store of courage. I dreaded going downstairs to meet the rest of the family: three blue-eyed, blond, cold-looking young girls, ranging from sixteen to twelve, who shook hands with indifference, and a sullen, skinny woman named Jeanne who worked as a housekeeper and cook. It was September and as the night grew cold, Nicole built a fire in the dining room, saying, as I later learned, that obviously no American ever could or would learn how to build a fire properly, and without fire, how could one exist, since there was no central heating? We were to live at Le Bois Normand until October, when the girls would go back to school in Paris, a temporary postwar schedule dictated by the lack of fuel. Normandy is never warm. Even in summer it can be chilly and damp. Since I always feel the cold, I had to sleep in my new, dusty-rose English sweaters. Finally I'd achieved my longed-for cashmere twin set and they had to serve as a pajama top.

Gradually the girls became individuals: Claire, sixteen, was bossy, intelligent, decided, and aloof, but in all fairness, she had a lovely face and perfect features. Jani, a plump fourteen, seemed almost disposed to be slightly friendly. Marie-Ange, only twelve, was the wild one of the family and might become, I thought, the most beautiful of the three.

Madame Bouchet de Fareins, in the old aristocratic fashion, addressed her daughters as *vous* instead of the normal familiar form of *tu* and they worshiped her, living for her infrequent smile or word of approval.

Her time was occupied mainly with creating extraordinarily beautiful and wildly lavish flower arrangements. Frightful anger was visited on anyone who dared to interrupt her while she was working on them. Other paying guests, her personal friends, came on the weekends, and the house, neglected as it was, boasted wonderful flowers in every room. There was even a small vase in mine.

Often Nicole, whom I called simply "Madame" as in "Oui, Madame," retreated to her room with a migraine that lasted several days, and no one dared to make a sound until she recovered. If a Monsieur Bouchet de Fareins existed, or ever had existed, he was never mentioned. Perhaps she was a widow?

I recognized that the little red ribbon Madame Bouchet de Fareins always wore on her lapel, or her cardigan, was the sign of someone who had the high distinction of being a member of the Legion of Honor. Only later did I learn that she had earned it early in the war. After Dunkirk, a dozen British soldiers who'd been unable to reach the evacuation beaches had been led by the Resistance, of which she was a member, to Le Bois Normand. Nicole had hidden them in the attic for nine months, until, one by one, they'd all been guided to Spain and back to England. If any one of them had been discovered, she and all her family would have been shot.

Finally the day came when we returned to Paris, where the Bouchet de Fareinses had an apartment on boulevard Lannes, right opposite the Bois de Boulogne, in the sixteenth arrondissement, the most snobbish and expensive section of the Right Bank. Carrying as many kilos of butter as we could—butter that started to melt in an alarming, unexpected heat wave—the girls and I endured the jerky trip.

Nicole had gone on before us and we were met at the station by a charmingly attractive and obviously mischievous young man of twenty-one named José Wechter. Only a few months older than I, he had the face of a devastating rogue and a most self-possessed grin as he stood on the platform slapping his chic suede gloves into the palm of his hand as the girls swarmed excitedly around him. I'll never forget the insouciance or arrogance or the self-satisfaction of that gesture on a steaming day. At that time, no well-bred man went without gloves in October.

José was a graduate of Le Rosey, the grandest boys' boarding school in Europe, where billionaires and kings sent their sons. He was an exotic mixture of Brazilian and French and spoke American English, with upper-class British slang thrown in now and then. I realized immediately that he was Claire's boyfriend, since she was so brilliantly happy to see him. The usually stern girl didn't try to disguise her joy.

The sprawling third-floor apartment I was to live in had clearly been decidedly luxurious in the prewar years. The large salon and Nicole's big bedroom faced directly onto the Bois. Although there were many rooms, I'd been given a drab little space that looked out onto an even more drab interior courtyard. Again there was a bidet, a sink, and a mirror. The toilet, which I shared with Nicole, contained a roll of that benighted item, French toilet paper, thin, scratchy, pale brown, and slippery. If I wanted a bath, I had to inform Nicole at least two days in advance and use the tub in her bathroom, limiting myself to three inches of hot water and, as she never failed to mention, depriving her of her own bath. A shampoo was only possible if I boiled a pot of water on the stove and carried it through the house to her sink. I rinsed my hair in ice-cold water, and there was no central heating at all during my entire year in France. Three days a week the electricity was cut off from dawn till dark in the entire arrondissement. Somehow, now that I was back in Paris, none of this seemed like a hardship, but rather another part of the adventure I was living each day.

Fortunately there was a large fireplace, the center of all family life, in the spacious, sunny salon, where we ate lunch and dinner. The Paris of abundance I'd known at the George V was gone. This was the way the French really lived at home postwar, although restaurants had all the food they needed.

At our first lunch we were joined by a silent, severe man and, astonished, I found myself being introduced to Monsieur Bouchet de Fareins. He and Nicole had long been divorced, but he lived in his own large room, which had once been the formal dining room, since a shortage of apartments had made it impossible for him to find a suitable place of his own. He added nothing to the meals, since he spoke only to his daughters, and that rarely. I soon learned to overlook him entirely except for a polite greeting. After lunch he vanished, not to be seen again until lunch the next day.

Nicole's sisters began to come to lunch frequently, joining the three girls, demurely uniformed, who always came home for lunch from their nearby convent school. Francette Drin, the youngest sister, had a merry, roving eye and a playful manner, for which I was grateful. Like Nicole, she also wore the ribbon of the Legion of Honor for her work in the Resistance. Francette was a widow whose husband had been caught publishing a Resistance newspaper and imprisoned. He died in prison right before the Liberation, leaving her with a young daughter. Anne, the third sister, and the oldest, was a schoolteacher, serious and exceedingly proper except for the fact, unheard of at the time, that she was an unwed mother who had proudly produced the only male child in the family. She never revealed the name of his father. These three sisters, whose maiden name was Joba, were half-Italian and one of their ancestors had been the last doge of Genoa. Monsieur Bouchet de Fareins had been of the upper class of Lyon, the heir to many silk mills that had been destroyed during the war.

After lunch, when the girls had returned to their convent and I sat drinking my demitasse and listening to the three sisters gossiping, as little as I understood, I realized that I had fallen into a family that could have been created by Colette. I felt immensely privileged to be allowed to join them.

José dropped in nearly every night, bringing with him a group of friends, all male, all young, all good-looking, all either graduate students or working at their first jobs. There was Philippe Hersent, son of one of the richest men in France; Comte Hubert d'Andlau; Comte Aimery de Comminges; and Comte Edouard de Moustiers, the oldest and grandest of them all since his mother had been born a princess de Bourbon-Parme, a collateral branch of the family that had ruled France. Edouard, it seemed to me, had the assurance and attitude of the Sun King himself.

Soon I found that I could speak a few words of French after all . . . motivation, motivation, motivation. They taught me to parrot insults that I later discovered translated into "bugger of mosquitoes" and "escapee from the bidet" and corrected, without mercy, all the mistakes I made in my first hesitant attempts at conversation.

Only once had the Jewish question entered into this new life. One afternoon after her sisters had left, Nicole, informed by Rosemarie Aubert, checked out her information by asking me if I was, indeed, Jewish.

"Yes, of course."

"Don't worry," she said hastily, in a reassuring tone of voice, "I won't tell anyone."

Shocked by this sign that she anticipated anti-Semitism, and surprised by her immediate impulse to hide my background, I used all the little eloquence at my command to insist that she tell everyone as soon as possible. If they didn't like it, too damn bad. I certainly had no interest in spending time on anyone who discriminated against Jews. I noticed no difference in the group of young men. They treated me exactly as before, as a curiosity, as someone to amuse them, someone to tease.

One night, in the course of a lively discussion, I made a threatening gesture at Edouard with the fireplace poker. Apparently this was an impermissible liberty to take because in an instant I found myself thrown over his knees and being soundly spanked. I quickly retreated to my room to hide my rage and humiliation. I found myself in tears and it was half an hour before I was able to return to the salon and act as if nothing had happened.

Perhaps a spanking seemed to Edouard to fall under the heading of another joke at my expense, but I'd been spanked only once in my life. It was an early memory, dating perhaps from the age of three and a half. My father had administered a few symbolic smacks after I'd deliberately broken his glasses because he'd given me a small toolbox and I'd been uncharacteristically furious at receiving what I considered to be a "boy's present." Daddy had been deeply reluctant to punish me and explained carefully why he was forced to spank me. I'd never before been so naughty . . . and never was again! Of course he didn't hurt me, but it had left an indelible memory. It was impossible to imagine an American boy daring to spank me now, but I hadn't been able to deal properly with Edouard, largely because the whole thing had happened so quickly.

To my great good fortune, José and I weren't attracted to each other at all, although we remained friends for more than twenty years. Slow on the uptake, I was utterly unprepared to understand or intuit the lives of these complicated French. One of the boys eventually explained to me that José was Nicole's lover, not Claire's boyfriend. I could scarcely believe it, because she was almost twice his age, and my thinking was deeply conventional. José was also the son of Nicole's for-mer—*very* former—best friend, a Brazilian heiress, and he had broken his engagement to a ravishing young American girl of great fortune because of Nicole. If he hadn't come to the house to be with her, bringing his band of pals with him, there wouldn't have been any young Frenchmen for me to meet.

I eventually understood that the only reason for Nicole's early dis-approval of me had vanished as soon as she realized that José wasn't going to be interested in me and I wasn't going to try to flirt with him. Even her usual migraines disappeared as she was reunited with this boy she worshiped.

Slowly Nicole and I began to become friends. Although she was never beautiful, she had a wild and potent charm when she chose to exercise it and a lovely, lulling, low, caressing voice, with which she could flirt with the best. Certainly my father, and later my husband, could attest to that. After a few weeks she invited me to call her by her first name and use the familiar form of address. The first time I "tutoyed" her at the lunch table, her daughters were bitter, openly angry and jealous of a sign of intimacy they were forbidden. This was probably one of the reasons she'd taken such an unusual step, since she loved to keep them off balance and pitted me against them, as she pitted them against each other, so that all of us were forever vying to be in her good graces. Of course, I was deeply grateful for this attention and a warmth I'd never dared to hope for. I fell for her, as she had intended I should, and added to the group of her devotees.

Soon Nicole began to take a hand with my clothes. There were almost no ready-to-wear stores in Paris at this time, but I managed to find one where I bought a jacket that I thought would update my old skirts. She took one look at it and, in an hour I've never forgotten, showed me the nine different places where it didn't fit. I took it back to the store the next day and, to the shopkeeper's unconcealed astonishment, insisted that he make nine alterations.

Shortly after that unforgettable lesson, which has served me all my life, Nicole revealed the name and address of her "little dressmaker." The names of their little dressmakers were normally kept a secret by French women—all but the richest of whom had one—because they didn't want her to have any more customers than she had already.

The little dressmaker was only a copyist who didn't provide any guidance about styles, merely fine workmanship. It was up to me to find a photograph or drawing of something I thought was suitable from the latest collections, then go to a fabric store and buy the right amount of cloth, lining, and trim, go to a button store for the buttons, and take all this to the dressmaker, who would, in the course of six weeks and at least four fittings, reproduce a couture garment made to my measure. Fortunately she was very, very cheap and very good.

In those days, besides sweaters, upper-class French women owned three essential outfits they wore day in and day out: a black suit, a gray suit, and a black cocktail dress. Even Ginette Spanier didn't order more than these three items plus an evening gown, from the Balmain collection. The American concept of owning a large variety of clothes simply didn't exist.

As I wrote in *Scruples,* a simple sweater, worn with the gray skirt and an Hermès scarf, was enough to make any woman, including the queen of England, well dressed enough to hold her own under any circumstances except those that required a cocktail dress or ball gown. Under orders from Nicole, I took myself to Hermès and spent an hour choosing a scarf that employed the classic motifs of stirrups and bridles, in bordeaux, green, and cream, with signature notes of gold, a scarf I was to keep for thirty-five years, the first in a still-growing collection. At the time it cost the equivalent of twenty-five dollars, which was much too much money for me to spend but absolutely worth the investment. I couldn't resist the temptation to buy a small Hermès "agenda," a date book with its own tiny silver pencil, an object that, when used in public, immediately conferred unspeakable status on its owner.

Fortunately for me, Balmain routinely employed a short model on whom clothes for petite clients were designed and shown. On the five or six occasions I was invited to balls in the course of the next year, I was able to borrow these glorious dresses from Ginette. After the afternoon fashion show was over, I'd appear and the dress would hastily be shortened, fitted to me, and accessorized. The morning after the ball I returned the dress, which would be put back into its original condition and worn at the collection that same day. Once, when I went to a *bal de tetê*, which required a headdress, the ladies at Balmain actually managed to fasten a small flock of white doves in my short hair—how, I'll never know.

Hubert d'Andlau persuaded me to take up fencing. Another prank? In a moment of folly, I, who can never tell one hand from another without thinking about it for a few seconds, joined a private fencing class in a famous Left Bank fencing club. I was utterly hopeless but the *maître* encouraged me, insisting on giving me additional lessons, because he needed the money, just as, years earlier, my piano teacher had told my mother I had talent, making me endure seven useless years of piano lessons. In a moment of insanity, I even went so far as to order a custom-made fencing jacket, which I was never to wear.

I still needed a job badly and Christmas was approaching in two months. Fortunately, Ginette continued to invite me frequently for drinks, and at her house I became friendly with a charming young Irishman named John Cavanaugh, a fine designer who worked as Balmain's assistant. Later, John opened his own successful couture house in London, where for many years he dressed Marina, the Duchess of Kent, then the only chic member of the royal family.

One early November night, John gave a cocktail party at his Left Bank apartment near the Eiffel Tower. All transportation in Paris had gone on strike, so I walked to the avenue Henri-Martin, the large street closest to boulevard Lannes, and actually had the nerve to hitchhike, a daring act that nothing but a party could have inspired. I got a lift on the back of the motorcycle of a tough-looking fellow who deposited me in a most gentlemanly fashion in front of John's place on the Champ-de-Mars.

During the party I noticed an exceptionally good-looking man, tweedy and obviously an American. I asked someone who he was. "That's Harrison Elliott," I was told. "He's the most charming man in Paris."

"Would you introduce me?"

Harrison and I chatted for a long while, laughing a lot. The important thing was that I could speak to him in English. The entire personality I'd been living without for months was suddenly mine again. Harrison was the first American I'd met since I arrived in Paris and I felt at home with him immediately. The way in which two Americans who have just been introduced to each other are able to communicate is entirely different in a dozen ways than it would be if they had to speak French. I'd forgotten how much more casual, intimate, easy, and relaxed I could be with a new acquaintance.

Harrison turned out to be a thirty-one-year-old Californian, from

June Street in Hancock Park. This meant nothing to me, but more than twenty years later I discovered that it was a conservative, old-money, highly respectable neighborhood of Los Angeles. Harrison looked exactly like my vague, glamorized idea of a Californian with a decided surfer twist: blondish-brownish surfer hair, surfer blue eyes, and regular, strong, masculine features. He wore large, horn-rimmed glasses and was tall and muscular. He'd been in the American army as an interpreter and had chosen to take his discharge in Paris when the war ended.

From there Harrison Elliott went to work at Dior and was in charge of public relations when Christian Dior invented the New Look in 1947 and created the greatest fashion revolution of the century, or the second greatest if you count Chanel, and I most certainly do. Every fashion editor in the world had depended on Harrison to let them photograph or sketch the dresses they wanted to feature. He'd done favors for all of them and was on the best of terms with everyone of importance in the world of fashion journalism.

Recently, he told me, he'd opened his own PR business, representing the powerful syndicate of the custom hatmakers of Paris—in those days no woman left home without a hat. In addition, he had a number of other clients who made various expensive accessories, such as handbags and umbrellas, and the city of Biarritz and Les Ballets de Paris de Roland Petit also were clients.

"Don't you have a job for me?" I asked eagerly as soon as I heard this.

"As a matter of fact, I might, except you can't speak French."

"But I'm learning more every day," I pleaded.

"Well . . . look, if you'll work for nothing until you're fluent, I'll find you something to do. I'll pay you once I'm satisfied with your French. You can come in tomorrow, thirteen rue Jean Mermoz, near the Rond-Point, and get started."

I all but danced the long way home from John's party, crossing more than half of Paris on foot in a dream of pure ecstasy. Now I wouldn't have to go back to New York, now everything had fallen into place, now I was truly on my way. I stopped en route and ate dinner alone in a small bistro, smiling at everyone in the restaurant. Most of the people of Paris seemed to be out strolling on the streets on that remarkable night of no transportation as they celebrated my new job, which was to determine the course of my life in ways no philosophy of my father's could have anticipated.

Chapter Eleven

THE NEXT MORNING I WALKED A FEW BLOCKS TO THE NUMBER FIFTY-two bus and took it for a twenty-five-minute ride, standing on the outside platform as I always did to get a better look at the city. I got off a short distance from Harrison Elliott's office, which was on a side street only just around the corner from the Rond-Point of the Champs-Elysées—at the center not just of the city but also of the fashion world of Paris. The office was on the ground floor, a simply furnished set of rooms with two secretaries, the most important of whom was named Annick. A part-time bookkeeper was the only other employee.

In France, no one can open a new business without a certain amount of registered capitalization that is disclosed on the firm's letterhead, and I soon learned, via Annick, that all the considerable capital invested in the PR firm came from a forty-one-year-old woman named Rosine de la Marre, known to everyone as Kiki. Kiki was famous, far and away the top designer of period costumes used in the French cinema. It was rumored that she was involved romantically with Harrison, just as often as it was rumored that he was only interested in men.

My knowledge of homosexuals was vague. I'd first heard of "fairies" in high school and I'd decided for myself that they all lived on Devil's Island, where they engaged in their odd practices because there were no women around. Later, at college, Harvard boys informed me that all "pansies" went to Yale, a tale I more or less believed for several years, until I went to a Harvard–Yale game with a Yalie. The topic didn't interest me much and I simply assumed, in Harrison's case, that where there was smoke there was fire.

I was immediately put to work running all kinds of errands, rushing from one hat designer to another to arrange to borrow new hats for photographers, picking up all manner of things, particularly photographs, and taking them here and there. At first I was no more than a human delivery service.

Quickly, I was entrusted with more important jobs, making myself useful helping out at hat collections, which were given at the same time and in the same daily way as the couture shows. Hat models, chosen for the way a hat sat on their heads, not for their looks, paraded in front of the customers, wearing absolutely plain black dresses and no accessories, the better to show off the new millinery creations that made headlines in newspapers and magazines all over the world.

Chic women, at this time, had a different hat for each outfit they owned. The hats were not designed by the couturiers but by custom hat designers. Women had three or four fittings on their hats, exactly as they had fittings on their clothes. Ordering a perfect French hat was a major and serious piece of feminine business, on which a woman's future might well depend. As Danny Kaye sang, "I'm Anatole of Paris, I reek with chic, my hat of the week caused six divorces, three runaway horses . . ."

Even I was required to wear a hat. My natural penchant for going hatless was decried as heresy by Harrison's clients, and the famous Susy, the house of Gilbert Orcel, the house of Maude et Nano, and several others made me free hats, for otherwise, of course, I wouldn't have been able to afford them.

My finances were in a desperately mixed-up state. Up until now my father had been paying my room and board and giving me a small allowance for general living expenses, including a few new clothes for my new life. Now that I had a job, he had reduced my allowance by the size of the salary I was supposed to be earning. I didn't dare admit that I wouldn't be paid until I learned to speak French well, since my parents wouldn't consider that a real job at all. But when my imaginary salary was deducted from my allowance, it meant that my living expenses had to be pared to almost nothing. Although I'd given up fencing the minute I got a job, I still had to pay for that ultra-elegant and useless quilted white vest.

The only answer I could find to paper over my permanent insolvency during the rest of my stay in Paris was to invent an elaborate history of major dental work that never stopped being necessary. My parents sent me extra money for the nonexistent dentist and dental specialists, and with great good fortune I had no dental problems at all during this time. Perhaps this was my first experience in writing fiction, but it felt like garden-variety, old-fashioned lying. However, I had no choice and I didn't worry about my crime, any more than I worried about changing my dollars on the black market, as every American in Paris did. It was amazing how many francs you could get for the dollar, at least four times the official ratio.

In the late fall, I received a notice that my old winter clothes had finally arrived from New York. I had to go to customs to pick them up and there I discovered that the big suitcase my mother had sent was locked and I didn't have a key. I tried to explain to the customs inspector that the suitcase contained only worn clothes, but he insisted on prying it open with a crowbar, breaking the lock and the frame and then proceeding to go through each and every item of my out-dated, all-but-useless Wellesley wardrobe.

Suddenly, as I watched this vandalism, something exploded in my head, detonated by his pigheaded stubbornness and sheer meanness, and, from out of the blue, I began to berate him soundly in loud, furious and fairly fluent . . . French! I was so clearly in the right that I soared to heights of angry eloquence. All the way back to boulevard Lannes, I never stopped talking to the taxi driver, violently informing him of my misfortune, without even realizing that I was speaking to him in French. After I'd lugged the suitcase upstairs—it was one of those days without electricity and the elevator didn't work—I related my story all over again, to everyone who would listen, in rapid, em-bellished, detailed, colorful French! They stood around listening to me in shock, disbelieving and delighted, for once at a loss for words.

It took me a while to realize why. Abruptly I understood that in the space of a few hours I had become a creature transformed. Everything had fallen together with that thunderclap of fury at the customs in-spector. I knew how to tell a story in their language, I knew how to complain in their language, I knew how to describe an idiot in their language. *I could speak their precious language.* The French adore French with a passion and a ferocity that no American can understand. No one is truly human to them who doesn't speak it. I'd fulfilled the promise I'd made to my mother, but, more important, I'd made the essential breakthrough without which I could never have become a real part of the life of the family or, indeed, of the life of France.

I never looked back. Every single day my French grew dramatically better and better. It turned out that I had a genuine ear for language, and now, as I dared to use it freely, all the lessons Mademoiselle Gaill-rand had drilled into me for three years came flooding back: vocabu-lary, verbs, even the use of the subjunctive. Total immersion in French for less than three months had done the trick, something I could never have guessed in high school, more than four years earlier, where we had had only written drills. My accent became that of the Bouchet de Fareinses, a pure Parisian accent, since I had no other accent to lose.

When I could really speak French, I discovered that it wasn't just knowing how to use the grammar or the vocabulary, it's in the pitch of the vocal cords, the head movements, the shoulder and hand move-ments, the shape of the mouth, the tilt of the head, the width of the smile, the play of the eyes. It's a strong verbal body language, as dif-ferent from my normal way of communicating as a Kabuki play, and it transformed me into someone I couldn't be in English. French gave me a second personality.

I informed Harrison that I now spoke French well enough to be paid for my work. But he was going through a temporary cash problem, he explained, and he'd have to postpone the day when my salary would begin. He'd already borrowed some of the little money I had in order to pay the office phone bill. Even I could tell that he wasn't charging nearly enough for his services, hoping to build up his business by working too cheaply, but I couldn't venture to give him business advice.

Instead, since it was close to Christmas, I told him that I'd be taking a skiing vacation over the holidays, returning on the morning of January 9, my twenty-first birthday. After that, I promised to continue to work as a volunteer, "until he could pay me," so that my father wouldn't drag me back to New York. I had few illusions about that promised salary, but I blithely chose not to think about it.

After I'd extracted some more money from my parents—God bless root canal!—I took off, by myself, renting a tiny room in a small hotel in Megève. There, for the sum of three American dollars, I could hire a private ski instructor for the entire day.

I'd learned to ski during my junior year in college, when I'd gone with Doris Sommer to the Laurentians in Canada, and I'd kept at it with Jimmy Kahn in my senior year. I truly loved skiing, the only outdoor sport I was willing to suffer for. Now I took myself and my leather ski boots and wooden skis down to the ski school at Megève and asked for an instructor for the next two weeks. The head of the ski school looked me over carefully, then looked around at his corps of dashing Alpine instructors, one more devastating than the next, and assigned me to the oldest of them, a plain, very married, middle-aged man, who was a local farmer the rest of the year. It was infuriating, but I simply didn't have the nerve an older and more self-possessed woman would have had to ask for another instructor, a young and handsome instructor.

I spent the next two weeks getting intensive ski instruction and nothing but ski instruction from Emile, who was kind and patient. I was essentially too cautious to ever ski really well, and the only time I could bring myself to let go and deliberately ski the fall line, straight downhill, was after lunch at the chalet restaurant on top of the Mont d'Arbois, where Emile and I shared a bottle of red wine. However, I survived the two weeks without injury and learned a great deal.

On the train going back to Paris, without the benefit of the courage red wine had induced in the mountains, I reviewed my life and determined to lose my virginity.

Chapter Twelve

As I've been writing this autobiography, I've finally come to grips with another, much deeper, and far more important reason for the decision I reached on my birthday eve. Joe, the midshipman, had effectively taken away my power when I was fifteen and forced me into premature sexual activity. My college career as a deadly resolute virgin, however technical at the end, was an attempt to regain that power. Now, in Paris, with all my own careful and sound logic, I was taking the decision about my virginity into my own hands. Without any prompting of feelings for any particular man, I was consciously planning to regain my sexual power in the straightest, most aggressive way possible, based entirely on my own decision. Once again, I was able to find myself inner-directed, the only comfortable place for me to be. My legal majority was an excuse I didn't need.

If I had come of age sexually in another decade, perhaps in the easygoing, permissive mid-1960s or, better yet, in the 1970s, the seriousness of virginity could never have been so intensely meaningful to me. However, given my age, virginity and its loss were crucial aspects of my coming-of-age. The proof of their importance to me lies in the fact that, without my realizing it until now, they have been a constant in every novel I've written, no matter how contemporary the setting.

On page 79 of *Scruples* my very first heroine, Billy Winthrop, loses her virginity and on page 194 Valentine O'Neill, the second heroine of that novel, loses her virginity. Princess Daisy; all three heroines of *Mistral's Daughter;* Maxi Amberville of *I'll Take Manhattan;* Eve and her two daughters, Delphine and Freddy, who are the three heroines of *Till We Meet Again;* Jazz Kilkullen of *Dazzle;* Gigi Orsini of *Scruples Two*—the list of defloration goes on and on. Even in my latest novel, *The Jewels of Tessa Kent,* written twenty-two years after *Scruples,* both Tessa and her daughter, Maggie, lose their virginity. The context of the scenes is never repetitive; only the eventual outcome is planned.

With few exceptions it is my heroines who decide exactly when they will choose to abandon their virginity, making for self-determined, independent sexuality, in keeping with their own strong characters. Unlike my decision on my birthday, their decisions are based on a specific man they plan to have sex with, almost always a man they're deeply attracted to, on whom they choose to bestow the "pearl of great price," as we used to call it in college.

No heroine of mine, except in Daisy's case of rape, is set free to have sex until I've given her permission, picked her partner, and set the scene. (And of course the rape was planned by me as well.) This endless compensation for the reality of my own life is clear. Amazingly, it's taken me until now to see how, in this particular area, my unconscious operates. "Relentlessly" would be the way to describe it.

As I look at my Hermès agenda for 1949, I see that on Monday, January 10, *the very next day* after my birthday, I've written, *"Le Commencement."* That night I'd taken my regular bus home and bumped into Edouard de Moustiers, whom I'd never seen on the bus before. If I were writing this in a novel, I would never dream of employing such an unlikely coincidence or such a short time frame. This was real life.

Edouard, who had a job at a large firm called L'Air Liquide, still lived at his parents' apartment on boulevard Suchet, only a short distance from boulevard Lannes. When we got off the bus, he asked if he could walk me home. As we reached the front door, he stopped, put his hands on my shoulders, and very simply asked, *"Est-ce que tu voudra être à moi?"* Would I be his? I answered that I would. Obviously my change in mental orientation had produced the necessary vibes.

I'd never so much as kissed him, never had a minute alone with him before, but it takes very little thought to see that of the possible men I knew, Edouard was the most likely. First, he'd already become a sexual figure in my life by spanking me, with all the erotic connotations I didn't realize at the time. There was even the connection to my father and my first spanking. But that obvious, and to me, in spite of being a veteran of psychoanalysis, unconvincingly Freudian aspect aside, Edouard was far and away the most impressive and mature of all the group that hung out at the apartment. He was tall and beginning to lose his hair, but that was compensated for entirely by his imposing features, his large, beautifully cut, distinctively aristocratic, aquiline nose, his heavy eyebrows peaked over keen eyes, his firm, rather stern mouth, and his expression of command and authority. He looked truly regal.

"We'll have to wait until my parents go away for a weekend," he told me. I couldn't imagine why that was necessary, but apparently Edouard, *grand seigneur* that he was, didn't believe that the deflowering of a virgin should take place in a hotel. And there was the problem of surrendering our separate proofs of identity when we arrived. (No one even today is supposed to so much as leave his house in France without proof of identity.) You couldn't rent a room in any French hotel without giving this proof to the local police, who, most inconveniently, kept it overnight.

Could there have been anything more anticlimactic? After all I'd gone through to retain my virginity, I expected, at the very least, to be swept off my feet, in a fanfare of trumpets.

Reader, his parents didn't leave home for an entire month.

Incredibly, on February 10, after drinks and dinner with Michel Paulmier-Peterson, a beautiful half-Swede-half-Frenchman, at Les Trois Canettes, a favorite Italian bistro on the Left Bank, I finally made my way to a *"rendez-vous with Edouard chez lui."* (His parents must have hung around for dinner.)

There is a highly significant star next to this date, the first time that star appears in my agenda. *Without even buying me dinner,* Edouard took possession of my body. No dinner? Which of the boys I'd known at college, boys who had never taken me out without feeding me at a good restaurant, would ever have bet that such a possibility—such a crime!—could ever take place?

The experience was, as of course it was destined to be, perfectly dreadful. Losing my virginity hurt very badly indeed, something I hadn't been at all prepared for in spite of all my reading. However, Edouard was determined to perform his part and I, God knows, wanted to do what I'd set out to do. I gritted my teeth and glared at the ceiling and thought bitterly about what a fool I'd been not to have allowed Jimmy Kahn to be the first. At least I was physically wild about Jimmy in a way I never felt about Edouard. At dawn that morning he drove me back to Nicole's in his ancient, open sports car. I crept up the stairs, stealthily inserted my key in the front door, and, making no noise at all, regained my room in my stocking feet, satisfied that no one knew that I'd not slept in my bed as usual.

My agenda shows that in the next two weeks I spent three more evenings alone with Edouard—his parents must have been away on holiday—and one afternoon hunting in the country. That was the only occasion on which I remember being able to have an orgasm, standing up, fully clothed, and necking with him in a barnyard, after fruitless efforts in bed. Although my memory isn't exact, this leads me to believe that he couldn't have known much about clitoral stimulation. Otherwise, it's incredible that I could have had full-fledged sex with him, with less and less pain each time, and not have had an orgasm at all on any of those four occasions. Edouard himself was not happy about the course of his seduction and, in fact, let me know that it was not only rather inappropriate of me to finally reach a climax in a barnyard but slightly ridiculous.

One day during this period, Harrison suggested we visit the ancient, out-of-the-way church of Saint-Julien-le-Pauvre. What we were doing sightseeing, I can't imagine, busy as we were, but in the taxi on the way back to the center of Paris, he suddenly leaned over and kissed me once, lightly and quickly. I was stunned. The man, as far as I knew, was either romantically involved with Kiki de la Marre or not interested in women, and we'd enjoyed a friendly, joking, easygoing but very daily business relationship. It was a familiar American relationship, not a complicated French relationship of the type I was consumed by.

If there was one man in Paris with whom I hadn't been flirting, it was Harrison. "What was *that* about?" I asked him, confused. "I think I could fall in love with you," he answered with a laugh. He's got to be kidding or teasing me, I thought, and shook my head at him in mock rebuke.

Sometime during the next week Harrison casually invited me to spend the next weekend with him in a little village named Bertenonville, outside of Paris, leaving Saturday afternoon in a car he'd borrowed from Kiki. I agreed, totally unaware that I was making any sort of decision at all. Nicole was curious enough to ask what I thought I was doing going away with my boss for the weekend. I answered that I needed to get out of Paris for a few days and just relax in the country . . . I was tired of chasing after rabbits who peed pathetically after they'd been shot and, anyway, he was a *pédé,* as homosexuals were known in argot. She raised a sardonic eyebrow but let it pass.

Harrison and I left Paris very late and drove out to Bertenonville, where we arrived just before dinner. We were staying at a very modest bed-and-breakfast where Harrison was well known to the owners. I just had time to use the downstairs bathroom and wash my hands before we ate a long, hearty, country meal. After dinner the owner's wife showed us to our upstairs rooms. Or rather to our room. There was only one guest room, a very cold one, on the second floor and it contained an enormous bed, which had been carefully opened and warmed with a warming pan.

Reader, what was I to do?

I'll make the best of it, I thought, not just amazed but slightly amused at the prospect of having to share a bed. I still assumed that since Harrison was, as far as I knew, homosexual, although I'd never personally witnessed any indication of this rumor, the situation was harmless. I was wearing my long johns, underwear, socks, and sweaters, hardly an outfit that would lead to seduction. I swear on the head of my only granddaughter, Kate Krantz, that when I climbed into that huge bed, I did not consciously believe that Harrison had any designs on me.

Of course, Harrison didn't know about my precious, closely guarded virginity. Unlike the discussions I'd had with Nicole, and she'd had with her sisters and José and probably every last one of the boys of his group, the condition of the "silly American virgin" had, of course, never come up in my business life.

I turned my back and prepared to sleep. "What are we going to do about this?" Harrison asked, tapping me on the shoulder. "This what?" I asked. "This," he answered, putting my hand on his penis. He was fully erect and enormous, much, much bigger than any man I'd ever touched before. "My God!" I cried, totally confounded and bewildered, both at his condition and his size. The sheer surprise of that moment has never faded. He wasn't *supposed* to be excited. And although I'd had plenty of experience judging penis size in the course of my college career, Harrison was astonishingly large.

The next few hours of earnestly attempted lovemaking certified two things: I had to be the most intact of intact virgins and Harrison was the most heterosexual of men. There was simply no possibility of penetration. None of my lovemaking with Edouard, who was perfectly satisfactorily proportioned, had prepared me to accept a man the size of Harrison, and I certainly couldn't pass up the temptation to use this heaven-sent opportunity to claim my virginity for a second time.

I don't remember any more details, but we must have managed to satisfy each other somehow because we finally fell asleep.

I woke up the next morning, saw Harrison lying beside me, and was totally engulfed by incredible joy. I was in love, madly, madly and completely, without any question in love, for the first time. Nothing was the same as it had been the day before. My first twenty-one years vanished as I lived only in the staggering happiness of the immediate present. It was a state of life-changing bliss.

There was no bathroom attached to our room and as I rushed urgently to the downstairs toilet, across an open courtyard, the romance of the situation was undimmed. Shivering, I returned to the bedroom for more hours of fruitless but desperately passionate sex. Eventually we had to get up for breakfast, but we returned to bed until it was time for lunch. Nothing, perhaps an inch of penetration, but otherwise he was just too big and I was just too tight.

We ate lunch in silence, goofily, exhaustedly, utterly content just to gaze at each other and wonder what on earth had happened to us after all these months of knowing each other in such a different context. If it hadn't been for José and the group of young men I met at Nicole's, surely I would have realized that we had been falling slowly in love for months, since the day we met. It certainly wasn't business that demanded that we spend so much time together. And yet I'd had no idea what had been going on between the two of us, or rather, it would be more accurate to say that I'd given it no thought. That night I wrote in my agenda, *"La plus belle matinée de ma vie—H, mon amour."*

Just as we were finishing lunch, in the mid-afternoon, the door to the dining room opened and we were astonished to see Kiki, who'd unexpectedly arrived with a group of friends, to claim her car. She was a striking woman, beautifully dressed, with a big warm smile and lots of dash, a handsome creature, tall, with olive skin, dark brown hair, and bright brown eyes. To me she was a perfect example of a worldly adult. In one brief look and a friendly greeting, this forty-one-year-old Frenchwoman of immense sophistication let me know that she was shocked to the bone to find me there, understood the situation completely, and was determined to show nothing.

I felt not the slightest embarrassment. What had happened to Harrison and me was too important to leave room for anyone else's feelings. His past with Kiki had nothing to do with his present with me. There was a certain amount of badinage and then Kiki and Harrison drove me home. I sat silently in the backseat, too worn out by lack of sleep, the expenditure of sexual energy, and the discovery of love to be able to think rationally about what was going on or what was going to happen. As soon as I reached Nicole's, I took to my bed and fell into a feverish sleep.

I only saw Kiki once again, quite by chance, during the rest of the time I spent in Paris. It was as if she'd disappeared, and, with the cruel, self-centered single-mindedness of first love, I wasn't interested enough to even ask what had happened to her.

However, Edouard didn't conveniently vanish from my life. Although the next time I saw him I told him, to his displeasure, that our barely started affair was over because I'd fallen in love with another man, he continued to be a part of the entire group around Nicole and José, and therefore inescapable. He was upset at first and kept inviting me for drinks at the Jockey Club, where women were only allowed at the bar, but soon he realized I was serious. Rather unsuccessfully, he tried not to show that he was wounded by being thrown over for an American. Or perhaps it was better for it to have been an American—one American condescending to lower herself with another—than another Frenchman?

Harrison and I continued to behave normally at the office, although Annick walked in on us one day when we were holding hands and that was the end of discretion. We were both so busy that we didn't manage to see very much of each other alone at night, and when we did, we still weren't able to make love, however ardently we tried.

I had three or four dates a day, lunch, tea, cocktails, and dinner—

fortunately I wasn't getting paid for the work I did on my job—and in spite of being overwelmingly in love, I didn't break a single one of them. Never again in my life until the day I got engaged, some five years in the future, did I confine myself to seeing only one man, another holdover from having worn the accursed crest of Joe, the midshipman.

Three full weeks later, Harrison and I decided to spend another weekend in the country. We missed the train we intended to take, since he could no longer borrow Kiki's car. Instead we ran through a rainstorm to a tiny, squalid hotel on the rue Monsieur le Prince, called the Hôtel du Paradis. Again, an utterly unlikely detail I'd never put in a novel. There, thank heaven, during a Thai dinner, I finally drank enough wine—a great deal of wine—to relax, at long last, and be able to be penetrated fully. I was giddy with relief and very proud of myself.

I truly lost my virginity, albeit for the second time, on March 19, 1949, almost fifty years ago. If I say it seems like yesterday, forgive me the cliché, but it does, oh, it does.

Chapter Thirteen

WHAT DID I REALLY KNOW ABOUT HARRISON ELLIOTT AT THE TIME I fell so totally in love with him in the space of one night? Very little, it seems to me, considering that we'd worked closely together for months. For the first time in my life a man's background was unimportant and, to him, my background was equally irrelevant, just as politics and the state of the world didn't hold our attention for a minute. Anything that didn't concern our daily lives together didn't seem to be happening at all.

The eleven-year difference in our ages, the fact that Harrison had been through the entire war while I was in high school and had lived in Paris during all of my college years, the distance that separated the cultures of Los Angeles and New York, vast in those days, gave us almost nothing in common about which to compare notes. Even if we'd been born in the same year in the same city, for me, the past had vaporized in the delicious bewilderment and enchanted poetry of my present. One detail tells me how little I was like my former self. After a lifetime of constant and habitual reading, and following four years of immersion in the best that English literature had to offer, I managed to finish only one book the entire year I spent in Paris. Which book? *The Fountainhead.*

Looking back, I recognize that Harrison spoke the most beautiful and polished French of any American I'd ever heard, although I didn't know where or how or even why he'd learned it. I knew his mother was a devout Christian Scientist and that he disapproved of her convictions, but I didn't know if he'd been brought up in any particular religion, although his looks were conspicuously those of a WASP. I knew he had a brother, but I didn't know what his father did for a living or where Harrison had been to college, or even if he'd been to college—I can't imagine that I didn't ask at least that particular question that had been so automatically asked for four years. Even after all his time in Paris, everything about his manner and clothes was preppy in a way I recognized was unmistakably Ivy League.

I understood that he was aware of his ambiguous sexual reputation, because, early on, in one of our rare serious discussions, he warned me that I'd hear about it on all sides. The rumor was, he said, based on his friendship with his longtime client, the ballet star and choreographer Roland Petit. On many occasions we had dinner with Roland and Margot Fonteyn, with whom Roland was romantically involved at the time in some complicated way I didn't comprehend at all. The very real world of bisexuality in which Harrison was at home was a mystery to me. I tried to hide how out of my depth I felt. Dancing with Orson Welles at a party or having drinks with another of Harrison's friends, Robert Capa, perhaps the greatest photographer of World War II, was on a level of reality I could manage to handle, with awe but still keeping my head above water. Double-dating with Margot Fonteyn, the ultimate ballerina in the world, was quite another.

I learned that Harrison's job in the army, once the war was over, had been to go out into the countryside and trade with the farmers. He bartered unneeded army surplus for fresh produce. He admitted, laughing, that this job had led him into playing fast and loose with a rather major piece of army matériel . . . a jeep. He either had or had not spent time in the army jail for this escapade—the denouement of the story was left deliberately vague, and, when I got to know him better, I suspected he had gone to jail. The few facts I knew about Harrison included the chip in a front tooth and his nearsightedness, which caused him to wear glasses. When he took them off to peer closely at someone with his huge blue eyes, which were already framed by faintly etched laugh lines, the effect was flat-out devastating, but I never believed that he did it on purpose. I discovered that many people called him "H," and soon I did, too, from time to time.

Harrison's charm came partly from the fact that he was, on a dozen levels, more constant fun to be with than anybody in Paris. As John Cavanaugh said when we met again twenty years later, "There was never again such a golden boy." Harrison could go to a café for coffee and make it a memorable occasion. He could cross a street and turn it into an adventure. He was as naturally joyous and high-spirited as a happy kid and he had an unfailing ability to tap into the fantasy and flavor of every moment. Effortlessly, he lured everyone he met into the irresistible world he created that made them feel as fascinating as he was. Harrison had an amazing gift for intimacy. There was something deliciously *collusive* in being with him that made people feel as if they were caught up in some wonderfully childish and exciting—if unknown and benign—wickedness. He was infectiously charming by nature, without calculation or forethought. Everyone he knew, in every circle he moved in, wanted to be with him. And he had chosen me.

I often think that only my assumption that he was homosexual kept me from falling for him as soon as I'd started to work with him. This natural insulation, which caused the purely friendly attitude I felt toward him, may well have been one of the reasons this devastating man came after me.

Years later, in *Dazzle,* I described a photographer named Tony Gabriel. "Charm, that unfairly distributed blessing, is essentially inexplicable and resists description . . . Gabe couldn't turn it on because he couldn't turn it off." Neither could Harrison.

Yet, somehow, even in a torrent of emotion I'd never felt before, I was simultaneously able to realize in some small part of my mind that in many ways Harrison was fundamentally unreliable. The tip of the iceberg was his absolute inability to be on time, ever, for anything, a matter that from earliest babyhood had been important and significant to me. I was, I knew, overly programmed to absolute promptness, but time was something Harrison had no concept of, nor did it bother him at all that he lacked it.

To me, it was unthinkable that someone wouldn't return borrowed money, but Harrison never even bothered to mention a hope that he might be able to return the small sums he frequently borrowed from me. They wouldn't have amounted to much under other circumstances, but because I was working without a salary, they were vital. He was completely financially irresponsible, not dishonest. He didn't pay me because he couldn't. He'd have given me his last franc if he'd had one, but as far as he was concerned, long before we found out we were in love, my money was his money. I could never refuse him whatever I had. I learned to pay Nicole my pension and buy a book of bus tickets the minute I got my allowance, so at least I had the essentials.

In these small but meaningful ways, Harrison's character was foreign to me. Many things about him made me uneasy. He was wrong for me and I sensed that fact in my bones from the first. I knew it as powerfully as I refrained from thinking about it.

I may seem incredibly judgmental for a girl of just twenty-one who was experiencing a rare, passionate—and long-lasting—love for the first time. Shouldn't I have been too blindly caught up in my emotions to even notice Harrison's faults? Perhaps I might have been, if I hadn't worked closely with Harrison for months before I found out that I was in love with him. However, I knew only too well how he operated in a business situation; I'd seen, over and over, how little seriousness he allotted to his obligations. It wasn't any one individual thing he failed to do, but all of them together. Quite simply, he lacked any trustworthy center.

Before I can feel that things are right in a love relationship, I need a man of thorough decency, a really good man, a man whose honesty runs clear and true through his character, an honesty on which I can rely. Harrison didn't have it and wouldn't have recognized it if he saw it.

His joie de vivre and grace were the reverse side of his lack of character, and, in the end, one canceled out the other. Of course, at the time I didn't dwell on any of this or explain it to myself . . . it existed but I ignored it.

I was hardly a paragon myself: I'd goofed off at college as much as I could, the opposite of the ideal Wellesley girl, and at the moment I was lying to my parents without shame, for reasons that were essential to me. However, I'd always followed through on the obligations I undertook, great and small, and I was, basically, a dutiful person who lived up to expectations. If anything, I was too good a girl. Although I didn't demand that other people be like me, Harrison existed, in too many ways, in another dimension of behavior altogether. He didn't have the slightest moral core I could ever discover. He was not the right man for a good girl, for a Judy Tarcher, to love.

I was, and remain, profoundly non-self-destructive. I can be carried away by my emotions, but only so far. At a certain point I'm stopped by my built-in common sense, a knowledge of what is appropriate behavior, a serious lack of recklessness, a keen sense of where the boundaries exist, beyond which I won't and can't go. Peter Duchin once told me, during a testy interview in the 1970s, that I was the squarest person he'd ever met.

Harrison would have been the least square.

As soon as H started to mention marriage, early in the spring, I told him that I hated the idea of marriage, was much too young to even think of it, and begged him not to mention it again. He did, however, return to the subject frequently, even trying to dredge up a totally unconvincing Jewish grandmother, as if that would have made any difference, but I always managed to deflect the question. Even in the dizzying excitement of my first true love, I realized, largely subconsciously, that given our characters, we could never make a life together.

In my least favorite moment with Harrison, I spent two hideous hours waiting for him on the terrace of the Café de Flore, ordering one mineral water after another to keep the waiter at bay, all but doubled up with intense menstrual cramps. Harrison was supposed to meet me, bringing a pair of shoes that I was having repaired. I'd given him the money for the shoemaker, and the shoes were vital: I'd never found any French shoes to fit me and these were the last almost-decent pair I owned. He finally arrived without the shoes. He'd bumped into the Orcels, our richest clients, had gone for drinks with them, and had paid for the drinks with my shoe-repair money. He'd simply "forgotten the time." He was thoughtlessly, almost compulsively hospitable. To grab a check with my money was necessary to him and he genuinely couldn't understand why I was so upset. This incident—this wrong, wrong, wrong incident—took place at the height of the enchanted spring when we were so happy together.

My love for Paris had only grown more intense, yet I had outlasted my six-month visitor's visa and I had never been able to obtain a work permit, which at that time was impossible for any American. My non-paying job with Harrison could not have appeared on his books even if he had paid me every week. Neither Ginette nor Suzanne Lulling at Dior, nor any of our clients, could have legally hired me.

Through a friend of my parents, named Viola Ilma, who had serious sexual pull with an official of the Paris police, I got an extension of six months on my visa and was able to persuade another official that my means of support was a form of barter: room and board in exchange for giving English lessons to Nicole's daughters. In reality, the three girls had spent many vacations visiting an English family, and once they realized I could speak French, they revealed that they spoke upper-class English themselves.

In spite of these hard facts, I managed to blind myself to the fact that I wouldn't be able to live in Paris forever. For me as for Maggie in *Mistral's Daughter,* "Each day was enough, round and full and as complete as an apple of the sun."

Whenever people asked me when I'd have to go home, I had only one blithe answer. "Never!" Amazingly, I actually managed to believe it. I continued to live in a kind of total denial that's completely opposite to my normal nature. It must have been the only way to fully experience my happiness. I didn't even collect memories. Each minute with Harrison was too alive to be trapped, and if I'd tried to pin down any particular moment, it would have been as good as an admission that this moment might not come again. I refused to allow myself to imagine that in time to come I'd long to remember specifics of any particular hour or minute. It was all going to last forever . . . I didn't ask how.

Again, as I wrote in *Dazzle,* "Forgetting any other reality, Jazz and Gabe lived through the . . . weeks without asking questions of the future or directing a thought to the past. Only the uncomplicated completeness of the lavish present existed, perfect days and perfect nights, which would mark all days and all nights to come in their memories; days and nights in which detail flowed into detail to make a seamless, splendid whole; days and nights that are granted to a few fortunate people once in a lifetime, but rarely twice."

Chapter Fourteen

A FRUITFUL, ALMOST TROPICAL AND SUDDEN SPRING CAME TO PARIS
that year. From April first there was never a day that wasn't glorious
and, as if to make up for the winter, finally warm.

Nicole and the family were going to Le Bois Normand for a four-
week spring vacation, decreed by the school authorities, but, of course,
I didn't intend to join them. Nicole, however, still expected my room
and board to be paid. I thought this was only fair since I had been
accepted as a paying guest for a given number of months, and she
counted on my money and ration tickets. Her entire family was able
to eat because of it. How could she manage if I suddenly left her?

Quickly, I found a tiny, unbelievably cheap hotel room on the Left
Bank, at the Hôtel Valence on the rue de Valence, near the Seine, a
short walk up the rue Saint-Benoît to the crossroads where the church
of Saint-Germain-des-Prés stands. I moved there on April 11.

This area had become my stomping ground. The Café de Flore,
where I had breakfast every morning, was *my* café—I never set foot
in Les Deux Magots, only a block way and equally famous. La Reine
Blanche and Le Montana were my bars, Les Trois Canettes and the
really cheap Aux Assassins were my bistros.

The Hôtel Valence boasted a bathroom down the hall where, for a
few additional francs, I could arrange for a bath. My room had the
usual sink and bidet in the corner, and the friendly lady at the front
desk assured me, when I asked her about possible visitors, that as long
as a gentleman produced his identity, I need not trouble myself. She
seemed to anticipate a veritable parade.

Harrison and I were almost always together, although I continued,
following my convictions, to date a number of other men, particularly
Philippe Hersent. At one point, thanks to naughty José, who put me
wise, I made a shocking and laughable discovery.

During that first autumn when I was still being ridiculed for being
an American virgin, all the adults in Nicole's world, including her sisters and the entire band of young men, had been watching me carefully
and waiting to see which one of the guys would be the first to get me
to bed. It had never been a question of "if," only of "who." They had
even been betting on it, something like an office pool. The night I'd
first tiptoed home so carefully from Edouard's, Nicole had been per-

fectly aware of it, actually watching me arrive on the street outside from her bedroom window. She'd spread the news delightedly. Perhaps Edouard himself had tipped her off, although it wouldn't have been like him to do so.

Yes, the French are an irredeemably cynical race. I had given them months of amusement, when I could have saved myself the trouble.

On April 21, Harrison turned thirty-two and I decided to give him a birthday party in my hotel room. I filled the bidet with dozens and dozens of daisies, bought a bottle of scotch and one of gin, and walked up to the Flore and persuaded a friendly bartender to give me a gigantic lump of ice, which I lugged back while it dripped all over my blouse. I invited everyone we both knew and they all came. Few parties I've ever given have been so successful, with the room wonderfully over-crowded and expensive liquor flowing as it rarely did in those days. God knows how I got the money for the drinks . . . some new dental emergency, no doubt. I drank very little during my life in Paris. Imported alcohol cost too much and wine and aperitifs didn't agree with me.

One of Harrison's closest friends was a disreputable, colorful guy of undiscoverable, almost certainly criminal, occupation named Robert Cagnoli, whose father owned an abandoned brothel that had been, after the world-famous Sphinx, the second most important *maison close* in Paris. Although it was now shut by the government, and officially didn't exist, Robert still had a key and lived there, illegally, with his tough girlfriend, Natalie. We all called it, without frills, "the whorehouse."

By the end of April, Harrison and I decided we had to live together. In order to save on rent, since he was totally broke, H had already moved to the Cagnolis' ancestral whorehouse on a decidedly unpic-turesque side street in Montparnasse, not far from the Opéra. I moved in with him there while Nicole was still in Normandy.

A female member of the French Assembly, one Marte Richard, had made all brothels illegal several years earlier, throwing hundreds of girls out on the street and disrupting businesses that had been going along peacefully for decades, if not generations. The only water at Robert's place was cold, and the few sticks of furniture remaining were on the top floor. To get to our room I had to toil up six flights of stairs, passing the empty rooms whose walls still were decorated in their varied and gaudy former fashions: Madame de Pompadour, Turk-ish Delight, African Queen, and, of course, everybody's favorite, Tor-ture Chamber.

There the four of us sometimes played at keeping house, shopping in the nearby street market and cooking a simple dinner on that rare occasion when we didn't have other plans. Or rather, Natalie cooked and I paid for the food. Harrison and I occupied one run-down little room, all but completely filled by a bed and an armoire, Robert and Natalie another, and there was a kitchen, a shower, and a joint living/dining room with a long dining table and a group of ill-assorted chairs. On weekends we sometimes invited a crowd to come over and supply us with food and drink. In return, Robert put on screenings of ancient, silent pornographic films in which the men wore nothing but black socks and dress shoes. They were deadly serious and unforgettably filthy films, sexually arousing in spite of their old-fashioned acting and the barrage of wisecracks everyone made while they watched.

Although I could indeed speak French and I had an engrossing job in PR, I realized, without the slightest guilt, that this current arrangement was not perhaps *precisely* what my parents had in mind when they gave me permission to stay on in Paris. I was living illegally in a shuttered whorehouse, living in all-out, full-bodied sin, working without a permit—and not even getting paid.

Reader, consider that less than a year earlier I'd almost been thrown out of college for the crime of drinking, not even on campus property but on an adjoining beach! If only Babs Butterfield could have seen me then.

One spring night Harrison and I lay on the bed, reading, without making love. Was *this* what could happen to people when they were married? I wondered, in a mixture of surprise and curiosity and a touch of dismay. Until that night I wouldn't have believed it possible that we could have had the opportunity to make love and not taken it. It didn't happen again, but my question to myself was so naive that I remember it far more vividly than most of the details of our lovemaking.

When the family Bouchet de Fareins came back from Honfleur, I finally had to tell Nicole about Harrison, since I had no intention of leaving the whorehouse. She showed little surprise. I think she'd suspected what would happen with him from that first weekend we spent together, and certainly after the time I broke things off with Edouard. She was probably pleased that my Paris education was now complete, just as long as my room and board continued to be paid. Ginette Spanier, of course, knew all about it and so did John Cavanaugh, Harrison's friend as well as mine, and unquestionably so did everyone else we knew in Paris.

Until mid-May, my life passed in a dream of love and work. I understood, every day, that I was happier than I'd ever known a person could be. I experienced my happiness fully, as it was happening. Wordsworth came close to how I felt when he wrote, "Bliss was it in that dawn to be alive / but to be young was very heaven!"

However, in a few weeks I received alarming letters from home. My father was flying to Paris on business, arriving on May 23. He wrote that he was coming over to visit the liquor manufacturers represented by one of his clients, the house of Julius Wile, who imported Bollinger champagne, Bénédictine, B and B, and a number of other brands of liquor. The next day I got a letter from Mimi, warning me of the truth. Daddy wasn't really coming only on business. Growing suspicious, he had decided to make the trip to find out what the devil I was up to. Mimi herself assured me that she knew absolutely that I couldn't be guilty of anything at all wrong, that I'd never sleep with a man if I weren't married. She was still living on American standard time.

Unfortunately, in those letters I had continued to send so faithfully to my parents all year, I had mentioned, when I first met Harrison, that he was considered to be homosexual. Months later, forgetting this entirely, I wrote that he wanted to marry me. It's easy to imagine the consternation this combination of information caused.

Blessing Mimi, I decided that although I had to continue to live with Harrison, I'd make it appear that I was living with Nicole. The problem was that as soon as my room had been vacated, she'd rented it to some other girl, although I was continuing to pay for it! So much for my fears about her ability to take care of herself.

However, I had to have Nicole's cooperation and I was stuck with a fait accompli. I was furious at her but essentially I couldn't afford to make a fuss. I finally figured out that while he was visiting, I'd get Daddy to drop me off at the door of Nicole's apartment house and I'd lurk on the stairs until he'd gone off to his hotel. Then I'd take a taxi back to the whorehouse, no matter how late it was. Believe it or not, this solution worked, although I often had to walk a good distance to find a cab.

When I gave the driver the address, he'd turn and look at me in undisguised astonishment. The name of the whorehouse had been the same as its address, which I now forget. After inspecting me carefully and muttering dubiously to himself, the driver would take me there and then wait to see what would happen. Since we had a prearranged ring that signaled when any of us came back, there was a wait while someone walked down six stories, stood behind the door, and opened it silently. As I disappeared inside, yet another Parisian cabdriver thought he'd seen a ghost of great days past.

Once my father arrived, I began to show him my Paris. He met all of my friends, Harrison first of all. Then we spent a weekend at Le Bois Normand which included José, Edouard, and Francette as well as the girls. Nicole took him to visit her gardens and cooed to him by the hour in her delicious version of English, conquered by him as so many women were. Daddy took me to lunch at Maxim's with blond Stella Adler, the great acting coach and one of the most downright gorgeous women I'd ever seen, in her magnificent, big black hat with a perfect veil. We went shopping for my mother and we took a jaunt to Fécamp, in Normandy, where Bénédictine was made. We were pressed to taste especially good samples from so many barrels that we all got loaded before lunch.

Sylvia Lewis, the woman who had introduced my parents, was living in Paris that year, and Daddy spent most of his time with her during my working day. Mimi and I never liked Sylvia, a contentious and unattractive person who'd made a special effort to convince me that Harrison, about whom she knew nothing, was homosexual. She was a born meddler.

Fanny Cohen, that most faithful of my mother's friends, who had appointed herself Mimi's much-needed mother figure from my sister's birth, shared many secrets with her after my mother's death and one of them was that my father and Sylvia had conducted a longtime affair. I don't doubt it. I know of other women for certain, so why not Sylvia, too, particularly since my father spent three endless weeks on his mission to Paris, far more time than he needed?

On June 2, the beginning of the Pentacost weekend, Harrison and I, with Daddy and Sylvia, took off in her car for a five-day trip to Normandy and Brittany, which included Mont-Saint-Michel and the fishing villages of Concarneau, Quimper, and Douarnenez. Harrison drove and I sat up front with him, but of course I shared a room with Sylvia.

Closely watched as I knew I was, Harrison and I managed to disappear for a short time every evening after dinner and make hasty love, once on the floor of a public hotel bathroom we discovered in a corridor, once lying in a grassy field with horses chomping around us. I made sure to be back in the room to greet Sylvia in my pajamas, never wondering what she'd been up to while I was gone. During the day Harrison and I presented what we wrongly thought was a perfect facade of mere friendship.

Throughout all this time, I was unhappily conscious of how little my father and Harrison spoke to each other. Daddy was the only person Harrison Elliott, famed for his way with people, was utterly unable to influence by force of personality. In fact, H was terrified of my father and all but tongue-tied with him. Although I tried to reason with him about it, he simply couldn't manage to break through my father's distance. It wasn't our secret sexual situation that froze him, it was something about my father's tundralike remoteness, which I saw operate often with other men in my life in the years to come. We even went so far as to give Daddy a big, riotous dinner party at the whorehouse, since I'd written home about Robert living there. Every sign of my habitation had been eliminated, and although Harrison sat next to my father at dinner, they talked to everyone but each other. When I reproached him, he told me in misery that it was impossible for him to communicate with Daddy.

On June 13, three terribly long, strained weeks after he'd arrived, my father finally left Paris. I'd been waiting for him to say *something* to me about Harrison, anything at all, but as we took the taxi to the Invalides, whence his airport bus left, he sat there, imperturbably, looking out of the window, clearly intending to maintain his majestic silence. The family's lifetime refusal to "upset Daddy" kept me from confronting him, from asking him what he thought about H.

Finally, as we neared the end of the ride, I was too frustrated by his habitual nonreaction to everything he chose to ignore, to stand it any longer. I thought also that it would be wise to try to put my parents' minds at rest. "Daddy," I said, gathering all my courage to break into his silence, "for your information, I'm not planning to marry Harrison." Some vague sort of noncommittal grunt was his only reaction. With one short exception, which took place four years later, this was the closest to a conversation about, or rather *around,* an emotion— one-sided as it was—that I was ever to have with my father in my life.

However, he took rapid action when he returned to New York. He must have observed more than I realized, but instead of facing me and discussing it, the way any normal father would have done, he dictated a letter. (Every letter he ever wrote me was dictated to his secretary.) This brutal, brief letter contained a ticket back to New York on the *De Grasse,* a French Line ship that left on June 27, giving me a mere week's notice before I had to be on board. My father added only that, unfortunately, I wouldn't be home in time for his traditional birthday celebration on July 3, since the *De Grasse* was an old ship on its last voyage and the crossing would take ten days. His promise to let me live in Paris for a year, until the next September, was never mentioned.

I've often realized, for much of my later life, that I NEVER HAD TO GET ON THAT SHIP. I could so easily have manipulated my parents by threatening to marry Harrison. If I'd written them that if I were forced to go home I would simply get married in order to stay on, they would have given me practically any amount as long as I promised *not* to get married. I could have squeezed years out of them— *if* it had occurred to me to do such a thing. *The thought never even crossed my mind,* so strongly shaped was I into a dutiful daughter.

There was another way as well. I could have sent back the ticket and lived hand to mouth, the way everyone else was doing. After all, no one had any money, we had free accommodations, food was cheap, we all survived, and probably, possibly, something would have turned up. Nobody had the power to force me to leave. But I had always been such a revoltingly good, sickeningly obedient, horrifyingly well-trained little girl, damn it to everlasting hell!

Only actual marriage to Harrison, a marriage I'd continued to reject each time he asked me, could have kept me from having to give in and go home, since I had no money and no valid visa or work permit. I had to face the fact that I simply couldn't bring myself to marry a man of Harrison's character. To me, no matter how much I loved him, marriage was far too serious and permanent a matter to be entered into with grave doubts.

Yet those months of a great love were more than enough to form my future. The rest of my life stemmed directly from it.

My parents ordered, "Come back," and away I went, reverting almost instantly to my childhood, as quick to comply as I was when my mother made her gesture of dismissal of her children after we'd been displayed to her guests. My prized, fought-for freedom simply vanished at the first summons home. I never considered that there was *anything else to do but what my parents expected of me.* At twenty-one, I was still absolutely under their thumb, in spite of my year of managing for myself, of having had the courage to take on France and the French . . . and win. In retrospect, although I horrify myself with my infantile reaction, I understand it only too well.

My world fell to pieces as I hastily arranged to pack my suitcases, pick up the innumerable items of perfume and gloves my mother listed for me to take back, and make the many visits to say good-bye to everyone I knew, all the clients and all my friends.

Harrison and I spent one last weekend at Bertenonville on June 24 and returned to Paris on Sunday the twenty-sixth to eat dinner in a little restaurant on the Left Bank opposite Notre-Dame. I gazed at the moonlight falling over the shadows of this splendid sight, one of the wonders of the world, and asked myself how such beauty could add to my desperate unhappiness.

The next morning Harrison took me to the Gare Saint-Lazare, from which the boat train left at nine-thirty. We had no words left, nothing to say to each other. We were mute and shy with misery. As the train pulled out of the station I suddenly stood up, grabbed my handbag, and rushed down the corridor with the desperate intention of getting off, but the train had picked up speed and was going far too quickly. At that last minute, when I'd finally discovered an instant of guts, it was too late. By the time the train reached the port, I'd lost my courage, and I boarded the ship, a robot again. In my agenda I find only four words: "The end of everything."

Clockwise from top left: My notorious grandmother Tilly, my uncle Max, my father, aged eleven, and my aunt Bess.

My mother at seven, wearing a prophetically Napoleonic hat that was made by her father.

My mother and father in 1924, the year of their marriage.
(Courtesy of Morris Coleman)

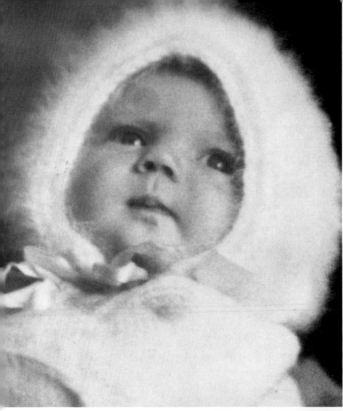

Me at three months, March 1928—already enduring a bonnet.

Below: The first picture of Mimi and me together, September 1929.

Enjoying life at seven months, summer 1928. Clearly, blondes do have more fun.

Me, my mother, and Mimi on her first birthday, June 13, 1930.

At one and a half, I'm already interested in the camera.

My brother Jeremy, about three months old, with me in the middle at four, and Mimi, two and a half, on the right, winter 1932–33.

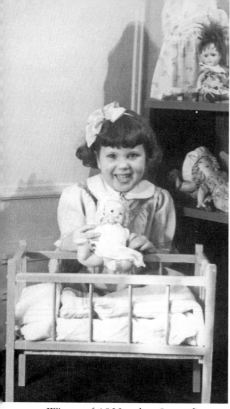

Winter of 1933, when I was five. The doll's bed was my most treasured possession.

On our way to school, spring 1932.

Below: Summer of 1934. I'm six and a half, Mimi's five, Jeremy's two and a half.

In 1943, I'm fifteen
and a half and in
full flirtatious mode.
At seventeen, I
enclosed this photo
in two dozen
Valentines I sent
to boys.

A middle-year picture: Mimi was eleven, Jeremy
seven, and I was twelve and a half, in the summer
of 1940.

Right: First spring at Wellesley, 1945—Toddy
Melvion, Marion Weis, and me at seventeen.

Jimmy Kahn, me, Mimi, and Mimi's date in a Boston bar, 1947.

Ginette Spanier, wearing Balmain, in Paris, spring 1949.

Hoop Rolling Day, senior year. I was twenty. The winner traditionally is the first in the class to get married. I ran slowly.

Nicole Bouchet de Fareins, showing her famous legs at Le Bois Normand, 1949.

Michel Paulmier-Peterson in Paris, spring 1949.

Edouard de Moustiers dressed for serious rabbit hunting, fall 1948.

Supervising photo shoot for hat PR, at the Place de la Condorde, spring 1949. Capucine, the model on the right, later became a well-known movie actress.

Paul-Emile Seidmann, me, Ginette Spanier
Seidmann, and her sister Didine Spanier.
Spring 1949, a chance meeting in Brittany.

Philippe Hersent, summer 1949,
sunbathing on a visit to Connemara.

Chapter Fifteen

THE SLOW PROGRESS OF THE *DE GRASSE* WAS MADE ENDURABLE ONLY by my finding three kindred souls to sit with at meals, two men and another girl. Each of them was being forced to leave Paris for reasons not unlike mine. One, a marvelous-looking young man named Yves Manuel, was being sent to New York to separate him from the unsuitable Juliette Greco, who later became Darryl Zanuck's lady love and something of a minor film star. We four formed a tight little band of forlorn woe, parting between meals only to go and mourn for hours in the privacy of our tiny staterooms.

What amazes me today is that in the middle of my emotional agony, I was still capable of thinking beyond the moment and looking toward the future. Nothing made me weep more violently than the admission that crept into my mind, an admission that was totally unwelcome, that in the distant future I couldn't possibly feel as utterly despairing as I felt at that moment. Someday, I realized, I won't care this much, someday this pain will become a memory, I won't live all the rest of my life yearning hopelessly for Harrison and Paris. This was the saddest thought of all.

It made me feel *old,* withered, a crone with no juices left. I cherished the acute pain of my convulsions of misery. The realization that I would never again experience the particular loss of parting from my first love was, in a certain bittersweet, horribly sorrowful way, almost as bad as the loss itself. It meant that I'd left behind forever a romantic situation that, since it was, by definition, a first, I would never endure again. I can still observe myself lying alone and sobbing for hours in the narrow upper bunk of the stateroom I shared with a girl I almost never spoke to. Is such a memory peculiar to future writers? I have no idea, except that I believe that without having lived through severe emotional loss, no one would become a writer of fiction.

I had no way of knowing that I would be in love only one more time, no way to know how deeply marked for life I was by my passion for Harrison, but a small rational voice still made itself heard in my storm of emotion, and it told me clearly that there would be a future. Looking backward, it was during this ten-day crossing that, through my pain, I began to understand and to acknowledge the limitations of life, the fact that it would be lived, for the most part, with dailiness, not drama.

Mimi and my mother met me at the dock. My father was working and Jeremy was teaching tennis at a camp in Steamboat Springs. Even before we joined Fanny and Len Cohen for lunch, I insisted on going to Bonwit Teller to buy new shoes. The black suede shoes I arrived in had big worn spots on the soft leather, flapping soles, gaping sides, and run-down heels, although I wore a black Paris spring suit that was an exact copy of one from the latest Jacques Fath collection. My shoes were left over from my last year at Wellesley and I'd worn them for every date I'd had in a year, since I'd never found a pair of French shoes that fit me.

Several pairs of new shoes took a bit of the edge off my hatred for New York in its July humidity. Two days after my arrival, I see in my agenda, I went dancing with Larry Goodman at the St. Regis Roof. Although my sister remembers that I returned "the saddest person she'd ever seen in her life," obviously I didn't intend to take the veil.

I would never have credited this entry about going dancing if I hadn't just seen it written down, but I quickly started going out a great deal with the same kind of conventional, rich, perfectly nice, usually Jewish guys I'd known at college. They were no different, although they'd grown a year older, but I had changed in fundamental ways they could never understand and I found it almost impossible to have any fun with them. My real life existed in another world than theirs.

To my great regret, I've never kept a diary, except sporadically during the first months of my first book tour for *Scruples*. The only actual Hermès agenda pages I've kept have been, providentially, for 1949 and for 1983, when I went to live in Paris for three years with my husband.

But even without my agenda, I recall a great deal about the months following my return. Not surprisingly, I needed a good deal of real dental work. I also took driving lessons in Stamford. When I finally passed my test, after three attempts, I took my mother for an afternoon spin to Norwalk, where she wanted to do some shopping. When my father came home and found out where we'd been, he turned white and made me promise never to drive again . . . it was far too dangerous. He'd done the same thing to my mother when she learned to drive. Why did he always want to clip the physical wings of the women in his family while encouraging them to use their intellectual ones? Another mystery about my unknowable father. Unfortunately, I kept my promise to him for some sixteen years, until I found myself spending the summers in Westport and had to drive the children everywhere . . . of course, I'm not a self-confident driver.

I knew that a job was waiting for me at *Good Housekeeping,* but I wasn't in a rush to claim it. I wanted to find out first if I could get a job on my own and I was interviewed by Leah Salisbury, a literary agent, and Mike Dann, a big shot at NBC. Neither of them seemed at all eager to hire someone with no experience beyond doing public relations for French hat designers. That struck them as almost too frivolous to admit, and English majors were thick on the ground.

I was utterly lackluster about ambition. Even being as animated as lackluster took an effort. I didn't really give a damn about what happened to me. Six years earlier, during the summer before I left for my freshman year at Wellesley, I'd worked for my father, creating a campaign for a new Coty lipstick intended for what were then called "sub-debs." The campaign and copy had been used successfully.

"You should become a copywriter," my father had told me then, but the last thing I wanted, I promised myself, was ever again to be shut up in a room with a typewriter and a lipstick.

Reader, what if someone had informed me that in the future I'd spend the better part of twenty-two years in a room with a typewriter, creating entire worlds, without even a lipstick for inspiration?

However, I went to an interview at an advertising agency and was told that if I were hired, I'd "have to eat, breathe, and sleep" advertising, not an enticing thought. Eventually I took the path of least resistance and went to see that greathearted, outspoken Texan Maggie Cousins, the fiction editor at *Good House,* who hired me to start in August.

This, of course, was out-and-out nepotism. Herbert Mayes, my mentor, who you may remember had bought me from my parents when I was four, had arranged it all. Herb had worked for the Hearst Corporation since 1927, a year before my birth. Maggie had worked for Herbert since 1936 and she, too, was a good friend of my parents. Herbert was an extraordinary man, a fantastically brilliant editor, far and away the greatest and most successful male women's magazine editor who has ever lived. He'd had to leave high school after three months to go to work . . . that recurrent theme of successful men who've been poor boys.

I don't believe it's an exaggeration to say that except for me and Maggie, everyone who worked at *Good House* was terrified of Mr. Mayes—and I'm not at all sure about Maggie herself. He was a giant among perfectionists, he was unrelenting in his criticism, he barked the most unbelievably insulting things to people, he had no sensitivity to any feelings, no matter how justified, his progress down a hall of the magazine was preceded by a wave of fear, editorial meetings were mass anxiety attacks. His employees spent entire lunches whispering together, comparing monster stories about him, unable to get away from their fascinated obsession with his latest dressing-down. If you could satisfy Herb Mayes, you could work for anyone, and the people he fired always went on to much better jobs. The trade magazine *Printer's Ink* said that he "ate an editor and a writer every morning for breakfast," and one writer said he ran the magazine "like the overseer of a chain gang."

I knew him as an often childish prankster, an adoring husband and father, the most faithful of friends to my parents, a man who delighted in telling the vilest jokes he could get away with—jokes we didn't yet know were disgustingly "politically incorrect" but that were too funny not to laugh at. He could be seriously funny, too. In 1927 he dashed off the first biography of Horatio Alger, a total spoof that, to his amazement, became the basic source material for four other biographies and every encyclopedia including the *Britannica*. Makes you wonder about source material, doesn't it?

Grace Mayes was an enchanting, uniquely wonderful woman with a very distinctive, sardonic wit. Her love for my mother was returned in full. She was delicately beautiful, too thin, fragile, elegant, and a brilliant editor herself, although Herbert, whose staff was mostly women, wouldn't permit her to take a job anywhere. At Christmas, Grace gave Mimi and me presents like satin bed jackets and gold compacts when we were far too young for them, which made them all the more glamorously thrilling.

Herbert loved to terrify us when we were little. He'd hide in our long corridor, behind a curtain, and when we passed, he'd grab our ankles, screaming "Boo!" We never learned, we never expected him; we always shrieked.

In the summer of 1949, I sat at a desk in the fiction department of *Good House,* wearily reading through a huge pile of unsolicited manuscripts, known as "slush," and listening to him enter the room, giving a tour to advertisers. There were three other readers, all girls, working in that room and I know I was the only one who didn't quiver when he asked, "Now, which of you wants to give me a big wet kiss?" I knew he was kidding; they didn't.

Herbert didn't just have hair, he had a "do," a coif that never failed to tickle me. His abundant, curly locks, first black and later silver, foamed perfectly and in the most elaborate shape around his keenly intelligent face. He was of medium height, immaculately dressed and supremely groomed; a most attractive man if you didn't happen to think he was The Great Satan.

Both Herbert and Grace were so individual, with such powerful personalities, that unlike most people long dead, they are as vivid as if I'd had dinner with them last night.

During Herbert's years at *Good Housekeeping,* the magazine was far and away the most influential women's magazine in America, with a circulation that easily topped six or seven million. The famed "Good Housekeeping Seal of Approval" was literally a money-back guarantee and we had floors and floors of test kitchens, a test beauty clinic, and labs in which to test machines. No product that didn't live up to its advertising was allowed in the magazine.

When I started work, I was unaware that the unrelenting monthly critiques of the magazine that I'd written for Herbert in my last year at college, from the arrogant, highbrow, and disrespectful point of view of an English major, had not been kept for his eyes only. No, indeed. He'd had them *circulated* to the heads of the departments of the entire magazine, thinking that it would do them good to get a swift kick in the ass from someone besides himself. This did not make my welcome at *Good Housekeeping* any warmer.

Everyone knew that I was there because I had major pull, in spite of the three busy, entry-level summers I'd put in at various departments of the magazine. The first summer, when I'd worked in the Beauty Clinic, my job was to carry around various new products, like underarm deodorants, and persuade the staff to use product X under one arm and their own favorite under the other for two weeks, and then answer a questionnaire comparing them. I could empty a room of typists simply by appearing in the doorway. Now that I'd returned for good, it was to an understandably lukewarm welcome. I simply didn't notice. I was too drowned in self-pity to give a rat's ass what anybody thought of anything, including me.

I commuted to work every day that summer from North Stamford with my father, who had never changed the name of our house from Connemara. Every morning we drove the nine miles to the station and took the dilapidated New York, New Haven & Hartford Railroad into the city. Daddy continued on to Grand Central Station, but I got off at 125th Street, took the streetcar across town to the Eighth Avenue subway, and then waited for the express to take me down to Fifty-ninth Street. There I walked a few blocks underground and climbed the stairs that opened right inside the lobby of the Hearst Building at Eighth and Fifty-seventh. What a schlepp!

On the way home, my father expected me to get to Grand Central early, fight my way into one of the few air-conditioned cars on the train, and save him a seat until he arrived for the trip home.

His own agency, stunningly decorated by Lucien Bernhardt, was conveniently located at 30 Rockefeller Plaza, where J. D. Tarcher and Co. occupied a half floor ten stories above the statue of Prometheus. Daddy's magnificent corner office looked directly into the towers of St.

Patrick's Cathedral. As he strolled over to the station, arriving at the last minute, I had been busy fending off hundreds of weary commuters, all men, who were ready to kill me. This ghastly round-trip was to continue for five summers, but whenever I had a date, of course, I spent the night at the apartment at the St. Urban.

At least three or four days a week, the three other young-lady readers of fiction and I went to the nearby Russian Tea Room for lunch, where we paid ninety-five cents for the set lunch, a large, delicious sandwich, a glass of tea, and a pastry. The Tea Room was owned by a man named Sammy Kaye, a superb raconteur who kept table after table enthralled by his nonstop wit. A year or so later we dated for several months until he called it off. "I can't stand going out with a girl who likes to talk as much as I do," Sammy told me. I'm still friendly with his widow, Faith Stewart-Gordon, who has plenty to say for herself but is on the quiet side compared with me. Most women are.

I renewed my close friendship with Sue Kaufman, who later wrote the landmark novel *The Diary of a Mad Housewife* as well as five others, less well known. Sue and I had become friendly during freshman year at college when we double-dated with some Harvard boys. We were so much more interested in each other than in them that, although she went to Vassar, we'd never let our friendship lapse, and now that we were both living in New York, we saw more of each other than ever.

Sue was stunning, very dark, with magnificent eyes and delicately flaring nostrils that made her look fully as neurotic as she was. Whenever a conversation became too personal, she'd say, "Dearie, let's not talk about *that*," and "that," whatever it was, disappeared immediately. I was perhaps her closest friend, but in many ways I never really knew her. No one did. Her sensitivity was too great for true intimacy.

Another important friendship that sprang to life was with Joe Eula, the painter and almost certainly the leading fashion illustrator of our times. I'd first met Joe in Paris when he arrived with an old friend of mine named Beverly Gaussen. Bev had worked for my father as an art director until she decided to change her life completely, got a divorce, and took off for France.

Beverly had been the office glamour girl: high, high heels, lots of makeup, big hats, a great bosom, lots of red hair. Mimi and I loved our biannual lunches with her because she was so raunchy and Brooklyn-hip. When she and Joe showed up in Paris, after a painting trip that had taken them for many weeks all over the French countryside, they both stank. Really stank. Disgustingly. Neither she nor Joe had had a bath in weeks. Beverly had gone native, chopped off her hair, and given up makeup.

Harrison and I let them use the icy whorehouse shower, I lent Beverly a few clean clothes that she never gave back, and off they went. Joe returned to the United States and the *Herald Tribune,* where he sketched every Paris collection covered by Eugenia Shepherd, but Bev stayed on to marry Bill Pepper, the head of *Newsweek*'s Rome bureau, and reinvent herself as a famous sculptor in monumental steel. Beverly Pepper bought the first castle in Todi, Umbria, starting a chic-as-hell trend, and never came home. She's now a legend, and her daughter, Jorie, has won a Pulitzer for poetry.

Joe was an Italian pixie, small, curly-haired, wonderfully handsome in his own impish way, totally wicked but never mean, the world's best gossip, an immediate accomplice, a perfect friend who knew everybody in fashion. He told me that he'd been a ski-trooper during the war. This was perfectly true. He also told me that he'd broken a leg during the war—also true—and while he was lying, suffering helplessly, in traction, this poor soldier boy had been seduced by a doctor, his very first homosexual experience. Not true. Not his first.

Even Joe, to whom I can still talk on the phone today as if no time at all has passed, has to laugh at the fact that I believed him. The two of us used to buy a bottle of wine and greasy bags of chicken livers and giblets, instead of popcorn, and take them to old Marlene Dietrich double features. Once, when he was in Paris for a month, Joe lent me his Third Avenue walk-up apartment, which didn't have any electricity. Unfortunately, I was between serious boyfriends and had no real need for it, so I gave a party there, entirely lit by candles.

Late in the summer, Philippe Hersent arrived, for a few weeks. He was studying to become a bridge builder and, for bridges, there's no place like Manhattan. I immediately took him to the top of the RCA building to give him an idea of Manhattan the island. He went up to Connemara for the weekend and, at last, although not at Connemara, his yearlong devotion to me and all those hot baths he'd provided paid off . . . for both of us. He was the first man I slept with after I left Paris, and an astonishingly vigorous lover he was. The first night we spent together he made love to me five times. "You won't find many men who can do that," Philippe told me proudly and accurately, "not even on Sunday."

Interestingly, although my parents had dragged me home from Paris, once I was home, living under their roof again, they gave me a key and absolute liberty. Until I got my own apartment, years later, I was entirely free to lead the wildest life I could conjure up in my very own room—or in someone else's apartment—as long as they were away. They spent all summer nights at Connemara and every other weekend of the year as well. When they were actually living in the apartment,

I was free to come and go as I pleased, as late as I pleased, as long as I woke up in my own bed. That left me a lot of latitude . . . a version of the Blanket Permission. In fact, it was the same way they'd behaved when they left me alone in the city with Joe, the midshipman. They never seemed to wonder or suspect that I might have a sex life, or, more likely, I thought, they didn't care and the only reason they'd yanked me back from Paris was the possibility of marriage to Harrison.

Chapter Sixteen

IT WOULD BE A LONG TIME—YEARS, IN FACT—BEFORE I WOULD BE ABLE to take American men seriously. If I couldn't have Harrison, a man had to be French to really interest me. My husband tells me that he was given my name by a mutual friend who advised him to call me for a date during these early years. "Judy's really cute," the friend said, "except that if she hears 'La Vie en Rose,' she'll burst into tears and you won't be able to get her to stop." Fortunately, although he phoned, I was never at home.

Joe Eula led me into the world of New York fashion photographers that was to fascinate me and lay the groundwork for my interest in photographers. A large number of photographers appear in my novels—so very many that finally, while planning *Dazzle,* I asked myself why my photographers and photographers' assistants were always men. I created a new heroine, Jazz Kilkullen, a woman photographer, and then, unwittingly, spoiled the purity of my intentions by adding three male photographers to the story, to one of whom, the charming Tony Gabriel, Jazz . . . yes, yes, you guessed it . . . loses her virginity.

Themes . . . themes . . . every writer keeps returning to the same themes time after time, and doesn't even know it. But imagination is so much more powerful than a writer's real life. I finally had a brief affair with a photographer, but it wasn't an important one and his profession had nothing to do with it.

Back in the summer of 1949, Joe Eula introduced me to the late Milton Greene, the well-known fashion photographer who would later become world famous through his partnership with Marilyn Monroe and his superb pictures of her in the last years before her death. Milton was a humorous, happy-go-lucky, Jewish version of Huckleberry Finn, covered with freckles and seemingly born in his uniform of jeans and a blue work shirt. It was at Milton's studio that I first found out that there's absolutely no workplace as exciting as a photographer's studio. It's an ongoing aphrodisiac of a party with music always playing, exotic ethnic food and great deli laid out in abundance, and a heady, slightly hysterical, distinctly erotic atmosphere created by the mix of models, stylists, editors, assistants, and photographers. A fashion photographer's studio is, in real life, the way movie sets are ideally imagined to be but never, ever are.

Milton and I became good friends, nothing more, since he had a complicated love life, and he often drove me home to Stamford in his tiny, open, antique MG, knowing that my mother would invite him for dinner before he drove on to his own converted barn in nearby Wilton.

It was a world of interrelationships. Milton's ex-wife, Evelyn, was engaged to Dick Avedon, who had just come back from shooting, if not his first, then almost his first haute-couture collection for *Harper's Bazaar.* Ginnette had given me Dick's phone number and insisted that I call him.

Dick immediately invited me over and tried to teach me how to play poker, but Evelyn hovered much too closely for me to flirt with him, although I would have very much liked to try. He already had an aura of a vast future about him, a photographer version of the young Leonard Bernstein, and he was surprisingly handsome when I scrutinized his features behind his heavy glasses. Later, when I became a fashion editor, I was always galvanized when we worked together. Dick was the inspiration for a character named Falk, a great fashion photographer in *Mistral's Daughter* to whom Teddy Lunel, the future mother of Mistral's daughter, loses her virginity. But of course. And a damn good scene it is, too, erotic, sexy, funny, and emotional.

At *Good Housekeeping* I advanced to reading agented manuscripts, although we all had to pitch in and read our share of over-the-transom "slush" as well. I wrote a short paragraph on the contents of each of the agented stories, included my own opinion, and turned in a tall pile of them to Maggie Cousins every day. Maggie herself was a top short-story writer, the most talented of those working in magazines in those days, when every women's magazine included at least four short stories in every issue.

I was soon asked to write a full-page monthly column called "Tips to the Teens." It had been established for years and whoever wrote it signed it "Helene Wright." As Helene Wright I added one hundred dollars a month to my pitiful salary of sixty dollars a week. Magazine work, except for top editors, was and is scandalously and disgracefully badly paid. Magazines take full, unfair advantage of the prestige that supposedly goes with an editorial job. When I left *Good House,* seven years later, at the age of twenty-eight, my base pay was seventy-five dollars a week. My mother, as a secretary, had been making forty dollars a week four years before I was born! However, I had been made an associate editor on the masthead. This meaningless sop was supposed to make up for the loss of income.

"Tips to the Teens" was a financial lifesaver. The powers that be at *Good House* believed firmly that teenagers waited eagerly for their mothers to be finished with their copies of the magazine so that they could read the latest bulletins in proper behavior from Helene Wright. It was, after all, the eve of the 1950s. Each month I went into a trance for a few hours and imagined myself as a bad teenager, a teenager who, let's say, had stolen her best friend's boyfriend. I scolded myself firmly and then gave myself a strong motivation for behaving in a thoroughly decent manner, all in one hundred tightly packed words.

I also started, from the first month of my work at *Good House,* to send Herb Mayes memos about possible ideas that I could write or cause to be written for the magazine. I see some of them noted in my agenda: Don't Jump on the Engagement Bandwagon; The T-Shirt: Anatomy of a Status Symbol; Behind the Scenes at the Paris Ritz; What Is It Like to Be a Model at the Art Students' League?; What Causes Claustrophobia?; The Problems of Being a Great Beauty; Jealousy, and What Can You Do About It?; Little Boys Design Their Own Rooms; What Makes a Woman a Gold Digger?; An Emergency Cookbook for Husbands; Astrology, Is There Anything to It?; A Divorcée's Code of Ethics; Everything a Woman Should Know About Serving Wine; Mrs. Huntley, Mrs. Brinkley, and Mrs. Cronkite; Christmas at Tiffany's by Truman Capote; How to Save a Neighborhood; The Ten Easiest Household Economies; Diane Vreeland, the Tastemaker of Our Times; Friendly Hostility, the Hardest Kind to Handle; The Fair-Weather Wife; How It Feels to Be a Has-Been by Barbara Stanwyck. And on and on, many hundreds of ideas. These ideas were often fresh, some of them highly original, and they're still being recycled in one form or another today. The amount of text the mass of magazines requires is so immense that it's rare to find anything new under the sun.

This was the beginning of a pattern that continued for many years as I thought up ideas and wrote those that were suited to me. I continued to develop ideas after I left *Good Housekeeping,* during ten years for John Mack Carter at *McCall's* and the *Ladies' Home Journal.* However, during the nine years I worked for *Cosmo,* right up until the day I started *Scruples,* most of my articles were assigned by the editors.

In the course of these years I hired and fired three different agents because I generated all my own work and I saw no reason to pay them ten percent when I fought successfully (not negotiated but *fought*) with each of these editors to get paid at the highest possible level. John used to suck his unlit pipe, twinkle his eyes at me with that smile that had half his staff in love with him, and look totally puzzled. "I certainly don't remember agreeing to that price, Judy. How sure are you?" Helen Gurley Brown, the editor of *Cosmo,* who loathed giving up a penny of Hearst's money, would spend an hour on the phone long-distance from L.A. to New York, fighting—no, haggling—over paying me a hundred dollars more than the last article had been bought for.

However, I knew the worth of my work and never hesitated to demand as much as I thought I deserved. In this aspect of my life, of which I'm very proud, I foreshadowed all my future heroines, not one of whom undervalued herself in business. By the time I turned to fiction, I had long been earning the $3,500 per piece that was then the top pay in women's magazine writing.

Chapter Seventeen

To my bewilderment, less than five months after I'd left Paris, on Saturday, October 29, 1949, Harrison arrived in New York. Somehow, after I left Paris, everything about our idyll seemed to belong entirely to another time and another place. I'd worked hard and tearfully at trying to convince myself that it was truly over. Our worlds were foreign and far apart, and I hadn't dared to dream that we could see each other soon again. Harrison wasn't a letter writer and I had only a few days' warning of his arrival. He'd come for two reasons: to marry me and take me back to Paris with him, and to get a new business off the ground.

Although it's been almost fifty years since that date, I can still feel, as I re-create those days, the fog of ambiguity I lived through at the time. None of the reasons I couldn't marry H had changed, and after I'd managed to endure four desperately hard months without him, and finally made a start at emerging into a workaday life, it was deeply disturbing to know that he could simply materialize and I'd immediately plunge back into the same intensity of emotion I'd believed was diminishing.

I was so thoroughly inexperienced that I'd imagined that such a powerful love could be dissipated just because I'd made a rational decision that it wouldn't work out. I wouldn't have believed then that it would take almost three more years to finally stop being in love with Harrison, three years during which I would not, could not, care for another man.

For the next week, I saw H for lunch and dinner every day, and although my parents, in a complete departure from their usual practice, stuck around in the city over a perfect fall weekend, we managed to be alone together in his hotel room every minute he wasn't working or I wasn't working . . . which didn't add up to much. Even when we were making love, I was aware that the lighthearted, fresh, wondrous mood of our Paris romance couldn't be recaptured. Too much had happened. This was too serious.

The Paris of the past spring had not been Paris the city, I realized slowly, but Paris the *time*. It had been a springtime of passionate love, a time in which we'd never find ourselves living again, a time that had become forever unreachable, no matter how long the city itself endured.

Harrison was staying at the big, gray Barbizon Hotel on Central Park South, a nondescript place that presented a sad contrast to my little hotel room on the rue Valence, where the sunlight striking a single vase of tulips at the foot of our bed was enough to make me weep with joy. We didn't feel an ounce of the clear conviction that we owned New York as we had owned Paris. We had to plot and plan and hustle to be alone together and still try to present a decent facade to my parents, who, diabolically, kept inviting H for dinner and cutting down on what little time we had. A vast amount of easy freedom and naturalness had disappeared from our relationship with the introduction of my parents into our lives together.

The new business Harrison had come to set up was something he'd thought up that he called "a boutique," a word that didn't then exist anywhere in the United States. It was his idea to open a chain of small-ish, elegant shops in which a woman could find all manner of French luxury items: handbags, umbrellas, costume jewelry, gifts, hats, sweaters, gloves, and perfume.

I was highly dubious. I'd never heard of anything like a boutique. Nobody had ever tried such a concept. I had well-founded doubts that Harrison, the worst businessman I'd ever known, could pull off such an ambitious enterprise.

Harrison Edward Elliott had everything necessary to make a great PR man. He knew, quite literally, everybody important in the world of fashion, and everybody adored working with him, which was fifty percent of the business. He was brilliant at creating publicity ideas and presenting them with persuasion to magazine editors, the other fifty percent. Yet because of his fatal inability to raise his fees to their proper level, he never managed to make any money, no matter how many satisfied clients he had. Years later, when Art Buchwald's wife, Anne, took over Harrison's PR business, she quickly made a huge success out of it.

H spent Christmas weekend at Connemara and my mother grudgingly admitted to me, "Well, I have to say I can understand what you see in him," one morning after they had shared a breakfast alone together. My father continued to maintain his impenetrable coldness. The happiest times Harrison and I had together were when we managed to get away to Milton Greene's barn in Wilton, where we could behave naturally with each other, where nobody gave a damn if we came in, said a quick hello, and disappeared into one of Milton's many guest rooms. There, time belonged to us again, there we could recapture a flavor of the rapture we'd lost. Milton even let us use the house when he wasn't there.

Harrison managed to borrow five thousand dollars from his father. He was alight with joy. He was convinced that with such a sum we could marry, return to Paris, and start up the boutique business. This new proposal, which he was so heartbreakingly certain would finally sway me, had just the opposite effect. I knew how short a time that amount of money—*borrowed* money, as always—would last. Even worse, sickeningly, I could guess how soon he'd be trying to borrow from my parents if I were his wife. In the cold light of a New York winter I saw again, all too clearly, how deluded he was about reality.

It was truly, truly heartbreaking to look at the man I loved and realize that he didn't understand the way the world worked on one of its most basic levels, and never would.

If I'd been a different kind of girl, a less grounded girl, a less self-protective creature, and certainly a crazier and more foolhardy one, I might have been tempted to talk myself into this chance to return to the place I missed so deeply, with the man I loved much too much. On the face of it, it was not a totally impossible proposition and I could have talked myself into it.

But with my clear and realistic vision of the future, the idea of getting married because of a loan of five thousand dollars was fatal. If anything could have made me comprehend, more than I already did, that I had to say farewell again to Harrison, it was this.

Harrison left for Paris on December 26 after a tearful, passionate afternoon alone at Milton's. We drove back to New York and I waved good-bye, standing on the steps of that fortress of bourgeois safety, the St. Urban. There was a small, detested, but undeniable element of relief mixed in my tears. I knew that I'd made the only possible decision.

BACK AT WORK, after Christmas, I was told that there was a financial crunch and I'd have to read manuscripts for *Cosmo* as well as *Good House*. I was to deliver my reports to the executive editor, David Brown. Thus, in the early days of 1950, we started a friendship that has lasted to this day. David Brown was not yet the producer of *Jaws* and *The Sting*. Not yet the man who became the husband of Helen Gurley Brown and wrote all those alluring cover lines for a completely new version of *Cosmo*. Not yet a famously successful phenomenon of eighty-three who's still working as hard as ever, producing movies and plays.

David was vastly higher than I was in the office hierarchy, but he was a most kindly and always gallant gentleman, in the true sense of the word. What I didn't know was that David was secretly dating one of my best office friends, Wayne List, the *G.H.* copy editor, who was the most beautiful woman at the magazine and the most mysterious. No one knew much about her . . . she was either still married or getting divorced, just as David was either still married or getting divorced.

I had started to hang out with a bunch of thirtyish writers who always met in the cheapest of New York's French bistros. Their hero, of whom they loved to tell amazing tales, was a semi-legendary kind of fellow named Harry Salzman, who had actually become friendly with the great writer Colette. One night they were excited because Harry, whom I'd never seen, was going to join us for dessert. "Don't get your hopes up, kid," one of them, Merle Miller, told me in a snide manner that instantly irritated me. "Harry's much too sophisticated to be interested in a little girl like you. You think you've been around? Well, Harry's a guy who's really been around, not just one quick year in Paris."

Harry arrived and sat down next to me. He resembled a giant panda as much as a human can. He looked at me, we exchanged a few words in French, and Harry instantly announced to the table, "Judy and I are leaving. We're going to get dessert someplace where we can be alone."

For a few months we saw a great deal of each other, but sexually, I couldn't enjoy him. He simply wasn't my physical type, which was a shame because Harry was a wonderful companion, with a fantastic imagination. My father, oddly enough, was intrigued with Harry and never tired of talking to him about his adventures. I think he simply assumed that Harry was too plump to constitute a threat to his daughter. Harry was just about penniless, but somehow he managed to be broke in a most picturesque way. His business consisted of wooden horses that he rented to carnivals and vacation hotels. For a dime, the horse would buck for three minutes with a child on its back.

When I refused his proposal of marriage—remember, it was the era in which girls were forever being proposed to, and I was the kind of girl who garnered proposals like a butterfly being chased by nuts with nets—he thought it was because he didn't have any money. "Listen," Harry assured me, "I'm going to make money, I promise. I can make ten thousand a year, twenty, thirty—I could probably make fifty thousand a year!"

Not long after that, Harry went into the movie business with a partner, Cubby Broccoli. Their debut venture was *Dr. No,* the first James Bond picture.

Years later, multi-multi tens of millions of dollars later, Harry invited my husband and me to his New Year's Eve party in his great London house. It must have been very early in the 1960s because when I was introduced to a gorgeous, dark-haired young man named Vidal Sassoon, I asked him, "Are you related to the Sassoon family?" meaning the eccentric intellectuals of Bloomsbury. "No, I'm just a poor Jewish haircutter," he answered. I still see Vidal getting his hair cut every once in a while in Beverly Hills, where I go to Sassoon's to get my hair done, and he's as good-looking as ever. Although his hair is gray, he's kept it all, he's a father of five, and I know both his first and second wives.

Harry Salzman's daughter, Hillary, married and eventually divorced young Baron Hubert de la Bouillerie, the son of an old friend, Elinor Marcus, whom I'd met at Milton Greene's studio. Elinor was the prettiest girl I've ever seen in my life until I met Jill St. John. The la Bouillerie property included the world-famous gardens of Villandry. Elinor's sister, Carol Marcus, who was Gloria Vanderbilt's best friend, is now married to Walter Matthau, and Hubert, who inherited his father's title, although he doesn't use it, has worked as a film editor on a number of my husband's movies and miniseries.

I'm fascinated when I trace the web of just a single one of the relationships that developed in my life over the years. This web included Harry Salzman, a fabulously successful film producer; Milton Greene, a great fashion photographer; Elinor Marcus, now Elinor Pruder, an American girl who married a French baron and then married twice again, meanwhile becoming a well-known decorator; her sister, Carol, who married both William Saroyan and Walter Matthau; Vidal Sassoon, the world's most famous hairstylist; Hubert, the baron's son who learned a trade and went to Hollywood . . . mix them all together, add a plot, and they could make a novel, couldn't they?

As I write about people who were, after all, important in only a small corner of my life, although they've been there many years, I've begun to understand how seriously lucky I've been. I met, early on, and largely before they made their marks, friends who gave me the comprehension of fame, glamorous personalities, and the struggle for success that was essential to enable me to write my novels with a sense of security and familiarity about the worlds I was creating.

I've lived, for fifty years, in the background of what eventually came to be known as "a Judith Krantz novel," or, as *Town and Country* magazine recently called it, "Planet Krantz." If this world didn't feel like home to me, I couldn't write my novels with conviction. What many in the publishing business and many interviewers suspiciously consider to be a shrewd commercial move on my part is simply following that oldest of adages, "Write about what you know."

Chapter Eighteen

IN 1950 AND 1951, I SPENT TWO MONTH-LONG VACATIONS IN PARIS with Harrison. We were supposed to have parted, but we simply couldn't manage to make that decision stick, either emotionally or psychologically. We had our separate lives but we kept trying to have a life together.

It's impossible, at this distance in time, to separate each one of my months in Paris from the others, but certain moments stand out with vivid clarity.

Harrison's fortune seemed to be looking up, although the boutique idea had come to nothing, and he'd moved to a small apartment near the rue du Faubourg Saint-Honoré. I lay lazily in bed one morning, thinking about getting dressed for lunch. Immediately after Harrison left for his office, I heard high heels, tapping as loudly as possible, mounting the stairs and approaching his front door like a cavalry charge. With as much noise as possible a letter was jammed under his door. Curious, I got out of bed, picked it up, and saw Kiki's name on the back flap of the envelope that was addressed to him.

I understood that, of course, she wanted me to read it or she wouldn't have lurked around until the minute he'd left to deliver it. I opened the letter and read an impassioned plea for him to realize that the American girl was not for him, that she could do him no good, that he had to come to his senses and put her out of his life forever. After what the two of them had meant to each other in all these last months, after all the passionate joy they'd had together, after all their closeness, their long and marvelous love affair, their history together, after he'd told her so often that she meant everything in the world to him, how could he let the American girl come between them again for as much as five minutes?

I read the letter twice and felt sorry for her. To me, it seemed that she had completely humiliated herself. Nothing on earth could have made me write such a letter to someone who didn't want me. No one but an utterly desperate woman would have plotted for me to see this, I thought. The awful and unbeatable arrogance of youth had everything to do with my reaction. I couldn't have been more than twenty-two or twenty-three. Harrison was eleven years older that I was, and Kiki ten years older than he. So she had to be forty-three or forty-four, unimaginably old to me at that time. What sort of passionate joy could a woman of that age possibly be talking about? Not only that, I'd once asked Harrison why he and Kiki hadn't married and he'd answered, with uncharacteristic severity, "A man doesn't marry a woman ten years older than he is."

I gave him the letter that night. The only time I remember ever seeing Harrison shocked was when I told him that I'd opened it and read it. "It was intended for me," I told him, serenely, and never bothered to question him further about Kiki. She wasn't a rival. I had no rival, that much I felt sure of. That he would have gone back to Kiki didn't bother me at all. A man had to have someone in his life, I reasoned, and better Kiki, who had financed Harrison's business, than anyone else.

However, each return to Paris was a little less wonderful than the previous one had been. Paris itself was changing, getting more crowded and more tourist-filled; the citizens were far less happy and more difficult. Nicole had major money troubles and seemed sad and apprehensive. José had gone from her life. "I'm finished with all that now, forever," she told me. Only Ginette Spanier was unchangingly vital.

The Paris of 1949, that Paris of only a year or two earlier, that Paris that had existed for an enchanted moment in time, was wiped out of existence. Even the smell of the air seemed different, and the cab rides in from Orly no longer made my heart beat as madly.

First love, once it has been brutally severed, doesn't, can't possibly, return again as first love, but only as love of another kind. Second love, perhaps, but in any case, a heartbreakingly different kind of love. All my dates as a girl on the town in New York, my several lovers, all my efforts to become a successful workingwoman had changed me from the just-out-of-the-egg girl he'd known.

On the second of these trips I had dinner with Viola Ilma, the friend of my parents who'd been so helpful in getting my visa extended a few years earlier. During dinner she told me, with considerable insistence and detail, that she and my father had had a long love affair. I assumed that she must have been drunk and waved her off, much to her annoyance, but nevertheless I was concerned enough to speak to my parents one day soon after my return from Paris.

"You two really ought to stop being friends with Viola," I said. "That woman's really nuts. She tried to make me believe that she and Daddy had an affair. I think she's a dangerous liar."

Neither of them reacted by a shrug or even a blink. My mother asked me to pass the salt and we talked about something else. At the time, it seemed to me that the accusation had simply struck them as too silly to be worth a word, but later, when my father's bequest to a stranger in Philadelphia was discovered, I replayed the conversation in my head. Shouldn't both of them have said *something?* Shouldn't they have asked, "She said *what?*" or exclaimed, "Good God, that damn woman's out of her mind!" Of course they should have been angered and surprised by my account, I realized, and there was only one reason why they weren't. They both knew the truth of it and weren't good enough actors to have put on a realistic display of normal emotion.

One more glimpse into my father's secret life, and my mother's certain knowledge of it.

ON MY LAST trip to Paris, in 1951, an event took place that definitively ended the long, intense romance between Harrison and me . . . although not its memory. I was staying at the Hôtel du Théâtre des Champs-Elysées, a cheap but chic little place with a bar that was filled with models at lunch and cocktails. Harrison and I had arranged to meet at Ginette and Paul-Emile's apartment at seven o'clock that night so that we could both have a drink with them before we went out to dinner. That coming weekend we planned to spend together in the country.

Harrison was late, of course, and although I knew his habits, I was embarrassed for the Seidmanns to see how he kept me waiting. I'd had a drink or two—Ginette always poured a stiff shot of scotch without ice, due to her British upbringing—and then I had another. Time passed, he didn't even phone, and I had yet another drink . . . four drinks on a stomach empty since lunch. Finally Ginette and Paul-Emile had to leave for the theater, and lock up behind them. It was almost eight-thirty by that time, but I assured them that H would arrive at any minute and that I'd wait for him downstairs, next to the concierge's loge. As always, in a French apartment house, the light that you press when you enter the building is on a timer that goes on and off, giving you just enough time to get into the elevator and press the button for the floor you want.

I spent three-quarters of an hour, in an intensely cold entrance hall, standing by the timer and pressing it each time the light went off, while I struggled to fend off the agitated concierge, who came popping out to stop me. Eventually I waited in the dark for a few more minutes before making up my mind to return to my hotel.

I don't even have to close my eyes today to still see Harrison when he finally showed up, just as I was about to leave, bounding into the dark hallway, smiling and insouciant. He was two and a half hours late and I was very drunk and violently angry. I screamed furiously at him as he bundled me into the taxi he had waiting, making some ridiculous excuse. We drove off to the Left Bank to a bistro called La Petite Chaise for dinner. I drank a lot of wine, getting more and more outraged as time passed, telling him exactly what I thought of his hideous rudeness and his impossible character flaws. By now I was far more drunk than I had ever been in my life, or have ever been since. Harrison got me back to my hotel somehow, but as far as I was concerned, and as far as he was concerned, our long love had been destroyed. The adventure was over.

He sent me a huge box of flowers the next morning.

I never saw him again.

I was violently, almost impossibly sick for the next three days, unable to leave my hotel room, barely able to drag myself to the bathroom. It was a hangover of the body and a hangover of the heart and a hangover of the soul.

More than five years later, in the spring of 1957, six months after the birth of my first son, I received a totally unexpected letter from Harrison. He wanted me to know that he and "good old Kiki" had finally been married. This was a little more than eight years after our first weekend together at Bertenonville, when Kiki saw us together. I was then twenty-nine, he was forty, and Kiki fifty.

At some time I can't determine in the next years, Harrison went bankrupt, causing his wife to lose both her investment in his business and all her other savings and possessions. H was in deep trouble with the French tax authorities for nonpayment of taxes, and he had to leave France in a hurry to avoid all sorts of legal consequences.

As far as I know, he was never able to return to France, although I may be wrong. He and Kiki were divorced sometime after that. Kiki's story with Harrison is the most French story I know . . . a sad Piaf song of a passion that lived on and on, a passion that I suspect must have endured even after their divorce. She had loved him so much more than I ever had. He had been the ruinous, fateful, too-young love of her life and she paid the price. A heavy, heavy price, in every way, but not necessarily unacceptable to a true Frenchwoman. She was bitterly jealous of me, as I would have been in her place, but I didn't destroy her. She fought for him and she won him. By default. I believe that whatever it cost Kiki in the end to have loved Harrison Elliott, flawed as he was, it must have been worth it to her to have hung in there, to have lived closely by his side for so many years, allowing herself to be so bewitched by his charm that her Frenchwoman's practicality was dissolved into blind obsession.

I'm not a Frenchwoman and I could never have permitted myself to become a character in a French story. Blind obsession wasn't within my potential. I was a fundamentally logical American girl and it was contrary to every fiber of my being to make a decision that could only end tragically. In the last analysis, unlike any woman in all the songs of Piaf, I was in control of my heart. The ability to completely lose myself in irresistible emotions was all to be released one day in my novels.

Eventually, through mutual friends, I learned that Harrison remarried and divorced several times and fathered a number of children. I hope he's all right.

It was not by accident that the blond Californian hero of *Scruples* and *Scruples Two* was named Peter Elliott, and he was a man who "deeply, hungrily, passionately and persistently enjoyed women in all their characteristics, not merely sexually." When I wrote *Scruples*, I borrowed far more from my own life than in any other novel I've written since then. This is very common among beginning writers, and, in my lucky case, turned out not to be a mistake.

Chapter Nineteen

ONE DAY IN 1952 I BUMPED INTO HERB MAYES, WHO WAS LOOKING for me. He was upset and unhappy. "You're the new accessory editor in the fashion department now," he told me hastily. "Go see Nancy White right away." "But Ann—" "Ann died of an aneurysm last night." "Ann! That's impossible!" "I have to call her father, just go! Nancy's expecting you."

Ann Gohagan, a lovely, gracious girl, daughter of a close friend of Herbert's, had died instantly in her early twenties. I'd never known her well: the fashion department was way at the other end of the long corridor on which our readers' room lay, and we rarely saw any of the fashion editors as they went about their busy ways, but everyone had been aware of the sweet and beautiful Ann. Only in researching my latest novel, *The Jewels of Tessa Kent,* did I discover that some people are born with this fatal condition and can die at any time in their life, in a split second.

Stunned, I reported to Nancy White. We were all in shock as she told me that from that moment, by Mr. Mayes's orders, I had been created her accessory editor. The fact that, as I later found out, a number of other women on the fashion staff felt that the job should, by rights, have gone to one of them—and they were perfectly correct—had nothing to do with Herbert's plans for me, or the way he ran the magazine. I'd never had anything to do with accessories and it took me many weeks to make friends with any of them. Eventually I shared a little office with the shoe editor, Eileen, but the old camaraderie of the readers' room was gone.

Nancy White was a fashion editor with a difference. She was crown princess of the Hearst Magazine company. Her father had been one of William Randolph Hearst's best friends and top executives, and her aunt was Carmel Snow, the editor-in-chief of *Harper's Bazaar.* It was an open secret that when Mrs. Snow retired, Nancy would take her place, as indeed she did, and remained for many years.

Nancy would arrive at the office in the middle of a storm, striking-looking as always, beautifully groomed and coiffed, her excellent figure encased in a bone or beige suit, fine bone pumps adorning her feet, and no visible means of keeping warm. It is doubtful that she ever had to do anything about the weather but run two steps, for a limo and driver waited permanently for her at the entrance to the Hearst Building, to take her on her endless trips to the Seventh Avenue showrooms, usually accompanied by Janet Livingston, the assistant fashion editor, a pleasantly dry, witty, older woman.

In those days, if a dress was picked to be photographed by *Good Housekeeping,* at least five to ten thousand of them were sure to sell immediately. We used dresses in the price range our readers could afford: from about $12.95 to an absolute maximum of $39.95, the price of a wedding gown. We were far and away the most important force in the giant market of fashion for real women.

Every accessory had to be in a comparable price range. I was in charge of finding new hats, gloves, jewelry, belts, artificial flowers, and handbags to go with each dress. As I was soon to discover, this job had to be done without any reasonable foreknowledge of what the dresses looked like.

Amazingly, right from the first day, Nancy and Janet gave me only a few words of guidance—"flowered dresses for spring"—so that the first time I saw the clothes was when I unpacked them at the photographer's studio to iron them, a skill I had to learn on the job.

I quickly realized that I needed to cover my ass with a vast choice of accessories so that I could always manage to make the clothes look decent. Nancy and Janet very rarely showed up at the sitting, so busy were they flitting about and spreading their presence among our major advertisers of medium-priced clothing. I discovered that if nothing else worked, twenty-five dollars' worth of fresh flowers, held in front of the dress by the model, would always disguise it enough to do the trick. In fact, I found out that I was, incredibly, and without prior experience, in charge of the sittings almost all of the time. Fortunately, I rose to the challenge quickly.

Although we only shot at a photographer's studio, or on location, once a month, that shoot, which could last as long as four or five days, took an immense amount of preparation. And oh, once there, the sheer fun of it all! I adored every second of it, from the ironing to dressing the models as if they were enormous Barbie dolls, and then pinning them into their clothes, which were always too big. I used to lie on the floor, holding the end of a string, the other end of which had a fishhook attached to the model's skirt, so that, with the help of a floor fan, we could inject some movement into the picture. Now, in these days of wildly elaborate fashion shoots, productions with a dozen stylists fussing about, this sounds as if we were making silent movies, but it worked, and most of the pictures were excellent.

I learned when I was working with models, a few of whom became real friends, that it was essential that I *never* look in the mirror by accident. After a few hours spent with models in a dressing room, as they applied their own makeup and did their own hair, a normal activity in those days before makeup artists and hairdressers, it was too easy to forget how beautiful they were compared to a normally attractive girl like me. Suddenly catching a glimpse of myself in the mirror was like turning into a giant lizard.

Over three years, I learned that these immensely beautiful women were merely ordinary people like everyone else, with the same problems that everyone had, knowledge that comes out somewhere in many of my novels, particularly in *Mistral's Daughter, Spring Collection,* and *The Jewels of Tessa Kent.*

Beauty is one of the themes that I have a constant urge to explore in fiction. While I absorbed the truths that lie behind the possession of rare beauty, I laid down a vital source of knowledge for a future in which I would deal, in fiction, with beautiful women. It gave me a certain absolute understanding very few writers possess. Unless you've actually had the experience of working woman-to-woman with models for several years, you can't begin to put yourself into their skin; you have no basis for being able to imagine how little—or how much—their looks matter to them in their real lives as human beings.

There was only one model whose beauty got to me: the great Suzy Parker. I was sent to Hollywood to write an article about her when she starred in her first movie, *Ten North Frederick,* with Gary Cooper. I spent three days interviewing her, having lunch with her every day and watching her, braless, casually stripped to her underpants, being fitted into her wardrobe. Every night I'd go back to my hotel room stricken with fierce, sickening headaches, the only ones of my life. She was simply too beautiful for a mere mortal to endure looking at for long.

The article was never printed. Suzy had presented herself as someone so independent that she'd never dream of getting married, but just before *G.H.* went to press with my story, she got into an automobile accident with a man who was discovered to be her French photographer husband, and, if I remember properly, not her first husband, either. Much of the article simply wasn't true, or perhaps it was just her Southern version of her own truth? Now she's married to actor Bradford Dillman and lives in Santa Barbara, a mother of four. But Suzy Parker in the 1950s! There's never been anyone remotely like her.

Good House worked with the best of the fashion photographers, although our clothes were the opposite of high fashion. All photographers like to do editorial work, as well as advertising, to keep their names in constant sight of other magazine editors, and there was the *Harper's Bazaar* connection in Nancy's future, too. So I found myself working with Avedon, Bill Helburn, Jimmy Abee, Lillian Bass, Gleb Durajinsky, Milton Greene, Paul Himmell, Bert Stern, and even the great Irving Penn. Remember, Avedon and Penn weren't yet the sacred creatures they've now become, but even then it was an extraordinary experience to be a part of a shoot, and an essential part at that, with these hugely talented people.

MIMI HAD GONE to live in Los Angeles after she graduated from NYU. She wanted the year on her own that I'd had, but she didn't want to learn a foreign language. There she became engaged to a man named David Karney, an Israeli whose father was the real-estate "Rockefeller" of Israel at a time when the Israeli pound was worth almost nothing in the United States.

She and David showed up to meet my parents for the first time one Saturday morning in 1952, at ten-thirty. It wasn't easy for a man to appear as the future husband of a Tarcher daughter, and I saved the day by bringing out a bottle of sherry at that indecently early hour. My nondrinking mother and my nondrinking father, Mimi, David, and I finished off that bottle long before lunch.

Mimi was married at a big wedding at the Harmonie Club. I was the maid of honor in a pale green Ceil Chapman dress and a miniature hat covered with tiny, dyed-to-match seashells by one of my hat contacts. The Harmonie Club was the stuffy, sumptuous, exclusive bastion of New York's absurdly snobbish old German Jewish families, the "Our Crowd" gang who look down on every Jew who arrived in America after they did. I have no patience at all with their viewpoint.

However, my father had become one of the first, if not the first, Russian Jewish members long ago. He'd been there for so many meetings for the Federation of Jewish Charities that one night, fed up, he announced that if he couldn't sign the check for dinner, they could forget about his showing up for the next planning session. He was hastily made a member and we went to the club on occasion for their lavish Sunday-night buffets. The best thing about the Harmonie Club was the bowling alley in the basement.

Now Mimi and David were living in Los Angeles, where he was beginning a magnificent career as a builder, and Jeremy was at college at St. John's in Annapolis. He'd had disastrous marks at Horace Mann, his high school, and hadn't been able to get into any other college. He'd been turned down by Rutgers, where my father's younger half brother had been an all-American quarterback, and even by Oberlin and Bard, those then-effete places that took just about everybody. Jeremy had insisted all along that he wasn't going to spend the best years of his life reading, so he simply didn't. Actually, he suffered from moderate dyslexia for reading and spelling. So did Mimi and so do I for math and spelling. Reader, didn't I say it wasn't my fault?

Now Jeremy found himself in an institution where the entire four-year curriculum was based on the University of Chicago's system of reading one hundred Great Books, and nothing else. Able, as he puts it, to "think freely and talk freely, without the element of competition and blessed with a great bullshit factor," he took to the Great Books with true fervor. One year, when I came back from Paris, I foolishly risked a certain jail sentence by bringing him, buttoned into my blouse, a copy of the utterly pornographic *Rosy Crucifixion* by Henry Miller, an erotic masterpiece that Jeremy rented out to his friends at twenty-five cents a day. I'm not taking all the credit, but eventually he became the first and best publisher of New Age books in the United States. It just goes to show . . . teach a man to fish . . .

Chapter Twenty

SOON AFTER I STOPPED GOING TO PARIS TO SEE HARRISON, I MET A Frenchman, then an American citizen, named André Sussman. André and his parents and his sister, Claudine, had escaped to the United States just before Hitler invaded France. There they had owned a thriving auction house and both Mr. and Mrs. Sussman had superb taste in art. However, in their hasty flight, like most French Jews, they lost everything. Only André's mother's recipe for making her own mascara enabled them to start up again.

By the time I met André, who'd served as a paratrooper during the war, Mrs. Sussman's home-cooked mascara had turned into a well-known eye makeup business called Aziza, which was later bought by Charles of the Ritz. André worked for his parents and one of his jobs was to demonstrate in department stores the application of mascara, something American women were just beginning to use. Until the early 1950s mascara was for the movie stars and hookers.

André was a blind date and came to pick me up at the apartment. He said a few polite words to my parents and we prepared to leave the house. Suddenly, from the front door, I heard my mother call urgently, "Judy, come back here, right away." I turned and asked why. "Are you wearing panties?" she yelled. "What! For God's sake! Of course I am!" I called back, annoyed and embarrassed by such a crazy question. When did I ever go out without my panties? What sort of thing was that to ask in front of a man I didn't know?

Yes, even my mother had been alarmed to the point of ridiculousness by André's unmistakable sensuality. He looked like one of those drawings by Jean Cocteau in which a man seems on the point of being transformed into a bull. André had remarkably prominent, full, and beautiful lips, a strong nose with wide, flaring nostrils, and deep-set eyes under a fine forehead. He was not conventionally handsome, but what he had was better than good looks.

I went out with him five or six times, even subjecting him to a weekend at Connemara. The fact that I made such a point of having every man I had any interest in spend a weekend with my parents makes me sick in retrospect. I'm forced to realize that I still needed their stamp of approval.

It was during that weekend in the country that I decided, absolutely, that André was not a candidate for marriage. I wasn't one whit more interested in getting married than I had been at college, but nevertheless, something in the air and water of the 1950s forced me to size up every man I went out with as either marriage material or not marriage material. I suspect it's still in the air and water whenever I read the cover blurbs of magazines designed for the young women of today. GET MARRIED! That's the bottom line, no matter how it's disguised as fifteen new ways to have an orgasm. It probably always will be.

However, what I was looking for was not eligibility but emotion. I had given myself enough time with André to be sure that I'd never fall totally in love with him. I knew what that kind of love felt like. I found him enormously attractive, though, and on that weekend in the country I decided that since I wasn't going to marry him, I was free to have an affair with him.

How clearly this decision shows that I was still deeply concerned with appearing to be a "nice" girl. Until there was no longer any chance for André to become my husband, I couldn't allow him to know that I might be sexually available. Once marriage was out of the question, it didn't matter if he no longer believed in the extremely effective manner in which I projected sexual niceness, a manner I'd unconsciously so refined and polished over the years that it's never disappeared.

When I went on my first book tour for *Scruples*, male interviewers were invariably and genuinely so shocked by me that almost every one of them asked me, accusingly, "How could *such a nice* married woman, of your age, with two children, write such an erotic book?" It didn't matter how hard I tried to explain the function of fantasy and imagination in writing sex scenes, or even the fact that women of any age, with any number of children, are not prohibited from including erotic behavior in their work. I might as well have been talking to myself until the day I suddenly thought of saying to one of these men, "If I only knew what was going on in your mind for the next twenty-four hours, I'd have enough material for another dozen sex scenes."

That stopped him cold and turned his questions to something else. Lately, I've found it even more effective, when this same protest appears, to calmly say, "But I've done it all, don't you see? I'm writing from my own experience. The heterosexual scenes, the lesbian scenes, the homosexual scenes . . ." By that time they're laughing. But I'm either blessed or cursed for life with a still-innocent face and body language.

André had a huge one-room apartment with an absolutely sensational Fauve-period Vlaminck over the fireplace, a picture better than many that have recently sold at auction for just under three-quarters of a million dollars. I don't know how he happened to own it, or even if he, not his parents, owned it, but at the time, it was worth about fifty thousand and he was struggling to hold on to it. His job didn't pay much, although he had a future, and he was thinking of doing something else, opening a cooking school with James Beard.

Since, as far as I knew, he couldn't cook, this struck me as highly impractical. Although we once had dinner at his place, it was based on a delicious cold roast chicken I was certain his mother had made. However, I didn't discourage him, since it seemed as if it would never happen.

In anticipation of such a venture, he had decided to change his name from Sussman to Surmer. I pointed out that while that sounded fine in French, it was hard to say in English, and suggested the alternative of Surmain, which was easier to pronounce. And so was born André Surmain, who opened a cooking school that quickly failed, but soon afterward bought a rather out-of-the-way brownstone for ten thousand dollars and became the owner of Lutèce, which instantly became the very best, most famous French restaurant in New York and remained right at the top for forty years, even as food fashions came and went.

I was wrong about his not knowing how to cook.

André wanted to marry me. If you've read this far, you've been expecting that development. It gets annoyingly repetitive, but I'm bound by the facts. He fell for me frighteningly fast. If sexual compatibility had been the prime reason for marriage, I'd have reconsidered my original decision; he was even more sexually exciting than Harrison. But he wasn't *the right one*. I couldn't have defined for myself what that meant, but I had to assume that I'd know it when I saw it.

Meanwhile, André showed me how to apply mascara and I was soon running around the fashion department sporting green mascara and green eye shadow, which he said made my eyes look greener. People used to stop me on street corners when we were waiting for the lights to change. "Excuse me, miss, but do you realize that you have green mascara on?" they'd ask with a worried look on their faces, as if I'd been held down and forced to have it applied.

That winter André and I decided to go skiing at Kitzbühel, in the Austrian Alps. I was determined to promote a free plane ticket. I had become wiser to the ways of the world, as every Christmas I was given gifts by the manufacturers whose accessories I used. Nancy White had to have her driver clear out the packages from her office twice a day. So many and impressive were the presents from Seventh Avenue, from kilos of caviar to mink stoles, that her office became all but impassable during the Christmas season.

Nancy herself had a room in her brownstone that was devoted, all year long, to the gifts she gave, baskets filled with marvelous things she'd wrapped herself. One year I had to return a Bergdorf's camisole she gave me because it was too big, and the credit was enough to pay for a new cashmere sweater. Sweet Nancy . . . it was rumored that she went to Mass every morning even though she'd been excommunicated, because she was divorced and remarried. When her first husband died, her excommunication was lifted, or so people said. I certainly hope so!

David Brown was still at *Cosmo,* although soon he freed himself to go on to Twentieth Century–Fox as story editor and start his glorious career. I asked him if it would be possible for me to be photographed for the editor's page of *Cosmo* climbing up to a plane on a ramp that bore the Air France logo, and include a brief story about how Air France was the perfect way for a fashion editor to start out a skiing vacation. No problem, he answered.

I took myself down to Air France and spoke to their public-relations people. Wouldn't it be worth a free, round-trip, first-class flight to Paris for me if I could deliver the *Cosmo* photo and story? Yes indeed, they answered, they could guarantee the ticket.

As soon as I returned from my ski trip, a worried David Brown told me that he'd found out that Mr. Hearst had never permitted the slightest mention of anything French in his entire empire. Mr. Hearst loathed and detested the *beastly, bloody* French. "But, David, I've taken the trip," I said plaintively. "I can't give it back, and how can I explain it to them?" Dave Brown, a gent as always, ran the picture and the story.

André and I took separate planes to Europe. Amazing as it seems, although we were engaged in a full-fledged affair, we didn't think it "looked right" to leave town on the same plane. Who, I wonder, would have seen us? We met in Paris and took a train to Munich and then drove overnight to Kitzbühel, where we planned to join other friends.

One of them was Sophie Malgat, a Swiss girl and a cherished friend of mine from Paris who had been, until very recently, the top runway model at Jacques Fath, the equivalent then of a Claudia Schiffer. Sophie and I shared a room, while André shared another room with an old skiing friend of his named Bill. Just plain Bill. Sophie, who couldn't ski and didn't intend to try, had at least a dozen pairs of ski pants with her and she changed her outfit at every meal. She was on her way, in a week, to another ski resort, to join the man who would become her second husband, the noted film producer Anatole Litvak. Years later, after their marriage, I had lunch at their magnificent Champ-de-Mars apartment, where he asked me suspiciously where my mother had been born. I answered, "She's a Litvak, Mr. Litvak." Sometimes—

rarely—you do manage to find the right words at exactly the right moment!

"What do you see in it?" Sophie asked me moodily one night in Kitzbühel as we were dressing for dinner.

"See in what?"

"See in having sex."

"Sex? What do I *see* in it?" I asked, doubting my ears.

"Yes."

"Oh, Sophie, if you don't know, I can't tell you."

One day, years later, when I heard a transformed Sophie joyously speaking on the phone with Françoise Sagan, I understood the mystery that lay behind her question.

The only problem about our vacation was that there was no snow for the first five days, since we'd gone before Christmas. We were staying at a hotel on top of the mountain, from which you skied down to the top of the cable car that brought people up from the village to start the thirteen-kilometer run downhill. We spent a lot of time in the typically slightly too-cute village, walking around and drinking hot chocolate, depressed and disgusted by the lack of snow. When it finally fell it took the form of a four-day blizzard during which we couldn't stir from the hotel.

After the snow finally stopped, there had been such a heavy fall that only the strongest, heaviest skiers were able to make any progress. Eventually, after another two days, I ventured out. There had been enough skiers on the slope to flatten down the worst of the snow, but it was still above my knees as soon as I left the narrow run that had been carved out. If I lost control, I'd be in instant trouble. I put on my gloves, grabbed my poles, and prepared to ski down with André. Instead, I was treated to a fleeting glimpse of his back as he and Bill took off at top speed, leaving me to negotiate the long downhill run entirely on my own.

It took hours. I alternately fumed and prayed as I descended the steep mountain, falling frequently. Never, ever, had I been subjected to such bad ski manners. Any lingering doubts I'd had about André being unsuitable for marriage vanished as I contemplated his disgustingly selfish behavior. You simply can't abandon even an expert skier to ski alone in such circumstances, no matter how eager you are to have a great downhill run. I didn't speak to him again until we were back in Paris, days later, when he'd finally humbled himself enough to satisfy me.

Our relationship continued. It was the one time in my life that I treated a man as men so often treat women. Although I enjoyed André enormously (off skis), I didn't love him. I kept him on the string for sex, and I knew it. I didn't tell him that I would never marry him, because if I had, the sex would have been over, and I simply wasn't ready to give up something so good.

If I was meant to be punished for this cold-hearted, hot-blooded behavior, I was. It happened thus. During the summer following our ski vacation, André and I spent the night at his apartment. A violent rainstorm blew up in the middle of the night. The doorman at the St. Urban noticed a wide-open window in our apartment and sent one of the elevator men up to close it. The next day, my father, who for some reason had gone to the apartment, was told by the doorman that I'd left the window open.

When Daddy joined me on the train back to Stamford, he said mildly, "You didn't sleep at home last night. You didn't close the window when it started to rain." "No," I answered, trapped, "I didn't." "I hope you know what you're doing," he responded, equally mildly. "I do." And that was that, not another word did he have to say on the subject. This was the second, and last, intimate discussion I'd had with my father in my life, the first when I'd informed him that I didn't intend to marry Harrison. At least this time he'd actually said something, not just grunted. We continued to read our newspapers side by side. Obviously, I thought, with great pleasure, my father realizes that I'm mature and have a right to a life of my own.

Three minutes after we arrived back at Connemara I heard my mother's voice raised in a tone that rang through the house. "Judy, come down here this minute!" Daddy had wasted no time in informing the enforcer. I went to her room and found her in a state of the wildest rage, a fury worse than any I'd ever witnessed. I just watched her, feeling cool and justified. When she'd finally paused for breath in her violent wrath against my evil, wicked, totally unheard-of behavior, i.e., sleeping with a man, I asked a single question. "Would you prefer me to *marry* André?"

She had nothing to say in return, not one word. It was the first argument I'd ever won with her. I knew she and my father didn't want me to marry André. He had almost no money, and he had an inferiority complex about never having attended college, since he'd gone directly into the American paratroops from his French high school. Consequently, he could be painfully shy in certain social situations. After one party at Connemara, Herb Mayes said to me, "Your French friend seems like a nice guy; too bad he doesn't speak English."

This was the way my parents discovered that their good little daughter wasn't a virgin, a thought they'd never entertained even while I lived alone in Paris for a year!

Soon afterward, that most cultivated woman, Mrs. Sussman, formidable and straightforward, asked me to lunch. She told me that if I didn't plan to marry her son, I should let him know quickly because I was breaking his heart. In all fairness, I had to agree with her, and soon André was gone from my life, although we've stayed friends ever since and to this day he sends Christmas cards, photos of him looking as sexy as ever.

After we broke up, André quickly married a lovely woman named Nancy, who'd adored him for years; adopted four children; and eventually moved to Majorca, where he opened another restaurant. André left Nancy for a twenty-one-year-old who drifted in for lunch, and settled in Mougins, near Nice, where he opened a restaurant, Le Relais de Mougins, which quickly won its Michelin star. His new young wife left him for a maître d'hotel, returned after a year, and then flew the coop again with a waiter. After that André gave up on her for good, or so he told me some eight years ago when we met again.

During all the years he ran Lutèce, before selling it to his chef, André Soltner, André had steadfastly refused to serve that American abomination, iced tea, to any of his customers. According to him, it would be a crime to serve it with French food. About eight years ago, when my husband and I were in the South of France, near Mougins, I wickedly phoned André and said that the two of us would like to drive over to see him, but only for tea . . . iced tea.

André deliberately made a mess of it—not cold enough, not sweet enough—but he somehow managed, for old times' sake. And we drank it . . . for old times' sake. Would he have treated me like Nancy? Perhaps . . . I'll never know, but that ski trip was a warning. Just last year he sent me a Christmas card and a photo of him alone, in Venice. He still looked as I'd remembered him, but I have no doubt a charming female companion had taken the photograph.

Chapter Twenty-one

EARLY IN 1952, I HAD A DATE WITH A CASUAL BUT LONGTIME FRIEND who told me that I'd never, ever get married while I was living at home, because I was too comfortable there to ever leave. This statement rang so true that the next morning I told my parents I was going to look for my own apartment. Granted, I didn't want to get married, but I didn't want to *never* get married. They tried to persuade me that it wasn't necessary, but I knew it was. Sometimes it takes only one word from an outside source to tell you something you already know but can't quite face.

In a few weeks I'd found a third-floor walk-up at 44 West Fifty-fifth Street, between Fifth and Sixth Avenues, at a rent of one hundred nine dollars a month. It was at the back of the house, with a view of a mildewed yard; it had a small living room with a rudimentary kitchen at one end, and a small bedroom, the length of the living room but only six feet wide. And a small bath. I thought it was heaven. I still do.

When I left home, my parents decided to move to 2 Fifth Avenue on Washington Square, since the St. Urban apartment was much too big for the two of them. I benefited from getting some of their leftover furniture. I furnished my living room with the Oriental carpet from the dining room, that all-but-historic and evocative Queen Anne sofa from my mother's bedroom, a yellow Victorian love seat, and a yellow painted desk. For the bedroom, I had a piece of carpet that was too wide, but rather than pay someone to cut it, I ran it halfway up the wall alongside my single bed. I hung a group of Milton Greene's black-and-white photographs of chairs in the Luxembourg Gardens, and I felt totally satisfied once I'd bought a window air conditioner, an absolute necessity in Manhattan that my parents, who retained some old-fashioned ways, had never installed in their apartment.

Although I'd never been taught how to cook at all, one night, when I found myself without a date, I bought two lamb chops, butter, and a frying pan. Anybody could do lamb chops, I figured. They promptly caught on fire, and reacting without thought, I threw the entire flaming frying pan out of the window into the backyard. Mimi's training in getting rid of food kept me from setting the apartment on fire. From then on, if I didn't have someone buying me dinner, I stopped at the Sixth Avenue Deli, around the corner, and bought myself a turkey wing.

My new liberty not only inspired me to write an article for *Good House* called "Why I Live Alone," but it seemed to demand a new hair color. I'd never been satisfied with being a plain brown and I didn't have the money to go to a salon, but I remembered that Daddy's sister, Aunt Bess, had been a natural redhead and I had red glints in my hair in certain lights. I bought a bottle of something called Superoxide, dipped a comb in it, and ran it artistically through my hair. I emerged a Lucille Ball orange, not the whole head, just the highlights. There was no upkeep problem; anytime I didn't feel orange enough, out came the Superoxide. With my green mascara I believed it looked very natural, or rather, that the two colors looked equally, but pleasingly, unnatural.

Entertaining had always been fun for me and now I had a perfect place for it. Whenever I went up to Connemara for the weekend, I liberated—not stole—a bottle or two of scotch from my parents' rarely opened liquor closet. When I had enough booze accumulated, I phoned Mamie, my mother's housekeeper, and settled on a date for her to bring over a giant bowl of her famous chopped liver. Then I called five times as many people as my apartment could hold and invited them for cocktails. The parties were always so jammed that they spilled over onto the staircase, and almost into the street, which made for a guaranteed success. Didn't Elsa Maxwell, who gave the greatest parties of the thirties, always say that the first requirement for a good party was too many people? I tripled that.

I also organized a subliminal man trap. Most of my dates came to pick me up at home and I always invited them for a drink before dinner. I had one bottle of Jack Daniel's, everybody's favorite bourbon, and when that was empty, I refilled it with Dant, the cheapest bourbon you could buy.

Such is the power of a label that no one ever said anything except, "Wow, I've got to admit that Jack Daniel's is really great stuff." I had a record player on the floor near the sofa, surrounded by a collection of the most romantic, evocative French music—Piaf, Trenet, Sablon, and Yves Montand (it no longer made me cry), plus a group of four records, produced by Norman Grantz, of Fred Astaire singing every great melody he'd ever sung in the movies, in his irresistibly amused way. When I answered the door, there was always music playing, and on my low, blue-painted Victorian coffee table, a filled ice bucket, the only use I found for my little fridge.

I was always careful to meet blind dates at a hotel bar, since I didn't want a strange man to gain admittance to my apartment. However, in spite of this precaution, I once got into a bad situation with a man I knew. I believed him to be gay and had taken him to a party where he could meet Jacques Fath, the famous fashion designer. They had indeed found each other more than interesting, but when my date took me home, he suddenly pushed me to the floor and tried to rape me. I screamed and he hit me so hard that I could taste the blood in my mouth. "Yell one more time," he threatened, "and I'll beat you up." Terrified, what did I do? I burst into tears and, amazing myself, sobbed, "Mommy, Mommy." This unexpected reaction—this atavistic reaction—proved surprisingly effective. The would-be rapist was too disgusted by my weeping to continue. I still believe he was gay.

My husband has always referred to my tiny apartment as a "rat's nest" from which he saved me, but I suspect he's just jealous. I preened myself with the thought that my place was very "me," whatever the hell that was, and I soon learned that it would take almost every penny I made to pay the rent, the phone bill, the electricity bill, and the laundry bill. With my limited math skills I nevertheless managed to discover two mistakes in my bank statements, both in the bank's favor. I was very pleased with my cleverness at being able to add and subtract.

The last few pennies I had left each week always went on fresh flowers, with which I filled one big vase: gladiolus, which I hated, in the summer, and chrysanthemums in the winter. I chose them because with care they lasted a good two to three weeks, longer than any other kind of cut flower.

Sometime in the early summer of 1953, I started to go out with a publishing executive who was in the process of getting a divorce. I had never dated a married man before, but Billy was officially separated. He was Irish, witty, sophisticated, and sweet, with an almost indecent appeal. He was forty, much too old for me, but I'd spent most of my new freedom without anyone at all in my life. I went out with dozens of men, but, ironically, not a single one I liked enough to kiss, much less go to bed with, just when it would have been so easy.

I ached in every part of my mind and body to love someone, I ached to pour out my deepest emotions that had been untouched since Harrison, and along came Billy, for whom I felt great warmth. We met in my apartment during lunch hour, since we didn't want to be seen together until his divorce was final.

One lunch hour, late that May, the day before my period was due, we made love without my diaphragm. Just that single, supposedly safe, time. A week later, when I hadn't had my period, I started to worry. I took a rabbit test and was assured that I wasn't pregnant. Another week or so passed and I went for another test. Ooops! It had been too early to tell the first time, but now there was no question. I was pregnant indeed.

I went home and stood under the shower, washing my hair and

considering what to do. Obviously I had to get an abortion; the question was where. I made a mental list of the people who would probably know doctors, starting with my old friend Gillis McGill, who ran Mannequin, an agency for runway models. It stood to reason, in that period so long before legalized abortion, that one model or another had to be turning up pregnant from time to time. I didn't panic but continued to add other names to the list.

Before I did anything else, it occurred to me to call Billy and tell him the bad news. Fortunately, this had happened to him before—he was as uncommonly fertile a man as I was a fertile woman. He knew a Park Avenue doctor who had an excellent reputation and who performed an abortion almost every day of the week before office hours. The code phrase was to tell him that "the man responsible refuses to marry me" or the doctor wouldn't do the operation. He charged three hundred dollars, par for that time, which Billy provided.

Soon I found myself in the doctor's waiting room. As I sat there, I was horrified to see a woman I knew well enter the room, Lillian Bass, a fine photographer herself and Paul Himmell's wife. She came straight over and sat down next to me. "Hi, Judy, what are you doing here?" "Oh, I have some kind of a stupid itch." "Well, you've come to the right place, this guy's delivered both of my kids and he's just wonderful. He'll cure you in no time." "I certainly hope so," I said, much relieved to get such an endorsement.

The doctor made an appointment with me for the week after the Fourth of July, at eight o'clock in the morning. It was several weeks away, and while I was waiting, a friend named Selig Alkon, whom I'd known since Wellesley, called and asked me if I wanted to go away with a group of other people for the weekend of the Fourth. He was an old buddy and he needed a date for the weekend at Montauk Manor, a seaside resort at the tip of Long Island.

We were planning to go with Selig's first cousin, Barbara Walters, whom I'd known since Birch Wathen, where she was several classes behind me; her date, a man named Ted Cott; and someone I'd never heard of named Steve Krantz, who was program director of NBC Television's flagship station, WNBT, and was both Selig's and Barbara's boss. He'd just broken up with a girl and he'd been invited to cheer him up, since he didn't have a date.

I'm psychic from time to time, like everybody else, and when I heard the name Steve Krantz, something much more powerful than natural curiosity was aroused. A distinct and oddly insistent bell immediately rang in my mind. Nothing more than that, but somehow I was far more interested in meeting this Steve Krantz than I was in meeting just another eligible stranger.

I realized that although I was expected, as always, to be at my father's birthday party, I couldn't possibly endure it. It meant being asked questions about my latest adventures by my parents' friends, at a time when I was waiting to have an abortion the following week, coping with both conscious and repressed fears. I gratefully accepted Selig's invitation.

The morning of July third found us all in Barbara's mother's dining room, eating bagels and smoked salmon to sustain us for the drive. Steve Krantz wasn't there yet. He walked in finally, very tall, very tan, and very handsome. I immediately scooped up a small, fuzzy dog from the floor—I'm not a dog person—so that when he came over to shake hands I was cuddling the squirming creature like a madonna. "Hello, Judy," he said. Something about the way he said my name touched me. It seemed meaningful. But he's too tall for me, I thought, and then amended it hastily. He's not really too tall, I realized with relief.

Chapter Twenty-two

WE DROVE OUT TO MONTAUK IN TWO CARS: SELIG AND I IN ONE, Steve, Ted, and Barbara in the other, an open convertible. I was able to catch glimpses of Steve's profile during the trip, while I tried to find out as much as possible about him without betraying any unusual interest. He'd ended that important love affair because the girl wanted him to convert to Unitarianism so they could be married in church. Originally from Brooklyn, he'd been an officer in the Army Air Corps in the Pacific. Steve was twenty-nine, Selig told me, a graduate of Columbia College and a brilliant television programmer. He was executive producer of the *Steve Allen Show,* which later became the *Tonight Show,* and Selig liked working for him. He was a good guy.

I could have told Selig that. I knew Steve Krantz was a good guy from the instant I met him. There's an enormous amount to be said for the validity of first impressions, and I was positive, on the basis of a look, a handshake, and a few minutes over a toasted bagel, that he was decent to the core. Although this has always been the essential factor to me, in any relationship, it's not a quality that you can easily determine until you know someone well. With Steve it was sitting right there, on top of everything else.

Once at Montauk, Barbara and I unpacked in the room we were sharing. I was startled to find that she had brought along a half dozen beautiful and elaborate cocktail dresses, more elegant than anything I owned. I'd only heard "beach resort" from Selig and had no idea that Montauk Manor was a huge hotel where everybody dressed to meet potential mates. I'd packed sports clothes and simple cotton dresses for evening.

That afternoon, for some odd reason, we all played Ping-Pong. Croquet, Ping-Pong, and, of course, Monopoly had been my games since childhood, when my siblings and I used to spend the summers playing all day and bitterly accusing each other of cheating, with much justice. Alas, as far as I can recall, I didn't cheat, they did.

My first action, in regard to Steve, was to beat him soundly at Ping-Pong. I doubt that this is a tactic you'll find in any rule book on how to attract a man, but it didn't upset him. He thought it was funny. To this day, when he wants to annoy me, he says he threw the game. Like hell he did!

That afternoon there was tea-dancing and, after we'd danced a few steps, he looked down at me and said, comfortingly, "Relax." Just that one word and the tightness in my muscles dissolved. I trusted him.

Later, dressing for dinner, Barbara generously offered me a choice of her dresses. She's a bit taller than I am, but they were all mid-calf in length, so that wasn't a problem. Nor was the fit. I was about ten or twelve pounds heavier than I am now, but that weight was almost all concentrated in my breasts, so Barbara's very-low-cut dresses presented no difficulty . . . indeed they presented an opportunity. Today she says that because of them, "I owe her my life." But I know that even if I'd had to wear my little cottons—even if I'd had to wear a nun's habit—I'd still have had results.

In the course of the weekend, I didn't spend more than five minutes talking to Selig, who, old pal that he was, didn't even bother to complain. I think he recognized that it wouldn't do any good. Lying on the beach, looking at Steve's big, tanned body, I couldn't focus on anyone else. When he went in swimming I even went so far as to put on a bathing cap and join him, giving a convincingly sporty performance, although I was worried all the while that I was getting my hair wet, cap notwithstanding. Years later, as soon as we built our first swimming pool, I gathered my two sons and told them to watch me do something they would *never, ever* see me do again, to remember it well, and never to say I couldn't do it. Then I dove into the pool, swam to the other side, and climbed out triumphantly, never to dive again.

At one point in Montauk we were all talking politics and the conversation turned to Dwight Eisenhower, who had, the year before, beaten my idol, Adlai Stevenson. "Fuck Eisenhower!" I burst out. Steve's interest, already strong, was further aroused. Well-brought-up young women didn't say "fuck" in company in those days, and it seemed to him that I had conviction, energy, and guts . . . and he liked that. During the last evening of the weekend we exchanged our lucky silver dollars, mine the last one I had left from my parents' silver wedding anniversary. It strikes us both, more than forty-five years later, that this exchange was amazingly symbolic and important, considering that we barely knew each other, but at the time it seemed almost— but not entirely—casual.

Before we all had to leave to drive back, Steve had taken me aside and secured my phone numbers at home and at the office. "When do you get to work?" he asked. "Nine-thirty," I replied.

The next morning I was sitting at my desk at nine-thirty, more prompt than I'd ever been before, when the phone rang and I heard Steve's voice. I put my hand over the receiver and announced triumphantly to my office mate, Eileen, "Victory is mine!" Steve says today that if I won, that must mean he lost, but I point out that there's such a thing as a win-win situation. He asked me out for dinner the next night, Tuesday, but since that was the day I was going for my abortion, I settled on Wednesday.

The worst part of getting an abortion, for me, was certainly not the decision about having one. It was entirely clear to me that I wasn't about to ruin my life over an egg and a sperm that should never have come into contact. I don't believe that a soul is created at conception, and the issue of Choice, although we didn't call it that back then, is vital to me. I had no moral problem with abortion. It never even occurred to me that some people might find it a moral issue, and, in the climate of the early 1950s, it was primarily a pragmatic problem: how do you get one? Almost without exception, every unmarried girl I knew, at this time in my life, had had an abortion. The existence of an upper-middle-class *unwed* Jewish mother was, like a unicorn in the bath, simply not a possibility. No one had ever heard of such a thing. There must have been religious girls who went away to have their babies and gave them up for adoption, but I didn't know of any such cases.

No, the worst part was my habitual overpunctuality, which led me to be a half hour early for the appointment. The doctor's office was located on the first floor of a midtown Park Avenue apartment building, and I had to walk around and around the block until he arrived, trying to figure out what on earth I could say I was doing in that part of town so early in the morning if I met someone I knew. I kept my eyes on the pavement and walked quickly, trying to be invisible. Finally the doctor showed up. Before starting, he warned me that he couldn't give me anything for the pain because I had to leave before his office hours began and I had to stay alert. I clutched Steve's lucky silver dollar throughout the procedure. It was unpleasant, but far from unbearable, and I'd expected much worse. He was a quick, gentle, and expert doctor and I was incredibly lucky to have found him. In fact, I used him as my gynecologist for several years.

Afterward, I took a taxi home, walked carefully up three flights of stairs, and called in sick. Jeremy brought me a sandwich for lunch and I rested all afternoon, immeasurably relieved. The next day I was back at work, feeling perfectly normal.

Steve had asked me to meet him at NBC before we went out for dinner. I wore my favorite Claire McCardell dress made of pale green, finely pleated cotton, and cut in that great designer's famous Grecian style, with thin straps that wound around the body, outlining the torso and waist, tied in a knot at the front. Naturally I didn't wear a bra. I loathe, hate, and despise wearing bras. They're worse than hats. I've never found a really comfortable one, and to this day I never wear one unless I know people are going to see me at some public occasion.

According to Steve, when I appeared on the busy floor of the set of the *Steve Allen Show,* with my divine dress, my divine green mascara, and my divine orange hair, he thought I looked like a prostitute. He still insists that you could see through the dress, but, trust me, in 1953 no one designed see-through clothes. Only a man would imagine that he could see the shadow of a nipple through that dress. He'd asked me to meet him on the set because he was producing a show that night with the mayor of New York, Vincent Impellitteri, and thought I might be impressed.

After the show we went to a dark, excellent French restaurant, Jimmy's La Grange, which disappeared long ago. During dinner, I felt that our conversation was somehow lagging, growing difficult to sustain, and I was so concerned that I retired to the ladies' room to think about how to remedy the situation. After all, wasn't I in the advice business, with "Tips to the Teens"? Hastily I decided to tell Steve about all the things I couldn't do, a lengthy list that started with spelling, math, cooking, carrying a tune, and most sports, and proceeded from those basics. He perked up immediately. Apparently he'd been feeling a little intimidated by my sophisticated job and background—he'd remembered my year in Paris and the phone call he'd tried to make—and he was still taken aback, if intrigued, by the way I looked. My enormous list of defects was just the antidote Steve needed and we haven't stopped talking since.

When he walked me back to my apartment that night and kissed me, I had an indelible emotional reaction. I felt as if I were coming home. I didn't know what that meant, but there it was, unmistakable. Strong. Powerful. Deeply important.

Yet, as we began to see each other several times a week, I literally could not begin to think about the possibility of marriage, although any normal girl would have seen that Steve Krantz had everything, and would have had marriage on her mind from the start. I was still so firmly set against the idea of marriage, so unwilling to commit myself to such a frightening and final undertaking, that whenever I tried to sit myself down and think about it reasonably, my mind simply turned off. A mind I had counted on to be rational and able to make intelligent decisions refused to function. It was exactly as if there were a wall of prohibition smack up against my face, a wall that stretched up into the heavens, when the thought of marriage faced me.

I had always felt very strongly that no matter how many wild oats

I sowed before marriage, once I was married, all that would be over, for good. My class at college has only a ten-percent divorce rate. All of us, regardless of background, had the firm expectation that you only got married once. I was certain that I'd be a faithful wife, and I have been.

As much as I feared marriage, that didn't stop me from playing my cards very carefully. I wanted to hook this big, beautiful fish even if I decided to throw him back in the pond afterward. I felt that now, if ever, was the time not to give away any piece of my independence. I continued to have dates with never less than two other men every week and I limited Steve to two dates a week and one on the weekend. If I wasn't asked out on any particular evening, I stayed home and didn't answer my phone until after midnight, when Steve began to call to find out what I'd been up to with my imaginary date. "Oh, we didn't do anything extraordinary, just Le Veau d'Or for dinner, then down to the Village Vanguard to listen to Harry Belafonte," I'd lie from a carefully prepared note I'd scribbled so I wouldn't sound vague.

When Steve stunned me, a month or so later, by saying, "Maybe we're seeing too much of each other," I was quick-witted enough to agree with him immediately, even enthusiastically. I suggested that he take some time out and go back to the girl he'd broken up with just before I met him. "Really, darling, see her for a few weeks, or a month or two . . . I'm not interested in a man on the rebound." The only thing I knew about her was the religious conflict. Now, at long last, he's admitted to me that she was a tall beautiful blonde, a talented pianist, a model, and a Phi Beta. I'm glad I didn't know all that forty-five years ago, but I would have said exactly the same thing. In any case, he only saw her once before he returned to me, a little sheepishly.

We almost always met at the bar at the Sherry Netherland, the most romantic bar in New York, from whose windows you could see the horses and carriages waiting to pick up tourists in front of the Plaza, and the corner of Central Park and Fifth. From there we went on to dinner at restaurants like Sardi's and the evocative, unique Cafe Nicholson and often to the nightclubs that flourished at the time, particularly the Blue Angel. It was a real old-fashioned, horribly expensive New York courtship, the kind you see in a montage in movies. We drank bourbon, at least two doubles each, before dinner, and sometimes I reflect that I married a man who courted me largely when we both were fairly tipsy . . . but in those days everybody drank a lot, although not nearly as much as we did during college weekends.

At one point in the fall, following our meeting, my mother asked me if I'd bought any new clothes that year. I explained that I couldn't afford to because of paying my rent. "Here," she said, giving me thirty-five whole dollars, "get yourself a new dress." By going wholesale to a junior dress manufacturer, Judy and Jill, I was able to buy two good-looking wool dresses and hear another piece of advice that changed my life. The saleswoman looked critically at my inherited little pot belly, something like the Hapsburg lip, as I tried on a size seven, and said, "You could stand to wear a girdle." Gasping—the awfulness of a girdle!—I went on a diet and lost ten pounds, which I've kept off since then except when I was pregnant.

On the other hand, my mother made no secret of the fact that Steve wasn't a man she would welcome as a suitor. In spite of his excellent job and his obvious promise, he didn't have a penny of family money. On his first visit to Connemara, she symbolically gave him the evil eye. We'd never served lobster at home, although we often ate it in restaurants, but for Steve's first lunch with us, there was a huge, cold boiled lobster, in the shell, on each plate. GO AWAY! was the message. It was the first lobster Steve had ever eaten, although he coped with it so well that I never guessed it. His family wasn't particularly religious, but they didn't serve the most expensive form of *traif,* or ritually un-clean food, to anyone, much less guests.

Her feelings about the threat Steve presented were so strong that she made the single funny, now politically incorrect, remark of her life about him. Looking at Steve, very tan and tall, she said he resembled "two Puerto Ricans, one standing on top of the other."

My father, not surprisingly, wasn't accepting toward Steve either. He'd never liked a single man I'd brought home except for Harry Salzman. However, Herb and Grace Mayes fell in love with Steve on first sight, which was an enormous joy to me, because Herbert either loved people or couldn't stand them, and the Mayeses were such an important part of my life.

When I finally decided, after waiting ten times longer than would have been normal, to go away with Steve for our first weekend to-gether, late in the fall, I packed my clothes in two hatboxes so it wouldn't seem as if I were bringing a suitcase. What was *that* all about? This dainty precaution could hardly have made any sense to the hotelkeeper at the Black Bass Inn in New Hope. Did he think I was planning to stay up all night trying on hats? I spent a few un-married weekends at Steve's apartment at 20 Fifth Avenue, and until we moved out, three years later, when I was pregnant, I could never again look any of the elevator men in the eye, because they knew about those weekends. Good God, sex in the fifties! We both were and ab-solutely were not Ozzie and Harriet.

For Christmas of 1953, I gave Steve a gray cashmere sweater from Saks, the most expensive present I'd ever given any man, and he gave me a fitted green leather cosmetic case from Mark Cross, the sort of dramatically lavish luggage women carried then, no matter how inconvenient it was.

I still hadn't been able to think, either rationally or irrationally, about marriage, and we both avoided the word "love," preferring to say that we "adored" each other, a far lesser thing. On New Year's Eve, not quite six months after we'd met, Steve took me to Voisin and ordered lobster and a chocolate soufflé. Then we went back to my place and made love. Afterward, we were sitting around on that damned ubiquitous Queen Anne sofa, waiting for the stroke of midnight, when Steve suddenly asked me to marry him. I could not utter the word "yes"—I was struck mute. But I couldn't say no either, I couldn't think of a good reason not to marry him, so I just nodded. Nodded yes, not no. I was truly so surprised by the unexpected way he asked me, with no buildup, that I didn't have time to think, which is the only reason I didn't have my defenses up and running.

Almost instantly, instead of feeling wonderfully happy, both of us felt sick to our stomachs with the enormity of what we'd done. Only by telephoning as many people as we could reach with the news did we manage to lessen our queasiness. Could it have been caused by the combination of lobster and the soufflé? In any case, Steve said that we "had to pour concrete" over the decision, sounding as if he belonged to the Mafia, and we did so by phoning our parents and a few friends. Only my mother's cook sounded genuinely thrilled to hear the tidings.

We decided to get married on the first day of the Washington's Birthday weekend, which came on February 19, just a little more than six weeks away. We planned a small wedding, with both our families. Steve's father was dead but his mother, Rose, a marrying woman, attended with her third husband, and then there were his sister, Sunny Onish, her husband and her two sons, and Steve's uncle Leon. In addition we invited Herb and Grace Mayes, Maggie Cousins, and Fanny and Leonard Cohen to my parents' apartment opposite Washington Square Park. Ted Cott, who was Steve's boss and friend, acted as best man, and my sister was matron of honor.

Jimmy Abee, one of the finest fashion photographers of the time and a dear friend, took my wedding picture as a present, and on my lunch hour I went to Lord & Taylor, where I found a perfect wedding dress with a white lace top, a pale blue cummerbund, and a white ballerina organza skirt. To my delighted surprise, my mother saw fit to take me to Saks and bought me some pretty clothes and even a waist-length black Persian lamb jacket. Steve and I went to Tiffany's for our gold wedding bands—mine was twenty dollars and Steve's thirty-five—but I didn't want an engagement ring. It seemed a silly way to spend money he didn't have. The fashion department gave me a bridal shower at Nancy White's, all of them chipping in to give me a charming pair of gold Victorian earrings, and Ted Cott gave us a big, rowdy party, full of NBC-niks.

We needed a rabbi but we didn't have a rabbi stashed away anywhere. Fanny Cohen finally came up with the recommendation of Jonah B. Wise, the son of Stephen Wise, who had founded Reform Judaism. We went to his study for the obligatory visit, but I don't believe he gave us any advice, which in any case would have been lost on us. The whole meeting took less than ten minutes, but I was incredibly chagrined when Steve asked him, right in front of me, what his fee was. The good rabbi, not at all taken aback by such a direct question, replied that it was fifty dollars. A bloody fortune! And hardly something you could negotiate.

The morning of my noon wedding I washed my hair, touched it up with a dash of Superoxide, and was escorted by Jeremy in a taxi to my parents' place. Steve had to be persuaded to buy new black shoes because I wouldn't let him wear brown shoes with his blue suit, but otherwise those were all the special preparations we made.

I understand why people make such a major production out of weddings, spending months and a fortune planning them, but I didn't want anything like that. Mimi had the grand wedding, but I was twenty-six, if only just barely, and I'd never spent a minute of my life daydreaming of being the star of a big marital event. My Wellesley classmates were all busy having the third or fourth of their eventually larger broods, and my mother was already quite annoyed that the caterer was charging twenty-five dollars a person for the wedding lunch.

A half hour before the wedding was scheduled I got serious cold feet as I was dressing in my mother's bedroom. I asked Jeremy to get me a drink, and quickly! Thank God, at twenty-two, he wasn't an experienced bartender, and he returned with a highball glass full of bourbon, almost all of which I drank straight down. It was the only way I could have been pried out of the bedroom. I walked down the improvised aisle in my parents' living room, on my father's arm, saying out loud, over and over, in a loud voice that everyone ignored, "This is all a mistake, a terrible mistake."

The rabbi didn't even wear a yarmulke, so Reform was he, and neither did any of the other men. The ceremony took about four minutes—fifty dollars indeed!—and all I remember was that Steve's mouth was so dry that he could barely croak out a "yes." My main memory is the vision of his lips all but glued together—surely I was the most unromantic bride in history. Almost immediately after the ceremony the worried caterer came up to me and asked what the mistake was. "This whole thing!" I answered, gesturing wildly around the room. "Oh, I thought it was something to worry about," she answered, and walked away, relieved.

Steve and I were supposed to leave that evening for a weekend in Havana—yes, Havana before Castro!—so we had an afternoon to wile away. We went back to his apartment, a block away, and made love and then, since it was a warm and sunny day, we went to the Central Park Zoo. In the monkey house, a baboon with a brightly colored bottom, turned around, pointed his ass in our direction, and proceeded to let us know, in the most egregious and unmistakable way, what he thought of us. I'm sure that somewhere in Africa there must be a folk saying that a large pile of fresh baboon shit is a sign of good luck.

After a splendid dinner at the Barberry Room, we went merrily out to the airport, only to discover that our plane would be late taking off. In those days you had to fly to Miami and then take another plane to Cuba. The plane was not just delayed, it was many hours late, and, when the airport closed down for the night—believe it or not, it did that in those days—there was no place to sit. I had to stand, in a crowd, on my wedding night, for three endless hours, trying to be a good sport in spite of the awful pain in my flat feet. Somehow I succeeded. Once the plane took off, Steve went to sleep immediately and I burst into floods of tears that never stopped, not for a minute, for the entire flight. My feet were agony, I was frayed in every nerve, utterly exhausted—and what the hell kind of wedding night was this, anyway?

I didn't cheer up until we were settled in our oceanside hotel in Havana, around lunchtime, but the weekend was heaven. There will never again be any place that was as romantic and sensual as Havana before Castro. We returned there twice more, the last time a year after Castro. The outdoor lobby of our former honeymoon hotel was filled with men marching back and forth, clad in paratrooper boots and T-shirts and carrying fixed bayonets on their rifles. "What's that all about?" I asked the desk clerk. "Oh, they're Red Cross workers," he answered. "Didn't you notice those red crosses on their T-shirts?" I had my picture taken with some of these laughing, bearded soldiers. Several days after we returned from our trip, Cuba and the United States broke off diplomatic relations.

On our first, honeymoon visit, we deliberately took one single extra day besides the three-day weekend allotted for the holiday. When I got back to work a single day late, Herbert Mayes didn't speak to me for two months. Thank God he loved Steve, or it might have been a year.

Chapter Twenty-three

A MARVELOUS NEW YORK LIFE SPREAD OUT BEFORE US. WE WENT TO every good movie, we saw a lot of splendid theater, we gave parties and went to parties, and wonder of wonders, NBC sent us a color television set, one of the first ever made, with a huge, ugly cabinet and a tiny screen. I looked at it once or twice—miniature green people saying incomprehensible things—and then only switched it on to amaze our dinner guests who'd never seen color television before. Only a detail like this makes me realize how long ago all this was.

Steve and I lived in his bachelor apartment at 20 Fifth Avenue and we rambled in the Village after dinner, walking through peaceful Washington Square Park to Bleecker Street, where all the bohemian coffeehouses were located, or on less familiar streets where, investigating a new bar, we'd find ourselves entirely surrounded by friendly lesbians or gay men.

On the weekends, unless we had important plans, my parents expected us to go up to Connemara with them. We went, Steve driving, but why we went, when we didn't have to and didn't particularly enjoy it, only shows what a powerful hold my parents still had over me and, through me, over Steve.

In spite of my four years away at college, my one year away in Paris, a year and a half on my own in my apartment, and the fact that I was now a married woman in my mid-twenties, with my own home, I still automatically continued to fill the role of the child who absolutely *must* please her parents without question, remaining obedient to their wishes, particularly since Mimi was living in California and Jeremy was leading his own life. I was thoroughly neurotic. I just didn't realize it then, nor would I until the mid-sixties when I started psychoanalysis.

At some point in these first two years of marriage, Steve and I had to go out to Los Angeles on business, and there I finally met my legendary evil paternal grandmother, Tilly Janks.

Mimi had been in touch with her for years, for she went to visit her regularly at the Jewish Home for the Aged. There Mimi was known not as her granddaughter but as her great-niece, since Grandmother Tilly fiercely maintained the fiction that Mr. Janks had been her only husband—even that was questionable—and that she was childless. She and that home-wrecker Janks had gone to Canada after abandoning their mates and children, and there had made a fortune in real estate. Eventually they'd moved to California and again prospered mightily in real estate . . . a riff on the familiar California legend of the "grandmother who owned Sunset Boulevard until the Depression wiped her out" that I've heard from several friends. During her period of wealth, Tilly had become a major benefactor of the very retirement home in which she now lived, where she was treated as a veritable queen.

Mimi, who describes her as "manipulative, bright, lying, charming, and witty," soon became the connection who supplied a constant stream of Tilly's favored heart medication, Hennessy Five Star Brandy, bought with money my father sent Mimi. She shared the brandy with those friends who helped her organize get-out-the-vote campaigns for Democrats at every election. The nurses called her "ma'am," because of her status, and according to Mimi, she not only had a strong voice in how the home was run but was constantly held up by the staff as an example of the benefits of casting your bread upon the waters. When Tilly entered the Home for the Aged, giving them everything she still owned, she was supposed to have only a year to live, but she survived for twenty-seven years until she died of a stroke in 1957. Benefits, indeed.

Steve and I went to visit her, yet another great-niece and her husband. Nothing of importance was said, although I stared with avid fascination at this perfectly active and lively woman who had caused such havoc in my father's life. I felt nothing but curiosity, although she had photos of our family displayed all over her room. These were all changed for Janks photos when her other "family" came to visit.

Mimi tells me that on one exceptional and never-repeated occasion, Tilly went to Mimi's house to see my father, who was in L.A. on business. She touched him and he immediately went into the bathroom and threw up. Nausea, yes, but amnesia . . . somehow, I don't think so.

ONLY TRUE LOVE allowed Steve and me to survive the second of our two honeymoons. Havana had always been intended as a mere weekend; our real honeymoon was planned for mid-May to mid-June, when we would go to Europe for a month, Steve for the first time.

I, the expert, was in charge of planning this trip and I spent hours studying maps, figuring mileage, and making choices of hotels. Our plan was to fly to Rome, stay a week, and then drive for two weeks by easy stages to Paris, where we'd spend the last week introducing Steve to the city and my friends.

My first mistake, in all my overcareful calculations, was to decide to have the last of my wisdom teeth pulled right before we left. The other three teeth had given me trouble during the past year and had been removed successfully by a renowned specialist who did no other type of dental work. For someone with strong teeth, I seem to have suffered inordinately with them, both in real life and in my Parisian lies.

Teeth, hats, bras, the sun, soon a deadly allergy to the bite of a yellow jacket . . . while enjoying normal good health, I sound like a hypochondriac full of foibles. Of course, it didn't help that I suffer from the princess and the pea syndrome and things that other women can take in stride bother the hell out of me. (I've never claimed I was easygoing, have I?) How many people do you know who travel with a wide roll of duct tape to attach hotel curtains to the wall so that no ray of light enters in the morning? How many people do you know who persuaded the front-desk clerk at the Savoy in London to change her room four times in a single afternoon, even getting the clerk, in his tailcoat, to lie down with her on the floor to confirm that there was a vibration from the Underground that, with her super-acute hearing, would have driven her crazy in the first three rooms? Each change was to a bigger room, I hasten to point out, and at the same price.

I also have a deeply rooted streak of insanity about packing that just gets worse as time passes. In my imagination, there lurks a man with a full glass of red wine whose mission at all times is to spill it over me and ruin the foundation of whatever wardrobe any trip demands. My belief in this possibility means that if I take two pairs of white slacks for a cruise, I need another two pairs as backup to foil the red wine terrorist . . . who has yet to show up in real life. This craziness applies to every item in my suitcases. I don't try to fight it anymore, it isn't worth the struggle. My backups, by now, all have backups of their own. It goes with the territory of being a devout obsessive-compulsive. How I envy the smug insouciance of people who are able to pack easily and travel light.

Now, before our honeymoon, I worried that the remaining wisdom tooth would act up while we were in the wilds of Italy. Better to have it out ahead of time, like removing an appendix before a trip on camelback across the Sahara. Off I went and had a simple operation, in the course of which the expert dentist injured a nerve that gave me a severe, incurable toothache for the next month.

We flew to Rome by way of Amsterdam. This was in the days when it was legal for Steve to promote airlines on the air and get free tickets in return, so we had to go by KLM in a huge, four-engine plane that took eighteen hours. I had four to five pain-free hours a day, before, during, and after lunch and dinner, after I'd dosed myself with aspirin and a couple of scotches. I remember, during our day in Amsterdam, seeing the otherworldly vision of hundreds of acres of blooming tulips through a drugged, jet-lagged haze, trying to absorb as much pleasure as I could before the pain started up again.

Rome is a blur, except for a visit to Gucci, where I somehow managed to pull myself together long enough to choose the black alligator handbag of the most amazing grandness that Steve bought me, and then, with truly exceptional indirection, I somehow acquired a small, jewellike, burgundy alligator evening bag—I still have both of them. Steve woke up in the middle of the night and, in disbelief, found me up gazing at them gloatingly by the light of the bedside lamp.

After we left Rome, with Florence as our next destination, we found out, halfway to Florence and far too late to do anything about it, that the car we'd rented, a new Fiat convertible—the smallest one made, called the Topolino—was in a state called *rodagio*. This meant that its engine wasn't yet broken in, and a governor had been installed inside the motor that limited our speed to under forty miles an hour. All my carefully made mileage plans became impossible at that rate of progress. As we made this discovery it started to piss rain. The roof of that bloody-awful haunted convertible did not quite close and we spent the rest of the trip in company with a slow but permanent drip that landed on Steve's head.

Because of the *rodagio,* in order to get from one hotel in which we had reservations to the next, it turned out that now we had to devote about fourteen hours a day to driving, although we didn't realize it in time to drive that car straight back to Rome. Soon we were past the point of no return. This was in the early days of rental cars and you couldn't just change one car for another en route. Nor could we change plans and take a train; our intention was to see the countryside and we still had two weeks before our arrival in Paris.

Florence is another blur of toothache, but Venice is clear. We arrived on a cloudless day, the first in a week, left the accursed Fiat at the station, and rushed to a *motoscaffo* to take us to our hotel. Then, hurrying as fast as I could, I led Steve from the hotel to the entrance to the Piazza San Marco, pausing dramatically under the archway that opens out to reveal the vast magnificence of the piazza.

"Now," I announced, and we stepped forward and through the archway. Instantly a deluge fell on our heads. We turned and ran back to the hotel and after a frustrating day waiting for signs of a letup in the flood—Venice in the rain has nothing to recommend it—we repacked and decided to change plans and drive over what looked like a simple mountain pass to the seaport of La Spezia, the nearest town we could reach on our quest to arrive at Positano, where we had our next reservations.

Steve had volunteered for the Army Air Corps at nineteen, immediately after his graduation from Columbia, and had ended up as a lieutenant in an amphibious assault company in the Philippines, setting up radio communications with the Air Corps to guide them on their strafing and dive-bombing runs. However, accurately guessing at the meaning of an Italian map was not quite as straightforward an operation as waging war on an enemy-occupied island in the Pacific.

As darkness fell we found ourselves driving in heavy, threatening clouds on top of a narrow mountain road that was nothing but a series of hairpin turns, barely illuminated by our headlights. We were only halfway from Venice to La Spezia. I was too frightened to do anything but huddle in my damp clothes and wish I believed that crossing myself would do any good. In this desolate place, Steve somehow spied a little figure standing in the dark. He stopped and bought a tiny bouquet of edelweiss from an enterprising young boy who, it seemed to both of us, shouldn't have been out at that hour. This strange, magical encounter immediately seemed like a good omen and I clutched the flowers all the way down that hideous mountain pass until, at midnight, we reached the sordid port of La Spezia and found a room in a dive where there was no light except for a dim bulb that hung on a string over the bed.

The next day we grimly drove to and through Positano, not even stopping in the driving rain to cancel our reservations there. As we pushed on I happened to look at Steve and saw a stranger, a furious, disappointed man I'd never seen before in my life. "What the hell am I doing with this person and who the HELL *is* he?" I asked myself, a question every happily married (or unhappily married) woman is bound to ask herself thousands of times during her marriage. I remember it only because it was the first time this normal wonderment occurred to me.

We continued over the border into France, where we checked into La Réserve de Beaulieu, a small and utterly elegant hotel. In my planning I had remembered that my family and I had spent a few glorious days there in 1948, where we'd seen women wearing the newly invented and shocking bikinis at the hotel pool. The next day was May 20, Steve's thirtieth birthday, and we awoke to sunshine and a brilliant sky. I gave him the silk dressing gown I'd managed to buy for him in Rome without his knowing it and we both thought that the worst of our honeymoon was over.

Reader, as that horror movie ad says, be afraid, be very afraid. Our

next downfall was a portside lunch in Cassis, the following day. Whatever delicious dish it was that we ate, we both developed diarrhea at
about the same time, an hour or so later, on the road leading up toward Paris. This was not the kind of *tourista* that you can control. We
were lucky that we were nimble enough to jump out of the car onto
the side of the road before the worst happened, over and over and
over. It's moments like that that make you discover that shit takes
precedence over almost everything. Our malady didn't go away for
weeks, although it was augmented at Nîmes, where I remember actually biting a hotel pillowcase with the worst menstrual cramps I'd ever
had while Steve frantically tried to get medications from the concierge.
I've never suffered like that either time I gave birth.

There was one respite on this journey to Paris. We had a reservation
at a little hotel called Le Prieuré, in Villeneuve-lès-Avignon, where we
arrived after dark, as our slow-moving car always forced us to do. The
next morning we had to leave right after breakfast in order to get to
our next stop in time, but we were both overcome with the charm of
the little hotel across the Rhône from Avignon. If only we could stay
for one extra day, we thought wistfully, but then we'd never make
Paris on the appointed date, and I'd worked myself into a state of true
control-freak dementia, determined to get to Paris in time for our week
there, where I was finally going to show my husband the city I loved
so much.

I'd made a reservation in Paris at the San Régis, the preferred hotel
of the fashion crowd. I'd written them a long letter describing the kind
of room we wanted, and mentioning that Dick Avedon, Carmel Snow,
and Nancy White had all recommended the hotel to me.

We arrived, on time, by God, and were led immediately to a miserable attic, unquestionably the worst room in the hotel. I sat down
on the bed and started to cry. I have hated the French at many moments, but never more than at that one. Steve, in a more practical
mode, went straight back to the front desk and got us a good room.
That night we had a reservation at Maxim's and I finally got to wear
one of the many dresses I'd been dragging around idiotically for three
weeks. We drove there, instead of taking a taxi, and as we pulled up
in front of the door of the grandest restaurant in Paris, our Fiat died.
Probably of humiliation. The next day we called a garage to remove
it at any price, with a huge sense of relief.

Our table at Maxim's was excellent and we no sooner sat down
than an old boyfriend came over to say hello, Michel Paulmier-
Peterson, that most exquisite half-Swede. I proudly introduced my husband, who seemed somewhat less thrilled at seeing this lady-killing,
hand-kissing apparition than I was. Looking backward, for me this

was the best moment of our honeymoon. Steve says that for him it was getting on the plane to come home.

Meeting Michel was a foretaste of the problem with Paris. Everywhere we went I wanted to introduce Steve to my old friends. However, as the French invariably do, they'd start a conversation in English, which, by now, they all spoke well or well enough, and within minutes they'd quickly and rudely lapse into French. At that time Steve hadn't yet learned French, so naturally he felt utterly awkward and out of place, something I foolishly hadn't anticipated. Paris was the last place we should have gone and it had all been my idea. No question, between my teeth and my friends, I totally fucked up our honeymoon.

Steve's *tourista* hadn't gone away either and he went to see Paul-Emile for a cure. Paul-Emile, who practiced from his home, as most French doctors do, asked Steve to strip. "All I have is diarrhea," he objected. "Take off all your clothes," the doctor insisted. He prescribed enormous, dangerous-looking pills, which we flushed down the toilet, but from that moment on, Steve was cured.

I imagined for years that Paul-Emile was curious to see, in all his glory, what manner of man I'd married, until I met another ex-patient of his. As a girl of sixteen, suffering from a minor ailment, she'd also been told to get naked by Paul-Emile, who then invited her to sit down in a chair directly in front of his desk. "Mademoiselle," he asked, "do you read poetry?"

In the end we made it back to New York without having a memorable fight, but I'd realized that traveling with a husband was more complicated than I'd anticipated, something like an Italian road map. I did know I could count on him to protect me on mountain roads and from uncaring front-desk management and to go into a fit of divine spending madness at Gucci. Nancy White once asked me plaintively, "Why do you have a better bag than I do?"

About six months later, in the fall, up at Connemara, Steve was on the phone doing business with an agent who maddened him so much that his back went into a spasm. By the time we reached our apartment, he had to go to the hospital, where they promptly put him in traction. I was sent home, where I lay on the bed and howled and howled between floods of tears. "I knew it was too good to be true," I raved at the ceiling over and over. "I knew it was too good to be true!" I felt sure that my world had ended. It was an entirely uncharacteristic way for me to react. Usually I'm calm when faced by a threatened disaster. The only thing I could think of was to take Steve drinks in a cocktail shaker after work, but from his bed of pain, he quickly let me know that the last thing in the world he wanted was a drink. He left the hospital in three days, with instructions to sleep on a board, but this incident made me realize just how much I now depended on him for my happiness.

TOWARD THE END of two magnificent, radiant, remarkably unclouded and uncomplicated years of marriage, when I was just twenty-eight, Steve turned to me one day and said, "We should have a baby." "Do we have to?" I asked dubiously. "Yep," he said, and within an hour I was pregnant. That's the way people had children then, with less consideration than they'd give to buying a new pair of shoes. There was a law that reigned in the 1950s. If you couldn't have children, you adopted them, but you just had to have kids, automatically, like everybody else, and the end of two years of marriage was the time most people were bitten by the bug. It's like the story about the two people who've finally got their lives perfectly arranged. They look at each other, shrug, and one of them says, "Let's go out and buy an elephant."

Chapter Twenty-four

I KNEW I WAS PREGNANT LONG BEFORE I CHECKED WITH A GYNECOL-
ogist to make sure. Steve and I had been taking cooking lessons at
night from a teacher in the Village who had turned his entire living
room into a huge kitchen. He shopped for the groceries, we brought
the drinks and wine, and by midnight we'd learned to make such dishes
as duck à l'orange or beef Wellington, encased in foie gras and covered
by puff pastry. Our jolly, unrealistic teacher always wore his shirt-
sleeves rolled up, revealing the dark, coarse stubble of the hair he'd
shaved off his arms. Of course, by the time dinner was ready to eat,
we were always too far gone in drink to remember how we'd managed
to cook these elaborate feasts, but I had learned how to peel an onion
and use a chopping knife, and I felt a confidence around the kitchen
that I'd never had before.

Less than two weeks after I first tried to get pregnant, I found myself
unable to go to that cooking lesson we'd paid for in advance. I could
only eat white food, only imagine ever eating white food again in my
life: white bread, the white meat of chicken, sour cream, vanilla ice
cream . . . the list of white food is short. But the thought of anything
else made me feel sick.

Hilliard Dubrow, my gynecologist, confirmed my self-diagnosis, and
Steve and I were both thrilled at our immense cleverness in our accomplishment, first crack out of the box, as it were. We started looking
for a larger apartment and eventually sublet one on Fifty-seventh
Street, only a block away from a park on the East River. The number-
twenty bus across Fifty-seventh would take me directly to the office.

In my fifth month we took a trip to Paris because we knew that we
wouldn't be able to travel much once the baby was born. There was
nothing I could buy to wear. That left only gloves and perfume. If I
need any other proof that my husband has saintlike qualities, it's the
memory of his patience while I tried on gloves, my elbow resting on
the counter while the saleswoman carefully smoothed the fine kid
down over each finger to make sure that they weren't too big or too
small. Twenty-seven pairs of kid gloves, in every length and color, were
needed to satisfy me before I felt I had enough gloves, and indeed, I
didn't have to buy another pair for decades. Steve has never gone shopping with me since: the glove episode broke his spirit.

On the last night in Paris we went to a famous classic restaurant, Lucas-Carton, for a final meal and I sat through the entire dinner with tears rolling quietly but unstoppably down my face. "It's never going to be the same again," I said, feeling a deep, inconsolable sadness for our first years together. The waiters paid no attention. Weeping women are probably a familiar sight in all great French restaurants. I knew, and I was right, that once you have a baby, your life changes so much that it's the end of an entire chapter. No great love affair lost, no divorce, no change of profession, has any real significance in the long run compared to having a child. A child is the one thing in life you can't change or move away from or get over . . . it's the biggest, and only absolutely final, commitment you ever make.

But that was a momentary reaction, like the other time I wept through dinner with my parents at Voisin on my twenty-second birthday because I knew I'd never be really young again. Now I knew I'd never be free again. I was right both times, but, on the other hand, not that it's one hell of a consolation, does anybody stay young and free forever? At least I'd put off losing my freedom by not having my first child until I was twenty-eight.

As the birth date approached, we started a form of lottery. People could submit proposed names for our child for a dollar and the winner would receive ten dollars and a commemorative scroll. We had privately decided on Nicholas if the baby was a boy, and naturally that was the name Herb Mayes submitted. His first grandchild was also named Nicholas. Of course, we might have had a girl, but I was irrationally convinced that we would have a boy.

I was full of irrational thoughts: I believed I looked glorious with the thirty-three pounds I'd gained, all in front; I had maternity clothes custom-made because nothing I could find in the stores was pretty enough; I even snapped completely and went shopping, a major mistake, for *post*-pregnancy clothes when I was eight months and three weeks pregnant, after a lunch with Patrick O'Higgins, a darling pal who was Helena Rubenstein's right-hand man. This ultrachic, red-headed Irishman who'd been an officer in the Irish Guards paid a dollar to have us name the baby Ludwig von Krantz. "Von," he explained, would be the child's middle name. Patrick had often taken me to Madame Rubenstein's receptions, and the last time I went, very pregnant, that bejeweled and amazing idol took my hands and held them for a long time while she looked quietly and deeply into my eyes, saying nothing. And conveying nothing.

My most irrational thought was that it was necessary to prove my strength of character to give birth by the currently faddish method known as "Painless Childbirth," invented by Dr. Grantly Dick Reed

Me with Orson Welles at the Orcels'
Greek costume party, winter 1949.
He was then thirty-four.

José Waechter sporting his Le Rosey sweat-
shirt, spring 1949, at Le Bois Normand.

Spring of 1949 at the Café du Rond Point. The hat was a gift of the famous milliners
Maud et Nano.

Harrison Elliot and me on my first return visit to Paris in 1949.

Harrison at Bertenonville during the first weekend we spent there in March 1950.

Harrison and me at Bertenonville on another weekend, in spring 1949.

Natalie (girlfriend of Harrison's pal Robert), Harrison, and me leaning out of a window in the deserted whorehouse we all lived in.

With my father on the Eiffel Tower, spring 1949, during his visit to find out what I was really up to.

Mimi, Jeremy, and me, summer 1950. The photo was taken outside Milton Greene's Lexington Avenue studio and was a gift from him to my parents for their wedding anniversary.

Joe Eula, summer 1950, at Milton's converted barn in Wilton, Connecticut.

Milton Greene, me, and Sophie Malgat at his Wilton, Connecticut, country home, circa 1951.

André Surmain, 1952.

With Sue Kaufmann at Connemara, summer 1952.

Steve during WWII, 1944. He was a
lieutenant in the Army Air Corps.

Steve and me after a rainstorm during our
courtship, summer 1953.

Wedding picture taken
in January 1954 and
given to me by James
Abbe as a wedding
present. It appeared in
the *New York Times*
society section on
February 20, 1954.

Dressing hysterically for my wedding, in my mother's bedroom.

Below: Left to right: Jeremy, me, Mimi, my father and mother right before my wedding, February 19, 1954.

Above: Married at last.

On the beach in Cuba on our first
honeymoon, February 22, 1954.

Above: Left to right, front: me, my mother, my niece Aliza, my father, and Mimi. Standing: Steve, Jeremy, and David Karney, Mimi's first husband. Mimi and I were both about seven months pregnant in 1956.

Left: Eight months pregnant with Nick, September 1956. This was a fashion shot for *Good Housekeeping*. I'm carrying my own treasured Gucci bag.

Above: Left to right: The Dakota, 135 Central Park West, and the San Remo, seen from Central Park Lake, May 1964. Our apartment was on the right corner of 135 CPW, hidden by trees.

Left: Working on a fashion photo shoot in Central Park. Photo gift of James Abbe.

in England. It was taught up at Mount Sinai Hospital, where I'd decided to have the baby in spite of the warning of my gynecologist that it was a great teaching hospital but not one designed for the comfort of a new mother. "But it's the best hospital in New York," I insisted, "and what if there's an emergency?"

Painless Childbirth training was all about abdominal breathing to take your mind off your "discomfort," but without partners or coaches. No husband was ever admitted into a delivery room in those days, nor did such a mad and gruesome idea occur to anyone. Childbirth was strictly between the mother and the doctor. Why should a man have to participate in any natural sight or upsetting sound or see his wife in a less than romantic position?

However, at the end of the course, we were all invited, with our husbands, to see a film of an actual childbirth. The camera was positioned right between the widely spread knees of a woman whose cheerful smile never left her face as she handily produced a huge baby. All the men in the room stopped breathing and the women were hideously embarrassed. At one point the doctor gave the patient a local injection before he performed a surgical incision known as an episiotomy. The sight of that long needle made me feel a wave of faintness. I looked around at my fellow classmates and their husbands. They were all looking stonily ahead, their eyes on the screen. Perhaps they were in shock or hysterically blind. If they don't faint, I don't faint, I thought, putting my head briefly between my knees and taking deep breaths. I managed not to disgrace myself.

However, I insisted that Hilly knock me out before he gave me that needle. "You won't even feel the needle at that point," he assured me, but I had fixated on it, as if it were all of childbirth rolled into one, and demanded to be unconscious for a purely local injection.

I had only one more bad moment. Steve and I were at the movies about a week before Nick was born when it suddenly occurred to me, with staggering and total surprise, that, for the baby that was kicking me from the inside, there was only one exit. Until that time I'd been in complete denial in spite of the film I'd seen. *Only one exit!* How in the name of sanity had I gotten myself into such a predicament? How could I ever have agreed to be part of such a grotesque enterprise? The whole project was obviously impossible—how could I have failed to realize that in advance? I had a frightful panic attack, something I'd never experienced before, and dragged Steve out of the theater to go find peach ice cream, the only available medication, since I'd been unable to bear even the smell of alcohol from the minute I got pregnant.

I worked until two days before my due date of October fifth. One day, very pregnant, I stood chatting with another equally pregnant friend in the corridor of *Good House* when Herb Mayes bustled by. He stopped and gazed at both of us with the utmost disgust. "If I ever, *ever,* see the two of you together again, you're both fired!" he shouted, and stalked off. This, at a magazine that always had a child's face smiling on the cover. From that time on, we met in the ladies' room, the only safe house we could think of.

Although I had an easy pregnancy and only one panic attack about childbirth itself, my subconscious must have contained darker thoughts. One night, shortly before Nick was born, I took a cherished cache of old love letters, of which I'd kept only those that contained proposals of marriage, and destroyed them. What if I died in child-birth? I thought, temporarily insane. What if all Steve had left of me were these letters from other men? How much worse he'd feel about my loss when he read these letters that were preserved in my desk. Today, of course, I regret the loss of those letters, but Melanie's death in *Gone With the Wind* had had more influence on me than I was willing to admit.

My mother was away at an Aspen seminar and didn't plan to return until a few days after the date on which I expected my baby. I tele-phoned her and asked her to come home early. "Why?" she asked in astonishment. "What can I do to help? I'm not a doctor, after all." Embarrassed by my normal desire to have her support, however invis-ible, but determined, I told her that I wanted her there and eventually, very put-upon, she agreed to come home early. Unnatural? Yes, but very typically Mickey Tarcher.

A few days before my due date, following instructions, I put a rubber sheet on top of the mattress, and under the bottom sheet. In the middle of the night of October fifth, I was awakened by a distinct popping noise in my head. My water had broken. I was smugly thrilled that once again, I was right on time. I wrapped myself in three bath towels and slept peacefully between contractions. When they were about fifteen minutes apart I woke Steve. We called Hilly, who said it was too soon to go to the hospital. I went back to sleep, waking only for the contractions, and when they were about ten minutes apart we got dressed, hailed a cab, and went up to Mount Sinai, where Hilly's little red convertible was already parked. Steve was told to wait in the lobby and sat there, almost destroyed by worry when someone handed him a pathetic little brown paper bag containing my clothes.

Meanwhile I was actually enjoying myself in the labor room. I've rarely felt like such a champ. The breathing worked beautifully and as the sun rose I was visited by a persistent ladybug that had managed to enter the air-conditioned urban hospital . . . another strange and unusual sign of good luck, like the little boy selling edelweiss on the mountain pass. I was sustained by a triumphant sense of being in control of the contractions and I enjoyed visiting with all the nurses who came to check on me. Six flying hours later, with very little botheration except during the really nasty final half hour, I was given ether for the episiotomy and woke up a few minutes later to see Nicholas, already cleaned up and perfect, with an adorable pointed head.

Nick was whisked away too quickly, in the fashion of the time, and I was taken up to my private room, violently sick to my stomach from the totally unnecessary ether I'd insisted on. The people in the room next door were having a circumcision celebration, which involved lots of noise and an overpowering smell of pastrami, which would have been mouth-watering under any other circumstances. When I told the nurse how I felt, she said, curtly, "There's nothing wrong with you, you've only had a baby."

Hilly Dubrow was right: Mount Sinai was no place for a new mother. When I had Tony, two years and nine months later, I went to Doctors Hospital, a genial country club with great food and friendly nurses. He was born with the pace of a freight train in little more than an hour, without giving me any time to control my breathing, barely time to convince anybody to move me from the labor room to the delivery room. I tried with difficulty to persuade the nurses to wake Hilly from his nap, screaming, "Get that fucking shithead asshole in here right away! I swear to bloody Christ I'm having a damned fucking baby!" I wish I could believe that I'd made some kind of breakthrough, but I'm sure I sounded just like every other nice girl under those circumstances.

Chapter Twenty-five

I TOOK A FOUR-MONTH MATERNITY LEAVE AFTER NICK WAS BORN. I had been promoted, more than a year earlier, from the fashion department to the job of personal assistant on article ideas to Herb Mayes, *still* at a salary of seventy-five dollars a week. I continued to write articles constantly for the magazine, and although I was now genuinely experienced at this craft, I was paid about a third of what an outside writer would have been paid for the same work, an inequity from which there was no appeal. My new job demanded a very steady stream of new ideas, often difficult to find, but I managed, including a number of ideas that make me smile in disbelief because they were, when I grew interested in the subjects, so far ahead of their time that they seem like jokes. Examples picked from many dozens include an article on the unknown Mrs. John F. Kennedy, who hadn't yet moved to Washington as the wife of a new senator, and on Woody Allen, who had just become a hit as a stand-up comedian.

Herbert was obviously moving me around from one department to another with some kind of important future in mind for me, although we never discussed it. I thought that as my mentor he believed I would edit a magazine eventually, and I thought that I would, too. To this day I know it would have been a natural job for me. All of *Good House* was my province: I developed ideas for the test kitchen, the Beauty Clinic, the travel department, the decorating department, and every other department that seemed to me to need pepping up. I was a natural magazine person and even now I read as many of them as I can lay my hands on, frequently seeing my old ideas rehashed, often envious at the freedom editors have in these days of open sexuality.

My arrangement with Herbert was that after my maternity leave I'd go back and work a half day only. I'd hired a full-time, live-in housekeeper-cook named Rose, who was a refugee from the Hungarian Revolution. Rose, whose single fault was that she put sour cream on everything, was a sweet, bright soul who could perfectly well take care of Nick in the morning when I wasn't there.

This ideal arrangement lasted a week. At the end of that time Herbert called me in to his office and explained that every other mother working at the magazine wanted my kind of part-time deal.

"I can understand that," I said. "I don't blame them. So I'm afraid that I have to quit."

"Quit! Nonsense! You have to come back full-time."

"Full-time? And have Nick raised by a nurse the way I was? No, Herb, that's out of the question, it's impossible."

"You're making the biggest mistake of your life," he shot back.

"I don't think so," I said, calmly, preparing to go and clean out my desk.

He glared at me and just as I left his office he shouted in a terrible tone of voice, "You don't write nearly as well as you think you do!"

That was my only glimpse of the side of Herb Mayes everyone else had seen, but it was hurtful enough to make me not speak to him for the next five years. He'd been publishing my work regularly for nine years, yet when I had the audacity to put my new baby's welfare ahead of his precious magazine, he chose to insult me where he knew it would hit me hardest.

ABOUT A WEEK before Nick was born, Steve had left NBC for Columbia Pictures Television as head of creative development. He decided to take this new job, since he saw that the future of television was no longer live from New York but on tape or film from Hollywood.

I hired my first agent, the well-known and respected Harold Matson, and soon he was getting me assignments from other magazines, although nothing seemed important. I was more fascinated by Nick than I would have imagined, and working seemed beside the point for the first time in my life. As with most mothers, he became my passion. I was a classic case. Obviously there was nothing on earth more wonderful than this child . . . and in truth, there wasn't. Meanwhile, Steve was developing a number of Columbia's most successful series, such as *Hazel* and *Dennis the Menace.* We spent the summers at the guest house at Connemara to get Nick out of the hot city, while Steve commuted to work. On winter and fall weekends we took Nick everywhere with us, strolling up Madison Avenue to check out the art galleries each Saturday and ending up at P. J. Clarke's, where he sat in his stroller and drank tomato juice. Two years later I was pregnant again.

Once more we had to move to a larger apartment. We looked all over the East Side for something we could afford, but my destiny, which had allowed me two brief years on the East Side, pulled me back to Central Park West, in spite of my struggles to avoid it.

The twelve-room apartment we found was at 135 Central Park West, in an old, famous building called the Langham Mansions, which took up the entire block between the gloomy Dakota, where John Lennon was to live and die, and the luxurious San Remo. Our high-ceilinged apartment was on the second floor, facing directly into the trees of the park, with French doors instead of windows in both the living room and the vast master bedroom, which looked out on West Seventy-fourth Street. There were fairly large balconies outside of these French doors, the moldings were magnificent, and number 135 was a building with a theatrical dash, boasting tenants like Lee and Paula Strasberg of the Actors Studio, the British actor Cyril Richard, Basil Rathbone, and Merv Griffin. The apartment was "rent-stabilized," which meant that our landlords, three Iranian brothers, could raise the rent by only fifteen percent whenever we signed a new lease. We rented all this at under four hundred dollars a month, in the condition known as "as is."

"As is" was the catch. The enormous place had been occupied for the past thirty years by a man, living alone, who restored antique paintings. This hermit with filthy habits had vacated the apartment feet first. Every floor was covered by dried paint, the kitchen dated from long before my birth, and when I called a city electrical inspector to check it out, he found 203 fire violations.

We had exactly fifteen thousand dollars with which to renovate and decorate this place, a major amount of cash in 1958. Daunted by the size of the task, I went to see Yale Burge, a decorator I admired whose work was in a French country tradition. Gently he explained that he could do exactly two rooms for that amount. "Then, as you get more money, we could keep on going until it was finished," he said helpfully, not understanding either the condition of the apartment or the state of my womb.

I found myself on my own, but Steve's older sister, Sunny, was a decorator who was willing to let me use her resale card at the wholesale houses that were clustered in the D&D Building. I had no design experience, unless you count my little walk-up and the small amount of work I'd done on the Fifty-seventh Street place, but after getting the electrical work done, and putting in a new kitchen and laundry room, I decided that there was nothing to do but wade in and do it myself, for better or worse.

I boldly explored every wholesale showroom until I found the fabrics and wallpapers I wanted. The furniture we'd moved from Fifty-seventh Street was re-covered, and with Sunny's guidance I ordered a new sofa and chair for the library. On my own I found bargain antiques, and fixtures and rugs for very little money. Every time I went to see how the workmen were getting along, I had to limit the length of my visits because the smell of paint made me feel sick, but the apartment was almost finished in time for our fifth wedding anniversary, on February 19, 1959.

Since the library was still empty, we filled it with a five-piece combo, invited one hundred fifty people to come and dance, and served a late supper from that long table in the dining room. I was a little more than five months pregnant and very happy with my full and delicious life.

My father came to see the apartment and remarked, almost to himself, "This is the most beautiful place I've ever seen," a rare compliment that I still cherish.

Tony was born on June 16, 1959. Now I discovered that having two children is not like having one child and a second child, but something like six or seven children all at once; but I took motherhood more or less in stride, since the diaper pail was kept in Steve's bathroom, not mine. No, reader, they hadn't invented disposable diapers then.

Less than a year later, Steve came home one day to announce that we were moving immediately to Toronto for an indefinite period. In spite of the impression I may have given in this book, I'm truly not given to tears except under extreme circumstances, but my memoir concentrates on dramatic moments. Toronto was a seriously extreme circumstance. Floods! I couldn't believe that after having a second child and finally settling into our wonderful apartment, we had to go into exile in Canada. But the Canadian operation of Columbia Television was a mess and Steve was needed to set up their production facilities and run their distribution operation.

Grimly we sublet the apartment and rented a house north of Toronto for the summer. It was hot as hell, worse than Connecticut. There, I hit a new personal low when I discovered that the best place to take the children for the afternoon was the local air-conditioned supermarket, Loblaws, so that they could sit on the floor, look at comic books, and smear ice cream all over their darling little faces. No wonder I hadn't wanted to get married, I thought, as I contemplated this view of Mumsy Hell.

Things got better in the fall when we moved to another rented house in the suburb of Rosedale, which was in Toronto proper. I hired a nurse and a cook-housekeeper at cheap Canadian wages, and through Harold Matson I got an introduction to Ken Lefoli, the editor in chief of *Maclean's*, the Canadian national magazine, a combination of *Life* and the *Saturday Evening Post*.

I was given an appointment to go in and meet him. Ken was an intense, darkly good-looking guy in his thirties, a major hot shot, who had absolutely no intention of hiring an American to write anything for him. The Canadians were—and are—very sensitive to the domination of American culture, especially American movies, magazines, and television, and I represented, in one way or another, all three.

However, he offered me an article that I knew immediately he expected me to decline. The laughable subject matter was "The Noise Problem in Canada."

I murmured modestly that I'd try, and after a few weeks in which I'd made myself a mistress of decibel levels in Toronto at every important four-way street crossing, and talked to any number of Canadian noise experts, I returned with a snappy, funny article that revealed to the waiting world that, wonder of wonders, there was *no* noise problem in Canada!

Lefoli and friendly Peter Czowski, a Polish count and his second in command, gave in and started to give me regular assignments. Before I left Canada I was asked to become a contributing editor on the masthead of the magazine, an honor no American and no woman had ever held before.

Between my work and the new friends we made, we grew resigned to Toronto, which was then the old, dull Toronto, with heavy-duty blue laws, no movies on Sunday, no exciting new neighborhoods, no charming waterfront, no liquor stores except those run by the state—at which you had to show a license to buy a bottle. There was nothing new or fun about it anywhere until Eddie Creed, who ran the best clothes shop in town, and another man named Isadore Sharp, built a sizable motel that soon attracted a good lunch crowd and named it the Four Seasons.

I bought my clothes from Creed's and Eddie asked me to become public-relations director for the Four Seasons, a job I hastily declined because the motel had a well-deserved reputation as a place to go for an after-lunch quickie. That motel became the first of the enormous chain of Four Seasons Hotels. Does this come under the heading of the road not traveled, wasted opportunities, or things I would never have been able to do and still be a decent mother? Probably all of them.

Steve hired a tutor to come every day and give him French lessons, which enabled him to make inroads on Montreal television that would have been impossible otherwise. Virtually all Ontario businessmen expected the French-speaking businessmen of Montreal to speak English, so he was a huge hit. I was less so, with my Parisian French. To them it sounded insufferably snobbish, until I made a full explanation of how I'd come by it. We frequently went to Montreal for a weekend because it was a hundred times the fun of Toronto. We even went to Buffalo for kicks! Once.

Just as we really settled into Toronto life, making many interesting friends among the refugees from the Hungarian Revolution, Steve was told to return to New York and take charge of international production and distribution for Columbia Television. Our entire exile had lasted a year and a half.

I returned with a final assignment for *Maclean's,* a cover story on the new discovery, Robert Goulet, then playing Sir Lancelot in *Camelot.* I saw the superb production of *Camelot* with Richard Burton and Julie Andrews at least a dozen times, both from the audience and standing backstage. I still sometimes play a tape of the original cast album. Now, *that's* my idea of a musical, and I don't care how it dates me!

Toronto in 1961 was not Camelot. But to be realistic, knowing what we know now, I suspect that even Camelot—King Arthur's Camelot—was no Camelot.

In this prefeminist era I had, unwittingly, found a way to "have it all," to raise my children and continue to work part-time on my own terms. Of course, this was only possible because I was a writer who was not bound by office hours, and by the assistance of a successful, supportive, and generous husband who paid for the household help who gave me my freedom. I doubt that I knew then how outrageously fortunate I was.

Chapter Twenty-six

ONCE WE'D MOVED BACK TO OUR NEW YORK APARTMENT, STEVE began to make the unending series of business trips that his new job demanded. Columbia had offices all over the world, from Tokyo to São Paulo, and he was needed in all of them, sometimes simultaneously, it seemed to me. He was incredibly energetic, full of ambition and determination, but I remember far too well how I felt about staying at home with the children while he disappeared for six weeks at a time, only to reappear with his next trip already planned. He certainly traveled much more than half of each year.

I had once written an article about the wives of traveling salesmen who were, as a group, the most unhappy women I'd ever interviewed. I began to find out why firsthand. Not only did I miss Steve terribly, but I felt that the boys were suffering, whether they were aware of it or not, from the lack of a father who could be counted on to come home every night. I didn't know how to be a daddy, nor did I want to rely too much on the children to substitute for a husband. I was afraid of becoming a mother who looked to her children to supply the affection she needed. Sometimes I had to stop myself from having long, one-sided conversations with Nick, which he certainly was far too young to understand, about my feelings of sadness. Frequently my resentment about Steve's absence would cause me to greet his return with smoldering anger, which would soon erupt into a fight, for he, too, was deeply upset at the loneliness he experienced on his international treks.

By this time I'd employed Lori, a young Swiss secretary who was in the United States to improve her English. She moved in and helped me with the boys. She did their laundry and took them to the nearby playground, a task I frankly loathed. Nick started preschool when he was three, while Tony, just a baby, was still at home.

One day, out of the blue, Herbert Mayes called Steve to inquire if I might like to write for *McCall's*, where John Mack Carter was executive editor. "Why doesn't Herb ask me himself?" was my testy answer when I heard this from Steve.

Soon John Mack Carter was on the phone. "I've heard your name mentioned, here and there," he said, as if it were being bandied about in the men's room. "Would you like to come in and see me?" I allowed as how I might. I knew that Herbert had been abruptly fired by Hearst, in 1958, over a trifling difference of opinion with the new management, after all the magnificent years of work he'd done for *Good Housekeeping*. He'd been snatched up immediately by *McCall's*, owned by Norton Simon, and had, almost overnight, turned that magazine into the most glorious-looking women's magazine that has ever existed. Now Herbert had become chief executive of the huge McCall Corporation and had reluctantly turned his editorial duties over to John.

On my first visit to curly-haired John Mack Carter, of the irresistible grin, whom Herbert, in his memoir, *The Magazine Maze,* refers to as a "grits-nourished Kentucky squirt," I was determined to let him know that I wasn't born yesterday.

"I know, and I know you know, that if it weren't for Herb Mayes, you wouldn't have phoned me, so let's not pretend that you've heard my name 'here and there,' " I proclaimed, already spoiling for a fight. He looked astonished, as well he might, as he tried and retried to light his pipe, his favorite form of stalling for time. How often does the powerful editor of a riding-high magazine invite a freelance writer for a meeting?

By the end of our first hour together we'd agreed that I'd start to work for him in much the same way I'd worked for Herbert, dreaming up ideas and writing those that were suitable for me. I made one mistake in this meeting: I let John know that I'd been turning in a dozen ideas every month for *Good House,* when I should never have admitted to such a number. Twelve fresh ideas every month were far too many, but now I was stuck with trying to find them.

However, I'd be working from home, which was essential considering that I wanted to spend a great deal of time with my children. I've continued to work at home to this day. I also agreed to fire my agent since I'd no longer be working for other magazines. I've never regretted this, since unlike Herbert, John was willing to pay me what he paid his other top writers. Although I always wrote as a freelance, never on staff, and always without a contract, I preferred to work for only one magazine at a time and deal directly with the editor at the top. This gave me the freedom I wanted, as well as the personal contact I was used to with Herbert.

For the next five years I worked for John at *McCall's,* and when he went over to become the editor of the *Ladies' Home Journal,* I followed him for another five years, enjoying him and our friendly skirmishes thoroughly.

One month I had two articles in the same issue of *McCall's,* one in the regular magazine and one in the Metro section into which articles on New York subjects were put. Proud of this coup, I called my mother to tell her to be sure and pick up a copy of the magazine. A month went by and she still hadn't done so. I phoned and asked her why. "I'm just never near a magazine stand" was the answer of this woman who took the subway to work morning and night, passing newsstands constantly. I hung up the phone and sobbed bitterly at her lack of interest or caring. I swore to Steve that I was never going to let her do this to me again. Fat chance.

Mimi, as the mother of two outstandingly beautiful and bright, Harvard-educated daughters, Aliza and Susanna, tells me that this is an example of the sort of jealousy that all mothers of daughters have to deal with frequently as their daughters grow up. "It's a bad moment when you first walk into a room and no one sees you, only your daughter," she says, "and it's even more difficult to see them enjoying their youth and their accomplishments while no one pays any attention to you, and you're getting older. However, it's something you simply have to conquer and get over." My mother was never able to manage this— perhaps because she didn't have the benefit of psychoanalysis.

In 1962, I was having dinner alone with my mother. Steve was out of town, as usual, and after my father's death, she'd moved, at my earnest persuasion, from the now-unsafe Greenwich Village to an apartment on Fifty-eighth Street and Park Avenue, in a building bristling with doormen and security people, where she'd recreated the ambience of the St. Urban apartment. Just as we were in the middle of dinner, Mimi called from California, where she'd waited until five P.M. Los Angeles time to tell my mother that she'd asked David for a divorce that morning. "It's so typical of you to call at this time of night," my mother responded immediately, in outrage. "You should have known you'd ruin my dinner."

She did have a unique way with words. As for appropriate emotions . . . words fail me. When I think of how I, like other women, am concerned with developments in my children's lives, I simply can't understand this side of my mother, and I have long ago given up trying.

The next day I flew out to California to be with Mimi for several days and see if I could help her. She and David had, as people say to cover almost any kind of problem, "grown apart," but it wasn't until two years later that they finally got a divorce. Several years after that, Mimi married a marvelous man named Jacques Brien, who was that rarest of doctors, a French-Canadian Catholic (lapsed) who was also an eclectic-Freudian psychoanalyst. The Church sent him many high-ranking clergy in crisis who were going through psychological and, far more often, romantic problems.

DURING THOSE TWELVE years when we lived across Central Park from my mother, I almost always invited her to brunch on Sunday, and to dinner on another day of the week. She took a certain interest in the boys, particularly Nick, who was older and much more outgoing and verbal than Tony at that time of his life, and when we were out of town she occasionally invited them to dinner at her apartment, but of course she wasn't a normal doting grandmother.

Once, when both boys were still very young and had simultaneous cases of the croup, from which Nick, in particular, suffered, she telephoned me and happened to ask what I was working on at the moment. When I said that I wasn't working, since I was taking care of two sick children, she snapped, "Where's your self-respect?"

Even today, at a remove of thirty-five years, I find this an extraordinarily unfeeling thing for one woman to say to another, particularly about her own grandchildren. In fact, it's downright crazy. But it does give me insight into the kind of mother she had been—or rather had *not* been—during years I don't remember. Obviously she thought that the boys should have been in the capable charge of a nanny and I should have been working, as she always was when her own children were sick. She was primarily interested in female grandchildren: Aliza and Susanna, who lived in California, and in particular in Jeremy and Shari's daughter, Mallory, who lived in New York.

Shari Lewis, Jeremy's wife, was the only member of our family for whom my mother really showed respect. Whenever I telephoned her, I first had to listen to a recital of Shari's latest news and triumphs. I was as fond of Shari as I could be and rejoiced in her success, and I don't remember ever feeling jealous of her for a minute. Shari was a phenomenon with absolutely unique gifts, gifts I couldn't imagine having or aspiring to. How could I be jealous of a woman who worked as hard and as brilliantly as she did, all of her life, much harder than I would ever have been willing to work? How could I be jealous of someone I admired with all my heart? Shari was a wonder and a loving sister-in-law with whom I enjoyed a great deal of mutual affection and many belly laughs until her too-early death in August 1998. She even insisted on sending me to her singing coach, Stormy Saks, who managed to more or less teach me to sing the first verse of "Happy Birthday" so I would no longer disgrace myself at birthday parties. After our lesson, he told me that I "definitely had an instrument, but even if it were trained, there was no way to know how pleasing it would be." I, properly, took that to mean, forgetaboutit.

Now Mallory, who is brilliant, beautiful, sexy, deliciously funny, and seems to have combined all of Shari's and Jeremy's outstanding qualities in her alluring, dynamic, exceptionally warm, and utterly irresistible personality—no, I'm not prejudiced, merely observant—is married to a splendid man, Brad Hood, and has a very young son named James Abraham Tarcher Hood. She'd be totally perfect if her chosen sport weren't skydiving. She's as close to the daughter I've never had as anyone could possibly be, perhaps closer, since I didn't have to deal with her as a mother. I'm enormously grateful for her for filling a hole in my life that nothing but a daughter could fill.

However, I felt deeply sad that for all the years my mother knew Steve, until her death at eighty, she never even tried to appreciate him for his wonderful qualities, to enjoy his sense of humor or even just to show him the thanks he deserved for taking such good care of her daughter and her grandchildren. Or gratitude for his patience with her!

But Steve wasn't singled out. Why should she have been expected to treat her son-in-law any better than she treated her own son?

Shari certainly knew how to reach my mother in a way none of us children ever did. When my mother criticized Shari's taste in the placement of a painting on her first visit to the couple's new apartment, Shari didn't invite her back for a year. That kind of take-no-prisoners reaction was the only way to handle her, but it was utterly impossible for us.

The three of us, because we never learned, or became hardened or sufficiently pessimistic, continued to crave a mother who would be *more* of a mother to us, but it wasn't in Mommy's nature to be what is normally thought of as "maternal." It is, for example, utterly impossible to imagine her saying something in the nature of "You look worried, is there anything I can do to help?" And yet she spent more than thirty years giving ungrudging aid and comfort to poor strangers who were in legal trouble. A puzzlement indeed.

Still and all, my mother did the best with what she had *available* of herself to give us. I can understand, although it's difficult, how her bitterly hard childhood and the need to help support her younger siblings had left her with no concept of what a mother, and now a grandmother, might be expected to feel about her children and grandchildren. Other women have come from the same sort of background and managed to be warmly maternal. However, nobody can be expected to be or do more than she's capable of. My mother was Mickey Tarcher and that, in itself, made her an amazing woman. "Full stop," as the British say for the period at the end of a sentence.

It's fascinating for me, as a writer, to see how strongly my relationship with my own mother affected my work. In ten novels, six of my heroines' mothers die while the heroines are younger than eight years old. In two more, *Mistral's Daughter* and *Till We Meet Again*, my heroines, Maggy, whose mother is dead, and Eve, whose mother is neglectful, are introduced at the ages of sixteen and thirteen, and as they grow older they have daughters themselves, to whom they become good mothers, but *only* because they've started out life as heroines. At the end of each novel, they're both very much alive. In *I'll Take Manhattan*, my heroine has a frankly bad mother, Lily Amberville, with whom she reconciles just before the end of the book for plot reasons. In *Spring Collection*, there's a mother who dies young and a semi-decent mother who dies in middle age. In my tenth and latest novel, *The Jewels of Tessa Kent*, the heroine is a bad mother who has had a bad mother herself, but she becomes a good mother to her daughter at the end of the book, shortly before her own premature death.

Only Billy Winthrop Ikehorn Orsini Elliott, my very first heroine, whose mother died soon after her birth, is allowed—after three marriages—to give birth to twin boys in *Lovers*, the third of the *Scruples* trilogy, but my eighth novel. What's more, she's thriving at the end of the book!

As you see, unless she's cast as a heroine from the beginning, none of the mothers I've written lives very long. In real life I was a caring, thoughtful, forever-pleasing daughter to a difficult woman who lived to be eighty. My obedience to my mother was the direct result of my childhood desire to make her love me. However, in my fantasy life as a writer, that particular plot wasn't highly probable.

I was aware of my mother problem in writing fiction quite early in my career, but no matter how I tried to twist and turn, in the service of my plots, the mothers kept expiring. It's as if my heroines can't have normally loving, good, and supportive mothers, or else what *task* do they have, what *challenge* must they overcome, in order to become heroines?

However, I've written a number of mother substitutes: aunts, older women friends, and even a father's mistress who enter into the lives of my motherless heroines when they're in their teens and give them maternal affection.

Most important of all, I always gave my heroine the character I write with more delectation than any other (except perhaps a female villain), the heroine's best friend. To a woman, they're slightly naughty, they're oddball and unconventional, they give great, sensible, down-to-earth advice, they're loyal, ingenious, they have wonderfully crazy love lives and my heroines couldn't manage without them. I don't write my own point of view into my heroines one-tenth as much as I write myself into their best friends. There's a certain realistic modesty about this. In my own eyes, I'm not a heroine type but I make a damn fine friend.

I have managed to write a number of caring fathers, oddly enough. I think that's because my own father was so removed from my emotional life that it was easy to create a father from a blank canvas.

Whatever faults my mother had, she didn't deliberately fade almost entirely away from involvement in our lives the way our father had. She had strong opinions on what we'd done—usually done wrong—but she'd been interested enough to direct some of her immense energy toward us. If she'd been at home, entirely focused on us, instead of away at work all day, our lives would have been as unthinkable as hers would have been under such dire circumstances.

As I write this at seventy, about a woman who's been dead for eighteen years, I want to be as fair as possible to her memory. She left me with a number of qualities that shaped me immensely.

Until I became a mother myself, she was the role model who influenced my determination not to get married right out of college but to learn about life on my own and, above all, to have a career. She inspired me, once I started writing, to make all my female protagonists strong, independent women filled with fire and determination, qualities that made my readers respond to them.

Although, in the twinkling of an eye, memory of her example as an absentee mother let me know that a career wasn't as important to me as being at home for Nick, and later, Tony, I've never felt right unless I was working on something, even if it was temporarily on the back burner. The work ethic develops into a habit with practice, and I owe much of it to her.

My mother was also absolutely calm about her health. I don't remember ever seeing her spend a day in bed, although it stands to reason that she must have done so. She was the reverse of a hypochondriac without being a Christian Scientist, and she passed this absolutely invaluable lesson to Mimi and me. Whatever health problems come our way, we cope with them as cheerfully as possible and without making them into more than they are. (I'm not counting my demanding, compulsive behavior about travel conditions.)

Much as she may have wished it, Mommy never overtly encouraged me to marry someone I didn't love because he was rich, but instead, urged me to work as hard as I could at whatever was at hand. She had great integrity. I can't imagine her doing anything underhanded or petty. From an early age she taught my brother, sister, and me how other, infinitely less privileged, people lived.

My mother was, almost to a fault, fiercely loyal to her many women friends. All in all, this woman who never had the luxury of being able to take anything for granted until she was twenty-three left me a heritage of strength.

There's an unexpectedly happy ending to my mother's life. Shortly after my father died, when she was only sixty-two, she began an intense relationship with one of her colleagues at the Legal Aid Society, an entrancing and much younger Irishman whom she'd known for many years. It made her so happy that she couldn't resist telling us all about it . . . I admit it came as a shock, but a thrilling one.

This man was married and very Catholic, with five children. He stayed married, but they had a great romance for many long years. He insisted that my mother learn to sip one martini so that she could have a drink with him. She had never been *allowed* to drink by my father on the grounds that it made her face red, another of his small but amazingly effective ways of keeping her under his invisible domination. However, after one martini—and she never touched a second one— not only was her famously perfect complexion unchanged, but her personality was transformed into that of a warm, playful, and loving person I barely recognized, for as long as the effect of the gin lasted.

In one of the intimate talks that Fanny Cohen had with Mimi, she said that my mother had been like that all the time when she was a young married woman, before my father began to have his series of affairs. It's entirely possible that much of what I've never understood about my mother's lack of warmth, in fact a characteristic bitterness of mood, was caused by a deep, abiding disappointment in her marriage. This will always be the chief question I have about my parents and their relationship.

Mommy never understood why, when she came to California to visit, as she did several times a year, Mimi and I always had her martini ready when we opened our front doors.

Chapter Twenty-seven

IN THE EARLY 1960s I'D CHANGED IN CERTAIN MINOR WAYS FROM THE girl with the streaked orange hair whom Steve had married. Once he was supporting me and I didn't have to pay rent, my first move was to go to a beauty salon and become the blonde nature had always intended me to be. When I was a year old I had platinum-blond curls, which soon turned into ordinary light brown hair, but I never recovered—still haven't—from my early blond self-image, started by baby pictures and augumented by the strong inspiration of Shirley Temple, who was my childhood idol. How I yearned to be able to sing and dance, and oh, how I wanted her hair!

As soon as our honeymoon was over, I exchanged my homemade orange streaks for blond highlights, much to Steve's disappointment, since he'd fallen in love with a redhead. I've been blond mixed with my natural color ever since, with the blond dominating. I've fascinated my great-nieces, and recently my granddaughter, by informing them, when they were about six years old, about the power they will have over their hair as soon as they grow up.

A year after our marriage I began to go to a gym three times a week and I discovered with astonishment that I was naturally good at gymnastics, the only sport that comes to me easily. I spent five years at Nick Kounovsky's, standing on my head and whizzing about on the trapeze and flying rings, actually warned, whenever there was a new student, to hold down my expertise so I wouldn't discourage her.

Eventually I switched to a method called Pilates, which was originally invented almost a hundred years ago by German-born Joe Pilates to rehabilitate injured dancers. For the last thirty-two years I've done it for three hours a week. It keeps you supple and strong, with an emphasis on a flexible backbone, and it works out all the weight-bearing muscles at every lesson.

Pilates is a hot new fad now, but when I started learning it in New York it was taught in only two or three studios in the United States. My California trainer, Diane Severino, learned the system at Ron Fletcher's studio, where she became the top teacher. Ron, an ex-dancer, had learned it from old Joe Pilates himself, so Diane is in the direct line of Pilates trainers, as kosher as a third-generation Freudian, but far more limber. She and I have been together for almost twenty years and we talk constantly throughout the lessons. Our favorite subject? Food, food, food.

However, in those early years of the 1960s, when Steve was gone so much, my children, my haphazard magazine work, and my three hours of gym weren't enough to fill my lonely evenings. Unhappy, I tried, as often as possible, to meet Steve on his travels and spend a little time with him, while Lori took charge of the children. We went to Alaska together, at the time it became a state, and in Juneau, in spite of my terror of flying, I made myself go up with Steve and a bush pilot in a tiny plane that swooped up and down over the glaciers. Eventually I was so wet with sweat from sheer fear that I had to strip down to a shirt. That night we celebrated with vodka on the rocks, a drink made with chips of glacial ice that barely melted.

Once I joined Steve in Egypt, where I stupidly wore a wide skirt to ride a camel out at the Pyramids. Not only are the Pyramids much smaller and infinitely less impressive than they look in photographs, but a hundred generations of camel-saddle fleas feasted on the insides of my thighs and gave me an itching rash that lasted for weeks. Although I spent hours every day at the almost empty museum with a guide, looking my fill at the great treasures that later traveled to New York and caused lines to form three times around the Metropolitan Museum, I couldn't ignore the women on the street carrying babies who had flies crawling on their eyelids that the mothers didn't bother to brush away. At a bazaar, where we ventured with a car and driver, the crowd, seeing us walk around, started to look distinctly menacing. There were German scientists working in Egypt in those days, so I screamed at Steve, "*Achtung,* Werner!" in what I hoped was a German accent. "Werner, *mein* man, we'd better get the hell out of here!" The crowd started to rock our car from side to side with real menace, but somehow we made it through.

To do business in Egypt, Steve had to put something like Seventh-Day Adventist on his visa. We had dinner with an important Egyptian television executive who told us that soon they'd go to war with Israel. "Why is that necessary?" I asked. "Because it exists" was his answer. Christ, I hated Egypt!

I tried to tread a fine line between leaving the children with Lori, who was absolutely trustworthy, and yet not leaving them for too long or too often. I particularly liked to join Steve in London because while he was working I could visit the museums and hang about the antiques shops on my own, never feeling lonely. Even if you're not a customer at the moment, there are no strangers who are as likely prospects for a good chat as London antiques dealers, or indeed, antiques dealers in general.

Occasionally I'd rent a car and driver and spend the day visiting one of the many great gardens that were open to the public. Sissinghurst Castle, in Kent, the home of Vita Sackville-West, the great gardener and lesser novelist and poet, was my favorite of all.

One day, in the very early spring, I went there and found that the only flowers in bloom were a bed of enormous white pansies in the "white garden." That sight was more beautiful to me than if the entire garden had been at its height of flowering. Afterward, I wandered around the pregnant garden and talked to the dozen or so apprentice gardeners from Kew Gardens, all women, who were working there, preparing the garden for spring.

I visited the library all alone and resisted the strongest urge I've ever felt to become a genuine thief and steal a book, any book, to keep as a souvenir of the entire Bloomsbury world, which I'd been reading about in biographies and autobiographies since college. Before I left, I stopped at the kiosk to legitimately buy some books, one the story of Pepita, the dancer who was Vita's grandmother, a flamboyant beauty, half-Spanish, half-Gypsy, who bore Victoria, Vita's mother, out of wedlock. (Real life so often surpasses any kind of fictional material.) I found out that the kindly, helpful man who sold me the books and spent a fruitless half hour patiently trying to explain the British monetary system to me, was Vita's son, Nigel Nicolson, who later wrote *Portrait of a Marriage,* the fascinating story of the strange but vital, loving, and strong union between his literary lesbian mother and his journal-keeping, snobbish, homosexual diplomat father, Harold Nicolson.

During the summer of 1962, Steve had to spend two months in South America, traveling all over at a quick pace. We decided that I should take the children and Lori and go to spend July and August at Le Bois Normand rather than stay alone in the heat of New York.

It was decidedly strange and sad to return after fourteen years to the place I had so loved in 1948. Nothing seemed to have changed superficially as we settled into that glorious house, yet everything was different. I had children of three and almost six, and a homesick Lori, who moped about, to concern me. The weather was a disaster, two months of cold and rain, and although the children and I walked into the village every time it wasn't actually raining, the boys were far from happy. The house was entirely filled with paying guests who were friends of Nicole's and often stayed for two weeks at a time. My sons quickly learned how to politely shake hands with everyone when they entered a room, but the entertainment of that novelty soon wore off.

Worst of all, Nicole was economizing to such an extent that all she provided for the boys' evening meal was vegetable soup, followed by bread, butter, and cheese. My kids were normal American carnivores and refused to taste the sophisticated Pont-l'Evêque and Camembert. I had to speak tactfully to her and insist that at least they get eggs for supper, since there was no question of the hamburgers they craved.

This doesn't sound as if it should have been difficult, but my knowledge of her frayed financial state, and her sensitivity on the subject, made the eggs into a tense diplomatic crisis. I could not under any circumstances offer to buy them special supplies of food, because that would have blown the whole fragile, unspoken problems of the arrangement sky-high. Nor could I take them out to eat in restaurants, because that would have been noticed by everyone and would have created a major scandal. The most I could do was buy them tomato juice and ham sandwiches on our village excursions. The only decent meal anyone had that summer was the night the village priest came to dinner and we were served tough roast duck. It fascinated me that in a family where no one went to Mass except on Easter, this simple priest was still treated with such exceptional attention.

One night, unable to sleep because of hunger pangs, I finally got up my nerve to go down to the kitchen. There, to my shock, was a roast chicken from which I boldly and defiantly carved myself a wing. I still can't imagine what such a fine bird was doing in the larder. When I got down to breakfast the next morning, I found a veritable inquisition going on. Who was the wretched thief of the chicken wing? Everyone was busy protesting their innocence when I arrived and quickly announced that I had taken it because I was goddamned starving. That ended the discussion. I was paying room and board for four people, the backbone of Nicole's summer's income, but those words could never be said out loud.

Unfortunately, others were. One day, near the end of our stay, Nicole asked if she could take the boys out on a yacht that belonged to some intimate friends of hers. Very pleased at the novelty of this outing, I agreed. When she came back she told me, quite unaware of the meaning of what she was saying, that she'd wanted to prove to her friends that it was possible for Jewish children to be well behaved. My years of loving friendship for Nicole evaporated almost completely when I heard this, an unconscious admission of an ingrained anti-Semitic bias I could not allow myself to recognize back in 1948 when she first assured me that she wouldn't tell anyone I was Jewish, as if that were doing me a favor.

In fact, rethinking Nicole, I wonder if my feelings for her were not largely an unconscious and very deep need for a mother substitute, particularly in a strange world in which I was struggling to make a place for myself. She really hadn't deserved my devotion. She was a woman who kept her children at a distance and off-balance, and used me as a ploy to keep her girls in a state of jealousy that made them hostile to me. Still, I had been utterly seduced by the sweetness of this intimacy. Nicole had a real lack of integrity, as she'd shown when she'd rented the room I was still paying for when I lived in her Paris apartment; she'd spied on me during my first love affair, and with her migraines and flower arranging she selfishly and ruthlessly dominated life at Le Bois Normand. She was adorable to my father and to Steve, calling him "poor darling" in a melting way, but I have to wonder if she ever played an honest game with me. Still and all, without Nicole and her sisters, her lover and his pals, what kind of life would I have led in Paris? Certainly nothing like the supremely fascinating atmosphere of a Colette novel I lived while I was her paying guest.

DURING TEN DAYS of that gloomy summer of 1962 I flew to London, where I had an assignment to write an article on Peter Sellers, who was still working for the Bolting Brothers in small British comedies but was soon to make his first Hollywood film. I stayed at the Savoy, in that fourth, quiet room the front-desk clerk had finally given me, and Theo Cowan, Peter's PR man who was to become a great friend, arranged for me to go out to the set on a Friday, the last day of the shoot. There I first interviewed the actor, who was playing a Cockney con-man who was passing himself off as a French fashion designer. Peter was into the role completely, hand-kissing, flirting, outrageously adorable and full of humor, all with a fake French accent, even during the interview.

On the following Monday, when I interviewed him again, he had started a new film in which he played a Church of England clergyman. He'd given up smoking over the weekend; he was dour, tight-lipped, uncommunicative, and raging mad that he'd been scheduled for an interview because, as he told me, he stayed in character throughout the film and having to talk to me "brought him out of his trance." And he *meant* trance. Once he'd worked out his character's physical traits, his walk, his hair, his clothes, and his makeup, he put himself into a trance every morning before he starting acting.

I discovered Peter was a firm believer in the world of the spirits and saw his medium three times a week. He spoke to his mother on an almost daily basis. Very filial of him, I'm sure, but alas, the lady in question had departed this world years ago.

I quickly decided to interview people around Peter, his friends and associates, rather than the man himself. I found out that this strange, strange man had no firmly fixed personality or character of his own at all. He simply became whatever role he played.

He had a childlike interest in all sorts of mechanical objects such as cameras and expensive cars, but if he took a new car out for a drive and was at all dissatisfied with it, he would take the jack handle and demolish the car with his own hands. He had done in some sixty of the world's finest automobiles. One night I had dinner with him, at a kosher restaurant in Soho, where I was so tense that I ordered chopped liver to start with and broiled liver for my main course. Whatever the nourishing properties of liver are, I must have needed them badly. I've known many actors, but none as weird, tormented, or talented as Peter. However, he had a seriously mean streak. He played around wildly while his wife stayed faithful. Eventually, when this long-suffering woman finally had a love affair with the architect-decorator who was doing their new apartment, he immediately sued her for divorce, as the injured party, on grounds of adultery! I call that bloody beastly. No gent he.

A year after this unhappy summer visit to Le Bois Normand, Nicole gave up the financial struggle and finally admitted that she had to sell the house. She and her divorced husband were now able to stop living together on boulevard Lannes and find separate apartments. He promptly married his mistress, much to her irritation, since she hadn't cared enough about him to know he had one.

WHEN WE GOT back to New York, the huge parade for John Glenn, the first American to orbit the earth, was being planned. I knew that I'd never be able to see my hero over the heads of the crowd, so I went to the maternity department on the second floor of Saks Fifth Avenue and secured a corner fitting room overlooking the parade route. While I steadily bought maternity clothes I didn't need, in order to keep the room, I was joined by all the excited saleswomen, and we enjoyed front-row seats for the festivities. In a week I returned the clothes and was stupefied to get a letter canceling my charge account because of the sum involved. This couldn't be! A charge at Saks was essential. After much thought, I realized that there was only one valid excuse. Reluctantly, I wrote the people at Saks that I'd had a miscarriage. My charge was promptly reinstated. Another step toward fiction? What's a short girl to do?

Years later, on the night the first man walked on the moon, I was alone in our fairly isolated country house, scared to death because the front door wouldn't lock. I armed myself with a long barbecue fork and knife and watched Walter Cronkite all night, calmed totally by his voice and his personality. Nobody but Cronkite could have given me such courage. How innocent, proud, and patriotic we all felt as those first steps were taken.

DURING THAT SUMMER of 1962 many more things went wrong. I wrote Steve almost every day, going to the Honfleur post office to mail the letters, but because of revolutions all over South America, he almost never received them and wrote me constantly, in a rage about getting no mail. With my history of compulsive punctuality and the strain of getting his angry, disappointed letters, I was driven to absolute distraction. The time difference and the rapidity of his travel made telephoning impossible. There was simply no way to reach him.

At one point during this miserable time, Lynn Tornabene, a friend from *Good Housekeeping,* and her husband, Frank, came to Paris. Lynn had an assignment to interview Audrey Hepburn, who was there to make *Paris When It Sizzles* with William Holden. I took a few days off to go to Paris and went to the set with her. There I discovered that my idol, Audrey Hepburn, not only smoked constantly but actually was human. She said "shit" with the casual air of someone to whom that word is common in conversation. I was genuinely shocked and shocked to be shocked. On my second date with Steve we'd gone to a premiere of *Roman Holiday* on board the *Andrea Doria,* and that was the Audrey Hepburn I still firmly believed existed in real life. Shit, indeed!

Later that day, Lynn, Frank, and I went to dinner at my old hangout, Les Trois Canettes, and I was so upset about the situation with Steve that I left them after dinner and wandered morosely around the Left Bank alone, finally stopping to sit and brood at an outdoor café table. A good-looking young Frenchman came by and very politely tried to strike up a conversation. "Can't one have any privacy around here, for the love of God!" I shouted at him, sending him scuttling away. In another mood I would have welcomed the diversion.

The only high spot of the two months was that I still had enough money at the time we left France to go to Deauville and buy my first, but far from last, Kelly bag at Hermès. My love of Gucci leather was transferred to Hermès, where it has remained ever since. In a changing world, for a woman who loves handbags, Hermès is a rock in a raging storm.

Once we were all back in New York and Steve wasn't traveling, we had a lively social life. My old pal from Vassar Sue Kaufman had married Jerry Barondess, an internist. The two of them became our closest friends and Jerry became our family doctor. On New Year's Eve the four of us would go to three or four different parties together. When Steve and I finally arrived home we'd see all the stars of Broadway trooping through our lobby, leaving the famous party given by Lee and Paula Strasberg.

We were part of an interesting group of young couples, many of them involved in the art world, such as Aaron Shikler and his wife, Pete. Aaron, who painted Jackie and Jack Kennedy for their White House portraits, painted me for my thirty-fifth birthday, wearing an oddly brave expression—a portrait I call "Nurse Edith Clavell About to Return to the Front." There were Terry and Roy Davis, later divorced, who, with painter-framer Bob Kulick, owned the finest picture framing shop in New York. Roy once offered me a painting by Prendergast, one of my most loved painters, but it was an indifferent example and I didn't buy it for nine hundred dollars—a mistake. There was David Levine, the now-legendary caricaturist; Bernie Owett, a brilliant art director at Young and Rubicam, and his fashion-editor wife, Trudy, who would become a psychotherapist; Betty Prashker, who hadn't yet become a famous book editor, and her lawyer husband, Herb, later divorced; Bob Loggia, who hadn't moved to Hollywood yet, and his wife, Marge, later divorced; Dick and Mary Stewart Krolick, the soap-opera actress, later divorced; as well as others who were on the money track rather than the art track.

None of them were as rich as Joanne and Alfred Stern, whose money came from Sears Roebuck via Al's mother, born Rosenwald, then Mrs. Max Ascoli. The Sterns were so rich that they hired the violently chic firm of Dennings and Fourcade to entirely redrape and recover the reception rooms of their huge Fifth Avenue apartment, from floor to ceiling, including all the furniture, in a wild and extravagantly flowered fabric, just for two days during which they gave huge back-to-back parties, at which only caviar, fois gras, and steak sandwiches were served.

Many of the others lived in the most magnificent East Side apartments, like Barbara (*Little Gloria Happy at Last*) and Jerry Goldsmith, later divorced, and the Stanton brothers, who owned all the Volkswagen dealerships on the East Coast. Frank and Judy Stanton later divorced, and so did Howard and Sunny Sloan, who gave the first dinner party anybody had ever gone to where the host wore an open shirt without a tie and the hostess wore blue jeans.

No guest at that dressed-up Park Avenue party understood it, but now I realize that the Sloans must have sensed that the sixties had started. So had Nancy Dine, wife of the painter Jim Dine, who wore jeans and a work shirt to one of Barbara Goldsmith's big parties. I looked at her, smashingly underdressed, upstaging everyone, including our hostess, looked down at my brocade suit, custom-made at Nina Ricci on my last Paris trip, and realized that, yes, I got it and didn't like it and would never like it. Why give parties if people don't dress up?

Among other acquaintances were a lawyer, Mort Janklow, and his wife, Linda, who was a granddaughter of Harry Warner, of Warner Brothers. Mort later became my agent on *Scruples*.

At the funeral of Mervyn LeRoy, Linda's father, some fifteen years ago, I heard Loretta Young give a eulogy that won the bad-taste prize of all time. She slithered exquisitely down the aisle of the Forest Lawn chapel, clad in a startlingly sexy, body-hugging black dress and the largest black garden-party hat I've ever seen. "Mervyn LeRoy discovered me," she announced slowly. Pause. "No. We did not have an affair." Long pause. "I was only thirteen," she added thoughtfully, as if in explanation of the omission. Who asked you, lady? I wondered to myself as the audience sat in stunned silence.

We had other friends like the Meltzers and the Crowns, who were politically far to the left of center and lived on Central Park West like us, but no one, as far as I knew, was a Republican.

It was at the Crowns' that I committed the most overtly aggressive act of my whole life, and only the two drinks I'd had gave me the edge I needed to act. Someone had carelessly spilled a drink on an expensive turntable and, seeing it, I snatched a pocket handkerchief out of the breast pocket of a particularly well-dressed dentist I knew slightly and mopped it up. "How dare you take my handkerchief?" he snapped at me. "The liquor was dripping right into the turntable and ruining it," I answered, amazed at his anger. "You should have asked my permission before you grabbed my handkerchief, you had no right to do that," he persisted, in a loud and furious tone. At that point, I threw my full drink right into his face. And that's the whole thing! It's so tame it's pathetic, but I can't think of anything more physically hostile that I've ever done to anyone.

I'd give almost anything to be Sandra Bernhard for a week. Oh, to have her total nerve, her ironclad attitude, her divine ability to do and say anything and get away with it, or if she doesn't, not to give a damn. I pray that it's all real, not an act, but act or not, I think she's wonderful.

I couldn't even flirt effectively. Marriage had destroyed my cherished come-hither ways. Steve denies this entirely. He insists to this day that I'd flirt with a flying pigeon and he was, for many years of our life together, frequently and unnecessarily, violently jealous. This made me self-conscious as well as angry, since I knew that if I wanted to flirt, seriously flirt, I'd do it in a way he'd bloody well never notice.

Once, that charming bad-boy A. E. Hotchner, the editor, novelist, and author of a Hemingway biography that was much disputed by Hemingway's wife, and who was later to become involved with Paul Newman in the "Newman's Own" brand of foods, invited me to lunch at the Plaza. Hotch's enormous and dubious expense accounts, while he worked at *Cosmo,* were the stuff of legend for decades. What that invitation was a prelude to I wasn't sure, but I accepted, only to decide to phone him the next day and say I couldn't have lunch because "I'd have to tell Steve and he wouldn't approve." Hotch was utterly disgusted, but Steve would *not* have approved, in a major way. On the other hand, I have to admit that in New York at that time, "lunch" was rarely just . . . lunch . . . particularly to an operator like Hotch.

Those were the days of much entertaining. I gave dinner parties for twelve, which I worked on for days, for by now I was an experienced cook. We also had hero-sandwich parties on a Sunday afternoon for a large crowd. One of the countermen from the Hero Boy on Columbus Avenue brought us the long Italian loaves straight from the bakery and then made the sandwiches to order at the dining-room table, which I had covered in platters of every possible choice of sausage and cheese and roasted red peppers.

One day in 1963, I was at a gourmet shop watching the clerk slice two sides of smoked salmon for a Sunday brunch we'd planned, when I heard something vague about Dallas and Kennedy on the radio. It wasn't much . . . not enough to keep me from getting my salmon, muttering that I knew he should never have gone to Dallas . . . but once I got outside on Madison Avenue I dashed to take a cab home, forgetting my other errands in a sudden panic. Unbelievably, the normal noise of the city had faded almost to silence. I rushed into the apartment and grabbed Nicky by the hand. As soon as I'd turned on the television I told him that he must watch and remember because this was history. Soon we heard the news of President Kennedy's death.

For my generation that was *the* great blow. I can't speak for other generations, but nobody had ever meant to us what Jack Kennedy did. Nobody would ever mean half as much again, not even Bobby.

That night we went to a long-planned dinner at Betty Prashker's. Everyone had telephoned to ask if she was calling it off, but everybody also needed to be with other people, like at a wake, so no one stayed away. During dinner, Steve and I left the table and went upstairs, leaving the others too busy talking and mourning to want to follow us. We watched the arrival of *Air Force One* and Jackie Kennedy in her bloodstained pink suit following the casket and heard Lyndon Johnson's speech. We went back downstairs and I remember telling everybody that I thought Johnson was maybe going to be okay, and then I went home and watched television, weeping as I've never wept since, uncontrollable weeping for most of the next four days.

Plans for our Sunday brunch weren't called off and I was sitting, still watching television and waiting for our first guests, when I saw Jack Ruby kill Lee Harvey Oswald. The first time, not the reruns.

Chapter Twenty-eight

In 1963 Steve left Columbia Pictures Television to start his own company. He had long been interested in the animation business, and he'd been instrumental in bringing Bill Hanna and Joe Barbera into the Columbia fold. Now he opened his own animation studio where he produced superhero cartoons, including Spider-Man and many others. He built an international distribution organization to market his own films for television and those of other major production companies.

That year we decided to rent a house for the summer in Westport, Connecticut, instead of sending the children to day camp and spending the summer in the city. During this first summer I rejoiced in a very old friendship, dating to my girlhood, with Rita and Herb Salzman. The Salzmans were practically part of the Tarcher family. Herb's much older sister, Sally Pepper, was one of my mother's close friends, and his parents were the people we'd all picked to fill the role of grandparents. Rita was four years older than I was, a glamorous Bennington redhead whose entire trousseau had come from Hattie Carnegie, then one of the most important and exclusive dress designers in New York.

The Salzmans were established in Westport, which was, at the time, a smallish town on Long Island Sound, where they owned a large summer house on the water and entertained almost constantly. They had a huge group of friends who made Westport their weekend home. We'd visited Rita and Herb occasionally while we were in Canada, especially for the Fourth of July, and it was there that I'd seen the first Nixon–Kennedy debate, thrilled to the core by JFK's brilliance.

At the end of that first summer, on the night of the Salzmans' traditional Labor Day party, I noticed Steve deep in conversation with Carol Fortas, the frightening wife of Justice Abe Fortas of the United States Supreme Court. What on earth could he be finding to talk to Carol about, I wondered? She was a tough customer, an important Washington lawyer with a salty tongue who wore a yachtsman's cap, smoked an occasional cigar, and terrified everyone with her sharp New England abruptness.

When we got home that night, planning to leave for New York and the city the next day, Steve told me that he'd agreed to buy the Fortases' guest house and an acre of land, subject to my approval. He and

Carol had established a price without using a real-estate agent. Neither of us had ever seen the house and I was to go and look at it the next morning. I was too astonished to have the conventional reaction at such news, which I believe is to either shit or go blind. Instead I went to sleep and had a vivid dream of a laden apple tree surrounded by newly fallen ripe apples that lay on the ground below.

The next day, after we cleaned the house we were vacating for the owners, I left Nina, our new Swiss helper, with Nick and Tony, sitting on the steps of the house with firm instructions not to go back in and mess it up because I'd be back in a half hour. I drove up Minute Man Hill to the Fortases' guest house. There was the tree, exactly as I'd dreamed it, and there lay the apples. I knew we'd buy the house before I even looked at it. It was the strongest, clearest psychic experience of my life.

Carol took me around the tiny, five-room house, which had all the charm of age, for it had been built in the 1840s for the chief cowherd, at a time when all of Minute Man Hill had been a large dairy farm. The owners of the farm had lived a few acres away in a huge stone house, where Carol and Abe now spent summer weekends, and only trees and broad green lawns lay between the two houses. Not far away was a red barn, which seemed to be falling down but came with the house. There was a little wood, and a good view of the bright blue waters of Long Island Sound; the house itself was located on the highest spot in miles. Compo Beach was a three-minute drive away.

I don't remember what I told Carol but it was some form of YES! Finally, I remembered Nina and the kids and drove back to find them patiently waiting. At least an hour and a half had gone by. I was in an alarming state of excitement. A week later we celebrated the purchase with a beach picnic with the Fortases. Carol provided the food: a large pitcher of martinis and one hot dog apiece. It was the most cliché WASP meal I've ever experienced.

We couldn't get into the house during the winter, because Carol had rented it, but by peeking in the windows and guessing at the dimensions of the rooms, I managed to furnish it from Bloomingdale's, and everything I bought turned out to be perfect.

However, the first summer we spent there all the plumbing decided to die at the same time and Tony, now six, with a stubbornness that defeated me, refused to go to his day camp, Singing Oaks, which he called "stinking goats." Nick had a great time there, but Tony hung around, bored and demanding. I began to wonder what mistake we'd made in buying a house. I remember looking out of an upstairs window at an army of plumbers replacing our septic field, and saying out loud in a miserable voice, "I wasn't meant to live in the country, I'm a city girl."

Carol Fortas was a famous gardener, but I hated the colors of the mournful garden she'd planted, all lavender, gray, and white and bristling with the thistles she loved. I'd never gardened in my life, so I hired a man to plant hundreds of bulbs for the following spring, of which only a few dozen came up.

I was furious at how we'd been cheated and treated like city slickers. I understood that I had to take matters into my own hands and I announced to Steve that I was going to take over the gardening, starting by planting a rose garden around the patio outside of the living/dining room. "How could you possibly do that?" he asked doubtfully. "Read a book and follow the instructions, like a cookbook," I answered.

I never had the slightest doubt that I could create gardens—perhaps a gene passed along from my gardening father?—but I did, to my utter satisfaction, without any help except that of a man who mowed the lawn and pruned the branches I couldn't reach. One night during the second year on Minute Man Hill I filled a dozen bud vases with different flowers in each one, lined them up on a table, and sat and looked at them for an hour, as proud as I've ever been of any book I've written.

For the next six years I dreamed about the garden in perfectly realistic terms many nights of the week. I could just about carry my weight in wet dirt; I dug like a man, and weeding became my joyous obsession. Almost every morning, as soon as Steve had driven off to the city, I went on the prowl for seedlings in the local flower nurseries. One of the handsome growers made my day by solemnly giving me a present of the biggest zucchini I've ever seen. I waited to laugh until I was alone in my car. I had a good idea what Freud would have said about that. Forget cigars—that zucchini was not just a zucchini!

The new seedlings were carefully concealed behind my potting bench until I could sneak them into the overflowing garden, and gradually the acre of lawn all but disappeared as I dug up the grass and replaced it with plants. Steve never noticed. My day-lily garden was planted from bare bulbs on the day of Bobby Kennedy's funeral. The bulbs had just arrived from the White Flower Farm and I decided that it was more important to get them into the ground promptly than watch the funeral train, although I dashed to the TV constantly.

I took every summer off while we owned our house, and worked in the garden at least five hours a day, wearing a hat, long sleeves, and long pants because of my allergy to the sun. When autumn came, what pure joy it was to fill my arms with dried steer manure and mulch my garden four inches deep before leaving it for the winter. Dancing with shit!

The house was too small for us and the kids when it got cold, so we had to drain the pipes of the house so they wouldn't freeze, and abandon our beloved place until the next spring.

Soon we'd rebuilt the barn, which now contained a Ping-Pong table. We put in a swimming pool in front of the barn, added a terrace, a dressing room, and a bar, and gave Carol Fortas the key to the swimming-pool gate. I kept a bottle of her favorite bourbon there for her and she swam mightily every day. In return she invited us to listen to Abe, a talented violinist, play chamber music with his friends Isaac Stern and Pinchas Zukerman. Those were magical evenings.

Steve hung wallpaper with professional results and painted and hung yellow shutters at every window of the little white house. We'd also started sending the kids to sleep-away camp, Nick loving it, Tony starting to protest at Christmas—without the slightest success—that he wasn't going to camp and no power on earth could make him.

In the afternoons, when it was too hot to work in the garden, I lay in the shade of a hat on a mattress that floated in the pool and read Trollope, an inexhaustible joy to which I still return and return. Once, when a precious little volume fell in the pool, I baked it dry in the oven, leaving it warped but still readable. I took more cooking lessons, becoming an accomplished cook, and we entertained a great deal. On the weekends we usually filled the boys' two tiny bedroms with guests and gave a party for them. Many Westport friends became New York friends when the summer was over.

When the kids came home from camp I arranged diving lessons for them with an astonishingly well-built and delightful local lifeguard. I'll never forget the moment I suddenly realized that to him—he was all of seventeen—I was that utterly sexless thing known as a "mom." It was depressing to realize this in my bouncing thirties, but I recovered. What else was there to do, since I wasn't the "Mrs. Robinson" type?

During our early Westport years a great scandal broke out surrounding Justice Abe Fortas. It was revealed that he was taking a retainer of some twenty thousand dollars a year to give advice to a businessman named Wolfson, and, with Nixon on his heels, he resigned from the Supreme Court in disgrace. Nothing will ever convince me that this was Abe's idea. Carol had literally forced him to sell his beloved guest house to us, as he admitted ruefully, and, unlike Abe, she was constantly, and unnecessarily, worried about money. I feel morally certain that the retainer was her notion. The agony they both went through was atrocious, but on the weekends when we joined them for a drink, there was never the slightest mention of an event that was making headlines in every paper in the country.

ALL WAS FAR from well with Steve and me, no matter how much we loved our summers. Sometime in 1965 Steve abruptly decided to go into psychoanalysis. He was in a deep depression. His success depended on his travels and his absence from home. The vast pressure he imposed on himself to make good and build his business and support his family only made things worse for both of us.

When I saw him depressed, it always seemed to me that his silence meant that he was angry at me and I would withdraw into my own, unexpressed anger and resentment, since I wasn't aware of having done anything wrong. This long-lasting misunderstanding was eventually cleared up, but not before a lot of painful learning had to be done. Neither of us was able to confront the other with our real feelings and clear the air, because we'd both come from homes in which we'd learned very young to lie low and avoid trouble. Our similarities worked against us during this period of our marriage. On the surface, all looked fairly calm, but underneath we were both thoroughly unhappy and afraid to admit it to the other.

I encouraged Steve when he told me about his decision to go into analysis, but I knew nothing at all about it. I'd never even taken a psych course in college. I'd always been of the arrogant and mistaken opinion that if I had a problem, all I had to do was phone three friends, talk it over, and it would disappear. I led a classic unexamined life, all the while interviewing people about their own lives and making a certain amount of sense about *their* problems.

As often happens, when one spouse goes into analysis, the other quickly follows, feeling left out and needing someone to talk to about this new situation. It was this way with me. I went to Jerry Barondess for a recommendation of a doctor. He offered to talk to me about my problems himself, but the last person I wanted to talk to was the husband of my best friend, who was also my internist. Finally Jerry gave me a list of shrinks and I went to the first one on the list, the late Dr. Benjamin Rubenstein. He was a strict, old-fashioned Freudian, for, in my ignorance, I wanted to go to the only kind of analyst I'd heard of. I knew that one of the rules of Freudian analysis was that the patient not make any major life changes while in treatment, and I suspected that I needed that kind of discipline at that unsettled time of my life.

It was a credit to Rubenstein's Freudian training that he didn't roll about on the floor shouting with hysterical laughter on my first visit. I'd made a neat little list of all the things I didn't want or need or even intend to talk to him about because they weren't problems in my life. I read the list out loud to him. It included my mother, my father, my husband, my children, my childhood—in fact, I informed him, in a no-nonsense tone of voice, the only reason I was there at all was that I knew I was spending too much money on clothes and lately I hadn't been as close to my sister as I used to be.

This was the equivalent of going to a doctor with an advanced case of leprosy and telling him you have a pimple on your pinkie. I was almost thirty-six at the time and knew very, very little about myself. In the next five years I was to find out a lot. The talking cure, as it used to be called, is indeed that. Dr. Rubenstein said so little that to this day—and I've had a lot more analysis—I'm convinced that, except for dreams which he interpreted very well, I more or less analyzed myself.

This balding, more-than-middle-aged Finn had been trained in England by Ernest Jones, who had written the definitive biography of Freud. Dr. Rubenstein did give me one piece of advice I still remember. There was a coffee shop opposite his office on Madison Avenue and frequently I had lunch there. One day I told him I'd finally figured out how to get them to make a rare hamburger by ordering two patties cooked together instead of the single one they always overcooked. "Good God, don't eat that meat rare!" he exclaimed. It was his greatest show of concern in the five years I went to him three times a week.

I'd traded one man who never said a word, my father, for another man who had been trained for years and years to speak as little as possible, to become as much of a blank screen as humanly possible. In retrospect, what I needed was a good, sensible, empathetic *female* analyst and I should have been sitting up, looking her in the eye, instead of prone, on a foam-rubber couch, in a position that guaranteed my feelings of lack of power.

By the second week of seeing Dr. Rubenstein, I'd dreamed that my father's real name was Arthur. "What does the name 'Arthur' mean to you?" Rubenstein asked. My only association was with King Arthur. It took at least a half hour to remember the pianist, Artur Rubinstein. The transference had been made, much to my blushing embarrassment. It seemed so incredibly corny! For the first two years of my analysis my worst fear was that Rubenstein would die, taking all that he'd learned about me with him. I shouldn't have worried; all that I'd learned was safely inside me.

Rubenstein's office, in the European style, was in his home, and was decorated like photos of Freud's office, with hundreds of small art objects. Often I'd ride up in the elevator with his wife, both of us looking carefully in different directions, and follow her by a discreet distance until we came to the entrance to his apartment. She'd go in one door and I'd go in the other to the waiting room. My doctor would never discuss her, of course, although I complained that it was a false situation since I could even smell what he was having for lunch. Naturally, I asked around and found out that she was a photographer of children, and that they were childless and went away each summer for a two-month vacation on an island in his native Finland.

On the couch my only form of control, since I couldn't see the man, was to make a ritual of taking off my shoes or boots and all my jewelry, and covering myself with the blanket that lay there. (At least I didn't put on pajamas.) For the first two years that I saw him, so much psychic energy went into the work (and into getting there on time) that I didn't write at all.

I mailed him his check every month for two years, since it seemed wrong to pay by hand for such intimate revelations, which I'd convinced myself he listened to out of fondness for me, not for the money. At the same time I believed that his name wasn't really Rubenstein and he was luring me on to talk freely by pretending to be Jewish! Talk about crazy! In the third year, getting slightly more sane, I delicately deposited the check on his mantel, and by the fourth year I had started to put it on his desk. By the fifth and final year I handed it to him directly. (One friend told me that I wouldn't be cured until I gave it to him in small coins, poured into his palm!) So some progress had been made . . . I'd admitted to myself that he did this for a living, not just because I was so adorable. Fortunately, I had twenty thousand dollars that my parents had given me, a one-time-only gift allowed by the government, so I was able to pay for my analysis myself.

Every summer Rubenstein and I fought about the fact that when Nick and Tony's school was over, we promptly moved to Westport for the summer, two weeks ahead of the time his vacation began. I offered to pay for those weeks but his position was that when he was in the office, I should come in from the country for my hour. And leave my garden? Not bloody likely! I was neurotic but I wasn't *that* neurotic. One day, as I bid him good-bye for the summer, I said, "Have fun on that island in Finland."

He almost turned blue. "How do you know about that?" "Oh, for Christ's sake, don't you realize that if you refuse to tell people anything, naturally they're going to try to find out?" I asked. That was the only vaguely serious peer moment I ever had with the man.

All of this was taking place during the second half of the sixties, and when I first appeared in a pants suit he looked as amazed as if I had announced that I was planning a sex-change operation. "Don't worry, Dr. Rubenstein, it's the latest style," I assured him, "and the zipper's in the back." My fall of long hair made him positively leap with astonishment when he opened the door to the waiting room. "Get a subscription to *Women's Wear* and you wouldn't be so surprised," I advised, delighted to have caught him in one more human reaction. Freudians!

However, any analysis is better than none and I had the need to know that my doctor was in a classic tradition and wasn't going to be experimenting with my mind. What I didn't know was that he was also Jerry Barondess's former analyst. One day, when this came out, sitting around the Barondesses' swimming pool, I spoke too quickly. "Hell, Jerry, you're the only other one of his patients I know and you're *still* so damn neurotic." Jerry was far from pleased. But it was true.

I do feel that my first analysis was a discovery of myself I couldn't have made under any other circumstances. It was a chance to reevaluate my life and my values, a chance to not keep on reliving the past in a destructive way, to ask myself why I was doing what I was doing and for what reasons. It caused certain harmful relationships to fade away and improved all my good personal relationships, especially with Steve, with whom I was now much more honest. One day, during the first six months of analysis, out of the blue, I told him about my abortion, something I would never have admitted to before. He was utterly understanding and not at all shocked. That was the beginning of both of us slowly revealing truths to each other that we'd kept hidden during ten years of marriage, and growing closer and closer as a result. The artificial mask of the nice girl he'd met was beginning to be stripped away.

The most important thing I learned was how strong my parents' influence still was, and how much I'd been leading the life I knew my mother wanted me to lead, rather than a life of my own. I'd started on the long, long path to becoming my own person.

Chapter Twenty-nine

I WAS TEN YEARS TOO OLD TO DO ANYTHING MORE THAN TASTE THE 1960s. I never could make myself do the Twist without feeling foolish, probably because I was too uptight to do it well, and not only did I not inhale, I was never offered a joint. I never even saw one. Would I have known what it was if I had? I certainly hope so.

A friend's husband, seeing me wearing my long blond fall, when I was only thirty-five years old, commented unforgettably and unforgivably, "Another old broad with young hair," which instantly put him in the ex-friend category. I did become expert at putting on false eyelashes, and I adopted the miniskirt and boots with enthusiasm, but for a woman with two children under twelve, the sixties always seemed as if they should be happening to someone else, someone still in her twenties.

There were some exceptions. Whenever we were in London, where we were making more and more friends, we felt part of both the era and the aura. In New York, through Jack LeVien, a friend of Steve's, we became members of the exclusive club that dominated the chic New York disco scene. It was called Le Club, and everyone wanted to get all done up in pretty clothes, go there, and dance. This was a decade before the Studio 54 scene and pretty clothes were still desirable.

Jack was one of those socially gifted men who seemed to know absolutely everybody in London and New York. His friends came from every possible group. He'd been an officer attached to Eisenhower's London staff in a PR capacity during the war, and later he'd produced the feature film *A King's Story* with the Duke of Windsor and a television series, *Winston Churchill: The Valiant Years*, under Steve's supervision.

Oh, Jack was *such* a deliciously silly man! He giggled constantly, a high-pitched giggle I can still hear, so easily that no one could resist telling him every word of the very best gossip. He knew more secrets than any woman who ever lived. He was a total lightweight but he added instant joy to every gathering.

Jack's home base was in London, where he lived with a lovely, calm woman named Lady Josephine Cato. He frequented Annabel's, that most famous of London nightclubs. When Jack introduced me there one night to Tony Shaftsbury, who had married one of Jack's ex-wives,

I tried, without much success, to make conversation with a stubbornly stuffy Brit. Finally, I was reduced to asking him if he lived in London. "No, in the country, we're just up for the night." "Oh," I said, "what a shame . . . London's so exciting now, you must hate having to leave it for the boring country." "Hmm," he commented, turning to someone else. Someone who would know that he was the Earl of Shaftsbury and earls lived in the country on their great estates and were never bored by owning vast chunks of England.

This sort of ridiculous encounter was typical whenever we saw Jack, who took nothing seriously and was always ready for a prank. He flitted in and out of our life for years. One day he got seriously sick and then had to be cared for at great expense for years before he died. The CIA took over his illness. Only then did we find out that he was an important member of the CIA, and had been actively employed since the end of the war. Watch out for silly men. They tend to hear a lot more information than men who take things seriously. Now that I know what Jack really was all along, I think of him as pure Graham Greene, but a sunny man in a sunny place.

In New York we were often invited to Barbara Walters's parties. Once I found myself deep in conversation with Barbara, Martha Graham, and Charlotte Curtis, who was editor of the *New York Times* women's page. Suddenly I realized how relaxed and comfortable I felt with these high-powered women. All I do is write for women's magazines, I thought, no one ever looks for my name on an article, but somehow I'm not intimidated. Damn, I *wish* I did something more important.

That's the only overtly ambitious thought that I can recognize from the sixties or any other time in my life until I was in the middle of writing *Scruples,* in 1976. However, I was frequently aware that I yearned to do *one thing,* anything at all, that would make me something less than ordinary. But I had no idea what that might be.

Years before, at one of the Mayeses' Thanksgivings, I'd met David Brown's brand-new third wife, Helen. (Wayne and he had been divorced for many years.) She was incredibly sweet, soft-spoken, a little timid, and somewhat out of her element, I thought, or else why would she not have realized that the top of her beautiful black lace bra was showing? Like silly men, never underestimate a woman who deliberately, as I realized in the years to come, shows a hint of her sexy undies.

In the later years of the sixties, I wrote to Helen Gurley Brown and suggested writing a short piece on the new word everybody was using, "funky." Helen immediately wrote back that "funky" wouldn't last more than six months—wrong, Helen—but if my letter meant that I could write for someone other than John Mack Carter, she'd like to talk to me about writing for *Cosmo*. Right! Thus began the most fruitful collaboration with an editor I'd ever had.

Cosmo printed an enormous amount of text every month and Helen had a large book filled with ideas just waiting for the right writer. She was the kind of editor a writer hopes for. No attempt to rewrite my work, no male editor saying unhelpfully to "put it through the typewriter again," but instead, crisp instructions: "On page five, paragraph three, line six, clarify the following three words." This was the kind of beautifully direct editing, and beautifully little of it, that I got from Helen or Bobbie Ashley, her articles editor, who became a good friend.

I did learn never to accept an assignment until I'd written Helen what my basic point of view was about it. Unless we agreed, I wouldn't even attempt to write the piece. There wasn't one word in *Cosmo* that didn't reflect Helen and her opinions, so if we differed, why start? Fortunately we were often in agreement and I was kept very busy. Soon she put me on the masthead as one of the six "contributing editors."

At some point in 1967 Steve sold his four-year-old business to a major cable television company. The offer was huge, and for the first time in our lives we felt truly secure about money. Steve also agreed to continue to run the company for them for the next five years. I was tremendously proud of what Steve had accomplished on his own, in only such a short time. He'd gone from a standing start to a worldwide business in animation and distribution.

I came home on Christmas Eve, while he was busy signing the papers that sold his business, and found a message that Mr. Maximilian had called, leaving his number. I called back out of curiosity since I didn't know a Mr. Maximilian. I found myself talking to a salesman at Maximilian's, the best furrier in the world, who informed me that my husband had just phoned him and ordered a sable coat to be made for me. "But sable will make me look fat!" was my immediate reaction. "I can promise you that it won't," he said, amused.

By the time my slender dark sable coat was made, I'd become a convert. Not only that, I'd noticed a fitted brown Persian lamb trimmed in suede while I was at Maximilian's for my first fitting, and when I'd mentioned it casually—yes, casually, I swear—Steve also gave it to me. It provoked a most unprofessional and judgmental comment from Dr. Rubenstein, losing his Freudian cool. "What, *another* fur coat!" I hope he was ashamed of himself after that session. If only I'd had the presence of mind to call him on his remark. Ah . . . "if only," two words I've promised myself to stop saying. Promised . . . and promised . . .

Typically, Steve had taken the time, while concluding this major business deal, to make the necessary arrangements to surprise me with something I'd never dreamed of owning. My sable became the first of three that I've worn so hard that two of them eventually lost their long hairs where I'd sat them out, grew shabby, and had to be turned into raincoat linings. When it became politically incorrect, years afterward, to wear fur even on a cold winter's night, I found that when it gets cool every night in California, at about four in the afternoon, there's nothing as cozy as sitting outside wrapped warmly in my surviving sable watching the golden evening light begin to dapple the swimming pool. It's only at these rare, quiet, not-working moments that I manage to feel almost—almost, but not quite—like one of my own heroines. An unworn sable sulks in the closet, the way pearls lose their luster if they're not worn around a woman's neck for too long a time.

Two years after he sold his business, Steve became unhappy working for anybody but himself, and he was able to settle his employment contract and start a new company, Steve Krantz Productions.

By 1971, both of us wanted to live in London in order to get out of New York, which had become increasingly dirty, sordid, and dangerous. Motorcycle gangs had taken over Washington Square Park. Our apartment had been robbed twice while we were away in Westport. Since we were on the second floor and there was an unguarded back entrance to the building, we had to put metal grids on all of the back bedroom windows and steel bars on the kitchen door so robbers couldn't slither over the transom. "Needle Park" was only two blocks west of the Dakota, on Seventy-second Street, and we had to walk by it on the way to the local deli.

Worse, both of our boys had been mugged four times each, surrounded on the street by gangs of knife-showing kids asking for money, watches, and bus passes. They were never hurt since we'd taught our kids to surrender everything they had at once and always made sure that they never went outside without provisions to turn over to muggers. Once Steve and I were in the park with Nick, and his bicycle was taken away from him as soon as he disappeared around the corner only ten feet away from where we were sitting. Another day, when Nick came home to report that he'd met "nice" muggers who had given him back his bus pass, I knew that it was time to leave.

We'd long had a dream of where we wanted to live in London. Friends of ours lived on a street called Ilchester Place, in Knightsbridge, one side of which backed up on Holland Park, a green island in that flowered, busy, evocative, and adored city. I was in constant touch with estate agents and eventually a house on the Holland Park side became available. I flew over at once to see it. The house was a perfect size and had a walled garden, behind which you could see nothing but well-tended parkland, with tennis courts in the distance. Built in a

Georgian style, of mellow brick, the house had been lived in by the same family for more than forty years and the entire electrical system was, to my experienced eye, a fire waiting to rage, with frayed cords trailing everywhere.

However, just at the time we bought our London house, Steve came home with a new project in mind. When he showed it to me I thought he'd gone quite mad. It was a comic book filled with tiny drawings in black and white, written and drawn by one Robert Crumb. It was something called *Fritz the Cat,* a underground comic, and my workaholic husband, who for thirty seconds says he had dreamed of actually retiring in London (as the French say, "permit me to snicker"), was now possessed by the idea of making Fritz into a full-length animated motion picture. In California, of course. London? Forget it. Every last production company turned Steve down on financing the making of *Fritz,* so he decided to finance it himself. When he'd owned his animation studio he'd hired an unknown art director, named Ralph Bakshi, whom he thought had great promise. Now he rehired Ralph and gave him a chance to translate Crumb to film.

Ralph was a wild man, loud, uncouth, gross, and dressed like a sloppy longshoreman. He was very street in his attitude and choice of words, but above all, he was unquestionably talented. He could be amusing, but I didn't like him.

Steve and Ralph left for California in a few days, to hire a group of Disney-trained animators, since Steve had decided that only the best were good enough for *Fritz.* I became the only person in 1971 to sell choice London real estate at a loss, unquestionably robbed by my most proper, stuffy estate agent. I also went about the sad business of selling our beloved little Westport house. I warned the buyer to either take up gardening or tear out everything I'd planted and replace it with lawn and trees.

I determined to sublet our New York apartment, on which we had a new three-year lease, because I had my silent, unexpressed doubts about *Fritz* and our move to California. A tenant presented himself, a smoothly elegant Englishman named Peter Brown who was willing to pay us two hundred dollars a month more than we were paying. "But why would you want to live alone in such a big place?" I asked. "You see," he answered most convincingly, "I give many large parties and this place is perfect for them." As soon as we moved out, Peter Brown moved in accompanied by a half dozen secretaries and a number of telex machines and proceeded to hold auditions for *Jesus Christ, Superstar* in our apartment, night and day.

Understandably, the landlords were able to get our neighbors to sign a petition to evict us. Peter Brown, that rotten, sneaky, lying cheat, worked for the Stigwood Organization and he'd made an under-the-table cash deal with our landlord to get us out of the way. The landlord had been in on the *Superstar* caper from the beginning. As soon as we lost our lease, the secretaries and would-be Broadway stars magically vanished, and Stigwood took over our apartment for six thousand dollars a month, more than twelve times what we'd been paying.

Occasionally in years to come, I'd see magazine pictures of John Travolta or some other Stigwood star, leaning happily over one of the balconies where, every year, we had entertained a group of children to watch the Thanksgiving Day Macy's Parade. I'd remember how, whenever there was a snowstorm, I used to go into the living room in the dark and watch the snow falling through the lights of the lamps in Central Park; how I'd gazed at the towers of Fifth Avenue, directly across from us, for long hours during the Cuban Missile Crisis and wondered if we all would really be vaporized in a second; how we used to put a large Christmas tree in the window of the library every year, decorated with bright paper ornaments Steve had bought in San Francisco and little white lights, until one day Nick said not to bother if we were only doing it for them, and I realized I'd been doing it for me . . . it was the tree my mother had not allowed at Christmas. I remembered how, with our beloved upstairs neighbors, Davis and Karen Thomas, we'd ridden bicycles through snow-covered Central Park in black tie, to get to Mayor John Lindsay's victory ball on the night he was elected mayor of New York and was immediately hit with a transportation strike.

When I told Doctor Rubenstein that I had to leave analysis because I was moving to California, he didn't seem at all disturbed. He never tried to wind down our work in any meaningful way, to lead to an official "termination." However, on my last day with him, he did express regret that I *still* hadn't realized that I must really want to witness the "primal scene" in which a child sees her parents making love. Freud has a lot to answer for . . . or rather, not Freud himself, that complicated genius, but those of his followers who interpret Freud far too strictly and reduce his teachings to a formula Freud himself would not necessarily agree with. For instance, rather than be a blank slate, Freud actually analyzed his own daughter, Anna. (Honey, I shrunk the kid!)

Nevertheless, I was deeply glad I'd been in analysis, even if it had been with a man I firmly consider was a less than satisfactory doctor, however orthodox. He was withholding to the maximum but he hadn't done me any harm, as far as I knew, and just being able to speak my thoughts and fears and fantasies out loud to someone three times a week had been tremendously helpful, helpful beyond imagining. It had brought me closer to Steve than ever. If we both hadn't gone into analysis at almost the same time, I'm not at all sure our marriage would have survived the difficult years of the 1960s.

The process had also made me far more mature. I'd learned that the list I'd taken in on my first day of analysis of the things that didn't bother me was instead a list of deep-seated problems. I had to discover and understand them as best I could in order to know what my part was in making them into problems, as well as what I could do to change them for the better. I'd learned to listen to people differently, to know them by so many clues I would have otherwise missed, to understand their motives and comprehend what made them behave as they did. I learned to forgive or ignore or deal with people who couldn't help being troubled and troublesome. I doubt seriously that I could have ever written fiction without analysis, since it's essential for me to know exactly why my characters act and react. They can do nothing without an inner psychological truth that satisfies me.

This truth doesn't have to be laid out in detail for my readers, but it must be there for me to trust in the validity of what I've written. Norman Mailer once said, "All writing is generated by a certain minimum of ego; you must assume a position of authority in saying that the way I'm writing it is the only way it happened." As far as I'm concerned, he's put it absolutely right, and that "position of authority" for me came from analysis.

Analysis also gave me a secret language of reference only other people who've been analyzed possess. Occasionally I wonder what coversation today would be without it.

Sometimes there were unexpected results that proved I'd changed. For years I'd been regularly petrified by a nightmare in which I was in an elevator that was out of control and about to crash through the roof of the building and disappear into the sky. One day, in the last year of analysis, I had the nightmare again, but this time I said to myself that the elevator probably wasn't even moving, and I opened the doors to find out that it was still on the ground floor. This was a distinct acknowledgment of important inner growth.

Chapter Thirty

As soon as the kids were out of school we flew to California and joined Steve on June 15, 1971. "Mommy," Nick said reproachfully, carefully picking up a tiny piece of paper on immaculate Wilshire Boulevard and throwing it into a trash can, "why did you wait so long to come here?"

We spent that first summer in a ground-floor suite at the Hotel Bel-Air. There was always an afternoon wedding on Saturday and Sunday, with receiving lines on the grass right outside our living-room patio. The boys would get dressed up in jackets and ties and go through the line, accepted as somebody's nephews, and bring back heaping plates of hors d'oeuvres to the patio where we were having a drink.

On the very second night we spent in California we were invited to dinner and a screening by Steve's lawyer, the late Gene Wyman. When the boys sat down in the deep armchairs of the screening room, with jars of candy on every table, and watched the giant screen rise up out of the floor, I felt as bedazzled as they did. It was purest Hollywood fantasy.

During that memorable week Steve and I were invited to our first California party at the home of Bill Dozier, a friend from his days at Columbia, who was married to Ann Rutherford, the effervescent star who'd played Mickey Rooney's girlfriend, Polly Benedict, in the Andy Hardy movies and one of the sisters in *Gone With the Wind*. After dinner, one of the guests passed around a batch of oddly shaped cigarettes that I knew had to be marijuana. I refused, on the basis that I'd never learned to smoke. *A weed virgin!*

The party immediately focused on me. While Steve watched, a trifle disapprovingly, I was coached by the entire group in the sport of smoking pot, to no avail. All I could do was cough. For most of the summer, at different parties, crowds of people vied to teach me how to smoke, but it wasn't until one friend invited us to dinner at her house by ourselves, with her boyfriend, that I finally caught on. Once high, I absolutely loved the feeling and found myself thinking all sorts of funny thoughts. Often I found myself saying them out loud without an audience, since other people were into their own funny thoughts, but grass only made Steve feel paranoid.

However, I eventually learned where to buy and how to clean my own marijuana and roll joints, since it was not the done thing to entertain, among the people we'd met, if you didn't have grass on hand. Nevertheless, whenever we were going to be out of town for any time at all, we'd flush the stuff down the toilet (not easy, it floats) so that in case we were both killed in a plane crash, our children would never discover it and think badly of us. Ah, innocence! Both boys had shoulder-length hair and probably, although I've never asked, could have shown me how to inhale, if not then, certainly in a few years.

Eventually, within a year, I had two bad trips, probably due to hash oil mixed in with the grass. Once I was up all night, making and remaking my bed, and another time it took me six hours to pin-curl my hair to my satisfaction. Even my bad trips were *absurdly* square and domestic. Since Steve still hated grass, I decided to stop smoking it, and we soon needed to make some new friends, friends who didn't consider an evening a success unless they were all stoned.

Years later, although I hadn't smoked grass for a long time, my brother and sister and I decided to have a sibling smoke-in, to see what insights we might discover about our childhood, since we were all born within four years and had grown up in the same environment. We chose to use Mimi's apartment, because she was unmarried at the time, and Jeremy and I arrived unaccompanied by our spouses. Steve had promised to pick Jeremy and me up and take us safely home at midnight.

It was a fascinating night. Mimi's memory was by far the best and she remembered so many surprising things that we agreed that if one of the other two of us also remembered, it should be considered true, since we didn't trust the well-known richness and invention of her imagination. She and I talked and talked while Jeremy sat and listened with an expression of complete contentment on his face. "Why are you just sitting there silently?" I prodded him. "I'm enjoying listening to the two of you," he answered, "it's like listening to great opera arias." At the end of the evening we had all agreed on almost all the important emotions any one of us felt about life with our parents. There is a great reassurance in knowing that my perceptions of my childhood were right on the button. Jeremy finally took the floor and told us that we were wonderful older sisters who were the only factor that enabled him to withstand the general neglect he felt from my parents. Oddly enough, although we planned to repeat the experience, we never have. Probably it was so complete that it didn't require additional affirmation.

———

I'D FINALLY GROWN accustomed to driving in Westport, with its sleepy little roads, but now I had to contend with aggressive California drivers. I was rigid with fear every time I got into the car. When I took the boys for tennis lessons with Pancho Gonzalez, the former champion whom I'd seen play in the forties at Forest Hills and who now taught at the nearby Beverly Hills Hotel, I'd check out their seat belts and warn them not to utter *one single word* while I tensely negotiated, barely breathing, the half mile of wide curves of the then peaceful Sunset Boulevard.

I had far more serious concerns than my driving as soon as we reached California. Mimi's husband, Dr. Jacques Brien, had been diagnosed with a brain tumor two and a half years earlier. He'd been put on an experimental group of drugs, given to only four other people in the country, because of his value to the medical community, and he'd remained alive and able to practice for almost two and a half years more. He'd told his analytic patients about his condition as soon as he knew about it, and had given them the option to stay with him or be referred to the best doctors he knew.

Those who stayed, and there were a number, made astonishing progress since they knew they had no time to waste. However, as soon as he realized that his faculties were starting to go, as soon as he couldn't speak or think as clearly as before, he decided to kill himself, since life without work, life that could only end soon in certain deterioration, gave him no reason to stick around. About two weeks after we arrived, and six weeks after he'd stopped practice, Jacques bought a gun and checked into a room in the newly opened Holiday Inn that overlooks Sunset Boulevard and the 405 freeway. There he shot himself. He'd told Mimi that he'd chosen the Holiday Inn because it was the ugliest building ever built and he wanted to make a statement. He also insisted that in his obituary it would say that he had "died by his own hand" since he felt strongly about the right to suicide.

Mimi, who had lived for years with this dying man she loved, was in a terrible state of grief, and of course I spent a great deal of time with her and her two daughters. Aliza was soon to start at Harvard and Susanna was a high-school sophomore. (David Karney, Mimi's first husband, had become an enormously successful builder and remained a devoted father to the girls.) My mother was deeply upset that suicide had been mentioned in the obituary, since, in what Mimi and I considered an old-fashioned way of thinking, she thought suicide a scandal that should be concealed.

Long before she met Jacques, Mimi had had a great romance with a man named Jack Dyckman, a famous city-planner. He was an unhappily married Catholic with children, but, like my mother's last love, he had been unwilling to get a divorce. Now, soon after Jacques's death, he arrived on the scene and accepted the James Irvine Chair at the University of Southern California, then the only endowed chair of urban planning in the country, and soon he was again part of my sister's life. Jack was recognized as an international genius as widely as he was recognized as a world-class alcoholic.

Jack and Mimi started to live together and in the mid-seventies he finally got a divorce and convinced Mimi he'd stopped drinking heavily. She agreed to marry him in 1977, a marriage that lasted only nine months after he resumed his drinking. It was almost unbelievable to watch a man able to drink so much and still function as if he were sober.

Mimi's relationship with Jack Dyckman continued after their divorce on a "same time next year" basis until he too died of a brain tumor. My father, Jack Tarcher, Jacques Brien, and then Jack Dyckman all died of brain tumors, and Mimi was half-convinced that it was something about *her*. I had to assure her that she didn't have that much power. After Jack Dyckman died, she vowed never to marry again and so far she's kept to her promise . . . although with my sister's charm, you can never be sure.

As soon as I moved to California, I started to look for a Pilates studio. From New York I heard rumors that one had just opened in Beverly Hills. I went in to discover that I was now the first and only pupil of one Ron Fletcher. Ron, who immediately announced that he was as gay as a coot, AA, sober for twelve years, half Native American and half Irish (so what could you expect from such a genetic heritage?), won my heart instantly. He'd been a lead dancer in Broadway musicals until he'd become a teacher.

The boys were now in camp, so I had Ron all to myself for two and a half hours every day that summer. He had a triple helping of the devilish charm of the Irish and by the time fall came new students were appearing: Ali MacGraw, Candy Bergen, Katherine Ross, Brooke Hayward, and a host of others, particularly Peggy Goldwyn, who became, over the years, with her husband, Sam, a lifelong friend.

Occasionally Nancy Reagan, the governor's wife at that time, used to drop in to visit with Ron Fletcher, whom she'd known when they were both in *Lute Song* on Broadway. They would shut themselves up in a private room from which we'd hear peals of startlingly wicked laughter ringing for hours. I've always known that there were two very different sides to Nancy Reagan. But aren't there at least five or six sides to every woman?

At the studio, we warmed up in front of a large mirror, and only my clear-cut superiority at the exercises I'd been doing for years kept me from feeling the way I used to when I worked with models and looked into the mirror by mistake. Our classes turned into a sort of group therapy, since, as always with beautiful girls, all they saw were their flaws. Candy, whose thighs might possibly have been a half inch smaller, referred to herself as "Helga the Hulk" and meant it. Ali, who'd gone to Wellesley and disliked it, was living in Trancas with Steve McQueen and could get dressed in one second, winding a long scarf around her head and another around her leotard, and emerge looking as if five stylists from *Vogue* had spent hours on her. Exquisite, gentle Katherine was the sunniest of the three, happily talking about her Malibu garden and bringing in flowering plants for the studio.

One afternoon, another regular, Brooke Hayward, daughter of the late agent-producer Leland Hayward, threw herself down on the machine next to me in a rage. "Damn that evil bitch, Pamela, she bankrupted my father and broke his heart and now she's just married the richest man in the world!" "Who'd she marry?" "Averell Harriman." Fascinated, I asked Brooke how to explain Pamela Harriman's success with men. "She keeps the world's most comfortable house" was the only understandable answer I finally extracted. From this hint I was later able to find the beginning point from which I constructed an entire character, the beloved mistress Annabel in *Princess Daisy*.

Ron was an unabashed star-fucker. One day he was concentrating on Barbra Streisand while Ali and I worked out on mats nearby. "If we both went into cardiac arrest right now, do you think Ron would notice?" I asked. "Not a chance," she answered.

That fall we left the hotel and rented an old house in Beverly Hills (built by Charlie Chaplin for Lita Gray, one of his wives) so that I'd have time to look around for a house to buy and find out more about the Beverly Hills school system. Tony, who was twelve, started junior high at El Rodeo, and Nick, at fourteen, became a freshman at Beverly Hills High, while I went house hunting, an endless process.

In our rented house we gave a party for the first anniversary of Ron Fletcher's studio and invited everyone who went there, known and unknown, even his landlord, the rather stiff grande dame Aida Gray, a minor-league cosmetics queen. I spent the night before the party rolling fat joints in case I needed to break the ice quickly. Before the party had gone on for more than three minutes I knew that the time for the joints had arrived, and started to pass them around. "What's that?"

asked Aida. "Marijuana, Miss Gray," I said, and watched her sprint away with her husband, as if the place were about to be raided.

Finally I found a house, on the corner of North Rexford Drive and Lexington, one block north of Sunset and one block away from the Beverly Hills Hotel, on a corner lot of over an acre. Edward G. Robinson lived across the street and a few blocks down Lexington was the corner on which both Jimmy Stewart and Lucille Ball had houses. Our house had a sunny lawn, huge trees, and a history, as almost every house seems to have here. It had belonged to the opera star Lawrence Tibbett, then to Mickey Rooney, and finally to Jane Wyman. Her fans kept ringing the doorbell and asking if Jane was in, until we built a wall and a gate.

With delight, I discovered that I could apply for a resale card at something called the State Board of Equalization, which would permit me to buy wholesale on prepayment of my estimated sales tax. Women like me were called AADs, which meant "also a decorator."

I went to apply at the board with Cynthia Lasker, a good friend from Ron Fletcher's. Her husband, the late Eddie Lasker, was the son of Albert Lasker, one of the greatest advertising men of all time, who was smart enough to take his fifteen percent commission in Philip Morris stock. Cynthia lived high up in Bel Air in a veritable mansion, the only woman I've ever known with a lady's maid who made her bed every night with fresh Porthault sheets and then ironed them each afternoon before her nap. When the resale-card czar asked her what she thought she'd be spending, in order to determine her sales tax, beautiful Cynthia looked demure and murmured something about "probably very little."

I knew I'd have to spend a lot to furnish our house, so when my turn came, I gave the man a realistic estimate. He slapped me with a huge sales tax and let Cynthia go free! When I told Steve this sad tale he insisted that I call the Equalization Board and change my story. Haltingly, I did so, saying that I'd probably been too optimistic. The man sighed, the sigh of one who'd heard that story before, and returned most of my sales-tax deposit.

While I worked on the house, Steve was busy finishing *Fritz the Cat*. It was rebellious and shocking, the story of young people (depicted as animals) breaking out of the fifties mold into the freedom of the sixties. It got an X rating by the Motion Picture Review Board for what they termed "anthropomorphic humping"!!! Someone with a sense of humor must have dreamed up that term, never heard since, but film critics considered it a landmark film that has never been duplicated. It did incredible business and it's still in distribution after all these years. Film students around the world study it today.

Fritz was invited to be shown at the Cannes Film Festival during "Critic's Week" and of course we went, staying at the Hôtel du Cap, an outrageously expensive experience I was able to amortize by using it in *Scruples.*

Shown in a little movie house on a back street in Cannes, *Fritz* quickly became the sensation of the festival and Steve became the darling of distributors from all over the world. I remember sitting by myself on the terrace of the Carlton while he sat at another table, receiving, one by one, like a Southern belle, distributors who wanted to make deals. I was glowering, pouring out my feelings of being totally unnecessary onto a postcard to Bobbie Ashley. It was my first experience of jealousy and I didn't like it, so the next day I hired a car and driver and took a trip to Grasse. I stopped for lunch at La Colombe d'Or in Saint-Paul de Vence, and there I noticed a gray-haired, heavyset woman patiently reading her morning paper while she waited to eat a solitary lunch like mine. It was Simone Signoret. God knows where Yves Montand is, I thought grimly.

In *Scruples* I made use of my few hours on the Carlton terrace in a scene in which Vito Orsini takes Billy Ikehorn to the Carlton and tells her what she's watching.

"That man over there with the hat on, he's made fifty million dollars making dirty movies in Japan. He's here to find some big-breasted Swedish girls who will agree to have their eyes made Japanese by plastic surgery. Then he will use body makeup and make even better dirty movies with them because he thinks that Japanese girls are too small-breasted. The man with him has fifty Swedish girls to sell—they are dickering over the price. The tall blond woman at that table over there is a man. He is waiting for his lover who is a woman casting director who only likes men in women's clothing. She spends forty thousand dollars a year at Dior to keep him well dressed. The three Arabs behind us are from Kuwait. They have nine hundred million dollars and dream of establishing a film industry in their country. But nobody wants to go and live there at any price. If they go home without a film industry they may be killed, so they are getting nervous. They are seriously planning to kidnap Francis Ford Coppola and possibly Stanley Kubrick but they're not sure they can afford them. The Russians who are waiting for a table are trying to induce George Roy Hill to remake *War and Peace* so they can rent him their entire army as extras. But they want it to be set in the future so they can use their air force and their new nuclear subs—"

"Vito!"

"If I told you the truth it would be boring."

"Tell me anyhow." Billy's dark eyes were as flirtatious as the sea.

"Percentages. Pieces of the gross. Pieces of the net. Pieces up front. Pieces deferred. Points and fractions of a point. Film rentals in Turin. Film rentals in Cairo. Film rentals in Detroit, in—"

"I liked it better the other way."

ONCE WE WERE back in California, Steve and Ralph started work on another animated film called *Heavy Traffic*. In the middle of production Steve discovered that Ralph, who was under an exclusive contract to Steve Krantz Productions, was conspiring with another producer to sell a film to Paramount. He had been using Steve's animation equipment and working on Steve's time. This treachery came at the worst possible moment and Steve had to lock Ralph out of the studio and shut it down, at the cost of hundreds of thousands of dollars, while he threatened Paramount and Ralph with legal sanctions. Finally they arrived at a resolution and Ralph finished the direction on *Heavy Traffic,* although he and Steve communicated only by memos. *Heavy Traffic* was a major success, but without a strong producer like Steve, Ralph, for all his talent, never again had another successful film.

Meanwhile, I was still writing for *Cosmo*. My most famous piece, about which I'm still asked, was called "The Myth of the Multiple Orgasm," inspired by a book written by a general practitioner, a Dr. Rubin, who insisted that any woman who settled for less than fifty orgasms during a single sexual session was being cheated. Another book that was also sweeping the country was written by a woman who signed herself "J, the Sensuous Woman," and who claimed the right to no less than one hundred orgasms. Every night. *One hundred?* Give me a break!

I beat the bushes and interviewed some fifty-five women, of whom only eight percent had multiple orgasms, as defined by Masters and Johnson. Only one of them, who needed almost an hour of foreplay before she had her first orgasm, claimed that she had never been satisfied and could always have another orgasm no matter how many she experienced. I also interviewed six well-known therapists to discuss my findings. They pronounced this woman an example of a true nymphomaniac.

Whenever I brought up my topic of research at a party, looking for women to interview, there would be a silence until someone would ask, "What's the normal amount of orgasms for a woman to have?" When I answered, "One, if she's lucky," there would always be a wave of greatly relieved laughter.

If I've ever contributed something solid to women feeling at peace with their own sexuality, it's that article. Nor are there multiple orgasms in any of my novels. Now, when I look at the post-Helen *Cosmo*, I see with disgust that the lead article is called, "How to Have Fifteen Orgasms Every Time," with the research done only through the *Cosmo* staff itself. I know for sure they have to have made up their statistics to fit the misleading title of the article. What a rotten thing to do to their credulous readers!

Under a pseudonym I also wrote "The Pure Vanity Face Lift," inspired by my own face-lift. One day when I was in my late forties, I was standing in front of a mirror at Ron's, minding my own business and exercising my arms, when Joanne Rydell, then the wife of director Mark Rydell, appeared behind me. "I saw the most fascinating thing on television last night," she said. "There was a plastic surgeon who stood behind a woman and put his fingers on her face, see, just like this, Judy, and showed how she'd look with a face-lift." "Do that again, Joanne," I asked. My developing jowls, which reminded me of my mother's, disappeared instantly. "Okay, I'm sold," I said, and set about interviewing plastic surgeons until I found one I liked and trusted.

Steve felt that if I really thought I needed a face-lift, I should have one, and so I did, a face- and eye lift that were so good, and had been done so early on still-elastic skin, that they lasted well over twenty years. I've never been coy in real life about my face-lift; in fact, I've inspired dozens of them, whenever women ask me about mine. However, I didn't want to put my name on the article, destined to be read by strangers, which gave a complete and honest guide to the process, step by step.

Yes, it's extremely uncomfortable for the first twenty-four hours until the pressure bandage is removed; yes, you're swollen and black and blue for about ten days, at which point you turn green, yellow, and finally back to flesh-colored, about three weeks after the operation; but good Lord, it's worth it! I don't understand any of the solemn moralizing that goes on about plastic surgery, with women, invariably too young to need face-lifts, writing that you should be "proud" of your wrinkles. Please! It's not living through difficult experience and hard-won knowledge that causes wrinkles, but plain old gravity, and there's no reason to be proud of the action of a natural force. Nor do "character lines" prove your strength of character. Your character is inside, established throughout your life, and there's no need to wear it stamped on your face to prove anything. But a face-lift is a matter of choice, a personal decision no one should make for you. I, for example, have never even had a facial and I'd flee swiftly from any chemical or laser peel. No "controlled burns" for my perfectly clean and delicate skin, thank you.

Most Hollywood women won't admit in print they've had any "work" done, the local term for cosmetic surgery, but anyone much over fifty who still boasts a lovely firm chin line has done so, I guarantee it. No one is immune to gravity. Five years ago I had another lift, done by the marvelous Dr. Frank Kamer, who's famous for "not doing too much," so I've never had that too-tight look. If I live long enough to need it, I'll have a third. Why *not* fool Mother Nature? That lady gets us all, sooner or later, and I'd rather lead her a merry chase.

For a few weeks after my first face-lift, I had a minor depression, the cause of which I finally identified. I deduced that since I was old enough to need a face-lift, that must mean I wasn't *really young* any more. Well, bless my soul!

Four years after we got to California, I decided to go back into analysis. I'd written yearly letters to Dr. Rubenstein (still hoping, I suppose, that he would take some interest in someone he'd seen three times a week for five years), reporting on what was going on in my life, but I'd never received an answer. This time I wrote him and demanded an explanation for his silence.

He wrote back saying that he couldn't imagine why I'd want or need to have any more analysis and, oh yes, he hadn't written back because he'd forgotten. FORGOTTEN! I still can't comprehend how he could have written such a thing, without quitting his profession in disgust at himself, but there it was, in black and white.

I knew then that I was right to start to seek another shrink.

Chapter Thirty-one

ONE DAY IN 1976, STEVE CONFESSED TO ME THAT HE'D SECRETLY BEEN taking flying lessons at the Santa Monica Airport and was not far from taking the test for his pilot's license. I was incredulous. When we got married we'd each given up something we loved: Steve, flying lessons, and me, skiing. Steve hated to be cold and fall down, two unavoidable elements in skiing, and I had a deathly fear of flying. In hindsight, of course, Steve should have learned to ski and I to fly. Oh, how I wish hindsight didn't exist. It gets you nowhere . . . but I can't shake the habit.

I'd blithely taken planes for nine years, from 1944 to 1953, before I became terrified of flying during a turbulent trip.

From that time on, I couldn't get on a plane without lots of tranquilizers and a couple of drinks. All our many years of travel had been tainted by the knowledge that I'd have to take a plane to get there, and once there, take another plane to come home. However, I hadn't allowed my fear of flying to ground me. On one particularly scary flight, from Seville to Madrid, I'd been so distraught that I'd managed to get Steve, normally utterly closemouthed on the subject, to tell me about his old girlfriends to give me something to think about besides the coming crash. Sadly, once we landed, everything he'd revealed went completely out of my head.

Now I decided that I had to take flying lessons too, so that I could fly with Steve. I'd seen *Airport*, the movie in which the stewardess lands the plane, and I vividly imagined Steve dropping dead at the controls and my having to take over. The alternative would have been to say, "Go fly, you underhanded, rotten, low-life bastard, for whom I gave up the one sport I loved, but count me out." However, I couldn't imagine our spending that much time apart.

I found a Beechcraft flying school out at the Van Nuys Airport and signed up. In theory it takes the average person eight to twelve hours, or less, to learn how to fly a single-engine plane. It took me an unheard-of forty hours. Reader, I was not a natural.

But I lost my fear of flying in the first hour! Once I understood what kept the plane up, and once I was in charge, with an instructor sitting by my side with dual controls, I began to enjoy it. The most fun of all was something called the "stall series," in which I deliberately put the plane up into such a steep angle that it had to stall and plunge down-ward, at which point I'd bring it back level again. Another fright I loved was when the instructor shut off the engine unexpectedly, forcing me to pick a field on which to land. I'd gradually guide the plane down in circles, using the air currents like a falling leaf, until, before we hit the ground, he'd suddenly switch the motor back on.

The part I didn't like was landing. It's utterly thrilling to take off into the sky, but so very difficult to land without "bending the plane." As I practiced landings I noticed that I rarely had the same instructor twice. I was so bad that they must have decided to rotate the danger among them. When I went for the required FAA eye exam, the doctor, a pilot himself, was incredulous. "You mean you've been flying with-out distance glasses?" "Do I need them?" "Good Christ, yes!"

Distance glasses suddenly turned the three runways I wasn't aware I'd been seeing into a single runway, and I progressed to the point of being able to land without smacking into the ground and sending the plane bumping down the runway in a series of huge hops.

Finally I soloed, taking the plane up by myself, circling the field three times and landing. When I arrived for the next lesson I heard the word "navigation." I should have seen navigation coming. Few pilots don't want to go somewhere. But navigation means learning a multitude of things, including judging your air speed, your fuel, your distance from the next airport—all of them requiring math. "You just have to learn how to use a slide rule," my instructor said patiently. "There's nothing to it." I shook hands with him and left, never to return. JUST a slide rule! Me and a slide rule in the same space? Never. Never. Never.

I couldn't have written *Till We Meet Again,* my fifth novel, with-out knowing how to fly myself, since one of my three heroines, Freddy de Lancel, later played by Courtney Cox in an eight-hour miniseries, was a pilot and part of the book revolved around flying. During the war, Freddy flew from 1943 to 1945 in the British Air Transport Aux-iliary, a group made up of hundreds of woman pilots who ferried every kind of aircraft from the factories where they were built to Royal Air Force and Royal Navy airfields. I dedicated that book to those brave women without whom the servicemen wouldn't have had a fighting chance.

Freddy, at sixteen, was born to fly and her solo was braver than mine.

"Yes, yes, yes," she said out loud, unconscious that she was speaking in a serious, imperative undertone as she taxied to the end of the runway and raced toward her takeoff point, her throttle full open, in an ecstasy of thrust, passionately urging on the plane as she approached that miraculous and logical instant at which she would have enough speed and enough lift so that her wings would rise irresistibly into the golden air, the beckoning sky, toward the setting sun.

As she took off, quickly rising, she was the archer, she was the arrow. She never glanced toward the empty right-hand seat. Time existed but not for her. Freddy's hands moved calmly as she reached the right altitude and began to make the necessary adjustments for turns and banks, her heart beating madly with a joy she'd never known as the light plane responded to her touch as if it were her own flesh. The patterns she had cut so often seemed to be made of a new material as she flew alone, the landmarks around the airport registered on her mind with new import. There was a divinity in the moment, a divinity in the edges of her wings as they embraced the night, in the steady roar of the motor, in the knowledge that one machine and one human being, aloft together and alone, made more than one entity. She heard herself laughing and she saw the evening star in the deepening blue of the sky. . . . How she longed to climb up into the heavens until she could see the stars of the constellation of Capricorn. The books said that they were far away, too far to be seen. She didn't believe it, would never believe it, for she knew that she flew now under Capricorn, the constellation of her birth.

I had called the novel *Under Capricorn* for months, feeling a connection to the words since I'm a Capricorn (slow, steady, trustworthy, determined, upwardly mobile, in case you care) but eventually I heard a World War I song called "Till We Meet Again" and fell in love with the melody and the lyrics and changed the title. My novels usually go through two or three title changes until I find the one that I think fits best.

Since I didn't have the passion of Freddy de Lancel, who actually enjoyed navigation, sometime in the middle of 1976 I hung up my wings and looked around me. Many things were going on in my life. My sons both had their driver's licenses, and, in California, when a boy gets that precious passport to freedom at sixteen, he's gone. Gone for good. You'll see him again when he gets hungry and happens to be near home, but essentially, once he gets wheels he's been elevated to a different place in the scheme of things, where there's little he needs from you and you're allowed to know almost nothing about his life. Nick was at USC but still living at home because, as a freshman, there wasn't room for him in the dorm, and Tony was finishing Beverly Hills High and going on to Berkeley the following year. In 1977 the nest would be really empty.

I realized that I was bored by writing magazine articles. I'd been doing it steadily since 1949 and there was nothing new for me to learn about the skill involved, and certainly no challenge.

My life seemed ready for a challenge. I'd recently found a new analyst, a Dr. S., whom I liked. He was nine years younger than I was, born reassuringly in Indiana. What could be less foreign than that? He assured me that he was not a Freudian, although, "like all analysts, he stood on the shoulders of Freud." He readily answered all the questions I'd asked before I would consider becoming his patient: his age, his education, his marital status, whether or not he had children, and his religion. He was Jewish and the second time I saw him I realized that I'd forgotten to ask if his wife was Jewish too. No, he'd married a Gentile and been disinherited by his religious family. He'd worked his way through medical school and earned the money to train to become an analyst by working in general practice in Long Beach. I found that admirable and I liked his casual, friendly smile. He was rather short but built like an athlete (he'd been on a college bike team), with curly hair and a lot of informal charm. All in all, although I was back on the couch, I thought I'd made a good choice.

I'd been running out of reading material lately. Whenever I went to Hunter's, the biggest of the six bookstores near or on Rodeo Drive, I'd find books filled with Nazis plotting to return or things like "The Crash of '79," not a subject I wanted to think about. My favorite writers, Colette, Updike, Cheever, Proust, Trollope, Roth, Robertson Davies, Iris Murdoch, Margaret Drabble, and George Eliot, were either dead or wrote too infrequently to satisfy my heavy reading habit, although I reread many of my favorites and I'm currently on my fourth go-round with Proust, discovering new wonders on almost every page.

Recently I'd had to fictionalize a small amount of material in a *Cosmo* article about the meaning of women's sexual fantasies. I couldn't find enough women who were willing to recount their fantasies to me, for a fantasy told out loud is too often a fantasy drained of power, so I'd added a few of my own, under an assumed name. Helen had called to say that the "boys upstairs," i.e., the Hearst management, had refused to print the piece unless she toned down certain of the fantasies. The only ones they objected to were *my* fantasies. I was proud of myself—too hot for Hearst—but it didn't occur to me that I'd been taking a step toward actually writing fiction.

However, I was often plagued by thoughts that started this way: "Once there was a woman who fell in love with her son-in-law." As soon as such a thought came into my mind, I quashed it, because where could it lead? I didn't write fiction. I was even more fearful of writing fiction than I had been of flying a plane. I hadn't written a word of fiction since those few short stories at Wellesley in 1945, and then I had found them difficult to do. I didn't know at the time that many writers have trouble with the short form and can write far better in the novel form.

Several years earlier I'd had an idea for a nonfiction book about women and their mothers, but my agent at the time, Roz Targ, had managed to screw matters up so completely with my prospective publisher that I'd dropped the whole idea of any book at all in my future. And dropped Roz, who would probably have been my agent today if she hadn't failed to protect me properly from a destructive publisher. Meanwhile, Nancy Friday had published *My Mother, Myself,* and that field was well covered.

I knew what good fiction was, heaven knows. I'd studied it and absorbed it for four years at college. Victim of too good an education, I was convinced that I could never be a fiction writer. It seemed to me that, at the very least, you had to be born wanting to become a writer, and start, like Truman Capote, writing stories when you were very young. I'd never even kept a diary or written a poem or shown the slightest sign of anything but fear of writing fiction. Letters were easy to write, everyone I knew owed me a dozen letters; but letters weren't fiction.

Only one person—my husband—thought I had the makings of a novelist, and he'd been saying so for many years.

For the twenty-two years of our marriage, Steve had thought of me as a natural storyteller, someone who could recount what had happened to me or to us in an interesting, detailed, and colorful way. From the moment in Rome on our honeymoon when he'd woken up and seen me transfixed by the sight of my new Gucci bags, he'd known how much I appreciated and understood the essence of a particular pleasure. He thought that I had an original sense of humor that would emerge in whatever I wrote and that I was as verbal as the entire House of Representatives. I also suspect him of wanting to put me to work because I spent so much time shopping.

I took a deep breath and told myself that the only way to stop Steve from continuing to persecute me with his notion that I could write a novel was to try and write one, giving it all I had. It was the only way I could prove to him that I *wasn't* a novelist and get him to stop nagging and pushing me.

I had never studied what was called English composition at college, but it seemed only logical to me that a novice novelist should try to find some sort of umbrella under which I could create a number of characters who would, at least, have the umbrella in common. A popular old novel, Vicki Baum's *Grand Hotel,* was the sort of thing I had in mind.

Puzzling over this problem, I continued to go to gym three times a week and get my hair done once a week at Aida Gray's. This meant parking on one side of Rodeo Drive and crossing the street back and forth eight times each week. Recently I'd been noticing the first beginnings of the arrival of boutiques on Rodeo.

At the time we moved to California, there had only been two places on Rodeo Drive besides department stores to buy clothes: Fred Hayman's Giorgio's, and Amelia Gray's, where Galanos and other high-fashion clothes were sold. Otherwise, the street was a hodgepodge of various stores, of which Gucci and Van Cleef & Arpels were the largest. There were bookstores, small hosiery shops, David Orgell for china and glass, Italian men's furnishings, estate jewelry at Frances Klein's, and tearooms.

Elizabeth's was my favorite tearoom, where I used to pick up a turkey-salad sandwich before going to Ron's because by the time I'd finished exercising, I'd usually missed lunch and be ravenous. Many of us used to sit around in a corner and eat and chat after our workouts. I could, and did, easily make almost an entire day out of one Pilates lesson.

One day the woman behind the counter at Elizabeth's told me that the store was being closed to make way for something called the Right Bank Clothing Company, an expensive boutique for fancy T-shirts and sports clothes for twenty-year-olds. I was still seething at this coming loss when I crossed the street, after gym, and suddenly had an illumination. It was exactly, precisely as if a lightbulb had gone on inside my head. Just like a *New Yorker* cartoon. *A boutique!* By God, if you can't beat 'em, join 'em! A boutique would be the perfect umbrella . . . a boutique on Rodeo Drive.

Excited at having an idea—perhaps an unconscious echo of Harrison's boutique idea of twenty-six years before—I went home and, using the desk I wrote on in the guest room, typed a few pages about a woman arriving at a madly luxurious boutique she owned in Beverly Hills, a boutique that had no name at that point. When Steve came home I showed the pages to him and asked him if this was fiction or not. It wasn't that I was a moron, but it had seemed so natural to write these first pages that I didn't think they could be that impossible thing called fiction.

"They're fiction, all right," he said in delight. "Now why don't you go back to the guest room and write some more."

This was better than flying, it was better than anything I'd ever done at a typewriter before; it was like uncorking a bottle of champagne, it was as if I'd been meant to do this all of my life, I realized, as I finished the first chapter of *Scruples*.

Nick at nine months, spring 1957.

Making eye contact with three-week-old Tony, 1959.

Tony on a balcony of 135 CPW, wearing the Adolfo hat I had had made to order for the Egyptian trip.

Nick and Tony at the front door of Le Bois Normand, summer 1963.

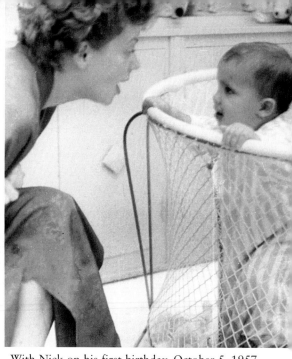

With Nick on his first birthday, October 5, 1957.

Nick and Tony at the port of Honfleur in the summer of 1963. Nick was six, Tony three.

Steve and me in a Cairo restaurant, circa 1965.

Above: Signs of the 1960s: the only existing picture of me with my long blond fall.

Above right: Steve and me on the lawn of our house in Westport, Connecticut, 1969.

Right: Our summer house in Westport, with Steve and Tony playing catch on the lawn, circa 1967.

Nick and Tony, circa 1965.

Steve and me in a photomatic booth in 1970, the year before we moved to L.A. This hairdo didn't last long.

The front door of our Beverly Hills house, 933 North Rexford Drive.

At Van Nuys airport in the days when I was learning to fly, before I wrote *Scruples*, 1975. *(Photo by Michael LeRoy)*

Above: My first PR photo, taken at Giorgio's, spring 1978, for *Los Angeles* magazine by Michael LeRoy.

Right: Steve in 1980, publicizing his hugely successful animated feature, *Fritz the Cat*.

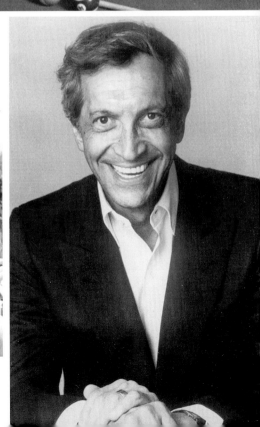

With Nick and Tony at Tony's graduation from Beverly Hills High, 1979.

Taken for *People* magazine the week *Scruples* became #1 on the *New York Times* bestseller list. I was writing *Princess Daisy*. The photographer told me to look thoughtful.
(Photo by Tony Costa)

Left: Opposite the Bridge of Avingnon while researching *Mistral's Daughter*.
(Photo by Pierre Boulat)

Below: My office in Beverly Hills, where I wrote my first three novels.

With actor Barry Bostwick on the set of the miniseries *Till We Meet Again*. He had leads in three of the miniseries made from my novels, which Steve produced.

Above: With Merv Griffin during one of my nineteen appearances on his show, 1982.

Below: At the publication party for *I'll Take Manhattan*. Donald Trump is giving me the keys to Trump Tower. My dress was a gift from Nolan Miller.

Below: With Joan Collins at a party at her Beverly Hills house in 1987, following Steve's production of her miniseries *Sins*.
(Photo by Eddie Sanderson)

Steve and I waltzing at our beach house, 1997. Part of a photo shoot for *House & Garden*.
(Photo by Tim Street-Porter)

Below, left to right: My niece Mallory Lewis Tarcher, Jeremy, and my late sister-in-law Shari Lewis Tarcher.
(Courtesy of People *magazine)*

A view of the Bel Air house we bought after we returned from Paris. Window is that of my office.

Chapter Thirty-two

EVEN AT THE PEAK OF MY ENORMOUS EXCITEMENT AT DISCOVERING this new ability, I was aware that one chapter did not make a book. Would I ever be able to get to the middle of a book, much less finish one? And if I could, amazingly, finish a book, would anybody want to buy it? At least I had no question about getting an agent, complete amateur at fiction that I was. I'd had no trouble finding agents over the years. Although I didn't realize it at the time, this sense of security did wonders to underpin my budding ambition.

I realized immediately that I couldn't work for *Cosmo* and write a novel in my spare time. I phoned Helen Brown and told her that I was about to attempt to write a novel "on spec" and wanted a leave of absence. I trusted her fully not to tell anyone, since, if I fell on my face as I expected I well might, I didn't want anyone else to know about it. She assured me that she'd keep my secret and so she did.

For a week I wrote about five hours a day, constantly interrupted by phone calls, my housekeeper needing instructions, and the boys barging into the guest room for one reason or another. After that week I made a large sign and Scotch-taped it to the door. It said, "Do not come in to say hello. Do not tell me you're home. DO NOT ASK WHAT'S FOR DINNER. Do not disturb me unless the house is on fire!"

Amazingly, it worked. I was free to write steadily from ten in the morning, by which time I'd organized the house, with time off for a quick lunch, until it was time to drive off to Dr. S. or Ron's late in the afternoon. I managed to produce about two thousand words a day or ten thousand words a week, and in six months the first draft of the book was finished. It was the most astonishing experience of my life to discover that I could write fiction. As my characters and their lives developed, I fell in love with them and with the process through which I created them, a process I tried not to probe or question, since I was afraid that if I did, it might disappear.

Beginner though I was, I discovered that I possessed a built-in story-telling kind of mind and I had particular ease and success in writing dialogue. I'd say the lines out loud until they sounded like real people talking. At times, writing was like crushing rocks with a toothpick, but most of the time, I was blissfully happy during my solitary hours in the guest room, alone with my characters. In more than twenty years of writing, this joy has never diminished, although after *Scruples* there was never again the sheer freedom of writing without a guaranteed audience, writing purely for myself.

Every Monday it was absolute hell to get started. I still hadn't realized that letting the story grow cold over the weekend is a dreadful way to write, since a story doesn't want to stop because it's Saturday or Sunday. I'd told my analyst that I was planning to write a novel but I didn't discuss it with him . . . it wasn't the sort of problem I talked about in analysis, since I didn't need his help or advice with it.

For several years I'd been doing transcendental meditation, or TM, twice a day after I'd taken the standard course at the local center. I loved the calm it gave me, like taking out my brain and dipping it in a bath of clean, warm milk. I taught Tony how to meditate and he used to come home from high school, meditate, and fall asleep until dinner (a year during which he grew a foot taller, so that now both my sons were about six feet three inches tall). Now I found that whenever I tried to meditate, new dialogue would fill my head and no matter how I tried to bring my mind back to the mantra, it didn't work. So I gave up TM for my growing obsession with my novel. My characters had become living, breathing people, and these particular first creations remain just as real to me today.

Whenever I completed enough new chapters to show Steve, he'd read them while I hid away in another room, not daring to look at his face. He'd call me when he was finished, and I'd creep out as slowly as possible and listen to what he had to say, teeth clenched, fists in balls. There has never been any editor as good as my husband and *Scruples* would never have been written without him, but new pages of a novel are so tender and personal that letting someone see them with a critical eye is a very special kind of mental agony.

When I hadn't drawn as much drama out of a scene as I could, he told me; when a scene was working, he told me; and when I didn't know what more to write in a scene, he very often pointed out the obvious: the scene was over. He was almost always right, and above all he was totally honest. He would never say anything was acceptable just to make me feel good.

Somehow we made it through the end of that book and through each of the following nine novels. It gets easier all the time, and long ago I learned to welcome his criticism. As a result of having an in-house editor, that essential second pair of eyes most writers must have, I've always sent my publishers a finished manuscript that needs little further editing. From my second novel on, I've always outlined each new novel in advance, but I've never shown any editor work in progress, with the single exception of my second novel, *Princess Daisy*.

I used carbon paper, which drove me wild when I so often put it in upside down. I wrote on an old Smith-Corona portable and I kept my finished pages in the freezer because if the house burned down, the fridge would be the last thing to go up in flames. When Steve and I went on a vacation to Ventana, in Big Sur, I took the whole thing with me and then spent each night worrying that someone would steal it out of the car. Somehow I never thought of putting it under my bed in the hotel. Also the project was so new, so homemade, that neither Steve nor I ever had the obviously sensible thought of buying photocopy machine, the first thing I purchased after the book was sold.

The first draft of this novel, which was published at 474 pages, took six months. In another three months I'd rewritten it and had it professionally typed. I took it to Pip's Instant Press, a forerunner of Kinko's, to be duplicated, and their machine broke down in the middle of the job, causing me a sleepless night before they finished it. I had accomplished a miracle on the way to Pip's. Only one door of our three-door garage would open and I managed, in a half hour, to completely turn my car around *inside* the garage, back two inches, forward two inches, turning the wheel with all my strength, until I could drive out the open door, such was my desire to get that book duplicated. I could probably have driven a freeway to get to Pip's!

When I had a finished novel, now called *Scruples*, I phoned David Brown. His response was immediately delighted. "Judy, how wonderful! I'm so thrilled for you! Doesn't it feel terrific to finish a book?" I admitted it did, trying to hide how I was taken aback at his enthusiasm for this unread, untested piece of work. I asked his advice about an agent. He first recommended Irving Lazar, but Irving was famous for not returning phone calls and the last thing I wanted was a busy, famous agent who'd keep me waiting to hear from him. I told David I wanted a new eager agent to whom I'd be important, not one who had hundreds of established clients.

"What about Mort Janklow?" David suggested. "I hear he's just started to represent authors." I told him I knew Mort and his wife, Linda, casually from New York. That evening Steve contacted Mort by phone and told him we'd be sending him a first novel, which he said he'd be delighted to read. The next day I finished packing the manuscript of *Scruples* in three boxes of typing paper. It made a lumpy package, so I added a Beverly Hills phone book to turn it into a neat rectangle, and sent it off.

Mort got *Scruples* on a Thursday, read it over the weekend, and called Monday morning to say that he was eager to represent me. His first attempt at selling *Scruples* was to send it to Michael Korda, at Simon & Schuster. After a while, Michael wrote back rejecting the book.

Mort read me the rejection letter, the first and last one I ever received in my career as a novelist. According to Michael, *Scruples* had "too much plot and too many characters." I was deeply upset. What was the raw material of a novel but plot and characters? I could add them but I could never take them out. The salt was already in the soup.

I was so uncertain, when I heard Korda's criticism, about what the future would bring that I called Helen Brown and asked for another assignment, planning to go back to magazines if no one wanted my novel. She gave me the job of writing about where the "beautiful people" work out in Beverly Hills and I bought a new leotard and made appointments at a number of gyms.

Before ten more days had passed, Mort sent the book, along with another one, to a publisher called Crown that has no connection to the bookstore chain. It was a strange but ultimately fortunate choice since Crown had published only a few works of fiction. They were the biggest clearinghouse in publishing for "remainders," other houses' unsold books, and they published art books and a lot of best-selling nonfiction like *How to Avoid Probate*. They were rich but not considered at all important publishers. I had no Crown books in my library.

However, the founder and sole owner of Crown, a picturesque, never-married, horse-playing, poker-playing, crafty elderly man named Nat Wartels, had decided that there might be money in fiction after all these years. Michelle Sidrane, his subsidiary rights editor, had suggested looking for women's fiction and recently he'd asked his executive editor, Larry Freundlich, to hunt around for some. When Larry received the two books from Janklow, he gave *Scruples* to his assistant, Drew Hart, to read. Drew was enchanted by the book and gave it to Michelle Sidrane, who also loved it. Finally Larry himself took it home to read. This was certainly the long way around to the only person entitled to make an offer.

By the time my agent next called me, over the Memorial Day weekend of 1977, he'd obtained a fifty-thousand-dollar advance from Crown. This was then a very large sum of money for a first book by an unknown novelist. It would still be considered a major advance today under the same circumstances.

Learning that my novel was actually going to be published was the most exciting moment of my life. When you're pregnant, you expect to have a baby. When you get engaged, you've had some preparation for the event, and when you get married, you know you're going to have a husband. But when you write a first novel, it's an act of blind hope and you don't know at all, no, never, not for a second, if you're going to get a publisher.

When I went to Dr. S. on that day of highest exaltation and told him about it, including the amount of the advance, he said he wasn't surprised because I'd said I was going to do it, and it was typical of me to follow through on what I'd decided to accomplish. I was very pleased at his reaction. But as I was leaving his office, he said, almost absently, "Amazing, isn't it, did you know that Herman Melville only got about six dollars and fourteen cents' advance for *Moby Dick*?"

As I drove home, my fury mounted. The hostility of his remark was too obvious to be overlooked. At this high point in my life, he'd deflated me completely by reminding me that a work of genius had been bought for so little, while my little novel had brought so much. The next time I saw him I sat down in the chair in front of his desk and said that we had a problem and unless he could come to grips with it, my analysis with him would not go on. I repeated his remark and told him how I felt about it. I added that since I knew what I paid him and could easily guess at the number of hours he worked a week, I knew what percentage my advance represented of his yearly income. He thought for a minute and then agreed that his remark must indeed have been an unfortunate reaction to my unexpected good fortune.

I had to admit that even shrinks have their human moments after all, and I resumed my analysis. Little did I suspect that Dr. S. would *never* be able to get over the money I'd made, and the much more money I was to make, and it totally tainted most of the eight years— yes, EIGHT YEARS—I spent with him. Why he didn't consult his own training analyst about this classic case of countertransference, which must normally be done in such a situation, is tragically mysterious, since he couldn't have helped but realize there was something very wrong in his continuing reaction to my good fortune.

But it wasn't just the money that bothered him. As time went by, and I most stupidly stayed in analysis with him while I wrote *Princess Daisy* and *Mistral's Daughter,* he never gave me any credit for having the ability to write successful commercial novels, but clung to the point of view that "I could do better work if I only tried." By better he meant more "literary," the kind of sensitive, serious, poetic "high" fiction that I didn't have the talent or desire to write.

He was, as I now finally realize, a version of my mother. "The trouble with you, Judy, is," Dr. S. was saying, in effect, "that you insist on making money by writing things that millions of ordinary people like to read, when you could be writing for the select few who really appreciate fine literature." I know this now, damn it to hell! Would I had known it twenty years ago. First, I had Rubenstein, an analyst like my father, and then Dr. S., one like my mother. How lucky can a girl get?

However, my understanding of this doctor and what he was saying was all in the future. Now I decided to go to New York to meet the unquestionably great human beings who'd had the brilliance to become my publishers. Sylvia Wallace, Irving's wife, gave me invaluable advice in one word: *Limo*. "Remember, you travel only by limo," she said, in the voice of experience.

I stayed at the Plaza and on the day I was to go downtown to the Crown offices I ordered a limo from the Plaza garage. I didn't specify what kind of limo, so they sent me the longest, most expensive one they had for rent, a gleaming dark-blue limo of truly embarrassing dimensions. I met Larry Freundlich, a convivial type, whose only suggestion was that I drop an entire, very dramatic section of the book, because Billy Winthrop was too nice a girl "to act like that." He thought it was immensely important that I tell everyone I was forty-six rather than my real age because by the time the book was published, I'd be fifty and "women wouldn't relate to a writer of fifty."

I agreed, reluctantly, but he seemed convinced of what he was telling me and I was such a novice that I'd have agreed to almost anything. Soon I asked to meet Nat Wartels. My brother had told me that Nat was a legend in the business, a one-man band who had seven desks in his office, each piled many feet high in papers, every one of which he could find in an instant. Not a single check was ever issued from Crown that Nat didn't sign.

Nat and I got on from the first. I told him what I'd heard about his filing system and he proved to me that it was true. Somehow the name of Herb Mayes came up, and it turned out that they'd been friends forever. When I explained my connection with Herb, I became instant family. Nat introduced me to Bruce Harris, Crown's director of promotion, and I asked him if I'd be going on a book tour. He answered, "Oh no, you'd hate it. It's absolute hell. You'd get to Cleveland and be bumped off every television show because Danny Kaye's personal co-pilot is in town." I was a little disappointed but I accepted what Bruce told me, never realizing that it was spending the money necessary for a book tour that kept him from planning one.

Larry and I went downstairs to leave for lunch. Larry waved for a taxi. "No, don't bother, my husband doesn't trust New York taxi drivers. He insists on a limo," I explained matter-of-factly, as my obscene limo swooped up, stopped, and the driver rushed out to open the door. Larry's face turned red and then white. We had lunch at Le Cirque and I offered to drive Larry back to the office but he insisted on taking a taxi. As soon as he'd disappeared I told the driver to get back to the Plaza as quickly as humanly possible. I couldn't wait to get rid of that car that was costing an indecent hourly rate, every penny of which was well spent. An indelible and important impression had been made on Crown, thanks to Sylvia's advice.

I spent a week in New York at this time and every day I called Sue Kaufman Barondess, trying to get in touch with her after the day's business was over. She and I had never stopped phoning each other and I often wrote to her. Only a few years earlier she'd written her last novel, *Falling Bodies,* which began with a dog falling out of an apartment to a New York pavement, where it was dreadfully smashed. I'd written her about the novel, which had many excellent qualities, and she'd replied in one of the few letters I ever received from her.

Suffice it to say, baby, it has been a very rough couple of months—almost, like Emma's, a Rough Year. The critical reception to *Falling Bodies*—with that maniacal review in the *Sunday Times*—did not help. I'm terribly happy that you liked it. So many people did, do, and I, undaunted, am glad that I wrote it. Although you won't catch me writing about the American family scene soon again, I felt I said something that hasn't been said—and have a raft of letters from women to prove it. The sad thing is that the Women's Lib movement has created a backlash of sorts—and the subject of the Unhappy Middle-Class Woman is almost taboo . . . Be thankful that you're not a fiction writer, baby—I know of five first-rate women novelists who say the last thing they want to do is start a novel at this point.

I kept calling Sue, but for three days I could only reach Jerry, who told me that Sue was busy and would call me back. One day he made a foolish mistake, saying that I'd just missed Sue because she'd flown to L.A. while I was in New York. I knew Sue would no more set foot on a plane than she'd cuddle a rattlesnake.

The next morning, I called her the moment I woke and finally reached her. We talked for ages, as easily as if I'd never moved to California, laughing as much as if we were still double-dating at Harvard, but Sue couldn't bring herself to see me in person no matter what time of the day I proposed, pleading the needs of her own work. I was used to this since she never went out when she was working, and she hadn't even been able to make time for my fortieth-birthday-party lunch. We spoke every day for at least an hour until it was time for me to fly home, each time enjoying easy, happy, long, intimate conversations, without a hint of trouble. When I got back to L.A., the first thing Steve had to tell me was that Sue had killed herself the night before, jumping out of a window from her eighteenth-floor apartment.

What I hadn't known, and what Jerry was trying to keep me from knowing, was that Sue had been institutionalized on and off for depression during the past years, and, on the day after she killed herself, she was due to go back to another institution, and she would rather die than endure that prospect. I'd always known that I'd never really understood Sue, but the shock of her suicide was devastating. I wrote Jerry, of course, saying what I could, but I never heard from him again, nor did any other friends of Sue's, of whom there had been many who adored her as I did.

WITHIN A FEW weeks, I got the news that Larry Freundlich had given Howard Kaminsky, at Warner Books, the manuscript of *Scruples* and Warner had made a preemptive bid to buy the paperback rights for half a million dollars. Was I willing to sell it for that or did I want Crown to look further? "Take it!" I screamed, disbelievingly, "before it goes away."

Suddenly Bruce Harris was on the phone. Crown, now reimbursed for their $50,000 advance and their half of an additional $450,000 profit in their pocket, wanted me to go on a fifteen-city book tour, starting on March 15 in Cleveland, with a book-and-author lunch at which I'd speak. "But you said I'd get to Cleveland and be bumped . . ." "Nah, I never said that," he insisted jokingly. An auction took place for the English rights, fifteen publishers got into the act, and the book was sold for a British record price for a first novel.

I spent many sleepless nights with rockets of speculation bursting in my head, but from Memorial Day, all through the winter of 1977–78 that followed, it *never* seemed to me that until after the book was published, on March 9, 1978, there was any guarantee at all that anyone would want to read it. I have a strong tendency not to count my chickens until they're almost too old for the pot, and never had that tendency been more in force than during the ten months from the sale to the pub date.

One day at lunch I got a surprise phone call from a stranger, the head of Warner's television, Alan Shayne, asking for an option on *Scruples* for fifty thousand dollars. Here I needed no advice. I knew at least that much about show business. "If the book's a failure, you won't produce it, and if it's a success, you'll pay a lot more than that.

No option, but thanks anyway." Steve had already taken himself out of the running for a miniseries production, saying that it would look like nepotism and that I'd earned the right to stand alone and unencumbered.

That January we spent two weeks in France and England for my fiftieth birthday, our first nonbusiness vacation in many years. In London we gave a party for all our friends, starting in our suite at Claridge's with drinks and hors d'oeuvres before a big, well-burning fire, and ending with a dinner at The White Elephant. Uncharacteristically, because usually I have no problem about my age, I didn't want to say it was my birthday—suddenly fifty seemed like too big a number to admit to—but once we got back to the hotel I felt depressed and finally had to realize that I was sorry I'd kept it a secret. You should never celebrate a landmark birthday and not, at the very least, admit it's a birthday. No need to say which one. Real friends won't ask.

In Paris, Steve went around like a lost soul trying to find out what the Super Bowl score had been but no one even understood his question. Finally, I thought of going to the imposing, dignified Ritz and seeing if they had a clue. "They're supposed to be able to do everything for their clients," I said. "But we're not clients." "Let's ask anyway." The three concierges who stand behind the front desk of the Ritz, serious, busy, and supremely conscious of their importance, were the first people we found in Paris who knew what the Super Bowl was. One of them kindly phoned the *International Herald Tribune* to find out the score, putting Steve out of his misery. I thought it was a good omen. "Let's stay here from now on, when we're in Paris," I suggested. And so we did.

We'd found our Parisian hotel after years of looking for one. During the three years we lived in Paris in the mid-eighties, I had a charge account at the Ritz Bar, I could cash personal checks at the front desk, I knew where to find its excessively well-concealed ladies' room, and on one memorable day, a young manager I knew asked me if I wanted to get a look at the new owner of the Ritz, the Sultan of Brunei. I followed him excitedly to one of the rooms off the lobby where a group of workmen were hovering around a hole in the floor. "Where's the sultan?" I asked. "That one," he said, pointing to a small man in jeans lifting a plank. "That one?" I asked in disbelief. "Yes, the guy wearing the T-shirt that says 'Galeries Lafayette' on it." The Galeries Lafayette is a huge, middle-level store, rather like Macy's.

Today Bill Gates is ten times richer than the sultan, who was then by far the richest man in the world, but neither of them will ever appear on a best-dressed list.

Chapter Thirty-three

WHILE I WAS COPING WITH THE EVER-GROWING AND EVER MORE mixed-up and elaborate preparations for the *Scruples* book tour, I had an idea for another book. I'd been looking for inspiration ever since *Scruples* had been bought, because I had a healthy dread of becoming a one-book author. I'd done it once, but could I do it twice? The thought tormented me.

In the middle of the night, sometime in the winter of 1978, I woke up and a line came into my head. "She was born Princess Marguerite Alexandrovna Valensky, but everyone always called her Daisy." With hair standing up on the nape of my neck, I scribbled it down on a scrap of paper and taped it to Steve's bathroom mirror, adding, "What do you think?"

I outlined the book in broad strokes and on January 24, 1978, almost two months before *Scruples* would be published and the book tour was scheduled to start, I signed a contract with Crown to write *Princess Daisy* by January 1, 1980, for an advance of four hundred thousand dollars for the hardcover rights.

It had been a once-in-a-lifetime experience to write my first novel on spec, in freedom and privacy, with courage and hope but without clear expectations, without an advance, without an agent or publishers or PR people breathing down my neck.

Looking back now, after ten novels, the chief joy of my career has never been, as so many people say "to have written," but rather the process of writing itself. To settle down in the morning in front of my computer, with an entire day of uninterrupted work ahead of me, to turn on my machine knowing what I hope to achieve in the scene I'm about to write, is as richly satisfying a state as I've ever experienced in a lifetime. It doesn't happen every day; the plot has to be fairly advanced and the characters well formed before this rare and precious condition can be reached, and it's often not repeated for a week or two while more pedestrian labor takes place. But oh, there is nothing better than those special hours in which imagination and craftmanship fly hand in hand and at the end of what seems like no time at all but is really at least six hours, I reread what I've written and say to myself, "I think I've got it right."

However, after a book is completed, goes through the publication process, and finally lands in the bookstores, there is no delicious basking in achievement as there is at the end of a good day's work, but rather an anxious wait to see how the novel will do during its day in the sun. The tyranny of the *New York Times* best-seller list is inescapable. No matter how hard I try to be strong enough to armor myself against it, the numbers game has always been present, from the day *Scruples* first landed on the list.

Except for *Scruples,* when a novel has become number one on the list, as Charlotte Brontë wrote, "Life is so constructed, that the event does not, cannot, will not, match the expectation." Yes, of course there is the thrill of reaching the peak, but that thrill carries with it the built-in question: how long will it stay at this volume of sales? Will it still be outselling every other book on the list next week? And the week after? Best-selling novelists are as competitive as tennis champs or baseball pitchers. There's always another new player coming up to take away your Wimbledon crown, and if you've pitched a no-hitter on Monday, can you possibly do it again on Tuesday? I can't imagine that a single novelist who writes for the large audience can be genuinely immune to this really terrible pressure, which leaches out so much of the pleasure of publication.

It's only after each new novel has run its course, and the paperback as well, that I've been able to think of each book with some measure of relaxed contentment in having created it. And even then, all too often, if I yield to the temptation to reread a page of it before at least two years have passed, I see phrases or whole paragraphs I'd give anything to be able to polish one more time! My tenacious obsessive-compulsive need to be perfect carries over into my work, but no matter how clearly I realize the truth and futility of this, I can't make it disappear.

Never, not once, as I wrote novel after novel, did I dare to think, "The last books did well, so this new one certainly will too." I regret bitterly that I never achieved that kind of calm confidence in my own powers, never reveled freely and unthinkingly for more than a minute or two in being at the top of my profession for well over a decade. The psychic means to feel such a healthy, optimistic, and enviable state simply weren't in my nature—on the contrary—and by now I've learned to accept that fact. I can, at least, look at my two-foot-tall pile of ten novels and feel a sense of absolute accomplishment, a feeling at once possessive, loving, and fairly well satisfied, particularly at the fact that the translations into so many dozens of languages—forty-seven at last count—means that I've communicated with millions of people I'll never know all over the globe . . . yet, in a real way, they know me.

Anyone who's read several or all of my novels knows the way I think and feel about just about everything that's important to me.

Fortunately, when the actual task of writing was going badly, I was able quickly to learn from experience and I could say to myself, "This hell has happened before, it's only to be expected, and even if today's work is terrible, tomorrow's will be better, and if not tomorrow, the next day."

As I work now on PR for my tenth novel, *The Jewels of Tessa Kent,* which will be published two months from now, before Christmas of 1998, I'm stealing every available minute to write this memoir, and I have no certainty that it will find a publisher. I most certainly hope it will, but the luxury of writing without self-censorship, without an eye to the reception of the public, which I haven't enjoyed since writing *Scruples,* is immense.

If I were sure this book would never be published, I'd still write it, just for the opportunity it has given me to look back at my life and learn things about myself. I wasn't fully aware of the events of my life until I wrote them down in chronological order. I've never been so alert, in historical perspective, to the way in which the people I've known and the experiences I've had led me along, under the force of influences I didn't understand at the time. No amount of analysis ever gave me the broad overview that allowed me to comprehend how my parents, the climate of my early life, my school days, my siblings, and my experiences with Joe the midshipman affected every aspect of my personality, including the way in which I've used fiction to work through these events. If one purpose of psychoanalysis is to live the "examined" life, writing an honest memoir can be far more of a self-examination. And a whole hell of a lot cheaper.

I conceived the idea of writing *Sex and Shopping* while I was re-membering, late at night, a party at which I'd met Jackie Sussan. The party took place in 1971, soon after we'd moved to California, and since Steve, as so often, was away, Bill and Ann Dozier took me to Joyce Haber's by myself. Joyce was then riding high with the success of her best-selling novel *The Users,* and the party was for the birthday of her then-husband, television producer Doug Cramer.

Ann and I approached the doors of Joyce's beach house, where two very attractive men were hanging about, looking at us with interest. We couldn't rudely pass by without introducing ourselves to them, so Ann extended a hand to one of them and I to the other, telling them our names. Our hands were rejected, without even a grunt of response. Ann and I looked at each other and shrugged with questioning looks. What kind of guests were these? We went on in and eventually, through the crowd, we spied Henry Kissinger and his date, the impossibly pretty Jill St. John. Ann and I had just tried to shake hands with Kissinger's Secret Service men. "Do you suppose they thought we had poison darts in our palms?" I asked Ann, who was a little taller than me but certainly just as unthreatening-looking.

As the party progressed, a very Hollywood party, full of celebrities, since Joyce wrote a gossip column, I noticed a tall, good-looking, dark-haired woman dressed amusingly in a T-shirt and a genuine pair of workingman's overalls. Our eyes met and I realized she was Jackie Sussan. Even I, with my taste for the classics, had read her work. Her glance was so extraordinarily friendly and personal that although we were never introduced in that mob, I felt somehow that we'd made some sort of definite contact. I've never forgotten the warmth she projected, and I was sad when she died almost three years later. No, I most certainly do not think she recognized a future writer in me, I don't think that she was trying to say anything with her interested look—that was just Jackie Sussan behaving normally.

But something about that memory made me realize that I'd had a life in which I'd rubbed elbows with more than my fair share of interesting people. A few weeks after I'd remembered a party that had taken place twenty-seven years earlier, a magazine asked me to write six hundred words about coming of age sexually in the 1940s. That request made me realize that it would be impossible to tell the truth about the forties in six hundred words, or six thousand. This, together with the old memory of Jackie Sussan, somehow jelled, in a split second, into the idea of writing this book.

One of the most delicious things about writing an autobiography is that you can rustle around in your life and find out how something that happened when you were six years old connects with something that took place sixty years later, and in a few words, skip from here to there . . . in a way you can never do in a novel.

So, to return to the publication of *Scruples*, Crown, with so much excitement going on, determined to publish the biggest first printing of any first novel in history. They researched it and came up with the figure of 106,000 copies. They created one of the great book jackets of all time and sent out a stunningly designed promotional announcement, received by all booksellers, that aroused a lot of attention.

For my part, I decided that I wanted a jacket photograph that would indicate to browsing future readers that this particular unknown author possessed a genuine background from which to write of the world of fashion. I could only do this through the choice of the photographer. By appealing to Helen Brown, I was granted the immense favor of an appointment with Francesco Scavullo, then at the height of his fame.

Crown would pay only one thousand dollars of the four thousand Scavullo charged. Nat Wartels was tight with a buck in spite of the hefty profit I'd just made for him, but I've always believed in investing in myself if someone else won't. I paid the rest of Scavullo's fee and flew to New York. Since the photographer had never heard of me, I was given a dauntingly cold welcome. A second-string makeup artist messed me about until I could hardly endure it, someone else rumpled his fingers through my hair, and I was told to wear the plain white blouse I'd arrived in, rather than any of the other clothes I'd brought.

After four hours of waiting, Scavullo told me to sit on the icy concrete floor of his studio, wearing only the blouse and a half-slip, and quickly, and most unsympathetically, he shot a mere three, or possibly four, rolls of film. Whenever I smiled he didn't shoot, so I kept my mouth closed and left, feeling abused, as indeed I had been.

He sent me only six contacts to choose from, a number so ridiculously tiny that no one but Scavullo could have been so arbitrary. Desperate and terribly disappointed, I picked the least bad, because there was no time left to go to another photographer. That black-and-white picture is still one of the best, and certainly the most honest, ever taken of me. In later years Scavullo fawned all over me when he was shooting me for *Harper's Bazaar,* and the photo was one of the worst anyone has ever taken of me. This is a story without a moral.

In January 1978, two months before pub date, I started keeping an informal journal for myself—no one, not even Steve, has ever read it—noting how I was feeling about what was going on. I always wrote at night, when I was too anxious or angry to sleep, so the journal isn't an accurate record of how I felt under normal circumstances. However, it's invaluable as the only record I have of those days full of a new-found ambition and determination. In one of the first entries I find these lines: "It's all out there but it isn't there *yet.* And I can't build castles on sand. I want to see those one hundred six thousand copies walking out of the bookstores and a second printing and on and on . . . but no one really knows yet. Most nervous making—yet I don't feel *too* worried."

I needed that spirit in the months to come, which would be emotionally and physically the roughest of my life. I was often driven to fury by Crown's lack of knowledge of how to publicize fiction. There were an incredible number of demands being made on me by Bruce Harris and Nancy Kahane, head of Crown's PR department, who would call almost daily with some new announcement, such as the news that she was going to "shoot me out" to speak at a lunch in Seattle, after which the Crown salesman would drive me to Portland.

A typical New Yorker, she had no idea that the two cities were at least a six-hour drive apart. I insisted on a plane.

Nancy had even booked a day of PR for me in New York on St. Patrick's Day, the one day you can't get even cross Fifth Avenue because of the daylong parade, much less get around with the rapidity PR demands. Nancy, who would later become a wonderful pal and a very fine PR person, had at this point far less of a clue than I did. And the fact that she was a former nun, a Sister of Charity no less, made her lapse about St. Patrick, for the love of God, even more inexcusable! Once I heard that, I realized fully that no one back at my publisher's had the right kind of experience. Neither did I, but at least I was sensible and could spot certain obvious limitations on their plans. Crown had never, *ever* planned a tour for a novelist before, and it was only too clear that they were learning on the job, at my expense.

I wrote, on January 27: "I realize fully, for the first time, that I must use my own judgment in every detail because they don't know shit. This is like being, at one and the same time, a Chinese Empress, much venerated, and a Chinese slave, to be used and used until she drops dead, uncomplainingly. Well they picked the wrong girl."

I'm astonished today that weeks before the book tour even started, I was able to see so clearly and accurately into a future that was altogether outside of my experience.

Meanwhile, I was having a hard time with Dr. S. I'd given him an advance copy of *Scruples* and as I told him about my struggles with some of Crown's most unrealistic and absurd plans, he said in a severe tone, "They can tell from just reading the book, without seeing you, that they can put any amount of pressure on you because of your own desire to become rich and famous, which can be read between the lines." "So, what's wrong with that?" I naturally *failed* to ask. However, I knew from his voice that "rich and famous" equaled "disgusting sellout." In addition, he told me that he felt that the character of Spider Elliott, my marvelously masculine hero, "was really afraid of women."

I'd written that Spider made insecure fashion models feel

cuddly, kissable, cosseted, hugable, teasable, pinchable, altogether adorable. He liked them all—the lanky ones from Texas who still had retainers on their teeth, which they religiously whipped on between jobs; the tough ones who loved to talk dirty even though it shocked no one but themselves; the ones who constantly lost their contact lenses in thick carpets; the sad ones of twenty-four who looked upon their twenty-fifth birthday as the end of the world; the lonely ones who had been discovered in Europe long before they were really old enough to leave their homes; he even liked the ones who didn't eat all day, ruining their nerves, and then expected him to buy them the leanest steaks for dinner. Quality protein for starving women was Spider's biggest expense. . . . To Spider, appetite was a sure sign of the female principle.

Reader, does this sound like a man afraid of women?

Dr. S. also told me that in a novel set in the world of retailing, the "clothes got in the way of the story." He added that since his idea of a good read was Kafka, *Scruples* really "wasn't his kind of book." What a total jerk, as we used to say in college. I certainly hadn't written my novel with him in mind as a potential reader.

I should have left that particular doctor on the spot, but I was too unsure of myself and far too vulnerable about my abilities. I didn't need a shrink who was an expert on commercial fiction, but I shouldn't have been seeing one who was so censorious, negative, and prejudiced that he diminished my shaky self-confidence. He certainly took much of the joy of my success away from me. I can only look back and assume that in part I must have stayed with him because I was incapable of adding to my inner turmoil at a time when my life was becoming so complicated and full of question marks.

During the first years of my career I should have—yes, "should have" again—drawn back, thought through his attitude, and left him. However, the process of transference had taken place and I projected my emotions on my analyst so that his opinions became the judgmental voice of my mother and I regressed to a childlike willingness to listen to him. Thank God I didn't allow his disdain to stop me from writing! I even brought him a copy of each of my first three novels, hoping for a crumb of approval that I never received. I would have been far better served by a Freudian, no matter how silent.

Meanwhile, back in real life, Steve had a terrible head cold, and our housekeeper was home, sick herself. On one dark night in February I found myself driving in the pouring rain to our local deli, Nate 'n' Al's, to buy chicken soup for Steve. I was feeling flu-ish myself but the next day Crown had arranged a dinner for me, without Steve, upstairs in a private room at the Bistro, then L.A.'s top restaurant, with twenty-six important local booksellers, and I was determined to be there. Before fatherly Ernie Greenspan, the local rep, came to take me to the Bistro, I sat, all dressed up, in the television room with Steve, frozen into immobility by the idea of the dinner. It was almost worse than I'd felt before our wedding, but I didn't dare have even a single drink.

The dinner was surrealistic and utterly dreamlike. Every last one of these highly professional booksellers was wildly encouraging, including the all-important Larry Todd of Hunter's, the best-known bookseller in Beverly Hills. Jim Zeidman, manager of the local Doubleday's, even insisted that the book would become a number-one best-seller, "because I can always tell and I'm never wrong." Another bookseller bet me five dollars that I'd get to the number-one spot on the *New York Times* list.

I wrote in my journal, "I still can't believe my calm last night at the party. It was as if I'd done this dozens of times before and I think that my ease is due to the fact that I can't envision the attention and praise I'm getting as being really directed at *me*—so I can move through it without being flustered. I don't believe in the success everyone predicts so I still haven't made that inner *change*. Maybe being a 'celeb,' as Tony calls it, isn't that different from real life?"

The weather got worse, we had water leaking steadily into our living room, roads were closed everywhere, and at one point, walking again from Nate 'n' Al's carrying a heavy shopping bag (chicken in the pot) to the parking lot, I didn't think I'd make it. The hideous sensory memory of that walk in the dark, in the storm, has never left me. I didn't know enough yet for it to occurr to me to hire a taxi to go pick up the food. I didn't know that my health was the most important thing for me to protect, no matter what, and I kept going as if I'd been brought up on Mary Baker Eddy.

There had still been no national PR. Book publicity is only useful once the book is available in the stores, unless it's a major publishing event and gets advance notice. Unless a book is eagerly anticipated, the distribution throughout the country is sporadic. After *Scruples* was published there would be a mass "lay down" of my future novels planned for the same day nationwide, but not so then. Nevertheless, our local bookstores had been promised that they'd all get their books on the same day.

However, Hunter's bookstore on Rodeo received fifty books early, because Larry Todd had asked for them air express. All unknowing, I went to Ron's studio only to have Don Henley, of the Eagles, sit on a mat next to me and tell me that he'd just bought a copy. I called Crown in alarm and they promised to send a salesman to buy the books back, but Larry Todd refused to give them up. A day later they were sold out.

Another small Chicago suburban store got thirty-seven copies in a blizzard, sold out in a day, and ordered five hundred more and soon Jim Zeidman had half-paved his window with *Scruples*, fitting it in between piles of Sidney Sheldon and Joseph Wambaugh. Every phone call from Crown was filled with semi-hysteria as they realized that the jungle drums of word-of-mouth had begun beating for my book.

However, all this building excitement was dampened not just by the weather but by the hurt of a total lack of any response from my mother, who had had a copy of *Scruples* for at least ten days and was a lightning-fast reader. She called Mimi and told her that she was very relieved that a friend of hers had read it and gone out to buy a copy for another friend, but I heard nothing. When she finally called, after two weeks, she was incapable of being happy for me. She explained her silence by saying that it was a "difficult book" for a mother to read because she kept seeing my "dear little face over Mrs. Glentz's shoulder," as the nurse was putting me to bed. "How old was I then?" "Nine months old." "But I'm fifty now," I answered, tightly, thinking in the back of my mind that at nine months it would have been nice to have been put to bed by my mother. A few weeks later she called to say that she'd decided that *Scruples* wasn't "really pornography but sociology." I'd rather hoped it was fiction.

By February 16 the weather suddenly changed into spring, *Scruples* was being reported as number twelve on the Dalton-Pickwick list, then considered the fastest in the country, and it was number ten in the Sunday *Los Angeles Times*. It had been in general distribution for only a week and I was awake in bed for an entire night with every kind of firecracker going off in my head. "Is this really it?" I wrote. "Is this being on the map, the big future, all those things I've always lusted after but thought I could never achieve? And, if so, so what?? Nothing will change in some ways, everything in others, and I don't know yet, which."

By this time I'd done a number of local interviews and, until I got used to it, I found that talking so much about myself, and answering the same questions so many times, left me with a feeling of real disgust, like a foul taste in my mouth. But, on the other hand, I could, with a third ear, listen to myself doing these interviews with complete ease, sounding relaxed and confident. Warner Brothers Television, now that they saw success coming, bought the miniseries rights for $350,000. With Barry Bostwick as Spider and Lindsay Wagner as Billy, it became the most popular miniseries of 1979 and is still being shown on cable today. The dramatic section of the book that Larry Freundlich had asked me to cut was the centerpiece of the miniseries. The television people had written the script from the original manuscript, not from the printed book. Absolutely no one noticed this mistake but Steve and me when we watched the miniseries on television.

In the middle of the night of our twenty-fourth wedding anniversary, February 19, 1978, I wrote,

> Steve is the most important person to me in so many ways that it's almost terrifying. I realize it so much more fully than ever in

all these years because we have both changed so much—*toward* each other—become so much more honest, trusting, vulnerable, dependent, needy, giving, utterly in agreement about all the most important priorities in life, that no one could ever be one tenth of what he is to me and I to him. He's so tender, so considerate, and so patient with my obsession with the book, with my anxiety attacks, one of which I'm having now, about maintaining my good health during these next few months. Oh, God, if only I could be sure of that I can handle everything else! How will I hold up on tour without Steve to counsel me, and yet I know I can do it because I HAVE TO. "New best-selling author on tour"—doesn't that sound wonderful? I think it's going to be the literary equivalent of war!

Herbert Mitgang, who wrote the "Behind the Best-Sellers" column for *The New York Times,* called for a forty-minute interview. I told him I was forty-six, thereby inserting a lie into the Paper of Record. He tried to trap me with questions like "How do you compare yourself to Colette?" I answered that "for a dose of instant humility I read a page of Colette," but something told me that the friendly local interviews would soon be a thing of the past. I was right. His piece was as nasty as possible, one big sneer, full of sexual remarks, and it made me promise myself not to do any more phone interviews, a resolution that I didn't realize at the time is impossible to keep.

My lie about my age came back to haunt me. Wherever I went on my book tour, interviewers referred to me as forty-six and members of the Wellesley class of 1948 immediately wrote to their local papers, saying that I sure as hell hadn't been sixteen when I graduated with them. By the end of the book tour, there had been enough of this mail to make a half page in the "Intelligencer" section of *New York* magazine, the best-read section of the magazine, which held me up to deserved ridicule. I wrote to the *Wellesley Magazine* correspondent for my class that I wanted to thank all those who had felt the need to rat me out and I was henceforth rejoining the class of 1948.

One night I had an enchanting dream of John Mack Carter offering me a job at seventy thousand dollars a year and having to refuse because I couldn't work for so little. Whether it was John or Herbert Mayes I was dreaming about, even my subconscious was getting the idea that I was making money. At a party at Fred Hayman's, I met John Dean (yes, the Watergate John Dean), who'd toured with his book for almost a year. He told me I wouldn't have any trouble on television because of my personality, but never, *ever* to look at the camera. He should know, I thought, and filed the useful information away. I became literally blind to cameras. I have not, to this day, so much as seen a camera on a television set, although I assume they're around somewhere.

On March 3, the day of publication ("pub date" is an artificial term, for in reality, books are often on sale long before the designated pub date), I found myself spending up to six frantic hours of the day on the phone to Crown, trying to straighten out the book-tour details, which, impossibly, were getting increasingly complicated and unrealistic. The people at Crown didn't seem able to comprehend that if I had to do three early-morning television shows on three successive days, I'd be getting up at 4:30 A.M. each day to have breakfast, do my makeup, dress, and get to the show, not a possible schedule for someone who could never sleep until after midnight and who'd be jet-lagged to boot. My inability to make them understand this was a source of immense frustration.

During this time I posed for a great number of photos for various publications for articles that were in the works. In a terrible storm I drove out to the San Fernando Valley with Betty Shapian, an efficient blond veteran of the PR wars who was handling my local PR. In some small radio station the interviewer asked me, in the anguished voice of a frustrated writer, "Why you? Why, with all the novels that get published, *why you?*" For once, I didn't have a ready answer.

The next Sunday, *Scruples* was going to be number eleven on the *New York Times* list and number six in the *Los Angeles Times,* and Peter Barsochini, of the *Merv Griffin Show,* then of vast national nightly importance, had come to the house to preinterview me as a possible guest. In my journal I wrote to myself, "I always thought wild success would be the ultimate. I never was imaginative enough to know how tough it would be. What a lousy character I have, where are pluck, guts, sense of fun, adventure?" (That must have been written on a particularly bad night!)

I was booked to do a speech at a Brentano's author lunch in New York and my mother now planned to come with some of her friends, since the *New York Post,* her favorite afternoon paper, had given me an excellent review. She asked me not to use any dirty words in my speech and I assured her that I'd announce "that my mother was in the audience and I'd promised her not to say 'fuck.' " In horror, she said, "Then I won't come!" For once she really made me laugh.

Finally, on March 6, the tide began to turn and instead of resenting the demands and pressures, I'd begun to thrive on them and feel that I was moving ahead with all flags flying, instead of kicking and screaming as I had been. Dr. S. was of the opinion that the reason I was able to be so calm through the publicity and pre–book tour storm was that

I knew it "really didn't *mean* anything." I told him that success, so far, wasn't what I'd thought it would be, but it was a damn sight better than failure. He chose to remain on the side of art for art's sake.

The *Merv Griffin Show* booked me and then, a half hour later, un-booked me. I decided to get my hair done anyway, and pick up a new turquoise silk dress I'd had shortened. When I arrived at Dr. S.'s that afternoon, I found Betty Shapian, arms barring the way, announcing that I couldn't see my shrink, I had to be ready to leave for Merv in two hours. They'd rebooked me. "I have to go up and tell him." "He knows, I went up to his office and told him myself."

I went home and considered my moves. First I took a Miltown, that oldest of tranquilizers that I'd been taking since Dr. Rubenstein told me not to take sleeping pills. Then I tried on the dress to make sure it looked okay, accessorized it, washed my turquoise earrings, did my eyes carefully, and finally took a bath and put the dress back on.

I'd never done a television interview before, but I decided not to wait in the green room and watch the first part of the show, since I was on last, but stay in the dressing room I'd been assigned, turn off the other distracting guests, and go over all the details of the growth of Rodeo Drive I had at my fingertips. When I got out on the stage I was startled to hear the well-organized applause from the audience.

I just looked right into Merv's eyes for twelve minutes, never dropping or raising my gaze, so I wouldn't see a camera, and kept answering questions, feeling no nerves at all. None. Merv was a marvelously attentive listener and so easy to talk to, as smooth as old satin. He did TM every day before the show started, which might well have explained his calm and openness. I was to do his show nineteen more times before, sadly, he decided he'd had enough of it and called it off after twenty-three years.

Merv held up the book himself—every author adored Merv for that—and told people to go out and buy it right away. Most interviewers will, at the best, allow a five-second shot of the book jacket lying on a table. Back in the green room I found Betty Shapian and Nancy Kahane, who'd flown out the day before, high as kites. Liquor was most definitely served in Merv's green room and they'd had a nervous hour in which to consume a whole lot of it. They danced around me like maniacs, screaming, *"You're a natural, a natural!"* I thought they were overacting to the alcohol, but I was, I later realized, indeed a natural for interviews on television. It's not surprising if you love to talk, don't get stage fright, and never see a camera.

I relaxed a little after the show but my emotions remained in a wait-and-see mode. I was too anxious about the future sales of the book to feel anything but firm caution not to expect too much, mixed with the absolute intention to do everything possible to make the book sell. Ambition, an emotion I'd never known before, consumed me, making me calm, resolute, and ready.

When the boys from Crown called the next day they all asked, after congratulating me, "You weren't wearing a bra, were you?" Of course I wasn't. I'd thought the top of my new dress, cut like an oversized blouse, didn't require it, but if they'd noticed, on a small television screen, maybe it did. Maybe.

Chapter Thirty-four

THE PUBLICATION PARTY FRED HAYMAN HAD GENEROUSLY OFFERED to give for me at his boutique, Giorgio's, took place early in March 1978. In 1991 he'd throw another for *Scruples Two*, but the one I remember best is that amazing first one. Fred had gone into retailing after being the banquet manager at the Beverly Hilton, and every detail was utterly festive and superbly organized, with the most lavish food and an elaborately dressed crowd of gorgeous people, ninety-nine percent of whom I didn't know. Somehow I was able to spend three hours on my feet without eating, drinking, peeing, or sitting down, while the entire Hollywood press went to town with cameras and interviewers. Fred had invited all the multitude of celebrities among his customers.

Two moments stand out. Charlton Heston and his wife, Lydia, arrived and she, poor lady, who was probably very used to it, was almost bodily thrown to one side by the photographers while he took my arm and posed with me. He looked straight ahead and smiled while I, not knowing the celebrity-photo drill, tried to make conversation. Finally, clearly at my wit's end, I idiotically asked, "What's it like to be a movie star?" Out of the side of his mouth he hissed, "It's a living," and continued to present himself full face to the cameras.

Now that I know better, I realize that no celebrity ever wants to be photographed talking or in profile, unless the profile is incredibly photogenic. The one thing celebrities detest more than anything is the photographer who says, "Just talk to each other naturally." If you see a picture of celebrities in any walk of life talking to each other, they almost certainly didn't know they were being photographed. It almost made me wish I'd asked Tony Shaftsbury what it was like to be an earl. A living too, I imagine.

The second moment took place outside on the street where Fred's huge, classic Rolls-Royce was parked, surrounded by models wearing his most lavish gowns, posing in a group for a mob of photographers. I was standing and gazing admiringly at them until I suddenly realized that this was *my* party and, with Pilates agility, I fairly leapt to the top of the hood, planted myself in the center of all the girls, and waved.

I was learning. But only baby steps.

The morning before the party, I had awakened to find a Tiffany's box on my bed with an enormously wide, round cuff bracelet inside it. The *Scruples* logo was engraved on it and on the other side three lines. A STORE IS BORN, said the first. Under that was the official pub date, MARCH 9, 1978, and then, in the third line, the words I AM SO PROUD—STEVE. Reader, remember that this was before *Scruples* became any kind of success.

I looked at it and immediately it took on two distinct meanings. It was both a little golden crown and a handcuff. It has indeed been both. I've never been photographed without it, I never leave the house without it, and it's the first thing I take off when I get home. Now, after twenty years, the engraving needs to be redone, but I'm too superstitious to allow it off my wrist for that long.

I finally departed on the long-planned book tour, leaving for Cleveland on March 14, and the next day I found myself with three back-to-back television interviews in the morning. There has always been a crazy but observant lady who lives only in my head and has nothing better to do with her life than to watch me on television and make sure that I'm wearing something different on each show. To fool that lady, I wore the ivory Chloé suit I was going to wear for lunch (the crazy lady never went out for lunch) on the first show, disguised the jacket with a large scarf on the second show, and did the third show just in my blouse and skirt. Someone who was leading me from one show to another said, "I've never seen anyone do that before except one other person. "Who?" "Danny Thomas."

At the packed hotel ballroom where the lunch was held, I listened to the author who preceded me, a former nun, describe vividly how she had been tortured for twelve hours in jail in Chile. My heart sank. How could I follow her with my big bubble-bath, chocolate-cake of a novel? However, I nervously managed to reason that torture probably wasn't what these well-dressed women had come to hear about and I spoke, using my now providential Charlton Heston story, and explaining that I was wearing ivory because this was my first author speech and I asked for their indulgence because I was a virgin. (Not again? Have I no shame? Apparently not.) In my journal, I wrote, "If I say so myself, to myself, I was SUBLIME." It's nice to see now that, along with all the self-doubts, discomfort, and anxiety, I had such high spots. God knows, I'd need them in a publicity process that took five months before it was over.

In Minneapolis the best moment was on a television show run by a famous local host, Henry Wolf. His first guest was a Baptist who ranted against gay rights, then two gay guys who talked about how their souls traveled in space. By the time it was my turn, I figured I could do no wrong, until I realized, after I was on camera, that the heavy mike the soundman had suddenly clipped onto my halfway-buttoned blouse was pulling so hard that my blouse was about to fall off my shoulder. Fortunately, I was wearing a bra this time, but the cameraman had a wonderful time shooting my fingers trying to do up my buttons while I talked to Henry, eyes locked, as if I didn't know what my fingers were doing. The audience, who could see the monitor, was in gales of laughter.

The third day of my first book tour was when the loneliness really hit, a loneliness I'd learn to get used to, but that was so unexpected at the time. I'd had the average media day: the two early-morning television shows; the interview lunch with the newspaper reporter during which I soon learned not to order anything to eat but scrambled eggs that I can easily swallow, because I can't answer questions with my mouth full; the three or four local radio shows, plus a number of trips to bookstores to sign stock.

When I got back to my hotel room—all the hotel rooms I stayed in were either overheated or freezing cold—I got marvelous news from New York. *Scruples* was number two in the *New York Post,* number two in the *Los Angeles Times,* number one for the Pacific Northwest Gill chain, and all the New York papers had now scheduled interviews. However, I found myself unable to react properly to the news because I was numb with the wretchedness of being all alone. I couldn't reach Steve, who was in a "mix," a three-day marathon in which the dialogue, music, and sound-effects tracks for a film are combined. He would never be free to travel with me because of his work producing pictures and television films, although, on occasion, he could fly out for the weekend.

I felt totally isolated and I had an hour of steaming out my clothes for the next day still to do. (My steamer was always the first thing I packed until I learned to wear nothing but wrinkle-free Adolfo knits on tour.) I ordered fried chicken for dinner, the only thing on the room-service menu that wasn't beef. It took an hour and a half to arrive and was so disgusting that I contented myself with bread and butter. Anyway, I was too tired to be hungry.

This sense of isolation and the attacks of lonesome blues after a tiring day of constant talking, attention, and staying up and animated were to become so familiar during the many book tours I've made that the only reason I can remember one particular instance now is that I wrote about it when it was fresh.

Next came Chicago, which was, and always has been, a bright spot on tour. It's a city of delightfully friendly, normal people, great buildings, wonderful food, and tons of media. I had a gorgeous blond Amazon of a limo driver named Roberta who spent all her free time glued to a copy of *Scruples;* a radio interviewer who asked me how to revive a flagging marriage, to whom I managed to say I didn't know because my twenty-four-year-old marriage hadn't flagged yet; lunch with a reporter who wore a golden sable coat like mine and said with a knowing, approving glance, "A golden sable is never a first sable"; and a visit to Water Tower Place, the great shopping center, where I looked around briefly and instantly fell in love with a doll. She was Victorian, dressed in taupe velvet, and had bangs, long brown curls, and a music box inside her that played "Hi Lili, Hi Lo," but of course I didn't buy her, because I was fifty and how would it look if I returned from my first book tour with a doll, of all things?

Steve tracked her down when he heard this story and she's been my one and only doll ever since, sitting in my office while I write, playing her song when I need inspiration, and put away carefully in my closet when I'm not writing, sporting a pink silk Chanel camellia and a little antique emerald and diamond pin. Every woman of every age needs a doll who can cheer her on and cheer her up.

A bookseller in Chicago gave me the best compliment I've ever had. "Look, I'm a pro," he said, "so I do my homework, I read everything and I mean everything, and I heard myself telling someone not to tell me how the ending of *Scruples* came out, and I thought, Oh, shit! I've been trapped."

Soon I was in New York, only two weeks since the *Merv Griffin Show,* and on the next day I was scheduled to do that Brentano's lunch with Jim Fixx, the runner who popularized jogging, and Erica Jong. My mother, Fanny Cohen, Grace Mayes, Sally Pepper, and several other women I'd known all my life were there. I sat on the dais next to Nat Wartels while my mother, getting more and more impatient with the other speakers, who were on before me, caught my eye constantly and gestured at me in irritation, as if there were something I could do about it. Nat turned to me and asked if I'd noticed the woman who was "trying to flirt with me, for Christ's sake." I put his mind at rest and spoke as calmly and well as if none of those women were there.

Nancy Kahane had finally joined me during the daytime. She'd received two job offers because of her work on *Scruples* and, even as I agreed to add Detroit, Phoenix, San Francisco, and San Diego ("they're just around the corner, once you're at LAX") to my overcrowded schedule, I fooled myself, writing in my journal that "Crown has finally understood."

On the day before Easter Sunday, knowing that the next week *Scruples* would be number four in *The New York Times,* following *The Thorn Birds, Silmarillion,* and *Bloodlines* by Sidney Sheldon, I decided to buy myself a pair of diamond earrings.

My reasoning was impeccable. If I didn't make it to the number-one spot, I'd need the earrings to console me, and if I did, I'd need them to celebrate. AA, anybody? I took myself to Van Cleef & Arpels, since that was the building that *Scruples* had replaced, and spent two hours trying on all the earrings there, assisted by two middle-aged, elegant, and friendly Frenchwomen. It was the most perfect way to spend a morning, speaking French again and trying on diamonds, and finally, when I'd found the right pair, bargaining as I could never have done in English for the price of "a friend of the house." I paid for the earrings but left them at Van Cleef because I thought it might be bad luck to take them with me before I knew, one way or the other.

When I talked to Steve that night and he asked me how I'd spent the day, I answered, "Oh, I bought some really lovely diamond earrings this morning." There was a slight but astonished silence before he said, "Good." Never in all the years of our marriage could I, nor would I, have done such a thing before, all on my own, and spoken of it so spontaneously. *I had changed,* I realized, thinking it over. I'd made enough money of my own to permit me to buy diamond earrings without even considering Steve's reaction, much less worrying about it.

My mother had finally allowed herself to feel better about my success, prodded into it by her proud-for-me friends, and she gave an afternoon party for me, inviting the Mayeses and a dozen of her other close friends, even giving each couple a copy of my novel. The brightest memory I still have of that happy afternoon is of Herb Mayes grinning at me in approbation while he held a copy of *Scruples* for me to autograph, a sight I'd never imagined I'd live to see.

On only one occasion have I seen one of my sons reading *Scruples* or any of my other novels. I'd knocked on Tony's door one day and entered, to find him reading the book. "Oh, Tony, what scene are you on?" I asked, beaming with pleasure. "Never you mind!" he replied, slamming the book shut, and I dropped the subject quickly, knowing it must be a sex scene. However, as Mother's Day approached, he kept bringing me copies of the book to sign for his high-school friends' mothers. "Are you sure?" I'd ask, wondering if it was an appropriate present. "Yeah, his mom's cool," Tony answered.

That is the *entire* extent of my knowledge of my sons' feelings about my ten novels. I give each one a copy and I know they read them, particularly Nick, who never fails to tell me how much he's enjoyed a novel. I know they're proud of me, but we have never talked about their contents, neither the plots nor the characters. Somehow the Judith Krantz who writes those books is not their particular mom, could not possibly be Mom, who can't know enough about sex to write about it. It's a natural taboo and I find it sweetly funny, although my sons are grown men now, not embarrassed adolescents. I nourish the fantasy, quite possibly an error, that if I had a daughter, she'd ask me all sorts of questions about who and how and why things happen in each novel, even the sexual goings-on, which are always carefully designed to reinforce character and further the plot, as well as give me and the reader vicarious pleasure.

This memoir should certainly give my sons a whole host of new things not to react to. When they read about a woman named Judy Tarcher who married Stephen Falk Krantz and had two children named Nicholas Tarcher Krantz and Anthony Falk Krantz, will they still believe that this character isn't *Mom?* Their mom? I must admit, this question makes me giggle. At least they'll know a great deal more about their maternal family history than they do now. I've deliberately written very little about my sons in this book because I respect their privacy. Their lives belong to them, not to me, and an account of all the many things, good and bad, that happen between children and parents over the course of the years would necessarily intrude on this.

THE DAY AFTER Easter Sunday, Nancy and I had lunch with Leo Lerman, fabled editor of *Vogue*. I was nervous with the fabulously knowing old legend until he told me with a kind smile that "all nice Jewish girls save their old copies of *Vogue* and still believe in it all." Then we were back on terra cognita. It turned out that he knew almost everyone my parents knew, including Lillian Poses, known as "Posy," one of my mother's oldest friends, to whom he was very close. As soon as I got back to the hotel, I called her in a panic to warn her about my age change. "Posy, listen, Leo—" "He's called already." "Shit!!! What did you say?" "I told him you were about Barbara's age." Barbara Kafka, the noted cookbook writer, was Posy's daughter and years younger than I was.

The next day, Nancy and I took a limo crosstown, eating twenty-two-dollar room-service sandwiches in a twenty-eight-dollar-an-hour limo, to squeeze in a local show, *Midday Live*. The other guests were the two well-known veteran actresses Arlene Francis and Alexis Smith, and a therapist, all discussing "Fear of Success."

Nancy and I sat in a small studio audience listening to the two stars rave on about how overly accustomed, indeed how almost bored, you can become by success. I was getting so furious at being in the audience and not on the stage that Nancy had to physically hold me down by gripping my arm. Finally, when I was beckoned up to join them, and bounded up to the stage, the therapist asked me if I hadn't felt trepidation while waiting my turn. I turned on him and practically howled, "My God, no!! I was infuriated because I thought you'd run out of time up here before I got a chance to talk about *Scruples! Scruples! Scruples!*" And from then on I was off and running, using up all of the time left on the program.

After New York I flew back to Los Angeles for a planned "rest" before the second half of the book tour. Actually, that time was so filled with furious phone calls I made for hours daily about the impossible lack of press Crown had for me in Atlanta and Texas (which instantly changed once they tracked down the culprit and fired her) that once, when someone with a wrong number called and asked if this was the "Flying Emery Board," I answered, "No, but I feel like it." Finally Steve and I decided that we weren't getting enough publicity from Crown and we hired Henry Rogers, the best-known and most powerful PR man in Hollywood.

In my journal I find, "I simply can't leave any stone unturned, still only number four in *New York Times,* this is Datsun, Toyota, and Avis time. I'm so different from the days when I wondered miserably why I had to go out and sell the book myself, that it feels as if I've had a sex-change operation. I drove 130 miles round-trip to Newport Beach just to sign stock in bookstores and I write a full-page dedication to any stranger I see buying a copy. I will do *anything* to become number one. Oh, probably not murder, but certainly arson."

Sometimes "doing anything" turned out to be the kind of embarrassment I hadn't yet learned to avoid. *People* magazine had decided to do a story on me, and during one of the times I was at home, they sent over one of their patented, I'm-so-adorable-I-can-make-you-do-anything photographers. After he'd inspected the house and taken the obligatory picture of Steve and me in bed, something the magazine absolutely demands of every couple, he looked disconsolate and defeated. "Gee, you guys aren't fun at all," he wailed, "there's no story in a married couple, not even a fun room in the house." "There *is* a sauna," my husband remembered, helpfully. "But we've never used it," I objected. The photographer brightened. "This could save the story. Judy, take off your clothes, get into a towel, and I'll shoot you in the sauna reading a book." "But, but . . ." "Keep on your underwear, don't show bra straps, nothing to it."

It certainly seemed harmless, put that way. I muffled myself in a large bath towel and the photographer prowled around looking for the right book, finally, after a long search, handing me an odd choice, *The Joy of Cooking.* As he shot me every which way but hanging from the ceiling, he kept muttering that I should relax, since the picture wouldn't make the magazine anyway, chances were. Of course, it was used as a full page, the chief illustration in the story, over the headline HER POT BOILETH OVER, and it was later reproduced by *People* as a full-page ad in *The New York Times.* My mother was mortified, but she told me that it was such a bad picture that my pot didn't look all that big, and nobody would recognize me anyway. Somehow, this didn't console me.

When the next *People* photographer showed up, after *Princess Daisy,* and asked me to pose with a daisy in my teeth, I'd learned that if I didn't pose, they wouldn't have the picture, and declined that particular honor.

Chapter Thirty-five

ALL TOO SOON, IT WAS TIME TO BE OFF TO ATLANTA AND THEN THE disbelieving awe of actually seeing just how big Texas is. Nothing I'd read had prepared me for the reality.

In Houston, the Crown salesman, Brad Fidell, who informed me that he'd been the "most eligible bachelor" in Houston for thirteen years (but certainly not the most punctual), managed to get me to the airport so late, after a busy day, that although I had time to check my bags, on a last-minute premonition I kept my cosmetic case with me. My bags weren't to return from Lubbock, where they'd gone to get lost, for three days, but there was no time in my schedule to buy any replacement clothes. There's a country-and-western song with the wonderful line that "happiness is seeing Lubbock in my rearview mirror." Count me in on that.

I did all my two days of Dallas, and one day of Fort Worth interviews, in the clothes I'd worn in Houston. I used my itchy tweed Jean Muir cape as a bathrobe and slept in my underwear and panty hose, which I couldn't wash because there was no time to dry them and it was too cold to sleep without them. At least I could bathe. I found out I could manage everything I had to do because I still had my mascara. The Red-Wine Terrorist had been vanquished, even if only for three days. Best of all, in Dallas, I did a local morning interview show with an absurdly handsome new young host who was tremendous fun. He had only half an audience, but by asking them to move around, he managed to make the studio look full. My memory tells me that he and I sat on cushions on the floor during a delightful, laughter-filled hour-long interview. I'd never heard of him before—a fellow named Charlie Rose.

My Dallas limo driver took me by the Book Depository Building without even asking, as if it were the first thing any visitor would want to see. It was such a pastoral, peaceful place, the old rose-brick building, almost Victorian, under such a blue, poetic, early-morning sky that it was impossible to reconcile the setting with the Zapruder pictures. I had to see it, but I was sorry afterward.

———

AFTER THE LONG, taxing swing through the South I had a short weekend at home to restore my blond highlights. In my journal on a Saturday, I wrote,

> So, so, *so* depressed. Have to leave again tomorrow for Portland. It's almost unbearable, the coming home, the feeling that real life is here, but I can only worry about hair, clothes, health, schedule. It comes with the territory but these weekends at home really destroy me, put me in such a terrible mood of resentment, it seems as if everyone is just using me to get the most mileage, now my pet fury is having to fly from Portland to Seattle and then immediately on to St. Louis, via a stop in Chicago to change planes, with a cocktail party planned for booksellers an hour and a half after the plane is due to land. Since we change at O'Hare, who knows when it will land? This directly plays on my sense of obsessive responsibility and need to be on time and in perfect shape. The cocktail party is like a fiendish obstacle race with standing around for two hours with strangers as the prize, drinking water, and remembering names. I'm so terribly blue I could cry, and everybody envies me and thinks I'm "so lucky" and I "should be so thrilled" and if I told them the truth, no one but Steve would understand. I must TRY TO SHAPE UP. Since I have to go, just go pull up my socks and DO IT! I was so good in Texas I amazed myself. It's coming home that breaks the rhythm. If it could be done physically, it would be better to just stay out— but only a man can do that, no hair worries, just shave, put on a fresh shirt, and remember to keep his fly zipped. And a man wouldn't be going through all the unpleasant and difficult symptoms of menopause that I'm having. My worst fear is that a hot flash will attack while I'm on camera and the sweat will just pour down my face. So far it hasn't happened, thank God, but I know it's constantly affecting my moods.

I was right to worry about the Seattle–St. Louis plan, the impracticality of which I had opposed from the beginning. I reached St. Louis after an endless and terribly tiring flight to find myself being animated in a freezing hotel ballroom, filled with more than a hundred booksellers. Alan Merkin, the vice-president of Crown and Nat Wartels's nephew, who was due to inherit his childless uncle's entire business, had flown out from New York to be there.

Afterward, Alan took me out to dinner with his daughter and a friend, and although they all found the restaurant comfortably warm, and I was wearing boots, I couldn't make myself take off my fur coat, or even my gloves, so that I could eat. I was shivering and shaking with cold and every time I mentioned it to Alan, he just said, "Oh, come on, you'll be fine," unforgivably paying no serious attention— no attention of any kind—to the fact that obviously something had to be wrong with me if I couldn't even eat at the end of a very long day. Alan was always a nice man . . . but also a publisher with a highly useful author who was getting tons of PR. He didn't want to admit that I was in bad shape. I was too worn out to make any kind of a scene but as soon as I got back to the hotel, I called Steve in a panic and said, over and over, "I just can't get warm, I don't know what's wrong with me, but I can't get warm. I can't stop shaking."

Steve had to leave L.A. on business the next day, but he immediately took over. "You're coming home tomorrow," he told me. "I'll call Crown and take care of everything, I'll make the arrangements for your ticket. If you can't do the media tomorrow, don't, cancel everything, but if you can, get on the plane right afterward, there'll be a limo to meet you."

"But I can't just leave," I wailed. "I have a schedule for the next two weeks."

"You can and you're going to."

I managed to do the day of media and got on a plane in the worst mental condition that I've ever been in. I was as close to having a nervous breakdown as I can imagine. And it was understandable.

On this first book tour, I was always in a strange and guaranteed-at-any-price-to-be-uncomfortable hotel room, where I had to unplug the magnifying mirror to plug in the alarm clock, where there was never a spot with enough light for applying makeup, where the heat never worked, the switchboard rarely worked, the room service never, *never,* under any conditions worked, so that the only safe thing to order was a sandwich, which started out cold in any case. Worst of all, the bed was almost always unsleepable, bad mattress, bad sheets, bad blankets. (I carried my own pillow.) I was constantly trying to reach people who were in other time zones, and I couldn't even try to go to bed until I'd steamed out the next day's clothes and put up my hair in pin curls.

At night I was always alone and lonely. There was no one to complain to, no one to comfort me, no one to say I was doing a good job.

The only time those conditions didn't apply was while I was actually on a plane, my jet-lagged body being hauled from one place to another, being fed plane food. My biggest problem was that, as a confirmed insomniac, trying to sleep in a strange and uncomfortable hotel bed meant daylong torments of anxiety.

The fact that Crown knew absolutely nothing about touring an author and providing any comfort beyond the limo I demanded, the fact that I was a thin woman with low blood pressure, low thyroid, and borderline anemia, the fact that I never had anyone to help me with my bags or cosmetic case, didn't help. Nor did the fact that I had to walk from one end of each airport to the other, and stand at all those constant cocktail parties on my flat feet, feet that have been my weak point all my life, feet that are the Tarcher curse since my sister, my mother, and my father had them, too. Every party in my honor was a nightmare of foot pain, but there was never any way to sit down and still fulfill the function of being a "guest of honor."

I came back from St. Louis determined not to leave home again, but on April 24, I wrote in my journal, "After a weekend of rest more or less restored to a normal condition."

A phone call came from Henry Rogers, who told me that he had "played down my *Cosmo* background and pitched me as a Beverly Hills housewife" who had more or less fallen out of bed writing a book that, lo and behold, turned out to be a best-seller.

I went bonkers with frustration. I'd gone to the Rogers and Cowan office weeks earlier and spent two hours with them, telling an entire group, including Henry, about every last article I'd ever written in twenty-four years on which they could hang a publicity pitch, yet here was a top-notch professional, a man I'd known personally for five years, who, in spite of my self-evident achievements, ignored my valid credentials and because of his perception of me, had devised a completely wrong and destructive pitch. In my journal I tried to figure out how this had happened.

It can't just be stupidity on Henry's part, because he's not stupid, so it must come from our prior relationship. No one *now* who meets me for the first time does so without some respect, but Henry saw someone, a typical Beverly Hills housewife, who has never existed. I have never, except when *angry,* taken myself at serious value. I know all the strong, good, tough things about myself but I overlook them. To me they're *expected* to exist. So instead, I concentrate on the surface, my looks, my funniness, etc. All very fine except if I don't do myself justice, others won't either.

Yet, when it comes to business I've always held out for a fair share. But that's business and the other is connected to approval. In business I don't give a fuck about approval because I'm not selling *me,* I'm selling my work, which is valuable. Obviously, I choose to write about the glamorous life in *Scruples* for good commercial reasons. The fact that the serious comments about the real limitations of glamour and wealth that I make in the book have been mostly overlooked is the price I've paid for writing about a beautiful woman with 250 million dollars—you can't have it both ways. *I must* get to the roots of my self-deprecation. So many women with no particular talent take themselves so seriously—there must be a middle ground. Is it the fear of seeming pretentious? Is it, as usual, my mother, who would only take me seriously if I smiled and tap danced? Or my father, who never took me seriously enough to talk to? But Christ, I hate those self-important, sacred-agony broads. I'm an entertainer—how to entertain and still be taken seriously? Perhaps impossible.

The next day I had lunch alone with Henry and told him how deeply he'd gone wrong. He thought about it for less than three seconds and admitted that he'd been absolutely mistaken. I told him that since he was being paid a flat fee, I expected him to start working from now on and not count the time he'd already put in, to which he agreed immediately. After that lunch, he never took me lightly again.

In a day or two I felt well enough to go gossip with my bookseller friend at Doubleday's, Jim Zeidman. When I complained about the tour's hardships he said merely, "Sidney would go out again," and this mention of the author whose book was just ahead of mine on the list made me know Jim was right.

Within a week I was off to Detroit, to Philadelphia for the then very important *Mike Douglas Show,* to Boston and New York again, and then to meet Steve for his birthday and go on to Washington, D.C., and later San Francisco.

In Detroit I was booked for the essential book show of that city, the J. P. McCarthy radio show. The host, peering deeply into the magnificent cleavage of another guest, paid me no attention at all, not even saying hello, until I broke, without invitation, into his conversational tryst with the announcement that *Scruples* was now number three on the *New York Times* list. That got his attention, but for the rest of the hour I had to compete toe-to-toe with someone I described in my journal as a "take-over talker, the toughest contest so far." We ended in a draw, Arianna Huffington and I. And that was twenty years ago, when Arianna was just starting. At the hotel that night I received a gift-wrapped copy of her book on Callas with a charming note.

Oh, that Arianna! She never left a possible stone unturned. Years later, Steve and I were invited to her birthday party in Santa Barbara, where she received her guests in a strapless, bright-red ball gown, totally Scarlett O'Hara, with a skirt so wide it filled the doorway, while the entire Santa Barbara Symphony played Strauss waltzes standing on the staircase behind her. Unforgettable. If this fierce Republican had been born here, with her excellent mind, wit, and driving ambition, she'd be running for president. As a Democrat, the thought makes me quiver. Still, we have so many less charming and less intelligent politicians . . . in that relatively new, irresistible but already overworked phrase, let's not go there.

The day *The New York Times Book Review* let publishers know the standing on their list was always a Thursday, ten days before the Sunday on which the paper came out. Steve and I and someone he was doing business with were eating lunch on a Wednesday, June 7, when Nat Wartels phoned.

I took the call in my office and Nat gleefully informed me that *Scruples* would be number one on Sunday, June 18. I felt as if a soft, powdery, powerful, white explosion had lifted me into the air and was holding me there. I just held on to the phone, speechless. It didn't seem possible. After all the struggle, it didn't seem real at all. In a trance of bliss and relief, slowly, as if I'd forgotten how to use my legs, I walked back to the dining room and said quietly to Steve, "One, week after next," not wanting our lunch guest to know what I was talking about. Steve immediately got up from the table, lifted me up, held me very tight, and kissed me. Then he phoned Van Cleef in New York and told them to send the earrings posthaste.

This moment was just three months after publication and fifteen weeks since *Scruples* had started climbing the *Times* list. Such a performance for an unknown novel by an unknown novelist was a once-in-a-decade occurrence back in the seventies. *Scruples* remained at one for six weeks, until the new Michener came out, and stayed on the list for forty weeks, until the end of December. I'd done well over four full months of PR and I still had to go to San Francisco, as I'd promised, and then return to L.A. to make a number of speeches for women's charitable groups. In March 1979 I'd have to go on another tour for the paperback.

In my journal I wrote, "I've always wanted to be *best* at one thing and this week I am, best at writing commercial fiction for the hardcover book-buying public. It's a flower in my buttonhole forever. Thank you, Billy, Spider, Valentine, Dolly, Josh, Lester—thank all of you for making this possible. And Vito really was essential. My darling Steve. He's so proud it's wonderful. The work paid off!"

After I'd written my little Oscar speech to myself, on June 15, as I had planned, I started *Princess Daisy*.

Chapter Thirty-six

I PUT AWAY THE JOURNAL OF MY FIRST BOOK TOUR AND MADE NO entries after June 7, 1978. Six months later, on the night of January 12, 1979, when I was working on the seventeenth chapter of the rough draft of *Princess Daisy*, it occurred to me to reread the journal because I couldn't sleep, and to write a new entry.

> The way I worked, the way I *wanted* it, my God, to think I got it! Now I'm happy with *Daisy*—great plot, good characters, a heroine you have to love, good heroes, a terrific villain—Ram, that shit Ram, raping Daisy, his half-sister—drama, excitement, entertainment, and *Scruples* is now becoming a generic term with Richard Marek advertising a book as "*Scruples* on the Potomac." I see my limitations as a writer so clearly but I have an unquestioned "talent to amuse," as Noël Coward once said of himself.

At an unknown time after that entry I finished the first draft of *Princess Daisy* and put it away for a few weeks to get some perspective on it before starting the rewrite.

I was delighted that I'd managed to write a novel so different from *Scruples*. This time, I'd vowed, my heroine will be poor and struggling, a girl who has to financially support her identical twin sister, Danielle, born four minutes later than she was, four minutes during which a shortage of oxygen to Danielle's brain caused a retardation that left her with a mental age of six.

A critic had labeled *Scruples* a novel of "sex and shopping," a description that didn't do it justice in my opinion, yet an expression that stuck and has continued to stick until I decided to use it rather than fight it and make it into the title of this memoir.

With *Princess Daisy*, I was determined that, although a princess, Daisy would live in thrift-shop clothes, bought for next to nothing. Orphaned and unable to finish college because she'd been robbed of what little money she had by Ram, and responsible for Danielle, Daisy found an entry-level job as a production assistant in a company that made commercials in New York City.

However, I hadn't yet realized the way my natural style would affect Daisy's poverty.

Soon after she had learned her trade, she discovered that since someone was always looking for her to solve a problem, her jeans and work shirt made her difficult to spot in the denim-clad multitude of the crew. She had worked out an outfit that had three virtues: it was cheap, practical, and highly visible. In cold weather she wore U.S. Navy, World War Two, ordinary seaman's pants with their complicated set of thirteen buttons and their sturdy fabric. In summer she wore white Navy bell-bottoms. To go with these basic trousers she had a dozen boys' rugby jerseys in the boldest stripes and brightest colors she could find. In the huge, grubby, confused studio, she always wore tennis shoes and thick white socks and braided her hair into one fat pigtail that fell over one shoulder, but at least it stayed out of her face. . . . The meeting ended while Daisy was planning her look for tomorrow—the 1934 Mainbocher suit, she thought, high heels, a tight chignon, and *gloves,* you rotten bastard.

As for evening, yes, Daisy indeed bought her clothes at English church "jumble sales," but as she searched among her secondhand-Rose treasures for the right thing to wear for an evening in Middleburg among the horse people, where she drew sketches of children on ponies to earn extra money, Daisy consulted her best friend, Kiki Kavenaugh.

"Ah ha!" Daisy pounced. "How could I have forgotten? Schiaparelli to the rescue, as usual." Triumphantly she held up an ensemble from the late 1930s when the daring Schiaparelli was doing clothes which were four decades ahead of their time. There was a jacket in lettuce-green tweed touched with sequins at the lapels, worn with a pair of corduroy pants in a darker shade of green. "Just right, don't you think?"

"It's heaven—really a fuck-you number as in 'fuck you, Mrs. Short, I know it's tweed and I know it's sequins and I know you didn't think they can be worn together, but now you do.' "

"In a nutshell. I really need this commission, so it's important to look as if I didn't."

"Then you'd better take my fake emeralds again."

"Emeralds with green sequins?"

"*Especially* with green sequins!"

Oh well. A writer should never change her natural form of expression, especially when it gives me so much fun. Daisy was still a poor orphan. Was it her fault if her cheap wardrobe just happened to look smashing on her?

Recently I received a fan letter from Barbara Schar, who lives in Whitehorse, in the Yukon Territory of Canada, and is Coordinator of Victim Services for the territory. She wrote, "Not only have your books provided me with hours of reading pleasure, they have also become tools in my new volunteer work with victims, specifically battered women. Because your leading and minor female characters show strength and courage under adversity, I have no hesitation recommending your books to women rebuilding their shattered lives, and often they have helped a woman to take one more step in the healing process. One woman, for example, felt so much better about buying clothes in a secondhand store after reading about the character Daisy Valensky turning secondhand dressing into an art form." Rarely has any fan letter meant so much to me.

I spent many weeks researching *Princess Daisy*, hanging around a commercial-making company in New York; spending endless time in London, where Daisy lived as a child with her father, Prince Stash Valensky; many hours doing library research on the life of noble Russians before the Revolution and on the treatment of tuberculosis in Davos in 1925. (Daisy's grandmother had TB.) I'd even discovered that my new British publisher had a fiancée who owned the kind of Gypsy's dog I wanted Daisy to have, called a "lurcher," and I'd become an expert on lurcher habits.

Oh, there was nothing I left to chance to try to lose the detested reputation of being a sex-and-shopping novelist, which I now accept will unquestionably be in the first line in my obituary. This label, perhaps because it's so easy to remember, has been used in almost every interview I've given, no matter how few pages sex and shopping take up in any of my books, no matter how much other material I've covered in the course of my writing career. Today I'm completely resigned to it. On balance, sex and shopping are both excellent things, activities people love to talk about and read about—even do!—and if I'd been able to add only two words to that original description they would have been "working women."

During the time I put my manuscript of *Daisy* aside to cool off, I actually finished that article on "Where the Beautiful People Go to Work Out" that I'd promised Helen Brown so long ago. I felt an obligation to finish this assignment, which gave me at least six severe attacks of muscle strain and forced me to spend a day at the spa called the Ashram, a place where pain in the pursuit of fitness was worshiped and lunch consisted of tiny bits of chopped vegetables eaten with chopsticks "to make the meal last longer." Meal?

When I finally reread *Princess Daisy* I was utterly dismayed to discover that while I'd been away from it, the book had, all on its own, managed to screw itself up.

The problem, as I analyzed it, was that there were too many layers of generations, too many flashbacks that contained their own flashbacks. I had set out to write a saga of three generations and I'd been caught in my own trap.

For the only time in my career, I called Crown for help. Steve had no solution for my problem and I knew I needed another pair of eyes besides his. I had a new editor now, a woman I'd only met once, in passing, whose name was Carole Baron. In the middle of my writing *Daisy* she had taken over from Larry Freundlich, who was no longer employed at Crown.

Several days later, Carole Baron arrived in California. She looked like a former sporty college girl, captain of the soccer team perhaps, with her gleaming, straight, ash-blond hair held back by a barrette, although she seemed to be in her late thirties and was stepmother to five children. I liked her enormously from the minute I saw her again, and we quickly set to work at the dining-room table, stopping only for a sandwich lunch, working until long past the time I thought I would have to quit or faint. Carole was a total demon for work, easily able to outlast me at my best. As soon as Carole was finally willing to stop for the day, we'd have a drink and Steve would take the two of us out for dinner.

Don't ask me what happened during the three days we worked together. It was some form of magic. Carole, as she told me she wouldn't, never supplied a word or a suggestion. She just *sat* there and paid strict attention while I went over every page I'd written and, because I now had an audience, I talked to her as if I were talking to myself. I discovered, page by page, where I could cut, where I could rearrange, where I needed a new transition, where I'd gone off on a wrong trail, and where new material should be written. When I'd found a solution that satisfied me, and Carole had nodded her agreement, I noted the page number on a yellow pad so I could write it after she returned to New York.

Late in the afternoon of the third day, we finally finished the manuscript and sat exhausted in the living room, although what *she* had to be exhausted about I can't imagine, when the phone rang. It was Howard Kaminsky, president of Warner Books, who had published *Scruples* in paperback. Howard was a very bright and funny fellow, Mel Brooks's first cousin, who had originally objected to the title of *Scruples*.

"My secretary doesn't know what it means," he had complained to me.

"Am I right in feeling that you'd be happier with a title like 'Ten Nights of Passion'?" I had asked testily.

"Well . . . not exactly that, but yeah, that's the general idea."

"Ask your secretary if she knows the meaning of unscrupulous, as in Richard Nixon, or get another secretary, Howard," I'd suggested, and that was the last I heard of it.

However, during the ten years that Warner had the license to publish *Scruples,* they did an absolutely magnificent job of it, always reprinting whenever I had a new book out, and splashing the now-famous cover with "By the Author of *Mistral's Daughter*" or whatever the title of my latest book was.

Although *Scruples* in paperback had become number one on the *Times* list within ten days of publication, the top executives at Warner Books strangely, considering its extraordinary record, had refused to put up the sum of one million four hundred thousand dollars that Nat Wartels wanted for the paperback rights to *Princess Daisy*. An infuriated and insulted Wartels had then decided to sell the book at auction. Hence the call that afternoon from Howard.

"What's happening at your place?" Howard asked me, chattily.

"I'm, working with Carole Baron on a polish of *Princess Daisy,*" I told him.

"Could I speak to her?" he asked.

I listened keenly to her end of the conversation, I but didn't learn anything until I heard Carole say cryptically, "No negatives," and although I was quite a distance from the phone, I heard a scream of anguish from Howard Kaminsky.

"No negatives?" I said to Carole after she'd hung up. I felt disappointed. I'd thought the book was much better than such faint praise warranted. "Is that all you can say about it?"

" 'No negatives' is the highest possible praise."

"How come?"

"It's a technical term . . . it means that there's nobody in the world who won't want to read the book—men, women, teenagers, foreigners from Finland to Tokyo, you name it, everybody will want to read *Princess Daisy.*"

"You mean it's *all positives?*"

"You could say that, too," Carole agreed, with her stay-cool-let's-not-get-too-excited grin.

The next day Carole went back to New York, where she was kidnapped away from me about a year and a half later, as I was in the middle of writing my third novel, *Mistral's Daughter,* by Dell-Delacorte, who made her their wildly successful publisher, but we've been firm friends ever since our three-day marathon of Zen editing.

The powers at Crown were so pissed to lose Carole that they pettily refused to sell her the old desk chair that she felt so comfortable in.

Steve and I managed to take some sort of vacation in Europe after I'd delivered the manuscript of *Daisy* to Crown. We flew back from wherever we were for the auction, because I wanted to be home while it went on, and stopped first in New York for a day so I could see my mother. I found her looking very thin and persuaded her to visit Jerry Barondess for a checkup. My mother didn't believe in doctors—"What do they know?" was her kindest reference to the entire medical profession—and it had been eight years since her last visit to one.

We flew back to L.A., still jet-lagged, in time for the auction the next day. All book auctions are conducted entirely by phone, so we could follow the auction just as well from home as from New York.

For *Daisy,* a "floor bid" had been established, which was the starting point for the auction. In this case it was a million dollars, offered by Bantam Books. This gave Bantam the right to sit out the auction and then "take" the book by "topping" the last bid, if it chose to do so. The eight paper-book houses that wanted to take part in the auction—including Warner Books, of all people—each had had several weeks in which to read the manuscript and make the calculations that would give them a sound idea of what they could afford to pay for the book and still make a profit.

Michelle Sidrane ran the auction by telephoning, one at a time, the subsidiary-rights editors of all eight houses. She told each of them what the last bid had been and gave them time to raise their bid or drop out. After each round of bidding was over, it was expected that some publisher or another would drop out of the auction. The day before the auction, each of the eight interested publishers had received baskets of daisies, a charming touch I was tickled to learn about from Michelle, whose idea it had been.

During the late morning of that day I received a phone call from Marc Jaffe and the famed Oscar Dystel, the top executives of Bantam. I didn't know either of them but nothing reminded me so much of the preliminary joking and slightly nervous banter with a prospective blind date as that conversation with these two strangers. Nothing of substance was said, and nobody mentioned the ongoing auction.

When I hung up I asked Steve, "What the hell was that all about?" "They were just making sure you were real," he answered, smiling at me with a look of pride, "and were you ever!" Fortunately, the phone has always been my instrument of choice for any sort of communication, especially flirting, which was exactly what I'd been doing.

After each round of bidding, rounds that took endless hours, Michelle would call Mort Janklow to tell him the latest sum bid, since he was the person who officially communicated with me. Mort would call me, invariably starting the conversation with the words "You'll never guess what just happened!" My nerves were stretched so tight that I *implored* him not to ask me to guess, just to tell me the bottom line, but he never saw fit to spare me the suspense. The auction dragged on and on. By two in the afternoon in California, it was time to leave the office in New York, and some of the publishers wanted to postpone the auction until the following day, but Michelle refused to allow the momentum to die and told them they had to keep at it.

Eventually Mort went to a dinner party, where he took over the bedroom telephone so Michelle could phone him with each new development. Between calls, without the knowledge of any of us and contrary to an understanding with Crown and Bantam, Mort was in communication with a reporter from *The New York Times*, giving him a play-by-play report of the progress of the auction.

I tried to keep calm by unpacking from the trip and steaming out wrinkled clothes until the last sum bid broke the previous record held by Mario Puzo for the paperback rights to *The Godfather*. Then I told Steve I thought we should have the drink he'd been trying to make me have, because steaming wasn't doing the trick.

At some point that evening, the last bid was made—by Warner Books, playing catch-up and offering twice what they had refused to pay Nat Wartels when he first asked for it. Bantam then exercised its topping privilege, paying three million two hundred thousand dollars and change for the right to publish *Daisy* in paperback.

I was too tired to feel anything but a sort of glazed, goofy surprise and a slim quiver of remote pleasure, largely mixed with the intuition that I wasn't having an appropriate reaction to this triumph. Try as I would, I couldn't get *into* any feeling of emotion the way I had when I'd learned that Crown had bought *Scruples* or that it had become number one. I kept telling myself that this might possibly seem real if somebody would come to the house with a handful of twenty-dollar bills and just hand them to me, or even throw them on the carpet at my feet. However, three million dollar two hundred thousand dollars wasn't a sum I could take in and comprehend with any part of my mind.

When I woke up the next day, it still didn't seem real, until I picked up my copy of *The New York Times* and saw the auction story on the front page. If I'd only thought to frame that page, or even just keep it, I could tell you what it said, but basically it announced to the world that Judith Krantz had just received the most money any human being in history had ever been paid for paperback rights. As Coco Chanel said, quoting Byron, after her first collection, "I woke up to find myself famous." So did I, at least in the world of publishing.

Now, I finally felt something. Not joy, not excitement, not pride, but rather a deeply resonating shock. If that sum of three million two had just been between me and Bantam and Crown and Mort and Steve, fine, but to have everybody know how much money I'd made? Nobody had any idea what *Scruples* had earned and there was something deeply embarrassing about this exposure. I'd gone public in a way I couldn't control and wouldn't have wanted if it could have been prevented. However, when you break a record, it's not something you can hide. No matter how accustomed I was to fighting with editors for a couple of hundred extra dollars for payment on articles, nothing had prepared me for such success.

It was so much money! Even after my agent's ten percent commission was taken off the top, even after the forty percent that was Crown's part of the total, and even after the income tax we paid on what was finally paid me, it was a hell of a lot to earn, and as I was to find out, nobody thought that anyone at all *shared* that money with me. I felt something close to guilt myself, since I'd never been trained to compete openly and to believe that worth and money can go hand in hand.

Everyone, it seemed to me, imagined that the entire sum, intact and probably in gold bars, had been delivered to me by a Brinks truck that very afternoon. For several years, in the publishing industry, I was the equivalent of a Bill Gates, and I was as thoroughly detested as he is by everyone who didn't have a piece of my pie. It was a relief when James Clavell broke my record about four years later, without any fanfare or disapproval. His auction seemed entirely appropriate to the book world, for Clavell was an excellent writer who had been a major figure for many years. Most important, James Clavell is a man, not a woman. I KNOW that if I'd been a man, and not an upstart female with only one lighthearted book to my credit, the fury directed at me wouldn't have existed. It took me a while to understand this, but what the hell . . . it *remains* a solid satisfaction to break a record and I'm very grateful that I did.

My mother, shocked and verbally disapproving—perhaps envious at my going so far beyond her own success—cut me out of her will on the grounds that I didn't need an inheritance. Believe it or not, at the time I didn't disagree with her.

As for Crown, they had become instantaneous players in publishing fiction with *Scruples*. Now *Daisy* established their position and enabled them, with their share of the auction money, to publish twenty first-time novelists, one of them Jean Auel, who had just written *The Clan of the Cave Bear*. All in all, a great return on their initial fifty-thousand-dollar investment in me.

Chapter Thirty-seven

ALMOST AS SOON AS I'D SEEN THE *TIMES*, NANCY KAHANE WAS ON the phone telling me that Steve and I had to fly back to New York in two days because the Bantam and Crown executives didn't know each other personally and wanted to arrange a get-acquainted-with-each-other and get-to-know-Judy dinner in a private room of the Rainbow Room restaurant.

Back in New York, the day of the dinner, I called Jerry Barondess. He informed me that my mother had pancreatic cancer. I had been right to be concerned about her thinness. This diagnosis was her death sentence. Unless this cancer is discovered almost as soon as it occurs, and the pancreas is removed, it is always incurable. Chemo and radiation can only add a year or two, at the most, to a patient's life and my mother had already decided that she had no interest in taking these measures. She had no pain because of the position of the cancer in the thin end of her pancreas, and she serenely refused any medication. She had an indefinite time to live, but certainly less than a year.

It was with this knowledge fresh in my mind that I sat through the endless, toast-filled dinner, of which I remember little. We all sat at a long table and goodwill reigned supreme, and if anybody happened to notice that there was anything very strange about me, they must have attributed it to fatigue.

Steve and I spent several days more in New York to be with my mother, who, at seventy-nine, had resumed her years of taking conversational French lessons, her work with young lawyers, her lunches with friends, and her reading. I knew she was aware of the prognosis of her illness, but she refused, with her customary strength, to pay any attention to it at all, much less discuss it with me. Without words, she conveyed that the subject was off-limits. For her, denial was the only way to carry on and, certainly in her case, she was right.

I found that I was obsessing about the one thing I could remember doing to her that had turned out to give her a severe fright. Several years earlier, when I was learning to fly, and she was in California visiting all of us, I invited her to go with me on a round-trip training flight to Catalina. We were flying with a pilot-instructor, so of course it was perfectly safe. She accepted readily, rather to my surprise, and then sat in the back of the plane, reading a book for dear life, scared out of her wits. Not once did my mother so much as peek out of the window, and not once did she complain. Obviously the reality of flight had overwhelmed her. I couldn't get this unwitting occasion of cruelty out of my mind.

Some months after her diagnosis, in late December, my mother came out to California for one of the customary two-week visits she made several times a year, looking slightly thinner perhaps but otherwise as full of energy as ever. Once she'd left, I went to my gynecologist for a regular checkup and was told that I had an ovarian cyst, which, of course, had to be removed to find out if it was benign or malignant.

I asked my doctor to do a complete hysterectomy while he was at it, so that I wouldn't have to worry about another cyst or uterine cancer, to which he agreed. I had exactly one day between the examination and the operation, a day I spent at Porthault, buying six sets of flower-printed blanket covers and pillowcases to match so that I could recuperate from the operation in style. It was a wild extravagance I would never have allowed myself under any but such extreme circumstances . . . so now I know what I'd do when faced with possible cancer. Shop! During her last months my mother also shopped for clothes and jewels more than she ever had before.

The *Princess Daisy* hardcover book tour had to be postponed, since the aftermath of a hysterectomy demands, as the old expression goes, two months of doing nothing heavier than "lifting a teacup." This postponement started a rash of rumors that I was dying of cancer, and I asked Rona Barrett, who had a television gossip show from Hollywood, to tell her audience that all I'd had was a hysterectomy without complications. Rona instead announced mysteriously that I'd been operated on and that I'd be out of commission and unable to travel for two months. At the last minute she was unable to actually say the word *hysterectomy*. Perhaps it was too blunt for Miss Rona's delicate stomach, but I was appalled, since the rumors only grew worse.

I had already agreed to be the guest of honor at a "Princess Daisy Ball" that was to be given in the early spring by the Lighthouse for the Blind, a ball with a White Russian theme, since Daisy had been a half-American, half-Russian princess, and I was able to promise the Lighthouse people that I'd be fine by that time. However, I had a strong psychic premonition that my mother would die on the night of the Lighthouse Ball, many months away. Mimi thought that I was being utterly ridiculous—"You don't have that much power," she said bluntly—but somehow I couldn't talk myself out of the feeling that these two events would come at the same time.

After the operation, in the recovery room at Cedars-Sinai, quite early in the morning, I tried to find out if the cyst had been benign or malignant. The nurse, understandably, couldn't tell me, but when my doctor didn't show up to give me the news, I began to get angrier and angrier, and more and more apprehensive. When he finally waltzed in at 8:00 P.M. with good news, thank all the gods, I would have killed him if I'd had the strength. I threw a fit that impressed even me, on the subject of letting someone lie around all day long wondering if she has cancer or not, when a quick visit or phone call would have answered my question. No doctor should ever be that busy!

A hysterectomy is not an operation that's dangerous in itself, but if gas pains could kill, you'd most certainly die afterward. There's no agony that compares, and I've had four abscessed teeth at once, so I have a basis for comparison. Fortunately no individual pain lasts very long, although it seems forever at the time.

One night, on January 3, 1980, I was in such pain that I took recourse in my journal yet again, describing how I felt about the fact that in two weeks every bookstore in the country would have copies of the 240,000 first printing of *Princess Daisy*.

> What will happen? Will they just fly out of the stores or will they move more slowly? I'm entitled to hope for the best, but I simply *can't* count my chicks till hatched, no matter how good it looks. The critics will *really* be out for blood, reviewing the money, not the book, but much as it may—will—hurt, I *know* it's a good book. I wish the next few weeks could be over so I could see some action in the stores, but now the important thing is to get my strength back and begin to think about the heroine of *Mistral's Daughter,* a fiery redhead with lots of temperament, guts, and determination. I *am* getting a rest, if not the kind I had in mind, but as soon as I can function I'll be besieged. It's great to beat off PR with sticks but not with farts.

I'm glad I have these words on record or I wouldn't believe them. *Scruples* had *already* sold five million copies in paperback; *Daisy* had been the "book of the year" at the international Frankfurt Book Fair, earning a half-million advance from England, an equal sum from Germany, and enormous advances from some thirty other countries; but even with all that evidence, plus the record-setting auction, I still could *not* manage to allow myself to count on success.

Granted, I'd only been in the publishing business since March 9, 1978, less than two years in all, but after my wild ride, wouldn't you have thought I'd be more of an optimist? Just how overcautious can a person get? I suppose that the truly unexpected success of *Scruples* and the equally unexpected record sale of the rights to *Daisy* had made me feel that I'd had too much good luck for one person. I've always been quick to substitute superstition for religion, and every discussion of a promising outcome to any project with Steve will find both of us knocking on wood at every third word. Perhaps my journal was just a reflection of that familiar state of mind, plus the gas pains. When I was feeling wonderful it never occurred to me to write in my journal.

Oh, how deeply I now wish that I'd been able to indulge myself in unbridled self-confidence at a time when I was on top of the world and could have wallowed in the thrill of it. Alas, I've never been the wallowing kind, much less the unbridled kind, and I found it impossible to change. I'd had such outrageous success after fifty, such utterly unexpected success, that it didn't alter anything fundamental about my character.

This, as a matter of fact, is a truth that interests me. A majority of people expected me to change with success, to become snobbish, to get a swelled head and believe my publicity, to lose my interest in anything but my new glory, to become, in short, another obnoxious celebrity who only wanted to socialize with other celebrities.

What they had a hard time realizing—what too many of them *never* realized—was that if you come to a *late* success, when your character is already fully formed and your life experience has made you the person you are, these changes just don't take place. The changes that do happen are internal. For example, I was able to be introduced to a celebrity without worrying what we'd talk about, because I knew they were ordinary people like me. When I found myself alone in a corner with Jack Nicholson at a small cocktail party, I knew that as two Lakers fans, we had a lot in common, and the fact that he was, oh dear God, *Jack Nicholson!* didn't keep me from having an easy, lively conversation with him. This would have been impossible before *Scruples,* Lakers or no Lakers. I also became accustomed to strangers being more interested in meeting me than they'd been in the past. I grew able to accept compliments as validly belonging to me because I had the work to prove it, and I had an inner thrill of accomplishment when I looked at my books in print.

The discouraging but inevitable part were the friends I lost. Some people simply couldn't endure my new success; their envy was too much for them, and they disappeared from my life, to be replaced, eventually, by people who met me first in my current incarnation. Everyone who's ever had a success, even a very small one, knows that this happens, but it's sad nevertheless, especially the first few times. Mimi was wonderful. "If it couldn't happen to me," she said, "I'm so glad it happened to you." Now that's a healthy reaction! I feel the same way about the daughters she has and I don't.

PRINCESS DAISY, IN its third week on the *Times* list, became number one, on February 17, 1980, displacing John Le Carré's *Smiley's People,* so my chickens hatched after all. I had all the poultry luck Grandfather Ben never had.

However, before I was finally able to make the hardcover tour for *Daisy,* I could see that my mother was getting worse and worse. I'd been able to fly to New York several times to see her before the tour began, and found her finally admitting to herself that she was dying, since she took out all her jewelry, most of it antique, piled it in her lap, and asked me if I wanted her to leave me this or that piece, or should she leave it to Mimi or Shari? It was all but unbearable to see her indomitable spirit finally losing the battle of denial that had sustained her for the past seven or so months. I certainly wouldn't answer her questions, considering their implications, but I couldn't stop her from asking them, either, so I chose the middle ground of declaring that I didn't want any more jewelry, and tried to get her to put the pieces away for the moment.

Back in Los Angeles, I was busy trying to get together a wardrobe for the *Daisy* tour. I still felt too weak for the ordeal of shopping, and I'd gained at least ten temporary but indisputable pounds around my middle, so I decided to ask Nolan Miller to make me the clothes I needed.

Nolan, enormously tall, enormously handsome, and enormously sweet, had the only atelier in town that I knew of where custom clothes could be ordered and the best of European-trained dressmakers could make them.

The one major item I needed was the ball gown to wear to the Lighthouse Ball. I wanted something white, very simple but draped carefully to hide my new weight, and easy to wear. I shouldn't have gone to the *Dynasty* designer for that. When Nolan had finished with the complicated dress, I could only put it on with Steve's help, because it had such an assortment of unfindable hooks and eyes.

At the last minute I realized I didn't have anything to wear over it and I asked Nolan to make a cape to go with the dress. When I arrived for the first fitting I found the cape already totally finished, white chiffon by the acre, cut on the bias and edged everywhere in six inches of fluffy white fox. "Don't you think this looks exactly like Lana Turner in the thirties?" I gasped, faint with dismay at the idea of wearing this über-Hollywood creation in sophisticated New York. "Absolutely," Nolan beamed. "Wasn't that the idea?"

No, darling Nolan, that was never the idea. That outfit ended up at the L.A. County Museum, in its costume department. I wore it for photos for all the New York newspapers, and it looked marvelous in the pictures, as uncomfortable and overdressed as I felt in it. But Nolan must have understood, because a few years later, when I needed a dress for a party for *I'll Take Manhattan*, given in the atrium of Trump Tower, he insisted on making me a free gown, "because you know why," and this time it was the most perfect dress I've ever had, lilac chiffon, plain, simple, and ornamented only by a collar of stiffened chiffon flowers around my neck.

Once I got to New York, every day as soon as I was released from the PR treadmill I went to see my mother. She was in a coma now, at home, in her own bed, with round-the-clock nurses. Jerry Barondess, who was still her doctor, deliberately did not come to see her, since there was nothing he could do but order "heroic measures" and she had definitely not wanted that.

I talked to her at length, recounting the details of what was happening, although I was almost positive that she couldn't hear me. This kind of communication, which reminded me of the times I used to report to her on my day at school, was a great comfort to me. It was just the two of us together in her room, as it had been so often during my early life, and I had things to tell her that I knew she would have approved of.

The night before the Lighthouse Ball I asked Steve to visit my mother in my place the next day, because I felt that I needed every ounce of energy, physical and psychological, that I could summon up, to get through the next evening, the evening of the ball, particularly in view of my premonition about her death. I was afraid that seeing my mother lying there, looking so terribly small and yellow, yet still so much herself, although she was unable to open her eyes or say anything, would affect my obligation not to disappoint the Lighthouse people, who expected many hundreds of guests at the Plaza ballroom. However, several times during the day Steve was able to phone me wherever I was doing PR and reassure me that her condition was stable.

The ball itself was extraordinary. As Steve and I walked up the steps to the Plaza, the blinding lights of hundreds of flashbulbs exploded, something I'd never had happen to me before. Since I didn't know the correct response to this barrage of photographers, if there is one, I looked straight ahead and concentrated on not stepping on my skirt.

The Plaza ballroom had been magnificently decorated in white and gold, as if it existed in the days of Imperial Russia, and the orchestra played waltzes. As the evening wore on and dinner was served, course by course, someone would come and ask me to dance just as my plate arrived, and bring me back to the table just as the waiter took my untouched plate away. I was too busy being polite to bother to protest at my vanishing food, but I learned that night always to have a sandwich before any dinner in my honor.

As soon as the last guests had disappeared and my role as guest of honor had been fulfilled, Steve and I went to the Edwardian Room of the Plaza for something to eat. Once I'd ordered, I turned to look at Steve and suddenly I heard myself asking, "My mother's dead, isn't she?" "Yes, she died sometime last night. She was dead when I got there this morning."

I started to weep, but I pulled myself together as best I could when I realized that, sitting there in my Lana Turner cape, sobbing away, I was attracting notice from the other diners. As I questioned Steve further, it turned out that he had spent an entire frantic day making the funeral arrangements, phoning Mimi and Jeremy, ordering the flowers, calling the boys at their colleges and arranging to get them on planes to New York, as well as tending to all the other details of notification of my mother's friends, so that the funeral could take place the next day in accordance with Jewish custom. Whenever he'd had a chance, he'd made his reassuring calls to me, aware that if I'd known, I could never have gone to the ball and would have had to let the Lighthouse down at the very last minute.

Less than twelve hours later, as the oldest of the children, I was leading the family down the aisle at Campbell's Funeral Chapel, toward a casket entirely covered in a wonderfully vivid and gay blanket of spring flowers. It is the only moment I remember about my mother's funeral.

We stayed on in New York for the few days my taskmasters at Crown allowed, and then Steve had to go back to business in California and I was off to Toronto and full-court PR press. I'd already interrupted the book tour with my operation and now there was no question of a second delay. The laws of publishing decreed that the mourning process had to wait until the ultimate amount of PR could be extracted.

As I sat on the plane to Canada, wrapped in fur, with a limo waiting in Toronto, where a three-day triumphant Canadian welcome was to follow, all I could think about was Mickey Tarcher, who had a map of the New York subway system engraved on her heart and could never bring herself to get into a taxi with me unless I guaranteed to pay for such a useless luxury, as she always considered it.

She was unique, and none of her children would ever stop being influenced by her example. She always was, and in so many ways she still is, an extraordinary woman.

Chapter Thirty-eight

AFTER THE HARDCOVER TOUR OF *PRINCESS DAISY,* I HAD BEEN AN-swering hostile questions about the auction for months, coping as best I could but always feeling I could do better.

"Natural" or not, I realized that I needed some sort of special train-ing to help me deal with the media, and fortunately I heard of a com-pany called On Camera that specialized in solving my sort of problem. Kristen Brown, who ran it, trained people to do their best on television: candidates for office, actors who were promoting their movies, and speakers for causes, as well as writers on tour.

There may be other operations like Kristen's, but I can't imagine one that would be more effective. I sat on a platform, facing Kristen and her co-interviewer, always a highly experienced television news-man, and answered questions that they fired at me, with the closed-circuit camera running. Then came the deeply awful part, as I watched them play back the interview, stopping it at crucial moments to show me exactly what I was doing.

Watching myself on television was deflating and humiliating. On television you look the way other people see you, not the way you look in the mirror to which you've become accustomed, so it's a nasty shock to see yourself talk with lips that move and smile in the wrong direction. To this day I can't stand to watch myself talking. I've cul-tivated amnesia on this subject because without it, I'd rarely speak. What a loss to the world . . .

I discovered that I often used the index finger of my right hand, known as the "queen's scepter," when I wanted to make a point. This is the single piece of body language that people hate the most, a school-marm's gesture to which everyone has been subjected far too often. I didn't always sit in a receptive and open way, with my hands resting face up on my knees, but instead tended to twist my legs around each other into a protective position that made me look as if I were trying to hide.

Kristen told me, "People pay about eighty to eighty-five percent of their attention to your body language and barely bother to listen to your words with the rest of their brain."

After a few sessions I'd learned how to always gesture on a gently curved horizontal plane, and my index finger had become all but attached to the fingers next to it. I learned how to look when I wanted to make a vitally important point, putting my fingers together under my chin in a sort of open pyramid that is called, appropriately, "templing." (Think Jimmy Carter and don't do it more than once in any interview.) I'd also learned that if I could manage to keep a smile, or at least a pleasant expression, on my face while I was being criticized, no matter how unfairly, it amazingly deflected most of the criticism.

Kristen and her partner would take turns at playing good cop / bad cop. "You love art, don't you?" she'd coo. "And beautiful interiors and clothes, and all those things you describe so well in your books?" When I agreed, she'd smile seraphically and ask, "And when did you have your face-lift?" It was moments like this, which probably would never take place in a live interview, that were deliberately shaped to keep me on my toes.

I learned that absolutely any answer was equally acceptable as long as I was comfortable with it, but that I was incapable of lying on camera. When I experimented and asked them to get me to lie about my age, I referred to myself as an "old bag" in the next sentence, an ugly expression I've never used in real life.

Probably the most important thing I tried to learn, but never managed to master totally, was the knowledge that I could actually say no. In theory, I should always be ready to choose *not* to answer a question, as long as I did it in a pleasant way. It would be ideal if I could seem to be answering the question while making a point about something entirely different, taking the interviewer's agenda into my own hands and answering only what I would have liked to have been asked.

Every time I've done this successfully, I've felt triumphant, but this difficult tactic is really the weapon of a smart and experienced politician. I used to feel a stupid, nagging obligation to answer the question that's put to me. My old days of being the teacher's pet came back to haunt me. However, now, after twenty years of being interviewed, I'm adept at holding my own and I can usually have fun with an interview, playing with it and teasing the interviewer because it's no longer a matter of life and death. Recently I was a guest on *Politically Incorrect*, where every lesson I'd ever learned about not interrupting and not being rude is thrown out of the window. To be a guest on this show is more fun than I'd ever expected to have on television. You're a good guest only if you're naughty enough, and I was as wickedly naughty as I could be.

———

SOON AFTER THE success of *Daisy*, Nat Wartels sold Crown to Random House, which was owned by Si Newhouse, one of the richest men in America. On my next trip to New York, this unknown billionaire gave a dinner party to welcome me, inviting only executives from Crown and Random House. He and Bob Bernstein, who was his second-in-command at the time, quizzed me, a total stranger, trying to get a grip on exactly who this strange Californian was besides a suddenly successful novelist.

"So where did you go to high school?" Bob began.

"Birch Wathen."

"My God, did you know my cousin, Alice Bernstein?"

"Well, of course I did, we graduated in the same class," I answered.

"What did you do after college?" Si wanted to know.

"I worked for Herb Mayes at *Good House*."

"Herb? I've known him all my life. A great man" was Si's response.

"My father was one of his best friends," I said modestly, "and Alex is one of my oldest and dearest friends," I added, knowing full well that Si had dated their daughter, Alex, at one point in her life, and that Mitzi Newhouse, his mother, and Grace Mayes were friends.

Both men's faces beamed with relief. An absolutely perfect game of Jewish Geography had just been beautifully played and I had been squarely identified as a highly credentialed, super-nice New York Jewish girl, no potentially oddball Californian exotic.

Shortly after this dinner, I left for Germany to tour the major cities, since Bantam was owned by the enormous German company Bertelsmann, which also owned my English and Australian publishers. I'd been invited to make a partly ceremonial visit to their headquarters in Gütersloh, located in a rustic region with the unforgettable name of East Westphalia.

Steve was too busy to go with me, so off I went. I'd met one or two of the Germans who worked for Bertelsmann and they were all young, all born after the war, all easy to get along with, but something about venturing to Germany alone didn't sit well with me.

I was to be met in Munich by two PR people, one a baron whose ancestral lands were in the part of Germany still controlled by Russia, the other, Anna, a pretty girl of about twenty-five who worked for him. They greeted me with flowers at the plane and checked me into the best hotel in town, the hotel that had been Hitler's favorite. As I crossed the lobby for the first time, I had a long moment of clear vision and saw it, in an unbelievably detailed way, crowded with laughing, pleasure-seeking Nazi officers and their beautiful, bejeweled lady friends. I even saw their silver fox coats and the cigarette holders they manipulated languidly. It was a startling vision into an aspect of the war, the German home front, that I'd never considered before and a disconcerting experience, an incident of unexpected, decidedly unwelcome time travel.

I had a magnificent suite but I was determined not to go to sleep until evening to try to minimize the worst of jet lag, so I asked Anna to take me to a museum for the afternoon. There we walked about rather aimlessly, looking at nineteenth-century pictures, until suddenly she exclaimed, "Oh, look, here are the masterworks of the Dachau School of landscape painting."

"WHAT DID YOU SAY?"

"The Dachau School of landscape painting," she repeated in all innocence, showing me some charming paintings of rural countryside. "It was a well-known artistic movement."

Only then did I realize that Anna lacked the faintest idea of history. My mind whirling, I couldn't decide where to start her education, but as luck would have it, we immediately came across a painting of Judith gruesomely holding by his hair the decapitated head of Holofernes. I informed her that my name came from the Old Testament, as did that of Miriam, my sister, and Jeremiah, my brother (exaggerating slightly in the case of Jeremy), because *we were Jews*.

"Oh, I love Jews, they're so creative, they have so much feeling for music, such rhythm," she replied, full of genuine enthusiasm. Ah, Sammy Davis Jr., I thought, now, finally, I know a little bit more about how you feel.

Although all the Bertelsmann executives I met, and there were many, treated me as I were Princess Daisy herself, I found that whenever I had lunch with the baron, he stubbornly resisted acknowledging by so much as the blink of an eyelash any of the things I deliberately said to get him to acknowledge that I was Jewish. This fact, of course, he knew perfectly well. It was as if he were determined to be deaf and dumb on that subject, in order to be tactful. If it's more tactful *not* to accept that a person is a Jew . . . I had a suspicion that I understood his thought process.

I forgot about the baron's attitude as we toured Munich, Hamburg, and Berlin and finally took a plane to Gütersloh, the center of this vast empire. We passed a frightening, indeed sinister, cityscape of vast, windowless warehouses filled, I can only hope, with books, before I was driven to a magnificent, strikingly modern building where I met most of the chief executives. Several of them were outside to greet me very formally, with a huge bunch of flowers and much kissing of hands. We proceeded to the office of the founder of the company, which was a tiny, timbered, ancient room, perfectly preserved inside this giant edifice, where I signed the visitors' "golden book" and sipped a cere-monial glass of sherry.

Then came lunch, in a luxurious executive dining room, with menus on which was written, "Luncheon in Honor of the Visit of Judith Krantz," followed by a list of many succulent dishes and fine wines. The first course was barely served when the baron rushed into the room. "Judith, don't eat, the press is waiting for you upstairs, and you're late already," he said, grabbing me by the arm and hustling me away from the table. I waved good-bye to my hosts, reflecting that the grandest occasions in my honor were always good for my diet, and spent five straight hours with the local reporters.

The next night there was a lavish dinner at a local hotel, which hundreds of press and executives attended. Suddenly I was confronted by the most magnificent blond, blue-eyed young man, too exaggerated an Aryan even for a Ralph Lauren ad. "Have you been to Jerusalem, Mrs. Krantz?" he asked. I confessed that I hadn't yet. "Oh, how ter-rible! And for a Jew never to have been there . . . shocking! I run our book club in Israel and I tell you that it's the most marvelous country in the world, the most delightful people, I love it! You *must* go, I insist! Promise me you'll visit me there and I'll show you everything." Weak with laughter, I promised. He was a refreshing change from the baron.

I never touch liquor on any working occasion and I had, by now, attained a reputation, entirely undeserved, as a teetotaler. Soon the dinner drew to an end, and with it, the last minutes of my official trip to Germany. All the men around me ordered a local speciality, an after-dinner drink called a *steinhäger,* which, they assured me, would knock over anyone who so much as looked at it. "I think I'd like one too," I said. "Oh no, you must not" came a chorus of protests. "No one who isn't used to it can withstand it." I insisted, and a tall, stemmed glass of clear, icy liquid was put in front of me.

My normal drink is vodka, straight up, and very cold, and the *stein-häger* didn't strike me as anything I hadn't seen before. While my pro-tectors watched, holding their breath as they contemplated the demise of their new author, I held up the glass, made the Hebrew toast to life, "L'Chayim," in a loud voice, and tossed it down in one easy swallow. As I thought, nothing new. If anything, it was mild. "May I have another, please?" I asked, making a tiny piece of Bertelsmann history.

The day after the tour ended, back in Munich, at lunch, Anna sud-denly had a brilliant idea, inspired by the television series *Roots.* "Why don't you go to Jerusalem, Judith, and go to the city hall and simply look up the records of your family tree?" she asked. As I tried to explain the history of the Diaspora to this hopelessly ignorant girl, the baron at long last decided to join the conversation.

"I admire old tribes," he said. "I once traveled for weeks with Gypsies and I found them fascinating. You realize that the Gypsies have a tradition as old as the Jews, don't you?"

I confessed to ignorance of Gypsy tradition, but the next day, as the baron and I sat at the airport, waiting for my plane back to Los Angeles, I said thoughtfully, "I've been thinking about the Gypsies and the Jews, and it seems to me that for better or worse, the Jews have given the world Einstein, Freud, Marx, and for that matter, Jesus Christ Himself—but I can't think of many Gypsies who've changed the world, can you?" Even that bloody awful baron finally had to laugh and say, "Touché."

My Australian tour was a towering success, almost all of which I spent on the phone doing radio interviews for a week in Sydney and another in Melbourne. At that time most of the Australian public could only be reached through local radio stations scattered in small towns all over the country. In the press kit that they'd all received, mention had been made of my landmark *Cosmo* article "The Myth of the Multiple Orgasm."

Australians in general were then about twenty years behind the United States in speaking frankly about sex. When the talk-show hosts, and they were all male, discovered that I'd actually say the word "orgasm" out loud, they went bonkers with joy. A live one!

They'd keep me on the phone for as long as possible and then call the PR person who was assigned to me and ask if they could please call back tomorrow for some more yummy orgasm chat. "Ah, Judith, now what, ah, *precisely,* do you mean when you, ah, speak of the 'plateau stage'?" All in all, in a country that then had a population of some eight million, less than New York City, I did eighty-four radio interviews, and *Daisy* was number one on their best-seller list for a full year. Even now, whenever I do a satellite broadcast to Australia, the second question after "How are you?" is invariably about orgasms. I loved Australia as much as I'd hated Egypt.

In England the highspot was one night in Manchester. There I was to be on a show called *Live from the Old Mill*. It was a nationally televised BBC hour and people waited two years for a chance to be in the audience, seated around tables, behind their filled wineglasses, from which they were forbidden to drink until the show was over. The three other guests were Peter Ustinov, Petula Clark, and the real Baroness von Trapp, about whom *The Sound of Music* was made.

The show was a major production, with a full-scale dress rehearsal in the afternoon, and I had to wear a body mike concealed under my skirt for twelve hours. I was convinced that each time I went to the bathroom, it was broadcast. The elderly baroness was in a foul mood . . . "*Nein, nein,* they got the whole story wrong in the movie, *nein,* the children weren't nice at all . . ." Even the normally hilarious Peter Ustinov suddenly didn't feel like being funny, and it was left to Petula Clark and me to cheer things up. When I heard her sing "Edelweiss," I thought of the little boy selling edelweiss on a mountaintop on our honeymoon, and I felt chills down my spine.

THE SUMMER AFTER my trips abroad, Steve and I were able to finally go back to Villeneuve-lès-Avignon, that little town where we'd stayed one night during our wretched, misbegotten honeymoon, and spend a week at Le Prieuré, the hotel we remembered so fondly. One night, at the local pizza place, the owner told us about the region of the Lubéron Mountains, where he went hiking. You had to circle around Avignon proper and then drive straight out east into the countryside until you came to a sign that led you to the little town of Ménerbes, which he advised us to visit.

Ménerbes was a ravishing little fortified village perched on the high, north side of the Lubéron, *le versant nord,* only a few miles away from other such villages, which had been the scenes centuries ago of terrible religious wars, with French Catholics slaughtering French Protestants to the last child. (So, what else is new?) It was surrounded everywhere by lush vineyards. From the graveyard of the oldest church in the village, which was no longer in use, you could look around over vast distances of farmland that stretched in every direction. Roussillon, Apt, Bonnieux, Oppède-le-Vieux . . . these were some of the names of the towns, large like Apt or just a collection of houses, like Oppède, that lay near the village of Ménerbes. We were so fascinated that we were drawn back to Ménerbes over and over again.

In the coming decade, Peter Mayle would spend time there and write about Ménerbes openly in *A Year in Provence,* published in 1990, and *Toujours Provence,* published in 1991, but as we went about our tours of the region, always returning to Ménerbes, all the people we met, from the artists and writers who lived quietly there half of the year, to the local inhabitants who lived there permanently, *implored* me never to use the name of Ménerbes in a book, because it would attract too many tourists, run up the price of real estate, and ruin its charm.

Mayle, however, chose to ignore these heartfelt desires and in his widely read books brought the residents and their village to the attention of the world. All that they had feared came to pass, and worse. Now I read that he himself spends his summers in one of the Hamptons because "Ménerbes is too crowded." Whose fault could that be, I wonder, Mr. Mayle?

As Steve and I drove around the countryside we came upon the little city of Cavaillon, famous for the best melons in the world, where the green Michelin guidebook promised an ancient synagogue.

Since we were there, we decided, we should take a look at it. We located the old building in a small, empty square but it was closed for the next half hour. As we waited, it seemed to both of us that we must be the only people who intended to visit, but as soon as the doors were opened by a guide, a crowd of people quickly and mysteriously materialized, speaking at least a dozen different languages.

Eager to get away from the guided tour, we bought a little pamphlet about the synagogue, which had been built in 1499 and then rebuilt in 1774, and walked around, leaving the crowd behind.

In *Mistral's Daughter,* in a scene with my heroine, Fauve, and her Jewish boyfriend, Eric Avigdor, I re-created the experience we had when we entered the central part of the synagogue.

> [They] stopped abruptly . . . taken utterly by surprise . . . in an almost empty room that nevertheless gave an immediate impression of the most gracious harmony of spirit. It could have been a perfect small salon from some abandoned palace built in the style and at the time of Versailles . . . the architect and craftsmen of Cavaillon who had worked on its interior had been trained in the unsurpassably delicate formality of Louis XV . . .
>
> Fauve leaned carefully on the balustrade . . . and thought that from this vantage point the temple looked like a ballroom in which she could imagine ladies in powered hair and men in brocaded vests dancing. But the guidebook, again consulted, informed her that she was standing on what had been the rostrum of whoever conducted the service. Her vision of dancers faded as she looked down and tried to imagine the sumptuous little temple filled with benches, and the benches crowded by people dressed as they used to dress throughout Provence, in costumes that were now only worn by folk singers performing for festivals. . . . Like all abandoned holy places, in which once the human soul has poured out its deepest emotions, it hummed with a complex energy and silenced the visitor.

I realized, as we drove away from Cavaillon, moved and deeply touched by the little, jewel-like synagogue we had come across by chance, that my next book had to be set in Provence.

We asked Jacques and Marie-France Mille, the owners of Le Prieuré, if we could keep our suite for another week and then another, until we'd spent six weeks there in all, while I was doing research and planning my novel.

For the first time I built my outline on a hero, Julien Mistral, a great painter, instead of on a heroine. Mistral proved so powerful, even in my first thoughts about him, that eventually I realized I had to balance him with three heroines.

The book starts in 1925 when Maggy, the first of the heroines, has

the strong, bold beauty of a day in the future, of an era that wouldn't dawn for another quarter-century. . . . In a time when all women had cut their hair, hers was a long, straight fall of shiny stuff, the dark orange of apricot jam, and her thick, unfashionably unplucked eyebrows were only a few shades deeper over eyes that were set almost too far apart. They were frank and spangled and wide open, the whites fresh and bright, the irises the yellow-green of a glass of Pernod before it has been diluted by water. Maggy's lips were so full and well marked that they were the focus of her face, a signal as emphatic as a signpost. . . . She looked like a large golden cat who had walked into a breeze. Nothing about her self-confident stance would have revealed her age to an observer, but her skin was as tender and new as a baby's palms and . . . dappled with faint freckles.

Maggy's name was really Magali, a name found only in the Provençal language that means *marguerite* in French or "daisy" in English, linking her to Princess Daisy in a way that only I knew but that had a strong sentimental meaning for me. A baby born in the last chapter of my newest novel, *The Jewels of Tessa Kent,* is named Daisy, and her mother, I've just realized, is named Maggie.

I've never known a real-life Daisy, but certain names hold a strange importance for me that I don't understand or try to question. When a writer discovers a character's psychologically "right" name, it's a gift to accept without question. Maggy's last name, Lunel, was taken from the nearby city of Lunel, for many Jewish families, lacking last names of their own, named themselves after their native cities, and Jews had been settled in Provence for longer than two thousand years.

Maggy was my first and only fully Jewish heroine, although the other heroines of *Mistral* are partly Jewish and many of their closest friends and lovers in my other novels are entirely Jewish.

She was the only illegitimate Jewish girl in her hometown, and she ran away at seventeen to model for painters in Paris in order to escape an arranged marriage. Soon I realized, as I was outlining the novel, that after being Mistral's greatest model and his mistress, Maggy, too, would have an illegitimate daughter, Teddy, fathered by an American Irish-Catholic. (I like to mix a heroine's ethnic backgrounds with the combination of Italian and Irish, my favorite for pure charm.) Maggy would establish the first and greatest of New York's modeling agencies, and Teddy would grow up to be kicked out of Wellesley for drinking on campus . . . speak, memory. . . . and become the top fashion model of the 1950s. She would go to Provence on a magazine photo shoot, fall in love with Mistral, her mother's former lover, and produce yet another illegitimate daughter, Fauve, a talented artist, the third heroine of the story and the daughter of the title.

I'm telling you all this because it occurred to me that a novelist writing her memoirs should, at least once, briefly describe the construction of the backbone of a plot. By establishing Mistral on the one hand, and his dizzying but direct relationship to a family line of the three illegitimate redheads on the other, mother, daughter, and granddaughter, I had a solid basis on which to build the complications that would enrich my plot and thicken the stew. I always think of a novel as a stew full of many different ingredients, added slowly and with care— or quickly with unexpected invention—and then watched over with my most active and alert attention as I constantly readjust the flavor, coaxing everything to cook together slowly, simmering and simmering, until the entire succulent dish is ready to be devoured.

Now began the research as I gave Ménerbes the name Félice. Mistral and Kate, his rich American wife, would settle on a big farm with a large farmhouse, or *mas,* named La Tourello, based on a combination of the real farms we visited. I described Félice and La Tourello without sacrificing any of the true local color or charm, yet without pinpointing their location. The amount of research I needed was enormous, since besides an intimate knowledge of period life in Provence, it included the art world of Paris in the 1920s and 1930s, the world of New York fashion modeling from the 1930s through the late 1970s, and, most difficult of all, France as seen from the inside during the German Occupation.

I had an exceptionally important stroke of luck that made the book very different than I had anticipated. The Milles, who became wonderful friends, sent me to see a man named Jean Garcin, who held the office of president of the Conseil Général de Vaucluse, which is the equivalent of being the senior senator from Provence.

I had made the mistaken assumption that because Mistral would be forty during the war, he would be able to continue painting in Félice during the war years. As I told Jean Garcin my plot, he suddenly stopped me and asked if Mistral had been a collaborator. Indignantly I said that of course he hadn't. Garcin, who had been in the local Resistance from the earliest days of the occupation, told me that unless Mistral had indeed collaborated, as an able-bodied man, he would unquestionably have been sent to work on a farm in Germany, to replace a German soldier. Stunned by reality, I had to admit that the Julien Mistral I envisioned would never have allowed a mere war to interrupt his work.

Now, deep into my story, I found myself with a "hero" who had, in one way or another, been a collaborator and I had to deal with this fact. The story turned serious, the acts of collaboration became all-important, and the consequences of Mistral's wartime behavior were to influence the entire plot of the novel, particularly Fauve's reaction. When she discovered the truth about her father, especially the fact that Mistral had refused to give refuge to his faithful Jewish art dealer, Adrian Avigdor, Eric's father, she broke with Mistral entirely and never saw him again during his lifetime. This made the plot infinitely more dramatic and more meaningful than anything I had planned to write.

As we left Jean Garcin, he looked at me and asked, "Madame, are you Jewish?" When I told him I was he said, "So is my wife. We met in the Resistance." The next day he sent me an invaluable gift, a privately printed history of the Jews of Avignon and the surrounding countryside, by Armand Mossé, of which only three hundred copies exist. Without the facts I found in this book, I could still have written *Mistral,* but it would never have contained the many vital details about the lives of the Jews of the past that added great substance to my story.

After Mistral's death, Fauve is informed that in his will he has left her a group of works that are hung in his studio and called the Cavaillon series. Reluctantly Eric persuades her to go to see them.

Fauve . . . raised her eyes and faced the studio. . . . There was nothing in all that vast space but some enormous paintings, larger than Mistral had ever painted, each hung with an exactitude of placement that spoke of much thought. . . . Then, on the far wall she saw the largest painting of all and was immediately claimed by its magnetism. All the brilliant profusion of other images faded around her and she narrowed her vision, approaching the gigantic canvas on which a seven-branched candelabra blazed with a crescendo of essential light, a monumental menorah that radiated the glory of thousands of years of faith against a background of triumphant crimson. Fauve stood there speechless, looking upward, her heart leaping, her mind empty of everything but awe.

Out loud, from behind her, Eric said the words that Julien Mistral had painted in tall, bold letters underneath the base of the meonorah.

"*La Lumière Qui Vit Toujours. La synagogue de Cavaillon,* 1974—the light that lives forever . . ."

"He . . . he went to Cavaillon!" Fauve cried out in wonder and joy. . . . "But the other paintings? What . . . ?"

Together they walked the length of the studio and stopped in front of the first huge painting. . . . There two tall candles were set in polished candlesticks, a twisted loaf of bread and a silver goblet, brimming with wine, stood on a white tablecloth. Each of the simple, elemental forms passionately spoke of gratitude for the gifts of the Creator to man. A peace, a gaiety, a joyful solemnity poured forth from the painting and Fauve nodded her head in the beginnings of comprehension.

"*Shabbat,*" said the bearded art expert from Paris, translating the inscription that was written not in French now but in the letters of the Hebrew alphabet. "The Sabbath." Fauve searched the strong, unfamiliar evocative shapes of the letters and saw in them the brushwork that was distinctively Mistral's, vivid and fierce, yet contained within a discipline to which he had never bowed before.

In the course of this scene, Fauve and Eric look at the other paintings, which she discovers to be tributes to the Feast of the Exodus, on which Mistral used the symbols of the Song of Songs, of *Shavous,* the Summer Festival, and of *Sukos,* the Autumn Feast.

Something deep in Fauve opened and finally understood: Julien Mistral had crossed the green fields of time and lived in old Jerusalem; his pagan brush had been transported and he had expanded his last and greatest forces on painting these celebrations of a people who had—who still—worshiped an invisible God.

He had respected the invisibility of their God. He had not tried the impossible; he had not attempted to paint the voice from the Burning Bush, but he had reached into the heart of their festivals and painted the spirit in which they commemorated their God, and painted it in a way that all the other peoples of the earth could understand, for all men lived by the ever-turned wheel of nature.

As Fauve and Eric finally leave the studio she turns back as she passes Mistral's easel, "caught by the sight of a scrap of paper that was tacked into the wood. On it, in her father's familiar handwriting, was just one line. She paused. The bit of paper was worn, yellow and smudged by a rainbow of fading colors, as if it had been much handled, yet it flew from the easel like a flag bearing a motto.

"Hear O Israel, the Lord our God, the Lord is one," she said, reading out loud. "That's all it says."

"Isn't that enough?" Eric asks her.

I KNEW THAT I had never written anything better than *Mistral's Daughter*. It got wonderful reviews and became number one on the *New York Times* list on February 20, 1983. Dr. S.'s grudging reaction to the book was that it was "better than the others." This remark was said in a tone that made it yet another put-down of my first two novels.

However, it was less surprising than the reaction of Ivan Nabokov, my French publisher, nephew of Vladimir Nabokov. Although Ivan had made a great deal of money with *Scruples* and *Daisy,* he now flatly refused to publish *Mistral*. It was unthinkable, he told me, using an absurd comparison. "How would you feel if a Frenchman dared to write about your Civil War?" he asked me furiously. Did he imagine, I wondered, that Americans felt the same shame about the Civil War as the French did about events that had taken place during the not-so-distant Occupation?

The book was quickly bought for France by Edition Stock, whose publisher, Jean Rosenthal, as it happened, had translated my other novels into French. When *Mistral* was published it instantly became far and away the greatest success I ever had in France, a country where American novelists were not, at least at that time, generally widely appreciated—unlike others countries, such as Italy and Germany, where they were read with gusto. (Now my novels are published in forty-seven languages, including Mandarin Chinese, and I've just added Lithuania, my mother's homeland.)

One day, back in Beverly Hills, in the winter of 1982, Steve tracked me down by phone. He knew my favorite shopping routes and he was able to find me dallying at the Saint Laurent boutique. He told me to come home instantly, for he had a visitor who wanted to hear the entire story of the book told to him in French because his English wasn't strong. He'd heard about the unpublished manuscript.

For the next two hours I sat with Jean Chalopin, a quizzical, brilliant, eager, and oddball young Frenchman, and recounted every last in and out of all the almost sixty years of the plot. When I was finished, Chalopin, who worked for the European broadcaster CLT, headquartered in Luxembourg, immediately decided to finance the making of

Mistral as an eight-hour miniseries to be shot entirely on location in Paris and Provence. This meant, as I allowed the news to sink in, that Steve would be living in France for at least eighteen months. And so would I.

When I told Dr. S. that my work with him would have to be terminated almost immediately, he didn't express the slightest worry that any important insights might remain unrevealed or that I still possessed any unexplored neurosis. He'd certainly enjoyed a better education in the workings of the publishing business than any other shrink in L.A.

Like Dr. Rubenstein, he said nothing to try to put anything we'd done in the last eight years into perspective. Horrifyingly too late, I finally understood that I had become nothing but a three-time-a-week meal ticket and if the trip to Paris hadn't come about, Dr. S. might have let me lie on his couch telling him my adventures with this publisher and that editor for eight more years. The expression "better late than never" doesn't begin to cover how I felt.

For years, most of what he had been getting were constant updates on my business life as a novelist, and he'd been satisfied with that! Worse, far worse, I'd become accustomed to giving him that! He'd never pushed me farther, never made me work on the really difficult stuff of relationships and feelings, as a good and honest analyst is expected to do as a matter of course. Too many patients, including me, hate to work on the hard, unpleasant, painful, embarrassing, deeply private material of their lives and will drift, if allowed to do so.

Most unforgivably of all, Dr. S. had never deigned to use the three novels I'd written while I went to him to illuminate the raw material of my own neurotic problems, and yet a good analyst would have seen them as a gold mine of insight. My individual creativity should never have been ignored just because it wasn't Kafka. I wrote him to that effect some ten years ago but I have yet to receive an answer. I haven't been expecting one.

It should never be *comfortable* to see a shrink just because it's become a habit you can afford. I hadn't allowed myself to realize this. If I'd had to struggle for the money to pay him, I'm sure I would have given him up years earlier and been the better for it. I blame myself severely for my lack of introspection. I'd cheated no one but myself, and those analytic years, which could have been vitally important, were largely lost.

I suppose Dr. S. *must* have helped me with some important issues, but I can't put a finger on what they might be, although he was fairly good on the subject of my sons as they turned into men. I'd certainly discussed my deep and ongoing problems of self-esteem with him, but I don't feel that he'd helped me to understand and cope with them. If anything, he added to them by the way he rejected my work. I had recurring dreams of being horribly mistreated by a hairdresser while I was in analysis with him . . . dreams that were a play on words about him, dreams that he must have understood but never explained. No, indeed, Dr. S. was not—is not—an ornament to his profession.

It's an unfortunate fact of that particular profession that many analysts, like Dr. S., don't ask themselves if a patient really needs them any longer, not even when the patient is functioning well, working well, and is basically content, as I was when I left for Paris. Worse, many analysts *prefer* to treat such patients as long as they continue to PAY ON TIME. Needless to say, I paid on the dot! Dr. S.'s last words to me were perfectly in character, totally indicative of his attitude toward a woman of fifty-five.

"You'll be fine," he said. "You're a big girl now."

Chapter Thirty-nine

STEVE AND I DECIDED TO RENT DURING THE TIME WE'D BE IN PARIS, and to leave our Beverly Hills house without a tenant, since we knew, from having rented our New York apartment while we were in Toronto, that even respectable-looking tenants do amazing damage to a house not their own.

We went to Paris, apartment hunting, staying at the Ritz, and looked at the ads in the *International Herald Tribune*. One in particular attracted us, an apartment on the Ile Saint-Louis, on the Quai de Bourbon. It sounded as romantic, as historic, as utterly Parisian as any location we'd ever heard of.

On a warm and marvelously sunny day, we arranged to see it and discovered a dream of a three-room walk-up, three flights up a dark, curving staircase, with a large living room where four tall windows looked right out onto the Seine. Wonder of wonders, it came with a garage in the courtyard, as well as a two-room flat on a higher floor, for any domestic help we might hire. In the kitchen was a wealth of beautiful dishes, glasses, and silver, as well as sturdy pots and pans, shown us by Madame, the apartment's high-born and self-important owner.

How could we possibly have been so lucky? we asked each other as we sat at one of the cafés just at the point of the Ile Saint-Louis, from which you could see the towers of Notre-Dame on the Ile de la Cité. We were carried away, for we knew that these islands, lying in the middle of the Seine, connected to each other by a footbridge, were the spot where a tribe of fishermen, the Parisii, first established that tiny settlement called Lutèce that would grow to become Paris. Here was the ultimate heart of the city, a living heart inhabited since A.D. 200 We didn't even have to make a decision or ask anyone's advice; we knew we couldn't pass up this unique chance to live in the oldest section of Paris, with its almost two thousand years of history. We had to start paying rent immediately, although it would be months before we could move in, but we'd anticipated that.

My only fear was the gleaming, highly polished staircase. I'd managed to fall down two flights of stairs in my life, without damage, but I had a minor phobia about descending a steep staircase. I'd just hold on tightly to the banister, I decided, because there was no way I could imagine not living in that apartment.

We went back to Beverly Hills to pack up. I had two round plywood folding tables made so that we could eat at one of them and bring out the second whenever we entertained. Bright round tablecloths and napkins were made for the tables from a yellow and pink Provençal fabric I found at Pierre Deux. I imagined the second room as a combination library and dining room, since it had been almost unfurnished when we'd seen it.

A reliable friend of Mimi's was found to house-sit in Beverly Hills, arrangements were made to pay the gardeners and the pool man, and in the last days of 1982 we arrived in Paris, again staying at the Ritz until we'd actually moved in.

By this time, over many trips, we'd made a warm friend at the Ritz front office, or *réception,* a young man from the Italian Alps named Helmut Profensor, who was blond, lean, ironic, and incredibly efficient. The first thing Steve needed in our new place was a telex, and when he found he couldn't make it work, Helmut came over on a Sunday and figured it out, the two of them sitting on the floor and puzzling over the damned machine until we finally were back in touch with the world. (The fax did not yet exist.)

Meanwhile, I was making a few discoveries of my own. All the lovely tableware and kitchenware we'd been shown had been replaced by the cheapest possible stuff, so our "completely furnished" apartment now possessed one dozen plain white plates, one dozen ugly all-purpose wine glasses, and one dozen sets of plain stainless-steel place settings. Also the only pieces of kitchen equipment that worked were the fridge and two of four gas burners, making boiling water easy, if Madame the landlady from the lower depths had been kind enough to leave us a teakettle, which she had not. No sharp kitchen knives, almost no mixing bowls, not enough equipment to prepare a real meal. All the ornaments that had made the living room charming were gone, even pictures had been removed, and the second room was entirely bare, missing the television set that had been there before. She herself had prudently disappeared and only showed her face when we finally left that apartment to make sure we hadn't stolen her stainless steel.

The beds were out of *La Bohème*—no, we'd been too excited to bother to bounce on them before we'd rented the apartment. The towels had disappeared with the dishes; the living-room and bedroom curtains were filthy; the bedroom carpet revealed itself, now that we weren't looking only at the view and jumping up and down in excitement, to be so grimy and tattered that I preferred not to walk on it in bare feet. In short, we'd been ripped off. But there was still the wonderful location, the view of the Seine.

Oh, yes. That view. It started to rain hard the day we moved in and continued steadily throughout the winter and misnamed "spring." Soon the Seine was closed to all river traffic, since the water had risen so high that there was no headroom under the bridges. And as for the location, as one of the women I met explained, "It's utterly impossible to park on the Ile Saint-Louis, there's no Métro stop, no bus stop, and you can never get a taxi, so if you entertain, do it in a restaurant people can get to, or no one will ever accept your invitations."

Within a short time, I'd bought new beds and bedding and a comfortable sofa for the second room so we could sit and watch the fire—a never-realized fantasy, although I'd ordered wood—put down a new carpet in the bedroom; hung posters; bought flowering plants; had all the curtains cleaned; and gone to the Bazaar de l'Hôtel de Ville—the BHV, as it was known—the biggest hardware store in Paris, and bought new kitchen stuff, plates and all, some of which I'm still using.

Everything purchased on the Ile Saint-Louis was almost twice the price as the same thing on the "mainland" of Paris, from toilet paper to laundry, from a bunch of bananas to a cup of tea. The stores all enjoyed a monopoly, since most inhabitants chose never to cross any of the bridges that connected the island to the Right and Left Banks, because it was such a long walk and just too much trouble. Longtime inhabitants of the Ile Saint-Louis, unlike us, had actually chosen to be prisoners there.

Even when the apartment was in some rough order, nothing could change the weather, the worst, we were told by the papers, since the French had started keeping records in Napoleon's time. In the early days I used to stare out at the swollen Seine, where sheets of rain were hitting the waters, watching huge trees float by, waiting, engulfed in utter gloom, to see a drowned body go by. Only the croissants Steve brought me for breakfast from a nearby café made me drag myself out of bed in the morning.

This had nothing to do with Paris, not, of course, the Paris of my twenty-first year but the Paris we'd grown to know over our many visits since then. An acquaintance told me that if a house on the Ile Saint-Louis caught on fire, the whole place would go up, because the streets were too narrow for fire engines. Another asked me if I hadn't noticed the *coupe-gorge* atmosphere. Damn right I had! If you were going to have your throat cut in Paris, it would have been there, where the riverbanks and the single main street were barely lit at night.

For months we ate dinner almost every night at the friendly Brasserie de l'Ile, at the corner, putting up our umbrellas and making a run for it from our front door to the welcoming warmth of the big restaurant, at which we sat at long tables, covered with paper placemats, among hardy strangers who watched in amazement as I removed layer after layer of garments and hung them on a hat rack.

I finally found a young woman to cook dinner and a handsome native of Portugal, Alberto by name, to drive our rented car and help out around the house. He was really an experienced butler, he told us proudly, and this job was a comedown in the world. He and his wife lived in the little apartment across the courtyard.

Since Steve hadn't yet found an office to rent, his blond secretary temporarily worked at the only desk in the house, in the living room. Although I knew she'd soon be gone, and I wasn't ready to work anyway, not having my own desk was as bad for my morale as the menacing waters of the dark, racing Seine.

We discovered that Alberto was taking our rented car out at night and speeding. The French police have cameras that record the license numbers of cars going over the limit. It took a while to find this out, since Steve's secretary and Alberto, a revoltingly carnal pair, had wasted no time in flinging themselves into an affair and she was hiding his traffic tickets from us when she went through the mail. We were able to fire her, but he refused to be fired. Instead, he blackmailed us.

Why were we susceptible to blackmail? I'd given one cocktail party and asked Alberto to get me some extra waiters. He said he could, but only if I paid them in cash. Having paid in cash, all unknowingly I'd violated an important law. He said he'd turn us in if we kicked him out and he was just the type to do it. As new residents, in a country whose laws we didn't understand, we didn't want to risk the chance of trouble. Looking back, it's easy to see that we should have gone to the American embassy and explained our problem. Alberto would probably have been deported, according to French friends who heard about him later.

Alberto was also the antihero of my favorite French domestic story. When I finally had a cook, she refused to serve us at the table because that "wasn't her job." Alberto, the butler, also refused to serve because we were only two people, and a self-respecting butler serves at least three or more people, not just his employers. When I finally managed to get this Marx Brothers explanation out of them, incredulous but still hungry, torn between laughter and rage, I went into the kitchen and dished up dinner myself. The next day I fired the cook, but we still couldn't figure out how to get rid of Alberto.

Trying to keep house in France under these conditions was a full-time hellish job and I got no work done on my next book, which I called *I'll Take Manhattan*. I was often to think that never was a book more aptly titled.

However, a major and important difference between life in Beverly Hills and life in Paris became evident almost instantly. Our social life in Paris was exceptionally intense, almost from the day we arrived, and it varied from the bohemian to the aristocratic, while that of Beverly Hills had become predictable and overly oriented toward the film industry.

When we'd moved to California I was forty-three and had been forced to leave behind a large group of good friends, built up over the years, both before marriage and after, who cut through the life of Manhattan in a dozen different directions. When we arrived in Los Angeles we knew only a few people through Steve's business. We found ourselves almost completely uprooted. The first year in L.A. had been wasted with our new, grass-smoking buddies because once we no longer smoked, they stopped being interesting. From that time on, besides my sister, I didn't seem to meet women to whom I could become close. Although we entertained the many new couples we met, we discovered that there were only a few of them we enjoyed enough to get to know on easy, just-the-four-of-us terms.

It's difficult, slow work to make new friends in a strange city in your mid-forties. All the Beverly Hills women I met had known each other since the days they carpooled each other's children to school, and they formed a tight connection that didn't expand to admit a stranger.

Yes, I'd found women to chat with at my gym, but they were all movie stars, and as a civilian, I'd never yet met a movie star I could truly consider a real friend on a peer level, although Ali MacGraw came very close. Basically, they live in their own special worlds, and often their closest friends are in the film business.

After I started writing fiction my life became so busy that I didn't have a free minute for the kind of time that is needed to meet people and nourish friendships. This lack of close women friends was the greatest hardship of my new career, including book tours. Except for my annual birthday lunch with Mimi, and my lunches with my friend and superb public relations expert, Judi Davidson, I didn't have lunch with another woman from the time *Scruples* was published until we left for Paris, some five years later. For me, having a lunch in a restaurant killed a day I could have spent writing or rewriting or outlining or researching, to say nothing of all the time spent on PR. I was consumed by my work. My nonfamily, nonbusiness relationships consisted largely of phone calls to Alex Mayes, with whom I've never lost touch, who has been "family" to me since we grew up enough to be able to eliminate the difference in our ages. Carole Baron, who lived three thousand miles away, was the only new woman friend I made and only the fact that we'd both majored in "telephone" managed to keep us together.

The friendship of women is of inestimable importance to me. It's as essential as water. I'd spent eight of my most formative years yearning hopelessly for it, I'd had it during high school and college, and in New York, but in those first years we spent in Beverly Hills, true new friends eluded me.

I have them now, in sharp, welcome contrast to those early days, through my involvement with the Blue Ribbon of the Music Center of Los Angeles County, the most efficient fund-raising group of women in the arts that exists. I make time for the Blue Ribbon no matter how busy I am, and through it I've met an ever-expanding number of interesting, lovable, hardworking, and outgoing women, whose friendship means the world to me.

Although we'd arrived in Paris with only one contact, she was the perfect person to know and through her we exploded into an exciting, multidimensional social life. The summer before we moved to Paris, we'd been on vacation in Venice when Nancy Kahane had phoned to tell me that *People* wanted to do a story on me in Avignon for *Mistral,* and to go there immediately. There had been no use in protesting; a story in *People* is every publicist's dream.

The reporter's name was Pam Andriotakis—it was for Pam's birthday that I gave the cocktail party that made me vulnerable to blackmail—and we spent three days with her and the photographer she brought along, becoming more and more at ease each day. Pam was young and unmarried, in her late twenties, but she'd been working in Paris for some six years and knew a large number of people. Pam was a native of Detroit, highly intelligent, very mature for her age, with dark, curly hair and strong, attractive features. During the three days we spent together in the Lubéron, Steve and I quickly found her warm and delightful.

Pam was our lifeline. First she introduced us to a charming, informal couple, Pat and Fred Painton. Fred was the head of the *Time* bureau and they'd lived in Paris for twenty years. The Paintons quickly introduced us to Dimi and Yvonne Paniza, of *Reader's Digest,* where Dimi was chief. Super-sophisticated Yvonne turned out to be one of the key women in Paris. She'd gone to school in a worldly convent where she'd laid the groundwork for her vast network of future friendships, and through Dimi she'd made hundreds more.

Yvonne, whose brother, Vincent Fourcade, had decorated the Sterns' memorable party so many years ago, almost immediately gave a lunch to introduce me to eight of her friends and there I met Jean Bakker, the Canadian wife of the Dutch ambassador to France, and one of the dearest women I'd ever known.

Within weeks, I found myself lunching at embassies all over the rue de Grenelle, with an entire diplomatic corps of ladies available for friendship.

Leo Lerman of *Vogue* had insisted that I call a friend of his named Sybille Gaussen. "She knows everybody and everything," he'd told me. I phoned Sybille and, since she lived on the Ile Saint-Louis, invited her for dinner. She wouldn't eat, she informed me, because she was on a diet, but she'd come over if I promised not to offer her anything but water. I expected an overweight sophisticate in her fifties.

Early in April, tiny Sybille burst into our lives, not more than twenty-five, a wizard stockbroker, as pretty as she was devilish, with snapping black eyes, a divinely dirty laugh, and a wicked charm. She hadn't brought an umbrella, since she lived just down the street, but by the time it came for her to leave, the returning rain was almost a flood. Steve made her a rainproof garment out of a giant black plastic garbage bag, with holes for her eyes and arms.

That began a deep friendship with Sybille and a second important friendship with her parents, who were our age: Gérard Gaussen, a high-ranking, retired diplomat, and his impressive and beautiful wife, Solange. They invited us to spend weekends at their enchanted chateau, Saint-Antonin, right at the base of Mont Sainte-Victoire, in Aix-en-Provence, which was graced with a view so totally Cézanne that it existed on the verge of unreality.

Suddenly I had a phone call from Polly Platt Grchich, a Wellesley classmate from Philadelphia. I hadn't even known she was living in Paris, but she was installed in the very heart of the French aristocracy with her husband, Andi, a Serbian who would have been (at the very least) a grand duke if such titles still existed. Polly gave a big party for us and there wasn't a single person there who didn't have a title. When I heard a madly elegant marquise rush in and demand "le peepee room," I discovered the ultimately chic way to ask for the ladies' room in French, but I never used it myself. Something about the phrase demanded that I be, at the least, a baronne.

Michelle Tourneville came into our lives when we went to her little Russian restaurant, La Tchaika, for lunch and discovered her, the co-owner, a deliciously charming redhead from Brittany. We fell in mutual love and Michelle gave a dinner party for us that made us feel as if we were in the French movie *Cousin Cousine,* in which everybody was related. There was her boyfriend, Georges Delorme; Georges's first wife, who was the chef who co-owned the Tchaika with Michelle; one of Michelle's former boyfriends with his new love; her father with his girlfriend . . . we never wanted to leave her little apartment, and, in fact, we often returned.

Soon we knew an authentic combination of Auntie Mame and grande dame, Helyette de Rieux, a friend of Pam's and, we discovered, of Herb and Grace Mayes and of Muriel and George Marek, who had long worked for my father. Helyette received almost every Sunday in a lavish-luxe picnic style she'd invented, serving a buffet of all the best smoked salmon and foie gras and cheeses and little rich cakes, without a main course. The first time we went to one of Helyette's crowded parties, Steve spilled wine on her. Three times. First he spilled the white, then the red, and then the champagne. He was deeply embarrassed at being so clumsy until he understood that far from being annoyed, she read into these accidents a sign that he felt an enormous sexual attraction for her and was just trying to get her attention. From that moment on, she adored him.

Polly Guggenheim, a sculptor who'd lived in Paris most of her life, became our guide into the art world, just as Helmut, and his lover, a most beautiful Argentinian named Edouardo, became our guides into the gay world. The newspaper world was revealed by Carolyn Pfaff, whose husband, Bill, wrote for the *International Herald Tribune,* and one day I woke up to a phone call from Nicole, the duchess of Bedford, who'd been told to contact me by Jack LeVien. "Come to lunch at Maxim's tomorrow, and on Sunday, Gerard van de Kemp, the curator of Giverny, is having a party for us out in Monet's garden and you can't miss that!" she said to a perfect stranger. *Indeed not.*

Things like that don't happen in Beverly Hills, can't happen in Beverly Hills. Paris is New York and Washington, D.C., rolled into one. Little happens in the provinces of France; everything happens in Paris, from entertainment to art to politics to publishing to international relations to big business, and we were lucky to plunge directly into everything but big business and politics.

Steve and I were the new kids on the block and we had more dates than we could handle. Everyone was curious about us, this American couple who spoke French, the husband a film and television producer (*Fritz* had enjoyed a giant success in France), the wife a "best-seller." (In French I wasn't called a best-selling novelist, but was known, in Franglais, as a "best-seller" myself.) Almost everyone we met was interested and hospitable and friendly, totally different from the usual picture of the French as cold to all but their own kind.

Of course, if we hadn't been able to speak French, it would have been another matter entirely. The French judge you almost entirely on your ability to speak their language, and we passed that crucial test. Otherwise we would have been confined socially to the world of the other Americans living in Paris.

My French, now that I was using it again all day, every day, had become so fluent that strangers often assumed that I had a White Russian background, as in "You must know my friend, the Princess Karinskaya." Apparently White Russians are known for their gift for languages. I learned, whenever I met a stranger, to quickly and casually mention that I was of Russian Jewish descent because I knew that no matter how friendly our hostess, some of her guests would inevitably be anti-Semites and it was better to let them know I was Jewish as soon as I could, even if I had to drag the fact in from left field. The French we met were all of the generation that had been indoctrinated as children with the idea that the Jews killed Christ . . . the two of us included . . . and, in not a few of them, this impression still lingered. I wanted to get my background straight with such people as quickly as possible so we didn't waste time on each other.

The wisdom of bringing up my background was reinforced by a conversation I had with Nicole Bouchet de Fareins, who was now living alone, all her daughters having married. She made exceptional arrangements of artificial flowers, which she sold to a decorating firm.

"Tell me," she asked seriously, the first time we were alone. "You and Steve don't engage in any religious observance, do you?"

"None at all," I answered.

"Then why do you say you're Jewish?"

"Because we *are*."

"But look, Judy, you don't *have* to be since you're not religious."

"It's not a question of religious belief or observance or of 'having to be' or not 'having to be,' " I said, patiently, trying to explain to this Catholic who only went to Mass on Easter. "We were born of Jewish parents who were born of Jewish parents going back, I assume, for thousands of years, barring the occasional pogrom and rape. My ancestors were Jews as far back as you can possibly imagine. That alone is more than enough to make us Jews."

Shaking her head sadly at this persistent folly of mine, she answered, "I have *never* understood why on earth you would actually *choose* to be Jewish when you could so easily be something else."

To Nicole, Jewishness was a genuine misfortune, a terrible burden to carry through life, something you should deny if you could get away with it. She could never understand, no matter how I put it to her, that because you are born into a group that has been persecuted throughout history, you have *all the more reason* not to turn your back on it and live a lie, simply because circumstances could be twisted to make such a rejection possible. That conversation was, for me, the final death knell to a relationship that had started when I was twenty.

Ginette, to my sorrow, had gone back to live in her native England, after the death of Paul-Emile. They'd both grown to know and love Steve. Before we moved to Paris, one year we'd arrived by plane in London on the Boxing Day holiday, the day after Christmas. Steve and I had been taken to our suite at the Connaught and had only then been informed that room service was closed until the next morning.

Starving, we took a cab over to the Savoy, where the headwaiter looked at us in our traveling clothes and explained that a formal dance was taking place in the dining room and we could be seated only if we sat out of sight behind a screen in another room and promised not to dance under any circumstances. "Would it be all right if I hummed to the music?" Steve asked as we were discreetly hidden away.

A minute later I heard Ginette's voice raised in surprise and delight. She and Paul-Emile were sitting at the next table, not in dinner clothes either. "Darlings, how wonderful! Come right over here and sit down with us! What luck to see you! You know Larry, don't you?" she said, introducing me to Laurence Olivier. I gasped and gaped as I shook hands with Heathcliff, man of my dreams, but soon I realized that time had passed and Heathcliff had vanished with the passage of years. However, we had a memorable dinner and Sir Laurence insisted on taking us back to our hotel.

He put Ginette, Paul-Emile, and me into the backseat and arranged Steve in the front, between the driver and himself. Olivier then proceeded to make the most unmistakable pass at Steve that I've ever seen, completely ignoring the three of us. Ginette and Paul-Emile were clearly not surprised. As he dropped us off, he told Steve there'd be a ticket to the play he was currently acting in waiting at the box office for him the next day. "Oh, and I'll leave one for her, too," he added absently, after noticing that I was getting out of the car with Steve. We went to the play, but we didn't go backstage afterward.

On another occasion we'd gone to drinks at Ginette's to find that the only other guest was Marlene Dietrich. Ginette took me aside. "If she likes you both, she'll invite you to dinner tonight and you can't possibly say no, I don't care what your plans are." After a half hour Dietrich decided that she liked us. "I'm leaving now," she said, "to prepare a tiny little bite to eat. I'll expect you all in half an hour." "But . . . but. . . ." Steve said, about to tell her that we had dinner reservations. "We'll be there," I said, giving him a look he understood.

When the four of us arrived at her nearby apartment, she proceeded to cook and serve in the kitchen a superb five-course meal, including individual filets mignons she must have bought that morning, insisting that, since she was the cook, she wouldn't sit down with us. Dietrich was not only a fantastic cook but a glorious one, for she managed to spend an enormous amount of time climbing dangerously and with a great show of her legs up and down the kitchen stepladder, much to my husband's joy. The next morning we sent her six dozen long apricot tulips and she sent us a thank-you note on her proudest new possession, a typewriter.

If Ginette had still been in Paris now, it would have made life even more fun, but she had been glad to leave, for there was new management at Balmain and nothing was the same for her.

While I had the criminal Alberto to drive me from appointment to appointment, Steve had his own driver, Elie, who worked only on films. Elie was a gentle madman who would take one disgusted look at a traffic jam, quickly pull the car up onto the sidewalk, and drive straight down it, slowly and carefully, never hitting anyone on foot, but with the attitude that he owned Paris. He was never stopped by a policeman. Perhaps he was a policeman?

My husband was plunged into the problems of preproduction, complicated to the power of X times 10 by the fact that CBS had bought the American television rights and suddenly decided that they needed all eight hours of *Mistral* completed on an "accelerated basis" to fill a hole in their schedule for some future sweeps.

Steve realized at once that the only way he could deliver *Mistral* on time was to have two major *first* units working simultaneously, with two directors, two line producers, two editors, two sets of caterers, two of absolutely everything. Suddenly Steve found himself in the unenviable position of making two films at the same time, one shot in Paris and one down in Provence, with only one set of actors.

During the first few months, he flew back to Hollywood twice to cast the three stars, settling with CBS on Stacy Keach for Mistral, Stefanie Powers for Maggy, and Lee Remick as Kate, Mistral's rich American wife. They all were to work during the months of May, June, and July, wrapping the series by August.

Preproduction had started with the rain as soon as we arrived in Paris, and I soon discovered a husband who was horribly different from the man I had married and learned, I thought, to know. Steve had always discussed his business problems with me, and I had long ago realized that the glamour of show business was, for a producer, one long litany of shit. It simply went with the territory.

But now he was absolutely devoured by the problems of keeping everything and everyone on track. This was shit on another level entirely, a sewer filled almost to the top with it. It was sink or swim for him in a most drastic way. Steve was pioneering a new way to do a miniseries, entirely on location, using only foreign crews, and two of them at that, and although the show was largely financed by European money, he had to deal with the constant interference of CBS. There was only one person in his life who wasn't involved in the production, only one person with whom he didn't have to be calm, reasonable, and upbeat, the unflappable captain of the good ship *Mistral*. You guessed it.

I became quite terrified of this new Steve. I truly mean *terrified!* His mood was so grim that I felt I couldn't talk to him about it and add to his problems. I had no way to anticipate his reactions. He had fits of anger at such unexpected things, like my purchase of two green opaline bottles, the same green opaline we'd been collecting since our honeymoon, that I withdrew into the background as much as I could, afraid of arousing his unpredictable ire. I was in an impossible position. I'd lost my best friend and I couldn't tell him about it because he wasn't my best friend anymore. Once he was home, if we weren't going out for the evening, he spent all of his time on the phone or sending telexes, so my lack of vivacity didn't matter to him. Matter? He never noticed.

Those days of the most maddening kind of activity, those days of a million aggravations, were on a profound basis—and this is what I unfortunately did not understand—a *joy* to him. He never tried to explain this to me because he didn't even realize it himself while it was happening. No matter how he behaved, he actually *adored* every bloody impossible minute of it! He *loved* being away from Hollywood and working in French with people whose craftsmanship was so much better than anything he could have hoped for at any price in Hollywood; he *loved* the challenge of being a pioneer in his field; he *loved* all the hundreds of people who depended on him for final decisions; he *loved* every minute of running his own big show, no matter how crazily angry it made him on a daily basis. He wouldn't have missed a single infuriating second of it. He had no idea how gloomy and frightening he'd become.

If I'd only known, I would have stopped worrying about him. I should have ignored him entirely . . . although this wasn't a possibility for me. "Should have" should have been my middle name, instead of Bluma-Gittel. Unfortunately, I was deeply upset by his personality change, which made me feel abandoned and unloved, so I scurried around trying to smooth over whatever I could on the home front. I should have moved to the Ritz!

The noted composer Vladimir Cosma started to create a score for the series that would become an immense hit throughout the world. The title song, "L'Amour en heritage," which was the title of *Mistral's Daughter* in French, would eventually be the top song in Europe for a year.

I had picked the name Mistral because of the famous wind of Provence, that *mistral* that rules the countryside and can be both hot and cold, like a Californian Santa Ana. When it's blowing, women who kill their husbands can use it as an acceptable explanation in front of a jury. To me, during that production, the mistral was always blowing.

(It was a doubly unfortunate choice. When I came to do the book tour for *Mistral,* interviewers invariably called it "Menstrual's Daughter," "Minstrel's Daughter," or "Mistrial's Daughter.")

In the spring of 1983 the sun finally came out, the waters of the Seine receded, and Paris returned to itself. Overnight my fall and winter gloom vanished and I became myself again, feeling euphorically light-hearted and happy. I've always been unusually sensitive to weather. And to noise, and light and . . . you wouldn't want to travel with me.

"I know what's been making you so depressed," Sybille told me as we had lunch on the terrace of her club, the Cercle Interallié, where she swam every morning. "It's that apartment. You should get another place. Here's the name of my real-estate lady. Why don't you give her a call someday?"

That lunch was on June 23. On June 28, a rare, perfect day, the sort of day on which real-estate people make their income for the year, after seeing a few apartments, I fell in love with one. It was on the fifth floor, with a glorious view of a large garden, but Steve turned it down because he hates living that far above the street. The next day I found another apartment on a ground floor, and on June 30, Steve made a five-minute running tour of the place, approved, and disappeared back to the set as quickly as he could. Later that very day we signed the papers that committed us to buy it.

One week! One week only passed from our renting a small apartment to buying an enormous apartment on the Left Bank. (It never occurred to us to look on the Right Bank.) Obviously we had decided to settle permanently in Paris without realizing it, without sitting down and talking it through, especially since both boys were out of college and living and working on their own. We each had entirely different reasons. My reasons were based on all the warm new friends I'd made and the potential for a vastly more interesting life that stretched before us than we had yet found in California.

Steve, for his part, had done business with just about every important chief in European broadcasting during his years as head of international sales at Columbia, and he was still on the best of terms with all of them. He could tell from the six weeks of work done already on *Mistral* that he could become a major force in European production on a worldwide basis. As an American producer living in Paris and speaking French, he had more possibilities in Paris than there ever would be in Hollywood. In France he was one of a kind.

I didn't worry about where I'd carry on my own work. I had written three novels in the guest room of our Beverly Hills house, a room with French doors that opened out onto a garden, and that layout for an office had somehow become the prerequisite for creativity. Now I'd found an apartment whose four sides were built around a private garden, and my office, like most of the other rooms in the place, had French doors. It seemed an omen. The sun was shining again and, in addition to Saint Laurent boutique clothes, I'd discovered the new designer at Chanel, Karl Lagerfeld. His suits were perfect for a small woman and I started wearing them from the first collection he designed. What else was there to be concerned about?

Chapter Forty

THE ONLY WAY FOR STACY KEACH TO FULFILL THE DEMANDS OF HIS role as Julien Mistral was to leave Paris frequently after his day's work and fly an hour to Nice, where his driver would pick him up and deposit him at his country hotel, near the location in the Lubéron where he'd be working the following day. Stefanie Powers's scenes were entirely in Paris, Lee Remick's almost all in Provence, but there was only one Stacy and he was in the lion's share of scenes.

Although he was on summer hiatus from his CBS series, *Mike Hammer,* Stacy still had a few hours of voice recording left over to finish on a soundstage. He wanted to go to London to do them but Steve, who knew that all eight hours of *Mistral* rested on Stacy's being available until the very last minute of the very last hour of the last day of the shoot, insisted that he do the work required on an excellent soundstage in Nice. He ordered Stacy not to go to London under any circumstances, afraid of letting his star disappear into an airplane and another country, even for an afternoon.

Stacy had other ideas. On a day in early July, at dawn, he took a taxi to the Nice airport and boarded a plane for London. In London the police sniffer dogs quickly found that the can of shaving cream Stacy was carrying contained some thirty-six grams of cocaine. We'll never understand why he took it with him, particularly with Heathrow's reputation for detecting drugs, although people speculated that it was an example of an addict's irrational fear of being separated from his stash.

Stacy was arrested and Steve was immediately notified, fortunately in time for him to jump on a plane to London, put up the bail, and bring Stacy back to Paris with him once a court date had been set for him to return to London and be sentenced for his crime. The date set was many weeks *before* the shoot would be over.

We had no way to know whether the British judge would throw Stacy's moronic, irresponsible, criminally reckless, coke-head ass in jail or order him to pay a fine. This meant that for the remainder of the shoot, there was absolutely no guarantee that *Mistral's Daughter* could ever be finished. Depending on what that judge decided, the entire complicated process, the hours of magnificent dailies, the hundreds of people involved, and the millions of dollars it was costing might be utterly useless and have to be trashed.

We discovered, as soon as Stacy was caught, that all the wardrobe and makeup people and even the drivers knew he had a major coke habit. Production people higher up the line knew as well. This was certainly not the first or last film set on which cocaine was being used by an actor. The only person everyone kept in the dark was the producer and, of course, the producer's wife. Not "ratting out" a colleague is a way of life in show business. Everyone looks to save his or her own job before anything else and nobody wants to make waves. The very people I would have expected to alert Steve to the problem had kept silent. He tells me that this is the rule on every production, not just on *Mistral*.

Yet even at a distance of fifteen years, I still find it impossible to accept or forgive the fact that so many people participated in a cover-up that had such a serious consequence. That's one of the many reasons I'm glad I'm not in show business, although over the years, I've accumulated a short list of people in the publishing industry I'd quite like to pinch in a vulnerable spot.

Weeks before this happened, Steve and I had spent lots of time with Stacy and his now-ex-wife, when we all were on location in Saint-Tropez together, and if ever there seemed to be a solid citizen, it was this particular actor, bright and deeply involved in his well-maintained muscular fitness. I'd had a few casual acquaintances in Hollywood who, I'd eventually realized, used coke, but he showed none of the signs by which they betrayed themselves. He didn't talk too fast, he didn't have a running nose, explained as an allergy, nor did he disappear to the bathroom in the middle of dinner. He must have doped himself up to perfection right before we saw him.

One day, soon after the arrest, in Ménerbes, I sat at a distance on a headstone and settled down to watch three funerals being filmed in that high, windswept graveyard with its immense sweeping view of the Vaucluse, the familiar graveyard the company had rented as a location. For the sake of economy, three deaths, which had taken place at widely spaced intervals in my novel—those of Teddy Lunel, Kate Mistral, and Mistral himself—were all being shot on a single day, one after the other, in the order in which they happened in the book. Only the costumes and makeup of the mourners and the coffins and the actor who played the last priest needed to be changed.

I was caught up in a sudden realization that three scenes I'd written in a converted guest room in Beverly Hills were being enacted in front of my eyes. I was filled with a sense of awe and wonder at the fact that if it weren't for me, none of this complicated film project would be happening. I'd constructed the story that contained these deaths, I'd written the book, the book had brought us to France to live, and now I was about to see the funerals I'd imagined in my workroom take place in the same graveyard that had been in my mind as I wrote. I found this circle of events hard to contain in my mind as something that was actually happening to me—it was almost an out-of-body situation—but I also felt a rare sense of unadulterated exultation and pure pleasure at my own accomplishment. I'd shut myself into a room for nine months, thought and dreamed, worked patiently at a typewriter, and *made today happen!*

Of all the moments I've ever spent on a film location, this was the most deeply gratifying. It was ten minutes of pure, thoughtful happiness, until Stacy appeared, mourning the death of his beloved mistress, Teddy. As I watched him weep over her grave, I wanted to jump up from my headstone and push the bastard in.

For the next five or six weeks Steve and I barely had a thought that wasn't connected to Stacy Keach. I went to bed wondering what was going to happen to him and to the production and to us, and I woke up thinking the same thing.

Steve, working like a demon, found an excellent British lawyer to represent Stacy, and the judge in London, thank all the gods and goddesses, remanded Stacy, ordering him to return in a few months. Before they had passed, *Mistral* was triumphantly completed.

There was a scene in the early part of the novel that called for Mistral and Maggy to brawl in a tub in a public bathhouse. Steve couldn't find a suitable period bathhouse to rent, so he decided to film it in an outdoor fountain. Prudently he saved the scene until the last day of the shoot, since he didn't want to risk Stefanie catching cold. On a freezing, raining night in August the scene was completed, Stefanie showing what a trouper she was by volunteering to repeat it three times until they got it exactly right. Neither of us would leave until we were sure it was in the can. Only then could we relax.

The next time Stacy went before an English judge he was sent to jail for six months, which put an end to the *Mike Hammer* series.

We had been incredibly lucky.

STEFANIE POWERS WAS so delighted with the whole production (in which she aged convincingly from seventeen to her sixties, with the aid of many wigs and makeup), and with her producer in particular, that she invited the two of us to dinner at Caviar Kaspia, a tiny, elegant Russian restaurant on the place de la Madeleine above a famous delicacy shop. The Kaspia menu lists little besides caviar, smoked salmon, blinis, and vodka served in individual carafes frozen into small blocks of ice. "Two hundred and fifty grams of Beluga each," she ordered, "and a carafe of vodka each." She and Steve had their caviar with blinis, and I ate my huge helping straight off an icy plate with a mother-of-pearl spoon. Then Stefanie ordered another round, which only I had no trouble polishing off. While the two of them watched in disbelieving silence, I ordered a portion of white Norwegian smoked salmon for dessert. That was the best meal I ever expect to eat.

As soon as the shoot was over in August, there was a chance for Steve to get away from Paris while the rough assembly of the eight hours was being made by the editors. We went to Klosters, in Switzerland, where Herb and Rita Salzman lent us their apartment. It was raining there, too. That brief, lovely glimpse of spring had turned into an extraordinarily rainy summer that had plagued the production day after day, and Klosters was a sea of mud.

I spent most of my time working on *Manhattan* on the Salzmans' kitchen table. One day we had such cabin fever that we decided we simply had to see an afternoon movie, and since the only thing playing was *Goldfinger,* we went, only to find that it had been dubbed into German and subtitled in Swiss-German! Shrugging, they gave us our money back at the box office and I bought a splendid gold watch as therapy for my disappointment. Steve's therapy? I can only hope it was in paying for it.

Back in Paris, Steve plunged into postproduction and I started working on the apartment. It had a truly extraordinary location: 17 rue Cassette, right around the corner from the place Saint-Sulpice, with its cathedral and huge central fountain spouting water in four directions. Catherine Deneuve, that most French of actresses, had an apartment on the place and shopped daily in the local markets. The place also boasted a major Yves Saint Laurent boutique as well as cafés, the city hall of the sixth *arrondissement,* and the local firehouse.

Our apartment was only a short walk in two different directions from both of our favorite Paris brasseries, Lipp and La Coupole, and it was two blocks away from the Luxembourg Gardens. We were only a few minutes from Saint-Germain-des-Prés, from the Café de Flore, and from Les Trois Canettes, which hadn't changed since 1948. If I could have asked for the best location in Paris, this would have been it, surrounded by all my beloved old haunts. I was wild with joy and excitement at the luck of finding this superbly Parisian nest.

The building that contained our apartment was ancient, so historic that it was protected by the Beaux-Arts, and only interior decorating changes could be made. Someone had already created a huge, new, perfectly appointed, modern bathroom and built many closets off the master bedroom.

The long salon had a row of French doors onto the garden and at the far end there was an enormous fireplace. In addition to a magnificent entrance hall and lavishly paneled dining room, there were large offices for Steve and me and a very comfortable apartment on another staircase for a cook or housekeeper.

The three stories on which our apartment lay rambled up and down around the garden. Hundreds of years ago the building had been a monastery that housed an order of Les Petits Pères Blancs ("The Little White Fathers"), and on its lowest floor it possessed three enormous wine cellars, a big laundry room, a two-car garage on the street, as well as an office for my new secretary, Florence, who had a view of the garden.

While we'd been on the Ile Saint-Louis and we had family visitors, we'd put them up at a hotel nearby. There, behind the hotel desk, I'd found pretty, blond, efficient Florence and enticed her to come to work for me. We'd managed to get rid of Alberto by straightforward hefty bribery, and Florence hired a responsible chauffeur. I set her to work locating a cook and a cleaning lady for the future, while I began to cope with decorating the apartment so that I could get down to serious work as soon as possible on my new book.

Eventually I managed to get the job done, but not without making a major mistake by totally overlooking the fact that the light of Paris is entirely different from the light of Beverly Hills. I was arrogant and headstrong in my ridiculous determination to create a Californian atmosphere that would transform and counteract the horrible Paris weather, an idea that went against every law of nature. It was as if I were trying to build a tropical island in Finland.

The perfect-for-L.A. fabrics and paint colors I chose were indeed ravishing by night, in artificial light, and our future guests were to find the apartment enchanting, particularly after we illuminated the garden. But during the day the whole place felt low in spirit, all gaiety washed out in the gray, northern light of what passes for a good day in Paris, and on a bad day it became the very definition of dismal.

Now, too late, I understand that to create a feeling of warmth in a cold climate with bad light, you have to use dark, rich, deep colors, reds, greens, and warm browns. I certainly proved that I was right not to have tried to become a decorator. In addition, we were about to embark on almost two years of weather, each one of which beat the record of the last one for sheer utter vileness and grimness. We had month after month of sleet, hail, freezing cold, and rain, lasting long enough to deny us another spring or a decent autumn, broken only by horribly hot, incredibly brief summers. They were, as the newspapers loved to remind us, THE THREE WORST CONSECUTIVE YEARS IN THE HISTORY OF THE FRENCH WEATHER BUREAU. (Emphasis is mine, not the newspapers'.)

Gradually certain drawbacks to the apartment I'd bought so hastily became clear. The grandiose salon was too big to heat properly, and the fireplaces could not be lit. We found special radiators in Belgium that we could use in our bedroom and offices and we had to put in an entirely new kitchen, which added so much demand for electricity that I asked for an official inspection, fearing that the whole place might blow up if I plugged in one more decent lamp.

Force is the French word for the available electricity, and the inspector told me, with distinct disapproval, that I had installed enough *force* to run a small hospital. When I got my first monthly electric bill, of more than two thousand dollars, I realized why the French are so stingy with their lightbulbs and their heating. Yet it was not then, to my recollection, that the first doubts about the wisdom of buying this particular apartment began to occur to me. Since it cost several thousand dollars a month to keep the place warm and bright, what choice did we have, I asked myself, with moronic but high-spirited bravado.

Later we were to find, on those rare days when the weather was decent and we ventured outside for a drink in the garden, that every one of our neighbors had flung open all their windows, as well they might on such an unusual occasion. Their phone calls, their calls of nature, their television shows, their musical moments, and their screaming arguments were all not just clearly audible but somehow resonated as if within an echo chamber, bouncing from one of the four walls of our garden to another. It was exactly like living at the bottom of a square well or inside a violin played horribly. Or, as I finally was forced to admit to myself, in a high-priced, historic tenement.

Whenever we sat outside, we could be, and often were, observed by dozens of people, many of whom probably made the mistake of envying us our garden. After two or three attempts to pretend that we were alone, feeling like amateur actors in a Noël Coward play, we stopped going into the garden on nice evenings, but there were so few nice evenings that it wasn't a hardship, or so I told myself, beating down thoughts that contained the words "you utter fool, why didn't you think of this before?"

Above our garden, on all sides, rose five stories of other apartments. On these top floors were dwellings high enough to catch the daylight, such as it was, light that we would get only in the summer and only for an hour or two, until the sun moved away and left us in the shadow.

We were locked into a claustrophobic situation and one that would always be dark, no matter what the season or the weather.

"Didn't you think," Sybille asked me as she sat and surveyed the garden, shortly after we'd bought the apartment, "that you might have asked me to come over and look at this before you decided on it? I would have told you never, never, *never!* In Paris if you want light, you must only buy on a high floor. But I suppose it's too late now?"

It was indeed. Sybille's words, to which I nodded miserably, only confirmed the doubts I'd been struggling to ignore. I'd literally snatched, without a second of mature consideration, without looking at more places, at the second possible apartment I'd seen in my eagerness to find an alternative to life on the Ile Saint-Louis. Now there were dozens of workmen busily transforming an expensive mistake into an even more expensive mistake. *If only . . .* In the matter of places to live, both Steve and I can, on occasion, be impulsive to the point of genuine mania. The rue Cassette was the worst real-estate decision I'd ever made.

But I couldn't tell Steve about my second thoughts. He lived only for the production problems that totally preoccupied him; he had not a grain of patience left at the end of the day to listen to my half-formulated doubts, and anyway, what change could we make? We were in mid-passage on the apartment, everything was half-completed, it was too late to do anything except press on. I resolutely put doubt out of my mind as much as I could and focused on the fact that as soon as we could move in, I'd shut myself into my office and really get down to work.

However, this plan was constantly being infuriatingly postponed by the fact that all the most essential workmen put down their tools on Friday by noon to go out and shoot deer in the countryside, which they regarded as a status symbol essential to their self-esteem.

The French work week was thirty-nine hours long, and God help you if you asked them to work overtime, at any amount of pay. Doctors only worked three days a week because if they worked more, all the money they made went to taxes. Whenever there was a holiday on a Tuesday or a Thursday, most workers routinely "made the bridge" over Monday or Friday and took a four-day weekend. Religious holidays in France are thick on the ground. During the entire month of May there were so many religious holidays and so many bridges that state banks were open only eight days of the entire month. Now the work week has been shortened to thirty-five hours!

Throughout our stay in Paris, no matter where we lived, by July 15 we heard the unmistakably sinister clanging sounds of iron shutters being fastened down over the windows of all the local shops as the shopkeepers made ready to take their six weeks or two months of holiday. When they reopened sometime in September, they called cheerily to each other, "Bonjour, Madame, Monsieur, did you have a good vacation? And when are you going away again?"

I saw the domino theory operate firsthand. As the food shops closed, the clients who depended on them had to leave Paris for their country houses or resorts, which enjoyed a tourist boom. This caused all the other stores or services, like laundry and restaurants, to close in their turn, turning Paris into a ghost town for the entire summer, except for the hotels, which were full of tourists disappointed to find so many restaurants closed.

Since Steve worked hardest during the summer, which was the only time actors on hiatus were available, each summer we spent there I persuaded my help to stay and keep the house running by paying them double wages and giving them extra-long vacations in the autumn. The only way to have food in the house was to drive to Le Bon Marché, a large department store that stayed open, and buy provisions in its food hall.

This approach to daily life, so different from that in the United States, was something I never could become used to. I spent hours appreciating the supermarkets of Los Angeles. I'd never before realized how easy life in California was.

Both Steve and I are blessed, or cursed, with a strong internal work ethic. We give ourselves to a project with whatever we have, we never begrudge working overtime, and we've never been late in delivering anything we've promised. But this is not and never will be the French way. To them the vacation, the long weekend, the downtime is utterly sacred. And who's to say they're wrong? Only twenty-five percent of them die of heart attacks compared to Americans. But four times as many French die of liver disease as Americans, because of a diet loaded with alcohol. Since everyone dies, perhaps they've found the most enjoyable way to go.

However, it kept me climbing the walls, not my favorite position.

Chapter Forty-one

Before I even began to write *I'll Take Manhattan,* I realized that I needed to research the magazine business. Although I'd been in it for so long, I'd largely been a writer, not an editor, like thrice-married, devil-may-care Maxi Amberville, my new heroine.

I decided that since no one would ever agree with me that my other heroines, except for Billy Ikehorn, had worked for their own money, I might just as well create an idle, rich, spoiled playgirl from a wealthy publishing family. While I was about it, I based the book directly on the plot of *Hamlet.* Maxi is galvanized by her father's death at the hands of his lustful younger brother, who proceeds to marry her equally lustful mother and take over the family business. By now I realized that no reviewer would ever notice, since they'd be skipping about, trying to spot the sex and shopping bits. And indeed, no one ever spotted the stolen-straight-from-*Hamlet* plot, except for one well-read television book reviewer, Connie Martinson—a Wellesley graduate, I'm happy to say.

In October 1983 I flew to New York to meet with Helen Brown, Amy Gross of *Vogue,* Cathy Black of *New York* magazine, Ellen Levine and Peter Diamandis of *Woman's Day,* Kate White of *Family Weekly,* Walter Anderson of *Parade,* and Bob Colacello of *Interview.*

While I was with Helen, attending a few days of editorial conferences, we went to look at the racks in the fashion department. "What's that?" Helen asked, pointing at some sportswear. "Guess," answered the fashion editor. "GUESS!" Helen said, outraged. "Guess," the editor repeated. I finally figured it out, from remembering those first ads that made Claudia Schiffer a star, and explained, bent double with laughter. Helen is not an editor you ask to guess anything you're supposed to know.

I set my novels in worlds where the work of the day happens behind the scrim, the veil of glamour. It's a totally deliberate choice; it's the world I write best about. The first question I ask myself before beginning a new book, with the exception of *Scruples,* is, What does my heroine do for a living? Each of them, in order for me to fall in love with her, must be hardworking, ambitious, and dedicated to her job, no matter how decorative she is or how glamorous her occupation seems to be until you've learned its details. And you can count on learning them. I realized this about my heroines only after I'd written several novels. It is so closely a part of my own attitude toward life that I'd just accepted it as normal.

If anyone were to ever ask what my rock-bottom subject matter is, the answer is "marketing." In every novel I return, drawn by my fascination with the subject, to how to best sell something. I think it's the genes of an advertising man's daughter finally coming out and having their way with me.

I know, although probably no readers will ever realize it, that in each novel, the characters, the plot, the details of how people live, and all of their adventures always depend directly on my core of interest in how to market a large number of varied products.

In *Scruples* I was concerned with the retail clothing business, the wholesale dress business, and making a success of a low-budget movie. All the aspects of making television commercials are covered in *Princess Daisy*, which naturally also deals in depth with the products themselves. *Mistral's Daughter* shows my readers how to be a great art dealer and how to run a top model agency, and in *I'll Take Manhattan* I invented a new kind of women's magazine. In spite of covering two World Wars in *Till We Meet Again,* I spent a lot of time on the champagne trade, and one of my heroines developed an air-freight business at a time when such businesses were just starting. *Dazzle* revolves around a commercial photography studio with three different kinds of photographers involved, one selling food, one selling automobiles, and the heroine creating celebrity photographs. The second part of the plot deals with the important issue of the right and wrong ways to go about real-estate development. In *Scruples Two* I focused on the inside story of making a big-budget motion picture and created in detail a new kind of clothing catalog, one that made Emily Woods, president of J. Crew, whom I interviewed at length, suspicious that I was going to start a catalog business myself. The story of *Lovers* takes place in and around two advertising agencies, and Gigi Orsini, my copywriting heroine, creates a winning campaign for large-size bathing suits, invents a new kind of chain of children's shops called The Enchanted Attic, and starts a new kind of cruise line; while Billy Winthrop creates a full home-furnishing catalog at least a year before Pottery Barn started to do so. *Spring Collection* concerns itself with the launch of a new Parisian fashion designer, and *The Jewels of Tessa Kent* deals with the inner workings of a major auction house and the promotion of a huge jewelry auction.

Glamour is the indispensable midwife for the birth of successful marketing. *Glamour sells.* That's why my novels take place in various worlds of glamour and why my heroines are women who present a glamorous exterior.

I've never, in real life, known a "glamour" girl who didn't have to work to maintain that illusion on a daily basis, for illusion it always is—with the possible exception of Suzy Parker in the 1950s. Being naturally glamorous is a contradiction in terms. Naturally beautiful, yes, naturally brilliant, yes, a naturally exciting personality, yes; but the thing we call "glamour" is a cloak of stardust, a spell of witchcraft that must be created. Don't take my word for it. "A magical or fictitious beauty attaching to any person or object: a delusive or alluring charm" is what that guardian of the language, the *Oxford English Dictionary,* has to say on the subject.

Once I was doing a segment of the *Today* show with Ivana Trump, who was married to Donald at the time, Beverly Sills, Iman, and Paloma Picasso. As the five of us sat and chatted in an orchid-filled sitting room at the Plaza, surrounded by technicians and invisible cameras, I asked myself if this was, finally, glamorous. Hardly. We'd all had to repeat our exits from our limos and our entrances into the Plaza three times for the camera, we'd all spent hours dressing and getting made up and having our hair done for this twelve-minute piece, and we were all *selling* something.

When I write characters who are, in some of their aspects, larger than life and more beautiful than normal folk, I'm entirely aware of what I'm doing. This heightened reality is a matter of personal preference, although some people deplore it, because for them, it's over the top.

"Over the top" for me is the line by Rupert Brooke. He described a woman as "incredibly, inordinately, devastatingly, immortally, calamitously beautiful." Over the top? And how! But I love it, for exactly that reason. I believe that I can succeed as a writer only by keeping to the instinct that tells me, "Follow your own path, don't be afraid to take it." With my passion for glamorous marketing, I never forget to whip up so much genuine entertainment through plot and character conflicts that it keeps my imaginary reader, the one I keep in mind as I write, who hates flying and is trapped in a plane circling O'Hare on a foggy night, from thinking of her plight. The only worry I want her to have is whether the book will last until she lands. Ordinary life-size just doesn't do it for me, and I believe it wouldn't do it for her, either.

I'LL TAKE MANHATTAN became my fourth novel to reach the number-one spot on the *Times* list, in May 1986. Three years and several months were to pass between the publication of *Mistral* and *Manhattan,* instead of the usual two-year interval I've otherwise maintained in the course of writing ten novels in twenty years, because of our move to Paris.

Normally writing and rewriting takes just about nine months, a natural rhythm that the use of a computer doesn't hasten, since it doesn't make my thought process any quicker. The rest of the time is spent in promoting the novel and thinking of an idea for another, as well as researching and outlining it.

On an unforgettable wet Monday I researched the half-built Trump Tower, where I had decided that Maxi would have an apartment. Donald Trump, who was then merely a bombastic builder named Donald Trump, not a household word, God help us—not yet even "The Donald"—took me all over the structure, proudly showing me the future apartments that were merely beams and holes. Finally he took me up to his own top-floor triplex and insisted that we tour his roof garden, where full-sized trees had already been planted.

"No, I don't want to," I protested, "it's too wet out there. Look, the clouds are covering the treetops. I'll ruin my hair!" This dread possibility, I thought, would surely bring him to his senses.

"Come on," he said, grabbing me by the arm, or was it the scruff of my neck? I felt as if I were in the grasp of King Kong, but see his trees I did, and ruin my hair it did, but later on, when Maxi needed money, I wrote a scene in which she sold her apartment back to Donald. I sent the scene to him for vetting, to make sure it could legally happen that way, and he approved.

Even later, when Steve was filming the miniseries, he was able to rent the Trump Tower atrium for the scene of the apartment sale. Donald played himself, with panache, speed, and an utter disregard of the script. When the time for the publication party came, where else could it be held but in that same rose-pink marble atrium, with Donald giving me the key to Trump Tower? As I danced by Peter Duchin, now married to Brooke Hayward, playing the piano in front of his band, I stopped and asked him if he still thought I was the squarest person he'd ever met, as he had in the sixties, twenty years earlier, when I'd interviewed him. He didn't answer me—he just grinned. Probably that meant that he didn't remember anything about a remark I'd never forgotten—or perhaps the jury was still out. Or perhaps he knew, as I knew, that I *was* still square. Square, but smart enough to know it.

Was anyone of my generation and background hip? After all, it's just a matter of pure attitude. How can you become hip unless you eliminate from your brain and psyche all the bourgeois values you've been raised with? Is amnesia the only way? Has anyone heard of a nice Jewish girl hipster who reached legal maturity in the late 1940s? I doubt it.

Norman Mailer was and probably is still hip and so was Robert Mitchum when he was arrested for smoking grass and photographed unrepentantly grinning in a police van. Mitchum ruled! Ali MacGraw and Steve McQueen were the height of hip while they were together. Judy Garland was too tragic to be hip and Madonna shows the wheels working too clearly to be hip. O. J. Simpson was still a little hip until he, unhiply, murdered his wife, but Nicole Simpson was never as hip as Faye Resnick. My idea of a hipster today is Chris Rock. I was irritated by a recent article in *The New York Times Magazine* by forty-four-year-old Luc Sante, who describes his infatuation with the Citroën DS, a car he first saw in Paris in 1963. After he writes of the way in which the "car's angle counterposed the wisdom of age" (huh?), he announces that "my generation, make no mistake, is the last hipster generation."

I take issue with Mr. Sante. Hip isn't about admiring an object, even such a great one as the Citroën. Although he's most amusing on the associations of the car (the first miniskirts, early Godard movies), that doesn't make him one of the last hipsters, just as I wasn't an early hipster because I lived in sin in a whorehouse fourteen years before Luc Sante laid eyes on his dream automobile. I was a square girl in a hip-as-hell situation, that's all.

Nope. I was never even close to hip. But with my green mascara and orange hair, I believe that I had my "cool" moments. At the time, of course, I didn't know what cool was, nor did anyone else in the 1950s, that most uncool decade. Alex Mayes tells me that when she was six and I was nineteen, she watched me brushing my hair in front of a mirror and thought I was the most glamorous woman in the world. Oh, how I cherish that image. She must have been a particularly bright six-year-old! Today I'd settle happily to be Cameron Diaz—who wouldn't?—but the offer hasn't been presented yet.

SINCE I WAS in the United States, Bantam sent me on a two-week book tour for the paperback of *Mistral* as soon as I'd finished my research. The only thing I remember about it was a moment in Cincinnati when I had to go on a live morning show with no warning because their first guest failed to show up. A soundman put a body mike around my waist as quickly as he could, not concerned that we were in full view of the audience. He simply went for it, stripping me without a by-your-leave. I was wearing a suit with an easily removed wraparound skirt, panties, and panty hose, fortunately impeccable. Afterward I shared a brief exchange with the next guest, Bill Blass, who had just arrived from Tokyo, totally exhausted and jet-lagged half out of his mind. "Isn't it fun being Bill Blass?" I asked him. "Isn't it fun being Judith Krantz?" he responded, deadpan.

The answer to both questions was yes. Jet-lagged or not, manhandled by a soundman or not, it is fun, great glorious fun, to have successfully poked your head up and been recognized for your achievement, and we both knew it.

WORK WAS PROCEEDING slowly on the rue Cassette. For Christmas 1984 we went to Los Angeles to see our children and to escape the gloom of a Parisian Christmas. The next year at Christmas we went to Klosters again and stayed in a hotel, seeing the Salzmans and their friends every night. We became friendly with Irwin Shaw and his great wife, Marian, in spite of initial coldness on his part. After *Scruples* no successful male writer, not even an Irwin Shaw, with all his achievement, has ever liked me without a struggle . . . a boys' club knee-jerk reaction.

Christmas is the opportunity for the French to take their traditional and much cherished skiing holidays. As many people ski as possible, in such masses that the government has to regulate how many people are allowed to go skiing and at what time of the month they may leave, dividing France into three geographic groups, each of which has its chance at the slopes. This is also the moment when the truckers traditionally pull an illegal strike, abandoning five or six big rigs across the highways everyone must take in order to reach the ski areas. Sometimes entire families were stuck in their cars for fifty hours before the government would decide to give the truckers what they wanted.

The lightning, unexpected strike is a way of life in France. Every morning we'd listen to the radio to find out who was striking, so we'd know if the electricity or water was going to be turned off or if the transportation in and out of Paris was going to disappear.

Once, in three years, after much difficulty about Steve's schedule, we finally cleared the decks for a visit to the Louvre. Here we were living in Paris and we hadn't yet been back to the greatest museum on earth, avoiding it on weekends for visits to galleries that were less crowded. We arrived to find that the guards had just gone on strike that very morning. "How long do you think you'll be out?" I asked the one guard who finally came to the barred door. "Until we get what we want!" he shouted furiously. Encouraging.

The frequent riots were more worrisome than the strikes. We were there in the early years of the new Mitterrand socialist government, and riots were common, with the heavily armed police, in full riot gear, including machine guns and tear gas, confronting various malcontented groups who disagreed with government policy. One afternoon, when I was shopping at the Saint Laurent boutique on the Champs-Elysées, the customers were all locked in by the police for their own safety. As we pressed our noses to the windows to see the pitched battle outside, my saleswoman said, "Oh, how I wish I could join them!"

"Why, what are they rioting for?"

"It doesn't matter—they're against this dreadful government, that's enough for me."

It was impossible to find out what was really going on in France without reading the daily *Tribune* and American newsmagazines, for which I made a weekly trip to an American bookstore. The news was so strictly controlled that on one occasion, when two exceptionally popular television anchorpeople angered the government, they simply disappeared from their show without any explanation and were replaced the next day, never to resurface. It was as if Peter Jennings, taking Katie Couric with him, had vanished without a trace. I could hardly believe that such a violation of rights had taken place, but my French friends didn't turn a hair.

Eventually we learned to take alternative routes when there was a riot expected on the bridge I had to cross to get to my Right Bank hairdresser; eventually we learned that whatever the government was up to, life in France continued, and that all strikes got settled in time. But, and it's a big but, living in a semi-dictatorship, for that, in my opinion, was what Mitterrand's government was, never became normal or even basically acceptable. As an American, I always had a slight but persistent feeling of deep discomfort, especially at the sight of the truly dangerous riot police menacing a crowd, or in learning that a mob of students had spent the night overturning cars all over Paris and setting them on fire. Every single day a French version of Kent State was fully possible.

I learned never to address French police in French, but to pretend that I was a confused tourist from dear harmless Canada. "Je, oh dear, je ne speak Français, not a word." You couldn't get into trouble that way.

Call me an unreconstructed Adlai Stevenson Democrat, if you will, but also call me a fan of a well-functioning two-party system.

On June 6, 1984, a startling realization made me see just how intensely and deliberately the French had rewritten history. It was a brilliant, breezy morning and Jean Bakker had invited me to lunch at the Dutch embassy. Before lunch I had an appointment at the hairdresser, near the place Vendôme, which meant crossing the most noble and historic parts of Paris, from the Left Bank to the Right Bank and back again to the Left Bank, where the Dutch embassy was located on the rue de Grenelle.

I noticed, as soon as we reached the boulevard Saint-Germain, that there were flags blowing from every tree, flags fluttering from every lamppost, flags flapping from open windows. The entire city danced with the red, white, and blue of tens of thousands of flags. Paris had never looked so festive or brave or beautiful. My heart lifted as we crossed the Seine and saw the Louvre decorated with flags. A spirit of celebration seemed to play even on the faces of the people in the street.

Suddenly I realized that it was the fortieth anniversary of D-Day. I started to look more intently at the flags, seeking the American flag, the British flag, the Australian and New Zealand flags—the flags of all the Allied forces who had landed in France and slowly, painfully, with great loss of life, begun the liberation of Europe.

Not one! Not a single one was to be seen. *Only French flags flew that day.*

By the time I arrived at the Dutch embassy, I was so boiling over with fury at the way in which the French government had dishonored and ignored the great facts of D-Day that I didn't give a damn about what I said. I walked into a roomful of diplomats' wives and, all but getting on a soapbox, expressed my passionate indignation that all the French were patting themselves on the back, exactly as if they had *liberated themselves,* instead of the majority of them following their government's orders and quickly surrendering to the Germans. I looked around, expecting some reaction, and met only the blandest, blankest of faces. It was exactly as if I were invisible, as if I hadn't yet entered the room.

These well-trained, dutiful, career-diplomat wives had long ago learned how to behave properly in a foreign country . . . like the three monkeys, deaf, dumb, and blind. My outburst was being kindly treated as a gaffe so great that it had to be utterly ignored. Conversation flowed smoothly around me and at no point in the lunch did anyone come up to me and whisper in my ear that she agreed with me. I simply hadn't said a word, as far as they were concerned.

Truth could not be allowed to shine on the doings of the French government. It could not even be mentioned.

That experience opened my eyes toward France and the French as no strike or riot ever could have. Just writing about it makes me seethe all over again.

Chapter Forty-two

TIME PASSED, RAIN FELL CEASELESSLY, LIKE PUNISHMENT, AS WE MOVED into 17 rue Cassette. I'd never fallen down that terrifying staircase on the lle Saint-Louis and I'd never given that happily imagined dinner party that would have required my second round table. When we entertained, we met our guests in accessible restaurants.

Florence had interviewed dozens of cooks, reserving only the most promising candidates for me to meet. I was immediately drawn to one, a former Parisian who had run her own bed-and-breakfast in the Dordogne, until her divorce. This middle-aged woman, named Monique Bovais, seemed to have just the qualities I was hoping for: experience, good sense, and a soothingly calm, reassuring personality. She started work immediately, the finest person I could have found. There was little Monique couldn't do in the kitchen, and she was an indispensable guide to choosing the all-important wines for each course of the small dinner parties I now began to plan. You can win or lose a reputation as a good hostess in Paris on the quality of the wine you serve, and, unlike me, no French guest seems to find it amazingly bad manners to stop the waiter and carefully study the label of the wine before allowing it to be poured.

That first year, on Thanksgiving, Monique cooked a memorable turkey dinner, a meal she'd never made before, even making her own stuffing and cranberry sauce. David and Helen Brown and Dimi and Yvonne Paniza were among our guests, and I'd invented a superb first fish course. With an electric knife I cut thin slices of bread from a loaf made with brioche dough, buttered it lavishly with sweet country butter, and then topped it with many delicate slices of Fauchon's best smoked salmon, garnished by a single caper. Even this experienced French cook was impressed with my version of lox and a bagel.

I had at last settled down to work, now that I had an office that looked out on a garden. In keeping with my utterly wrong-headed plan, I'd put down a wall-to-wall carpet that was the bright color of spring grass and covered the walls and windows with a glazed yellow-and-white chintz. I filled the useless fireplace with as many flowering plants as we could keep watered, and shut the too-bright, icy-looking draperies tight against the horribly depressing view of the garden.

It made me feel an all-pervasive, morbid, melancholy gloom to watch the rain falling on the pebbles under the trees, pebbles that were rapidly covered with happily growing moss. I told my driver, who had nothing to do when I was working, to scrub the moss off every week, which only seemed to encourage its regrowth. Even with the radiators turned on, I found I had to wear après-ski clothes to stay warm enough to write, and I was sleeping in ski underwear until June of 1985.

Of course Paris, even in the rain, had its wonderful side in spite of all my complaining. Our wine cellars were now partly filled with cases of that grand Bordeaux, Château Beychevelle, which we'd acquired at his own price from one of the owners of the vineyard. We'd met him on a long weekend at the Gaussens's chateau in Aix, and when he heard that we had no wine stockpiled, he was so thoroughly shocked that he kindly compiled a list of his best years for us.

Recently, in Los Angeles, I carefully picked up a bottle of Beychevelle in a wine store and held it up to see the price. Sixty dollars. We'd paid less than twelve. My Chanel suits, which came with their own exquisitely made silk blouses, cost eight hundred dollars apiece and I still wear them, especially the jackets, with white cotton shirts. New ones, without even a simple tank top, now sell for upwards of three thousand dollars. When I went shopping for an antique telescope for Steve's birthday, I was able to find a fine example at a reasonable price, and at the same time spot a superb bronze bust of a woman that I knew I had to have for myself. The model must have been a demimondaine, since one of her marvelous breasts was bare. I called her Sarah, since I felt it had been her name, and she immediately became the queen of the apartment, the center of the salon. Now Sarah sits in my Bel Air workroom on a round table surrounded by my framed bestseller lists. She's happier and warmer there.

I had taken the advice of friends and gone to Monsieur Massaro, on the rue de la Paix, for custom-made shoes for my flat feet. This master *bottier,* who'd designed the classic beige Chanel shoe with the black toe, took an incredible thirteen fittings to get the first pair right, but after that we had an easier time of it, and I slowly built up a wardrobe of shoes, some of which I still wear. I'd discovered a passion for a kind of ceramic called majolica and started to collect it for almost no money at all before an article in the *Figaro* Sunday magazine made it wildly fashionable, but still affordable by American standards—for the American dollar then was worth almost twice what it's worth in Paris today.

On Monique's weekends off, we went regularly for the treat of Sunday dinner chez Lipp, where Roger Cazes, the much-feared, autocratic owner, decided exactly who sat where. No reservations were ever accepted. One night, feeling particularly happy after a great *choucroute,* I informed him that we were now his neighbors and gave him a kiss on the cheek. To my astonishment, he smiled! From that time on we always had a good table. Perhaps too few women dared to kiss Monsieur Cazes.

When I wrote *Scruples Two,* some seven years later, I included a scene inspired by that night, a scene in which Billy, upset by events, decides to go out for dinner by herself, after a nap.

Single-mindedly, Billy entered the crowded, informal brasserie . . . and strode hastily through a mass of people who milled about right inside the door, holding drinks. Her cheeks were bright pink with the cold, her dark eyes deeply refreshed from the sleep she hadn't realized had overcome her, her hair whipped in every direction by the wind. Her mink collar stood straight up, framing the vivid drama of her beauty . . . the skirt of her coat flared out as she hurried in on a breath of winter air like a Russian princess who had crossed the steppes with a pack of wolves behind her. She headed straight toward a middle-aged, stern, unsmiling man with a mustache who was clearly in charge.

"Good evening, Monsieur," she said, smiling into his eyes, which were level with her own, "I hope you have room for just one."

The man with the mustache, Roger Cazes, the most courted and fawned-over restaurant owner in France, looked at this stranger in his usual expressionless way and made up his mind that there must be room, even at the most crowded time of the most crowded day of the year. All the people outside . . . had been told to expect to wait for as long as an hour, but this woman by herself, this sublime, wide-eyed unknown who had just asked for the impossible, with unquestioning faith that she would receive it, would be seated at once. Filling such an innocent, lunatic request made owning a restaurant a daily adventure for Monsieur Cazes. . . .

Billy was led immediately to the holy of holies, a small, mirrored, noisy nook that was always filled with Monsieur Caze's pets—politicians, writers, and actresses . . . where no one, not the most powerful men in France, was allowed to occupy the same table twice in a row for fear that they might think they had established a toehold on it. . . . Billy found herself squeezed in between two big, laughing groups on a long, black leather banquette, barricaded by a tiny table draped in white linen that had materialized in the magical way that can only happen in certain of the most desirable restaurants in the world. She glanced at the short, unchanging menu printed on a small card.

"Smoked salmon, roast lamb, and a carafe of red wine," Billy told the ancient waiter, unconscious of the glances of the other diners.

. . . Suddenly, unexpectedly, Billy felt herself relax into the coziness and the roaring vitality of the restaurant, a relaxation she needed desperately . . . she sipped wine while around her Frenchwomen with short hair were deciding to let their hair grow and tumble over their faces, and Frenchwomen with long hair were resolving to cut their hair to her careless, unnameable length and brush it with their fingers as she must have done . . . a woman is at her most distinguished when she dines alone in a chic restaurant, if her attitude shows that she feels perfectly at home and is unconscious of any embarrassment in being by herself . . . Billy had never been more distinguished than that Saturday night chez Lipp . . . eating with a sharply focused appetite . . . her lips curved in private amusement in a way that made half the men in the room sit up straight in a jolt of curiosity.

I rarely had a reason to eat alone at Lipp, although I did, for lunch, on several occasions when I was actively antique hunting, once even finding myself seated in the holy of holies. It made me slightly self-conscious. No Billy Winthrop, I.

I wouldn't want to actually *be* any of my heroines, but rather their beloved, relatively trouble-free, wise, and sunny best friends. Heroines struggle, heroines have difficult childhoods, important people die in their lives, nothing comes easily to them. They have many of the outward trappings of glamour but not the easy, self-confident happiness of their best friends. Heroines, in certain ways, none of them physical, are too much like me. No, I wouldn't choose to be my heroines, and I do manage to escape a lot of their turmoil by virtue of my age and marriage. But not all.

THE BUSINESS OF going to a French ladies' lunch is an art in itself and after a year I'd finally learned the ropes. First I'd receive a written note from my hostess detailing the names of the other guests and who they were, for all the world as if I could possibly remember all that information and attach it to the faces of the eight or ten strangers I'd be meeting in a short space of time. Once I realized the impossibility of that happening, I stopped torturing myself trying to remember.

Next, as guest of honor, since I was newest to the group, it would fall to me to take the first helping of each course. This had to be done with unhesitating panache. I learned to grab the serving pieces and plunge as rapidly as possible into whatever dish I was offered, as offhandedly as if I'd been doing it all my life. I was relieved when, as time passed, new guests of honor appeared, to be served first.

I'm a slow eater, but the other women all gobbled their food, no matter how delicious it was or how long it had taken to prepare. This was particularly difficult for me since I was aware that the hostess was waiting for me to finish before the main dish was passed around again. When I finally was driven to ask why such civilized people ate in such haste, every woman at the table agreed that it was because of their convent training. As schoolgirls, if they hadn't finished their meal in twenty minutes, they didn't get dessert. They didn't seem able to realize that it had been decades since they'd eaten lunch under the supervision of nuns. Nor, unlike me, did any of them ever have to go to the peepee room, again a question of convent training, which had made them develop formidably retentive bladders.

I'd learned to write a thank-you note to my hostess the very minute I got home and post it immediately, followed the next day by flowers from one of the two or three recognized top florists in Paris. The worst thing you could do was to send a flower arrangement, since that implied that you thought your hostess couldn't arrange flowers herself, but once I was guilty of the second worst thing, which was to send flowers *before* the lunch. I arrived to find my hostess hastily arranging my tulips, unquestionably cursing me as she tried to fill the vase before the doorbell rang. Eventually I arrived at a compromise: flowering plants.

The only way to tell if I had been a successful guest was if women asked for my card after lunch. (Of course, by that time I had the essential cards engraved with my address and phone number.) The greater the exchange of cards, if a number of your guests don't know each other, the better the party has been.

At the embassy lunches there was always a leather-covered board displayed before you entered the reception rooms. On the board I was able to find where my seat was located, as well as the names of my neighbors to the right and the left. This gave me only two names to memorize and as I became acquainted with more and more people, it became a little easier, but I've always had as bad a memory for names as I've had a good one for meals.

Dinner parties were far less tricky. The women at the ladies' lunches had finally stopped looking me over, asking me questions and trying to decide if I'd do or not. By now, many of them knew me.

Still there were permanent, built-in traps. At a dinner party, for instance, the greatest gaffe was to ask a man what his occupation was, something any American would do more or less automatically. However, since the answer would indicate how much money he made, such a normal question was utterly taboo. If he said he was a banker, he was certainly richer than a man who said he was an editor. No, *no,* never ask that essential question, which would automatically lead to an interesting conversation. I spent many dinners trapped between two men whose professions were entirely unknown to me and destined to remain so. I longed for forthright American introductions, for normal American informality.

There were ways, of course, for strangers to let you know their place in the scheme of things, like the dinner partner who complained non-stop about the problem of keeping the roof of his château repaired, all sixteen hectares of it, with one hectare equaling more than two and a half acres. There was also a woman at lunch who told us all that she'd shut off one entire wing of her château because it was impossible to heat such a gigantic space in the winter. As she left the lunch she said, by way of good-bye, "Now I must retire to my lands." I just may try that line some day.

The only people I knew who introduced people in the intelligent American manner were my publisher and the heavenly Michelle Tourneville, who loved to explain how, through carnal knowledge, everybody was somehow related to everybody else.

ONE DAY WE received a sudden all-cash offer on our Beverly Hills house, which we hadn't yet decided to sell. Now, cutting the final string to California, we accepted the offer that came from Hong Kong Chinese who were getting out early. It was for six times as much as we'd paid thirteen years earlier. As we telexed our old friend, the real-estate lady (like many real-estate ladies, a former high-fashion model), I felt a flicker of warning trepidation, but I ignored it, just as resolutely as I ignored the fact that I had yet to have a decent night's sleep in our bedroom, where I was illogically but thoroughly convinced some poor Little White Father had died in agony, punished for a mortal sin. To me a kind of tragic, freezing doom seemed to emanate from that particular room, as if the walls were impregnated with it, although Steve slept soundly. I should have had it exorcised.

Soon we heard that the buyers' astrologer had told them that to ensure good luck, it was essential that they move in before the end of the escrow. We telexed back that we'd consulted our own astrologer and he'd told us that it would mean very bad luck for us to permit this to happen. They waited, bought the house, and in a year resold it for *twice* what they'd paid. This was the beginning of the great Beverly Hills land boom and in the next few years that house I'd loved would change hands three times, until the last buyers tore it down, uprooted every tree, built a giant, out-of-scale house, and put in a north–south tennis court—paying *twenty* times what we'd originally paid. To this day, whenever I happen to drive past it, I feel a twinge when I remember my rosebushes.

However, in Paris I was charmed to see Monique rush out to the garden, managing somehow to slip between the raindrops, and choose the fresh vegetables she'd stored there, in her countrywoman's fashion, in order to make a fresh vegetable soup for our dinner.

She and I often had long conversations, since Steve came home so late and after my day's work I desperately needed someone to talk to. One day Monique asked me if she could have the next day off, although she gave no reason, saying merely that it was important. I answered that of course she could. Suddenly I realized that the next day was Yom Kippur, the most sacred of the Jewish High Holy Days. "Monique, if I didn't know it was impossible, I'd think you were Jewish," I joked. "Oh, Madame!" she said, bursting into tears, "I am. I am. But don't tell Florence, don't tell anyone, you must promise me."

Only after I'd sworn never to tell did she reveal her story, and even today, respecting her wishes, I'm not using her real name. She and her mother and her three sisters had spent the entire war hidden in an attic in Paris, fed by their openly anti-Semitic neighbors. After the war was over these same neighbors reverted immediately to the unpleasant treatment of the past. They let it be known that they had fed the Bovais family only out of Christian duty. At least their Christian duty had prevented them from denouncing the family to the Germans.

The experience of spending six years shut up in an attic, at the mercy of people she knew hated Jews, had left Monique with an understandable trauma she couldn't shake. She suspected that even Florence would change her good opinion of her if she knew the truth. I realized that the little surprise treats Monique occasionally prepared for us, the chopped liver and the matzo-ball soup that Steve and I had thought such delicate, shy tributes to our background, had been more than they seemed, but, for months, until she trusted us entirely, she hadn't said a word.

THE WAY STEVE'S home office was arranged on the rue Cassette made his telex totally audible on the other side of the wall from my bathroom dressing table. Every night as I was getting ready for bed, I'd hear the machine start up, spitting out rolls of paper all over the floor, which he'd read in the morning, since he rose early and went to sleep before I did.

Now, as a season absurdly called "spring" approached, in the continuing cold, the telex seemed to work overtime. Its tap-tap-tapping soon became a sound that I loathed passionately. I used to go into his office and glare at the endless stream of paper, as if I could make the telex malfunction through sheer dislike.

CBS had been so delighted with the success of *Mistral's Daughter,* which had gone on the air in September of 1984 and is still being played to this day all over the world, that they'd asked Steve to do another miniseries that would keep him busy for an additional year. The project was called *Sins,* from a book of the same name, and all that they had going for it in the beginning was the fact that Joan Collins had agreed to star in it. Both Joan, riding very high in *Dynasty,* and her new boyfriend, Peter Holm, had insisted on the titles of executive producer, which didn't bother Steve. He knew who would have to get the work done and his title of producer was sufficient.

While Steve started in on preproduction, casting Gene Kelly as Joan's costar, with a major role going to Timothy Dalton and lesser ones to Lauren Hutton and Marisa Berenson, I struggled to write about madcap Maxi Amberville. Often, at night, I'd go out in the dark, after I'd finished writing, and run wildly around the fountain in the place Saint-Sulpice.

I've never been known to run on purpose in my life, and indeed my running had something crazily frenetic to it. I couldn't stop until I was completely exhausted. I felt compelled to run to get away from the house and the problems of trying to keep up my spirits until I could lose myself in my work.

One night Steve came home early and Monique told him where to find me. He materialized out of the dark, caught me by the arm, stopped me in my tracks, and asked me what was wrong. "I don't know," I said, unwilling to complain about anything just when he was getting involved in another major piece of work. "I just don't know. It must be my book."

We returned to the apartment and Steve, concerned, consulted Monique. "Madame needs to get away from Paris," she said. "This is a difficult time of year. I advise a seawater cure at Quiberon, in Brittany."

"Oh, that's ridiculous. I can't take that much time away from my work," I protested, but in a few minutes both Steve and Monique convinced me that I needed a change. God knows, I knew I did, even though I didn't want to admit it.

I'd gone, without telling anyone, to a young French internist for antidepression pills, but when they hadn't done a thing for me in three days, I'd thrown them away, since I knew nothing about how long they took to work. The doctor's attitude hadn't inspired me to ask questions. "You're in good health, you're a best-seller, why should *you* be depressed?" he'd asked sardonically, while handing me a prescription. Why indeed? I asked myself, as tears filled my eyes as I walked down the staircase from his office.

I tried to blame my depression on the basically gray color of Paris, reminding myself that I'd always lived in full view of green or potentially green things, even when it was Central Park in the dead of winter. I blamed my depression on the lack of a good exercise class to go to; on the fact that we were so often obliged to eat in elaborate restaurants when all I wanted was a simple diet; on the fact that everyone in Paris smoked and after a dinner party I wanted to snatch off my hair and air it out as I did my clothes; on the fatigue of always being invited to dinner at eight-thirty and getting home so terribly late; on the non-existence of decent electric blankets—at home I'd slept with one for almost thirty years. However, in Paris, I had to try to generate body heat I didn't have under a heavy pile of mohair blankets, the wool of which wandered into my mouth—I blamed my depression on everything except the growing possibility that we'd made a big mistake and shouldn't be living in France at all.

I went off to Quiberon, which is set on the coast of Brittany, in a microclimate where it's clear and pleasant all year long. People taking the cure put on a toweling robe over a bathing suit, wear flip-flops, and spend the morning going from one hot saltwater treatment to another. There was the powerful hose wielded by uniformed women, the group exercises in the large Jacuzzi–swimming pool, and my favorite, a tub full of heated water with bubbles that rose up from the bottom, which made me feel that I was sitting in a bath of just-opened hot champagne. Between treatments, everyone flopped down in quiet relaxation rooms with walls and couches draped entirely with white sheets and either read or napped, or, since this was, after all, France, visited the handy bars.

Each afternoon people usually watched tapes of television movies in their rooms. I used that time to race out onto the steep but climbable rocks, alone in the bracing fresh air except for those few who were walking their dogs. I found perches in the rocks as close to the Atlantic Ocean as possible, where I'd settle for hours, emptying my mind, breathing in the sea air and watching the waves. Often I'd see the tide turn. After enough vacant contemplation, I'd think and think and think. One of the thoughts that returned often to my mind was something that Georges Delorme, Michelle Tourneville's lover and a publisher of Russian books, had explained to me. "It doesn't matter how long you live here, Judy, or how well you speak French, you'll never be anything but a stranger because you weren't *en classe* with us as a kid. You see, *you don't know our nursery rhymes.* Without that, you'll always be strictly a visitor."

At night, unrecognizable out of their robes, the other seawater-therapy inmates dressed for dinner in fashionable sports clothes. I sat happily alone, enjoying my book—a splendid novel called *Adieu, Volodia,* by Simone Signoret, to which Steve was trying to buy the rights—and eating the luscious *tourteau,* the large fresh local crab that was so in demand you had to order it days in advance. For once I let my hair go straight and didn't give a damn.

In two weeks I returned from Quiberon another woman. I was deeply rested and full of energy. I had discovered, in those hours of musing by the ocean, so wonderfully distant from Paris, that yes, we'd made a huge mistake, but there was no really sound reason to keep on living it.

Before I could discuss this with Steve, he announced that he'd found the cure for my blues, which he'd diagnosed as the seasonal disorder, recently discovered, that affects people who get too little light in winter. Apparently there was a special kind of strong lightbulb used to treat this malady, known as SAD. All that was necessary, he said, pleased with himself, was to find a way to attach these bulbs to the beams in my workroom above my desk, turn them on while I worked, and I'd be fine. Merry as a grig. I simply stared at him in disbelief. Did I look *anything* like a lab rat?

This absolutely insane and inhuman plan on the part of my normally kind, thoughtful, and loving husband told me how right I was to want to leave France and return to California. Choosing my moment carefully, I sat Steve down for a long, serious talk.

"Don't you find," I asked him, "that you've become tired of always being the *exception* in every single group? Isn't it difficult to live socially as the only Americans who happen to be considered acceptable, although not to everybody by any means, because there are just two of us, we speak the language, and we do work that people have heard of? Aren't you tired of being constantly judged against standards you're not even aware of? Aren't you weary of having to inform strangers that you're a Jew to avoid hearing a casual anti-Semitic remark? Haven't you found that you hate to live where we can't turn on the television news and expect anything but a pack of lies? Aren't you bored with the ancestor worship that is the basis for so much of the life of the French people we know?

"Don't you miss seeing our kids?" I continued. "Isn't it wonderful to take a free press and free speech for granted? Isn't it fun to meet a stranger you like and fall immediately into easy, open conversation, without worrying about keeping to a set of absurd rules? Wouldn't it be liberating to be able to drive ourselves again? Wouldn't it be amazing to fall asleep expecting a sunny day tomorrow? Isn't it important, on the most basic level, to live in your own country? *Have you ever felt truly, really, at home here?*"

Steve listened to me intently and eventually told me that considering that he spent almost all of his time working on the familiar, family atmosphere of a film set, he wasn't one-tenth as bothered by the things that affected me as I was, although yes, they certainly did get through to him. He had always envied me my year in Paris after college, but now he'd had the Parisian adventure himself. Since I felt so strongly that our joint future wasn't here, he could certainly work well back in the United States. He reminded me that he'd dragged me to Canada for his work and I'd adjusted, that he'd uprooted me from my lifetime home in Manhattan and taken me to California, because of his work, and he said that now, at this stage of our lives, he didn't want to be the cause of my having to live in a place where I couldn't be happy.

We both agreed that it wasn't only the apartment that was the drawback. If we truly wanted to stay on in France, we could sell the place after I'd finished my book, and buy another that had light and air and privacy. Indeed, when we did finally come to sell it, we broke even in spite of the fortune we'd spent fixing it up, *force* and all.

The first day it was on the market, our apartment was snatched up by the first people who saw it, Corinne and Patrick Ricard. He's head of the family firm, Pernod Ricard, who make the famous Ricard pastis and a soft drink called Orangina, as well as importing scotch and bourbon. According to my latest issue of *W*, the Ricards "live with their two children in a historic *hôtel particulier* on the Left Bank." In the photo, the beautiful, blond Madame Ricard, who is described as "the best female shot in France," was wearing Givenchy haute couture and posed in our former apartment against a dark green brocaded wall with a leopard-printed wall-to-wall carpet, sitting on a brown-and-beige-striped antique love seat. Clearly she had redecorated intelligently. Better her than me!

I was intensely relieved by Steve's reaction. Since I had seen him in a terrible fury so consistently, I didn't come close to realizing what this decision meant to him. He had to sacrifice the potential for European production that would have been his if he'd stayed on in a place where everybody in the business knew him as the American they trusted the most.

I did know, on the other hand, that if I stayed on in Paris, wherever we lived, I'd never write another book. There was too much going on socially—the aspect of life that halfway compensated for the rest—for me to stay seated in front of my typewriter with iron discipline during the nine months of six-hour days that are necessary when I write a novel. In addition, I wouldn't have found the inspiration for plot that was provided by my continuing observance of American life and women's careers.

We decided to settle in Santa Barbara, a place we'd both loved for a long time, after the filming of *Sins* was over. Since there was a chance just then, before production started, to travel to California, we took a week and flew back to Los Angeles. We spent a day in Santa Barbara, fruitlessly looking at houses with a real-estate agent. Toward the end of the day, seeing that we were drooping, she proposed showing us some raw land. Merely out of curiosity we agreed, and a few hours later we found ourselves the OWNERS of twenty-nine acres of the most extraordinary and exquisite, gently rolling hillside I've ever seen in my life, with an ocean view over a hundred miles of shoreline and a mountain view over acres and acres of green fields and avocado trees. The light was incredibly lovely—Santa Barbara is famous for its intensely golden and Grecian light—and the land was zoned for nine houses, although we only intended to build one. Several days later we'd found a local architect who was known for his innovative work and asked him to prepare preliminary plans. I took a series of pictures from the place on the hillside where we planned to build, covering everything in view, all three hundred sixty degrees of it, so that when we got back to Paris, I could tape my photos together in one long strip and have a panoramic vista of my future home.

Looking at that strip and dreaming of the house we'd build one day kept me going through the rest of the work on *I'll Take Manhattan*.

Reader, there was a massive drought in Santa Barbara the next year and all permits to build were revoked, so that we finally had to sell our hillside at half of what we'd paid for it. When we last drove up to Santa Barbara to have lunch, a year or so ago, we revisited that hillside and saw that it is still virgin land, as beautiful as we'd remembered it.

However, when we returned to Los Angeles for good, we prudently rented a really untempting house for nine months while I looked at one hundred twelve houses. My real-estate agent told me she'd never had a more difficult, reluctant, skittish client in her life, and only her old friendship for me and her knowledge that we had to buy a place to live eventually kept her going.

Finally I settled on a house that borders on the seventeenth hole of the Bel Air Country Club, surrounding us with great green vistas twelve months a year. From certain rooms we're provided with a view of our very own Deer Park, a constantly changing prospect of golfers, like groups of harmless visiting animals, whose only sound is an occasional shout of "Shit!" as they keep our pool well supplied with their sliced balls. I came back to look at this house five times, in all kinds of weather, to inspect the light, before we decided to buy it. I reached my decision on a rainy day. At last, at long last, I'd learned from my Parisian mistakes. It's the perfect house for us.

Of course, several years ago we did buy a beach house, so new it was just a concrete shell, in two fifteen-minute visits, but old habits die hard and long weekends at the beach have changed our lives immeasurably for the better, so being impulsive isn't always crazy. In our case, I figure it's much less than half the time.

Chapter Forty-three

"YOU'RE GOING TO BE ON PIVOT!" MY PUBLISHER ANNOUNCED, HIS voice filled with excitement. "Oy!" was all I could answer.

Imagine a television show that most people in France had watched without fail every Friday night for seven years, a show with an audience that was the equivalent of *Rosie, Oprah, ER, Seinfeld, Ally McBeal, Letterman,* the *Tonight Show, The Practice, Larry King,* and all our morning shows *combined*. That show was Jacques Pivot's *Apostrophe*, a show that lasted a full hour and a half without commercials, a show dedicated entirely to talking about books.

No matter what details about the French may annoy an American, they care deeply about all things cultural: they buy books like mad, and their ordinary high-school seniors leave school with a far better education than the vast majority of our college graduates.

The format of the show, which I'd often watched, consisted of five or six authors sitting around a table, talking with animation to each other, under the intense guidance of Jacques Pivot, a host who never failed to ask the very questions that would interest his guests as much as his audience; a dark, sparkling, roundish teddy bear of a man, a man as cute as any Frenchman ever gets, a man with a disarmingly humorous air, a man whose interests and whose life had just won him the annual prize given for the person who best personified *L'Art du Bien Vivre*. You can imagine how much pure pleasure a person who is judged the best in France at living well must have packed into his time on earth!

Once a year, Pivot did a show on foreign best-sellers, and since *Mistral* had made such an impact in France, this was a challenge I couldn't refuse, but one that made me tremble.

Apostrophe was not an interview show, it was a form of verbal Olympic event. The authors all knew that one of them would unofficially "win" in the eyes of the public, and the others would lose. Each author had to read the books of all of the others and be prepared to have intelligent opinions on every page in them, for when Pivot shot a question at you about any detail of the books under discussion, you couldn't fake it. It was the television equivalent of taking public oral exams for a Ph.D. thesis.

First I had to pass a preliminary test: having lunch with Madame

Pivot. Apparently they had booked several foreign authors in recent years who'd disappointed them with poor French, and Madame Pivot wanted to judge my command of the language.

That test passed—she drank a full bottle of Burgundy (*l'art du bien vivre,* indeed), I drank water—I settled down to read the five other novels that I had to all but memorize, studying them with far more attention than I'd given to any books since my senior year in college. I was constantly interrupted by anxious friends who called to give me advice.

"Don't get dressed up, don't wear Chanel, the public will detest you immediately."

"Wear a little Chanel suit, that's what people will expect, you must look like a best-seller; otherwise, they'll feel you're dressing down to them, and they'll hate you."

"Remember, the audience doesn't like a smart-ass, so, for the love of God, don't try to make a joke, you'll be misunderstood."

"Be as amusing as possible, that's what the people want."

"Keep in mind that it's important to be rigorously polite to all the other authors; the public will judge you by your good manners."

"Never speak until you're asked to."

"Jump into a conversation, that'll make you look intelligent."

Oy!

The only piece of advice that everyone agreed on was, "Above all, don't say a single bad word about another author's book. That's absolutely the one thing you must avoid. It's never, ever done."

I spent ten days cramming, shut up with those damned books, all of them translated into French. Wherever I saw something I wanted to remember, I marked it with a long slip of paper on which I scribbled the essential point.

One of them, by a British satirist, was about a publisher who became immensely rich because of his unusual ability to recognize a best-seller. The more nausea he felt while reading a book, the more likely it was to sell. If he finally vomited all over the manuscript, *voila!* a monster best-seller. I resolved to ignore this particular book and I decided to play it safe and wear an ivory skirt with a plain but becoming pink blouse, on the theory that every woman has had a pink blouse, at one time or another, and it couldn't affect opinion either against or for me.

The days leading up to *Apostrophe* were like waiting to open in my first starring part in a giant Broadway musical, knowing that I couldn't sing or dance. I'd never experienced such hideous stage fright, yet there was nothing I could do to hold back time. On the dread day itself, I gathered my little cheering section, Steve, Sybille, Florence, Jean Rosenthal, and Monique, all of whom would form part of the live audience, and went to the studio.

Naturally, given my time compulsion, I was the first to show up on the set, except for Jacques Pivot, who introduced himself and told me to sit at his right. He fell strangely silent, looking into the distance, humming to himself and twisting his legs around as if he couldn't sit still. To make conversation I asked him how many shows he'd done. "This is my four hundred and forty-fourth," he said, "and I'm still nervous."

My relief was tremendous. If Pivot himself was nervous, why shouldn't I be, too? In fact, why the hell should I be? What did I have to lose? We were going home eventually anyway. My future didn't rest on being on Pivot or on winning Pivot. I'd appeared on *Oprah* several times with almost no nerves, and that mattered so very much more.

As the rest of the guests arrived and were introduced to each other before we went on the air, I discovered that I was the only author representing herself. All the others were either the French publishers or the French agents for the authors whose books I'd been reading. Apparently the other writers hadn't "passed" lunch with Madame Pivot.

Suddenly the show began and Pivot, instantly assuming his on-air personality, lobbed an unexpectedly sudden question at me. I don't remember what it was, because at that moment I decided to throw away all the advice I'd been given.

I took a deep breath and said that before I answered whatever he'd asked me, I wanted to register a violent (*violent*) protest against the detestable (*détestable*) book that said you could recognize a best-seller if it made you throw up (*vomir*). I waxed eloquent about the virtues of best-selling novels—France's very own *Bonjour Tristesse,* for example—and heaped articulate and reasonable scorn on the English satirist for quite a while before I subsided.

The rest of the show is lost in euphoria. I knew I'd won Pivot handsdown in the first five minutes because I'd followed my instinct, broken the chief rule, and spoken my mind. I relaxed and remembered all the points I'd written down, so I was able to find something agreeable to say about everybody else's book. For the rest of the program I was Madame-so-agreeable-in-pink.

What a high! No PR I've ever done can begin to compare with it except for that first *Merv Griffin Show,* when I'd been too new to the game to have stage fright. For the next months strangers kept coming up to me in the street, introducing themselves and congratulating me on winning Pivot.

———

THE PREPRODUCTION ON *Sins* had been going on while I was neglecting my new book, yet again, to prepare for Pivot. Now I had time to learn that a suite had been taken at the Ritz for Joan Collins, plus an additional room for her clothes and yet another room for the exercise equipment she was bringing with her. Steve had made an arrangement with Valentino to make a large number of haute-couture outfits for her to wear in her role as a fashion designer, and the wardrobe department had created other lavish costumes. She would be spending the summer in France with her serious new beau, Peter Holm. With her too was her assistant and best friend, Judy Bryer, a delightful woman.

I'd only watched *Dynasty* once or twice, but of course I knew what kind of woman Joan Collins was. Her ultimate bitchiness was so well established that I never questioned it. I would never have guessed that she would turn out to be the major exception to the rule that a movie star can't be a real friend; that the day would come when we'd think of Joan as a down-to-earth, hospitable, cozy, terrific broad, with a sense of humor all her own and a platoon of loving friends, and as a totally devoted mother who has an admirable fortitude that has enabled her to survive a lot of difficult moments.

The first time I met her revealed nothing. She was calm, cool, and distinctly reserved during a welcoming dinner at the Tour d'Argent. Peter was tall and blond, not faintly attractive to my eyes, a Norwegian hulk (reported to be wanted on criminal charges in several countries) whose eyes only betrayed interest when I brought up the subject of the rising price of real estate. The late Douglas Hickox, who had beautifully directed the Parisian part of *Mistral,* and his wife, Annabelle, also were part of the party.

On the first day of shooting, Joan was two hours late arriving on location. Nobody said anything to her about it. On the second and third days, she was also two hours late. Finally Steve decided that he had to intervene and had a serious discussion with her about showing up on time. The following day she was three hours late.

She made her point. It was decided to rearrange the schedule around the star, since anything else was counterproductive. However, once she was ready to work, nobody could be a more thoroughgoing professional than Joan. She gave her best every minute she was on the set, and her best was compellingly watchable. The important thing to understand about her was that she had an absolute daily and addictive need to shop. Those first hours in the morning were the only time during the day when she could look in store windows and spot things she'd later have sent to her hotel to try on. Without this opportunity, she simply wasn't happy, and Joan not happy . . .

The entire *Sins* company would, later in the summer, spend ten days in Venice. There, Joan worked in costume and showed up right on time for nine days, with only one day off, a Sunday during which we bumped into her on the Lido dressed in jeans. However, the day before we were due to leave, I discovered Judy Bryer buying seven new Vuitton suitcases for Joan.

"How could she possibly need them?" I asked. "She hasn't had a minute off to go shopping since she's been here." "You'd be surprised," Judy answered, with a mysterious smile. I later realized that the Venice shops were sending boatloads of things across the lagoon to Joan's hotel, the Cipriani, for her to pick from every night, after she'd finished working.

Her shopping addiction aside, I discovered that Joan could be irresistibly charming and deliciously funny. That side of her is best described by a story Tony Newley told me one night, in the voice of a man who's just survived a terrible car wreck without a scratch. "You know, Joan and I used to be married and before our divorce I was quoted correctly as saying that I'd rather kiss Hitler than her," he said. "Well, this afternoon I had to spend several hours with Joan discussing our kids' schools and, Judy, so help me God, I damn near fell in love with her all over again."

(I think the first person to use the line about Hitler was Tony Curtis about Marilyn Monroe, after making *Some Like It Hot,* but no matter.)

The real difficulty on the production of *Sins* came from Peter Holm. His title of executive producer went to his greedy, dishonest head and one day he actually stole the books from the production office and took them back to the Ritz to study, looking to find places in the budget where he and Joan had been cheated. Of course he found nothing. Steve told him to come by any time and just ask, the books would always be available. Twice more Peter made laughable surprise raids on the production offices, but he never found anything to complain about. However, he fomented trouble whenever he could.

The period of the production of *Sins* was so infernally impossible, for business reasons far too complicated and boring to relate, that Steve was beset every moment he was awake. If I hadn't known we were leaving Paris, I like to have a fantasy that I would have moved to hotel to get away from the telex and the all-pervasive storm of problems in which my husband was enveloped. But that defiant thought belongs under the large catagory of "should haves" in my life. No matter how upset I was, I could never have added to his troubles by disappearing.

During the shoot in Venice I reached a low point. It's the most difficult city in the world to film in, since every piece of equipment has to be loaded onto barges and slowly, *slowly* moved through the narrow canals from one place to another. Meanwhile, the actors, except for Joan, were behaving exactly like rotten, hormone-filled teenagers on a rampage. They took the *motoscaffos* and boatmen that had been rented for them and disappeared in every direction, up to all sorts of mischievous, childish tricks, ignoring all instructions to stay put where the director could find them when he needed them. It was hell on everybody except for the actors, who were having the time of their lives, treating Venice like a summer sex camp.

I simply went to ground, wandering around the back streets in a solitary funk and taking long *vaporetto* trips to nowhere, all by myself. Being on my own in Venice could have been delicious, but it turned into one long, lonely, miserable pout. I could barely communicate with Steve and I tried to keep out of his way. I told myself over and over that his preoccupation had nothing to do with me. It didn't and I knew it, but that didn't help the reaction I had to him. I made resolution after resolution to tell him how much he frightened me, but then, when I watched the pressure he was under, I found I couldn't bear to add to it. I had no reason to even watch the filming. *Sins,* thank God, wasn't my book, and I felt, rightly or wrongly, unwelcome on the set.

As far as Peter Holm was concerned, Joan was to marry this perfectly dreadful man—we went to the wedding reception she gave at her house back in Los Angeles—and soon divorce him. Call it a giant lapse in judgment. I'm sure she'd have a more colorful term.

The evening after her divorce from Peter was granted (with Joan being ordered to pay him alimony), Steve and I hid out with her from the press, along with our mutual friends Don Quine and his wife, Judy Balaban Kantor Franciosa Quine, who'd written a truly excellent book about her long friendship with Grace Kelly, one of whose bridesmaids she'd been. I had the inspiration to suggest we eat at the one place nobody would think to look for Joan, the quiet, secluded dining room of the Hotel Bel-Air. It was a dreadfully sad evening for Joan. She had genuinely loved Peter, God knows why, and the summer of *Sins* was the height of their romance. But that was a long time ago, and she's had a lovely man in her life ever since. Nothing can get Joan down for long . . . she's an ultimate survivor.

The night that the first episode of *Sins* appeared on television, in February 1986, Joan gave a party at her house in Los Angeles and Timothy Dalton brought his lady love of ten years, Vanessa Redgrave, whose pro-PLO politics made me loathe her on principle.

Tall and lanky, Vanessa was shorn, her hair only an inch or so long, since she was working in a film called *Playing for Time,* about the concentration camps. I wanted to stay as far away from her as possible, but Timothy, who'd become a real pal in the course of filming *Mistral* and *Sins,* never left her side.

Eventually I had to go over to congratulate him and he introduced me to Vanessa. Thank God women can always talk hair! At the end of a twenty-minute discussion about her hair and my hair, I'd found her so intensely enchanting that as we parted we kissed. She bent forward and I bent forward and Vanessa ended up kissing the top of my head while I kissed her collarbone. *Oh, the power of personality.* Personality is as indisputably real as glamour is fake, and Vanessa Redgrave, approve of her or not, can't help being an utterly lovable creature, as long as politics is left out of the equation.

ONE MORNING IN the late spring of 1985, Duc Patric d'Harcourt called and invited us to a lunch party at the elegant apartment he shared with Thyra, his exquisite, dark-haired duchess. "Steve has to come too, it's boy-girl, boy-girl," he explained, "in honor of the comtesse de Paris. You can't say no."

I accepted immediately and hung up wondering how to break this news to Steve, who was still up to his eyebrows in *Sins.* He enjoyed the evening social ramble, but he'd never gone to a weekday lunch party, since they were for women only, and in any case, he wouldn't have had time.

However, this lunch was at the home of one of the three "first" dukes of France, the direct descendant of the man whose duty it had been to announce, "The king is dead, long live the king," and I damn well wasn't going to miss it. Finally I just announced to Steve that we were going, he had to wear a blue suit and black shoes, and he would have to make time for it because I couldn't go without him. I wanted to see with my own eyes the wife of the comte de Paris, the pretender to the throne of France.

In 885, Eudes, the comte de Paris, had been elected the first king of France, and as far as my royalist friends were concerned, his descendant was still king of France. This invitation, as surprising as it was Proustian, was an occasion on any level.

I'd met Thyra d'Harcourt several times and found her delightfully unpretentious and unstuffy, probably because she was born de Zayas, of a Spanish family, and retained a fresh Spanish spontaneity. We'd met the Harcourts through Comte and Comtesse Dominique Frémy.

Michelle Frémy was one of the most adept, surefooted hostesses in Paris. She and her quiet husband worked together publishing an amazing annual encyclopedia of more than sixteen hundred pages called *Quid,* which told you anything you needed to know about everything.

Their print order in 1984 was over four hundred thousand and since facts and figures changed so rapidly, all they could do was grow. They and their staff ran *Quid* from the former stables of their house, the loveliest I'd ever seen in the city. It was a classic little château surrounded on all sides by large gardens and ancient trees, an oasis of the deep country, with a church steeple the only tall building in sight, hidden behind a tall, blank wall on a street in the middle of the seventh *arrondissement,* not far from us.

Monique and Florence were just as impressed as I was by this invitation straight into the center of the center of the heart of the ancient royalist aristocracy.

"Madame, you must curtsy to the comtesse de Paris," Florence informed me.

"But I'm an American! Nancy Reagan didn't curtsy to the queen of England when she was invited to the wedding of Prince Charles."

"Madame, excuse me, but you are not Nancy Reagan," Monique said firmly. The two of them stared at me sternly, totally in agreement. Finally I decided to obey custom and practiced shaking hands with them, doing a slight inclination of the head and a tiny dip of the knees, until they were satisfied that I'd got it right.

Once we'd arrived at the Harcourts', we found nine other people standing around, chatting and waiting with an air of subdued excitement for the guest of honor. When she arrived, she did not disappoint. Divinely tall, with extraordinary posture and thick, lovely, wavy, gray hair worn in a chignon, the comtesse de Paris, who had been born a Braganza of the former royal family of Portugal, was the most ravishingly beautiful older woman I've ever seen in my life. It was impossible to believe that she'd given birth to a dozen children, known collectively as *Les Enfants de France.* She beamed with equal radiance at everybody, including the pretty, young socialist journalist who'd just written an autobiography of Mitterrand, the only woman in the room who didn't curtsy.

I was fascinated. The comtesse addressed all of the guests she knew in the familiar form, using "*tu*" instead of the usual "*vous*" while they addressed her in the third person, as in "May I offer Madame la Comtesse a glass of champagne?" Perhaps that's the divine right of someone who could have been queen of France, had there not been a Revolution. Curtsy I might, but Steve and I spoke to her in the first person, since we hadn't signed on to bring back the royal family, unlike almost everyone there.

At some point in the lunch the conversation turned to which of the group belonged to families that possessed a piece of the True Cross. (I know, I know.) There were so many claims that, in a pause, I heard Steve say, "The True Cross must have been as big as Noah's Ark." After a shocked split second of silence, he brought down the house.

Thyra d'Harcourt asked us to drive the comtesse home, and on the way she asked if she could send me her memoirs, and if I would advise her on an American publisher. Of course I agreed, but when I read them, I found that the two volumes covering hundreds of formerly royal births, deaths, weddings, engagements, and birthday parties— going back for several generations—totally displaced her own story.

There certainly might have been a fascinating account of what it had been like to be brought up a princess and granddaughter of an emperor and to become the wife of the pretender to the French throne. The problem was in finding it. I couldn't, try as I did. The memoirs could only have been published in English for the strictly limited number of people who care about endless details of a foreign and royal way of life that's gone forever, and I knew my publishers well enough to be positive that they wouldn't be interested.

I had no intention of stringing the comtesse de Paris along, so I wrote and explained exactly why I couldn't be of help to her. It occurred to me, in a perfect Henry James moment, that if I had wanted to, I could have dragged out an almost endless amount of time making fruitless efforts on her behalf, or even worse, pretending to make attempts, and become her New Best Friend. The way was positively clear to entertain for her and thus jump the highest fence in old French society. But even if I'd intended to live on in France, that would have been heartless and straightforward social climbing, a way of life that I've always despised.

I did enjoy the highly novelistic glimpses into a foreign world that I got from meeting people who belonged to a special and rarefied background, normally closed to foreigners, but that was as far as it went. I was almost over my head in aristocrats as it was, and the time had come to give my own lunch party to pay back some of my obligations.

Jean Bakker, Yvonne Paniza, Thyra d'Harcourt, Michelle Frémy, Polly Platt Grchich, Solange Gaussen—these were the names of some of my eleven guests you'll recognize if you're still with me.

Monique and I had a long discussion about the menu. "Salmon," she decreed, "for the principal course."

"Salmon? Listen, Monique, I've had salmon at every lunch I've been to this spring. We should serve something different."

"No, Madame, when salmon is in season, it's the understood thing that everyone serves it at every opportunity, like asparagus or baby lamb, and besides, it's the middle of Lent."

"*Lent?* Monique, be reasonable . . . even the Pope says Catholics can eat meat on Friday now. Why would you imagine that my friends have given up meat for a month?"

"But, Madame, it is more *delicate,* more *comme il faut,* to always observe Lent. You don't know who, among your guests, still follows the old ways."

So went the conversation of two Jewish women.

We served salmon, the only item I remember of what was unquestionably a splendid menu. I would never have dared oppose Monique on such a subtle point.

The next problem was seating. I was having a duchess and the wife of an ambassador, who in France is always much respected and given the title of *Madame, l'ambassadrice.* Which one should I put at my right? Finally, unable to decide, I called the protocol office at the American embassy and explained my plight. The officer I spoke to said, "Oh, both ladies are good friends, it won't make any difference at all." "You're sure?" "Absolutely, I get asked questions like this all the time."

But, I thought, that means that one of them will be served first and one next to last. Clearly that wouldn't do. (The hostess is always served last, unlike formal American service.) This detail was easily solved by hiring yet another butler so that one of them could start on my left and the other on my right, at the same time, and everyone's food would be hot.

I remember sitting in my salon, all pre-party details as perfect as they could be, blessing the sunlight that was just about to enter the room and might, at this season of the year, almost manage to last out the lunch. However, I felt most *infernally* nervous.

I'd been entertaining on my own since I was twenty-one, when I gave Harrison's birthday party in a tiny hotel room. That had been in 1949, thirty-six years earlier, but I'd never felt this kind of pre-party tension before. Was it just the ordeal of the French ladies' lunch that had finally fallen onto my shoulders, or was it because, in my heart of hearts, I felt like an impostor? Hadn't all my guests been most hospitable and forthcoming to me? Yes, they had. Weren't they among the best friends I'd made in my time here? Yes, indeed. *But.* My nerves were almost as bad as before *Apostrophe.*

Today, in Los Angeles, I don't feel a touch of anxiety before giving a ladies' lunch, and I've done it often. I know that there's simply no possibility that a roomful of women can fail to find a great deal to talk about, and very quickly, even if they've just met each other.

Back then, almost as soon as the party started, I could tell immediately that it was going to be a success, and when it was over, I watched women demonstrate the success by exchanging their cards as deftly as Japanese businessmen. However, I'll never forget the way I asked myself, before it began, why the hell I'd ever got myself into a position of such nervous agony. In retrospect, I think my impostor theory has a lot to recommend it.

It was my first lunch party, granted, and if I'd stayed in Paris long enough to give another, I'm certain I would never again have been one-tenth as nervous. Nevertheless. Before we left Paris, I had lunch one day alone with Polly Platt Grchich, herself a Main Line aristocrat, married to a European aristocrat, and she told me that after thirty years, as totally plugged-in as she was to Parisian life, she still missed America and still *didn't feel really at home* in Paris. This from a woman who's written a very successful book, *French or Foe*, on living in Paris for American wives who find themselves there for the first time.

Paris is one tough act. I'm pleased to know I can do it, and far happier that I don't have to.

Chapter Forty-four

WHEN STEVE AND I DECIDED TO MOVE BACK TO THE UNITED STATES, we resolved not to tell anyone of our intentions. We'd gone to such a major amount of trouble to install ourselves in Paris, and we'd made so many friends, that it would have seemed insane to them that we were turning our backs on it all. And our reasons, our deep feelings, couldn't possibly be explained. They didn't make sense to anyone but us. Also at the time that we made up our minds, our departure was so far in the future that we didn't want to live through the next year with one foot out the door.

There was still the production of *Sins* to finish. Only once did I go to the set. Joan Collins and Gene Kelly were supposed to be getting married at a large church in Paris and Steve told me I could take Monique and Florence and sit in the pews, as if we were wedding guests. The ceremony proceeded smoothly until Joan and Gene had to cross themselves. An argument broke out between the bride and groom as to which direction the second gesture is made, right to left or left to right. The priest, appealed to, said indignantly, "I'm just an actor!" The Anglican director wasn't sure. We held back our giggles as best we could while the argument raged. It seemed to me that Gene Kelly, an Irish Catholic, must be right, but I didn't dare to say a word. Finally they managed to agree, and as soon as we could get away, the three of us, dressed in our best so we'd look like wedding guests, retired to a local tearoom to laugh ourselves silly. No, it wasn't a smooth shoot, not even in the details.

On our next trip back to California to see our family, I made a quick tour of Rodeo Drive. Since the publication of *Scruples* I'd always had a ridiculous but unquestionably possessive feeling about the street that has been so important in my career, and I liked to drop in to various boutiques and see how they were flourishing.

At Pierre Deux I noticed some handsome, but by no means unusual, French provincial armoires. We'd made a few trips to the flea market, the Marché aux Puces, in Paris, concentrated at the permanent Biron, Vernaison, or Serpette stalls, which don't contain junk, and I'd resisted buying very similar furniture at prices that were less than one-third of what was being asked in California.

Since I'm a not an expert, I'd always had the suspicion that I'd be paying too much, particularly since French antiques dealers show up at the flea market when it opens, at four o'clock in the morning, and pick off the best pieces by flashlight, or else go out on trips into the countryside to find their merchandise in secret places known only to them.

"How come your prices are so high?" I asked the manager of Pierre Deux. He took me into his office and gave me an invaluable lesson on the subject of the markup.

"They're not high, they're realistic. We have to pay for our buying trip to France, counting every expense down to the last cup of coffee; we have to pay for having the furniture packed and shipped to Los Angeles; we have to have everything perfectly restored and put into impeccable condition; and then we have to pay our gigantic rent on Rodeo Drive and the salaries of our salespeople, to say nothing of advertising and public relations. Most important of all, on top of everything, we're in business to make a profit. A good one. When you factor all that in, it triples the price."

"So if I were going to be furnishing a house here, I'd be much better off buying in France?"

"Well, of course. You'd be paying the right price and only paying for the packing and shipping."

"What if I bought from well-established French dealers, since I don't have your special knowledge of antiques or the bargaining power you have as a regular customer?"

"You'd still be saving a huge amount," he assured me.

When we'd sold our house in Beverly Hills we'd given one of our sons the pieces of furniture he wanted, and sold the rest of it to the buyers, since we didn't want to put it in storage, so sure were we that we wouldn't be returning. Now, except for the modern, misbegotten Californian things I'd bought for the Paris apartment, not nearly enough to furnish a house, we owned nothing.

The information I'd picked up at Pierre Deux was the equivalent, in fashion terms, of being told that you're about to find yourself standing naked on the street in front of Neiman Marcus unless you buy a new wardrobe.

I returned to Paris with a fresh feeling about the antiques dealers who surrounded us in the neighborhood of the rue Cassette. Now, when I passed their provocative windows, I wouldn't be limited to admiring them from the street or playing the "just looking" role; I'd be a genuine client with a real need.

I resolved to look only for pieces of furniture on a scale small enough to fit into any house, and to go to well-known dealers with reputations to uphold. They would already have inspected the furniture, and I'd rather they made their normal profit than try to second-guess them at the flea market and judge for myself.

Antiques are like furs and jewels; no one really knows if they're what they're presented as being, except for the dealers themselves, who've spent their lives learning how to evaluate quality. Actually, the best place to buy antiques is at a "vetted" show, with many participating dealers, where a panel of experts examines every piece that's for sale.

I didn't have time to drift around the Left Bank antiques shops in leisure—I was still working hard on the so-often interrupted labor of *I'll Take Manhattan*—but I found a shop near the rue Cassette that was well known and trusted, and I started to buy, very slowly and carefully. When the *Sins* production moved to the South of France for two weeks, I saw my big opportunity to buy at non-Parisian prices, and I arranged for our driver to meet me in Nice, where the company was quartered.

From there, while Steve worked, I sallied forth on long, heavenly day trips to Aix-en-Provence, to Nîmes, to Avignon, and to Cannes, wherever there were concentrations of good antiques shops. My only mistake was a vast excess of caution. Although I knew that I was in the middle of a once-in-a-lifetime golden opportunity, although I was surrounded by a million choices, *now* I became difficult to please and found it hard to make up my mind. The lesson of 17 rue Cassette had frightened me more than enough to keep me from buying quickly. But everything I bought, when it finally arrived in Los Angeles, found a natural place in the house we were to buy in the future.

The deepest pleasure for me was in buying objects like a pair of lovely gilded Venetian mirrors, one of which had a crack right down the middle of the ancient, etched glass. "But naturally, Madame, most assuredly she has suffered," the dealer said. "But that is life, is it not? Look how beautiful she is." I quickly reached the point where anything that was in perfect shape looked all wrong to me. Signs of the proof of the passage of time were what drew me to a chair or a desk. Unlike many people who buy antiques, I wasn't buying for museum condition, but for sheer charm.

"First show me where it has suffered" became my request to any of the Provençal dealers, and that single phrase indicated to them that at least I wasn't totally unknowledgeable. Also, my assumption that there'd be something wrong made them willing to reveal defects to me more readily than if I'd walked in expecting perfection.

In *Scruples Two* I was able to use the knowledge I had never acquired, but I knew I could have used, in the characters of one of my favorite female villains, Cora de Lioncourt, and her husband, Robert.

Every good antiques dealer in Europe shuddered when they walked into his shop, for they bought the very pieces the dealer, against his own principles, had been covetously contemplating reserving for himself: antiques that were just on the verge of coming into fashion or objects so curious, so unusual that they had been overlooked until the Lioncourts started poking into the corners of the shop. Cora and Robert de Lioncourt would fly across Europe at a moment's notice to attend an antiques dealer's funeral, knowing that on such occasions, grasping families would provide the possibility of picking up something at half its value for ready cash. They became as adept at buying well at auctions as the dealers themselves, for they never allowed themselves to be carried away in the heat of the chase. Few estate sales, important or unimportant, escaped their attention, and they had cultivated dozens of little old ladies who had been collectors in their youth and now sold their precious pieces, one by one, to support them in their old age.

There are a multitude of joys in writing, but few equal the creation of an evil person, male or female. I'm just as interested in revealing what makes them tick as I am in delving into the psychological background of any heroine or hero . . . and there's so much more impure pleasure in writing a bad person than an admirable one! There's never been a rotten person I've created whom I didn't end up feeling sympathetic toward. I know what it is in their lives that has caused them to be so bad; after all, it's not their fault. It's mine. I dearly love a villain and far more, a villainess . . . they give me an opportunity to use my worst side, all the impulses or fantasies I've never even known I had, and then to exaggerate them, to give myself license to behave as I never would in reality. For seventy years I've been so bloody *good*, such a straight arrow, so concerned about presenting a decent face to the world, that it's thoroughly boring to me, but there's little I can do now to change my (near saintly) character. I'd rather write a great villainess than a great sex scene. I like to think I've done both.

My very favorite villainess, a heavenly bad-ass, is Susan Arvey, who first appears in *Scruples* and stays on the scene in *Scruples Two*. She's born-to-the-Hollywood-purple, and her husband owns the studio that produces some of Vito Orsini's films. She meddles in Billy's life, trying to keep her and Vito from marrying, but it's in *Scruples Two* that she really rumbles. She keeps her husband under her calculating, manipulative thumb, she sabotages Vito, and she carves out a secret life for herself that involves frequent trips to New York. There, in an apartment no one knows she owns, she thoroughly enjoys a complicated, dominating, totally shameless sex life with a series of hired young studs. Finally she turns her attentions to Vito himself and the two of them embark on an affair that starts as a glorious grudge fuck and promises unlimited future opportunities for them to enjoyably torture each other with a maximum of sexual tension. Ah, Susan Arvey, I could never, in my own life, do even a single one of the things you do so artfully, and get away with entirely. You are *unthinkably* wicked, untrustworthy, and depraved, dear Susan, but whose mind brought you to life? I may be hopelessly square and nice, but I've never claimed not to have a dirty mind . . . it's such a consolation for all the naughtiness I've missed!

Writing novels is the only way I know to live as a multiple personality for fun and profit. But I wonder, would a true multiple personality be able to stay focused for at least five to six hours a day manipulating all of the others, so that they can engage in specific dialogue and acts captured on paper that propel the plot of a novel forward? Nah.

BACK IN PARIS, I found my first Parisian friend, Pam Andriotakis, becoming more and more deeply involved in a serious love affair. She had met a charming young Pole, Arthur Gromadzki, the favorite nephew of Nella Rubinstein, widow of the great Artur Rubinstein. Nella, an ultimate grande dame, rich, powerful, and courted for all of her life, now counted on Arthur, her late husband's namesake, to devote himself to her wide public and private affairs. She had absolutely no intention of losing him to an American journalist from Detroit. Arthur was a promising but relatively penniless business student in graduate school, torn between his duty to his aunt and his love for Pam. His entire family, many brothers and sisters, all still lived in Poland, under the regime of the Communist government.

At the same time there were romantic developments with Sybille Gaussen, who had three unmarried older brothers and was an adored only daughter. Since I'd known her she'd been enjoyably tormenting her parents with a series of impossible, unsuitable guys. Now she had finally started to turn her delectably changeable attentions toward the patient direction of the Right One, a distinctly handsome, utterly prepossessing, and quietly droll young man named Jean-Paul Denfert-Rochereau. I'd met him at our very first dinner at the Gaussens'. His ancestor, the famous Colonel Denfert-Rochereau, had been responsible for the victorious defense of Belfort in 1870. (No, I have no idea what the defense of Belfort was. This isn't a history book.) A square, from which you can enter the catacombs of Paris, and a major Métro station bear the name Denfert-Rochereau.

In the course of ten novels, besides Dick Avedon as Falk, the photographer in *Mistral,* Sybille is the only person I've met in real life after whom I semi-modeled a character, in her physical characteristics—as Maxi Amberville, heroine of *I'll Take Manhattan.* I described Sybille, with an allowance for my normal exaggeration, through the eyes of Pavka Mayer, the artistic director of all the Amberville publications.

As well as he knew her he was always slightly amazed—as if he had sustained a small electric shock—by her actual physical presence, for Maxi was, somehow, more real than other people, more *there.* She was only of medium height . . . and her body did not take up a lot of room, yet she created a vibrating space around herself through sheer mesmerizing energy. Maxi was formed like a great courtesan of the Belle Epoque, with a tiny waist, excellent deep breasts, and sumptuous hips, yet she was not oppressively voluptuous and the masculine swagger of her garments only made her all the more feminine. . . . No photograph would ever capture the essence of Maxi because she lacked ruthless bone structure . . . but he never tired of looking at her wickedly undeviating gaze . . . she would have been riveting in a room full of beautiful women, for she made mere beauty seem not only irrelevant but uninteresting. . . . She had the mouth of a true-born sorceress, he said to himself with the well-earned judgment of a man who had successfully loved women for more than fifty years.

I was delighted by all these budding love affairs. As the mother of sons—who never told me *anything* intimate, which is, I realize, as natural as it is frustrating—I'd always craved daughters, and Sybille and Pam were not just friends, although they were still only in their late twenties, but daughter-substitutes, who didn't present me with any of the problems real mothers have. I never judged them; I gave the most sensible advice I could, but on request only; I listened with unfeigned, intense interest to every last detail; I never asked questions that might be intrusive; and my opinions were always open-ended. If they changed their minds, I was willing to change mine, too. It's so much easier, I suspect, when they're not real daughters.

At the same time that romance started knocking at our door, destiny announced itself unmistakably. One unfine day the apartment above us, which had remained empty for a long time, was occupied by the people who had owned it before we'd bought our place. Their name? *Fatal.* Not even Dickens would condescend to make up such an obvious name for these people.

Monsieur and Madame Fatal and the three little Fatal children had taken up residence only a few feet above our heads. If I had ever had the faintest doubt that we were doing the right thing in leaving, the Fatals would have banished it.

In very old buildings, like 17 rue Cassette, the rather fragile wood floor of one apartment is the equally fragile wood ceiling of another. When any Fatal walked, we heard each loud footfall; when any Fatal talked, we heard the sound of the carrying Fatal voice.

Monsieur Fatal was a diplomat from a Near Eastern country who had bizarre ideas on bringing up children. Unable to believe my ears, which recorded the sounds of heavy falls at regular intervals on the ceiling of my workroom, I rushed out to the garden to hear him commanding his children. "Now, jump! Good. Next one, jump! Not bad. Now your turn, jump! Excellent."

Reader, have you ever heard of anybody who spends an hour training his kids to jump from the furniture to the floor every day after school . . . or was it just the phantom of a bad Little White Father who had entered into the very soul of Monsieur Fatal?

I tried to make friends with the man, since the sounds couldn't really be heard at their worst in any other part of the house except my office. I introduced myself to him one day as his new neighbor, gave him French copies of *Mistral* and *Daisy* for his wife, and eventually asked casually about his methods of physical culture. He saw through me completely. "You are disturbed by my healthy children exercising their muscles, Madame? Then I suggest that you try to write in some other room. You have more than enough rooms in which to do so, I believe. Good day, Madame."

I bought some Boules Quies, the most effective wax earplugs in the world, and tried to write while using them. The jumping now resounded mostly in my body as if something heavy had just fallen on my head.

As summer approached, I realized that I had to know if the Fatal children would be going away to camp, giving me two months of peace—all I needed to finish *Manhattan*. From a window on the opposite side of my workroom, I saw Monsieur Fatal sitting at one of his windows. I rushed through the house and reappeared in the garden just under him, as if by chance.

"Bonjour, Monsieur Fatal, it is a delightful morning, is it not?"

"Bonjour, Madame. Indeed it is."

"Tell me, Monsieur, are your children, by any chance, going away on holiday this summer? Or to summer camp?"

"Do I inquire about your own summer plans, Madame? Do I concern myself with your private business? Do I allow myself that curiosity?"

"No, but Monsieur Fatal . . ."

"Then I wonder why you give yourself the right to be concerned with my plans?"

"Only because I have children myself, Monsieur, and I remember how good it was, how healthy, for children to breathe fresh—"

"Permit me to worry about my own children, Madame, without your advice. The Good Lord be thanked, they are strong and solid and in splendid form. They breathe beautifully. Life in Paris agrees with them. Good day, Madame."

Only the knowledge that I wouldn't have to live long with the Fatals on top of us kept me relatively civil with this fiend and enabled me to ignore the fact that he and his muscular progeny had to be endured. When I reread *I'll Take Manhattan,* I see no sign of the strain under which it was written. In fact, it's probably my funniest book. That must be because once I get into my work, I lose all track of time, comfort, hunger, thirst, eyestrain, muscle strain, or anything that might disturb my concentration, as long as there's someone to answer the phone. It's a writer's version of what's called the Zone.

Of course I had told Florence and Monique about our intention to leave. Florence was in love with a man who was about to move to California and she determined to follow us—and him. She remained as my assistant in Los Angeles for more than a year until the romance faded and family affairs called her back to Paris. Monique was far more desolate than Florence. She, dear and loyal creature, truly loved us. We still hear from her and write to her every year. She flirted with the idea of coming back with us, but she was singularly unfit for Californian life. She'd never driven a car, she couldn't speak English, and all her sisters lived in Paris. They were a close family and deeply important to her. How would she get to the market, how would she find friends, and, especially, how could she leave her sisters and their children? We talked it over for hours and we both realized that she would find it impossible to make a life for herself in Los Angeles.

Gérard and Solange Gaussen gave the first of the many parties that would eventually lead to the literally drenched glamour of Venetian-born Sybille's marriage in Venice, on a day of flooded canals and wet gondolas, which happened well after we had returned to the United States. We refused that invitation; six thousand miles is just too far to go to a wedding.

Pam and Arthur decided to get married, Nella or no, and their wedding took place in the Greek Orthodox Church in Paris. No one who was invited could have had any advance idea of the endurance contest they were about to undergo. The ceremony took place five separate times in five languages, with five different priests. There was the

English-speaking priest for Pam's American friends and her family, who had come from Detroit en masse for the occasion; there was the Polish priest for Arthur's huge family, who had all received weekend visas to come to Paris, although their children remained hostage in Poland; there was the Greek priest, I assume to make the marriage the Greek equivalent of kosher; there was the French priest for Pam and Arthur's French friends; and there was a priest who conducted the ceremony in Latin, I'm not certain why. I'd lost track after the first two.

Pam wore a long white couture wedding dress Karl Lagerfeld had made for her, with a long-sleeved bolero top for the wedding that when taken off revealed a wonderful strapless dress. The guests wore their best summer clothes, since the endless winter had suddenly turned into a hot summer. I wore my most elegant low shoes with my dress, not knowing that four of the long ceremonies were going to take place with the entire congregation standing! My shoes were off and my feet were planted flat on the cool stone floor of the church well before the second priest got started. Only the American priest told the wedding guests to be seated, blessings on his head. No two people could have been more thoroughly married than Pam and Arthur.

Now Arthur is very successfully working for a huge international investment company, they live in Geneva, and, like Sybille in Paris, they've produced three children, one more beautiful than the next. Pam, who visited me just the other day, has never looked better, and Nella is ninety-nine. So goes it.

After the wedding there was a most original and engaging dinner and dancing reception in a restaurant on an island in a tributary of the Seine. A fleet of little boats took the guests back and forth and I managed to get my shoes on in time to dance.

The following day, a Sunday, we gave a lunch party for Pam and Arthur and all their families . . . and Nella, of course, who was finally making the best of things. I'd hired Lenôtre, the best caterer in Paris, and tables had been set up all over the house. The food was served from long, white-draped buffets set up in our oversized entrance hall so that there would be a maximum of space in the dining room, and even the garden finally blossomed into its full potential on this wonderfully warm day. We were able to open all the many doors and use the garden as if it were an outdoor room. For once, everything looked as unreal and glorious as scenes from a movie about Paris. It looked the way I had imagined it would look when we first bought the damn place!

At this party I was finally truly able to turn off any personal relationship to the rue Cassette and see it through the eyes of Arthur's handsome and charming Polish family, and his distinguished, English-speaking father. The apartment was simply magnificent! Who could ask for anything more spacious, or more lovely? I felt ashamed when I realized how impossible, in the experience of these outstanding, highly educated Poles, who were returning to the restrictions of their homeland the next day, it must have seemed that two people actually had such a palace all to themselves. Like Tony Newley with Joan, I almost fell in love with it all over again . . . but I knew that the party was the reason, not the place.

Steve is convinced that we gave this party not just to celebrate the wedding of our first friend in Paris but because we had a subconscious desire to bring our French experience to a fairy-tale conclusion, in the same fairy-tale mood that had led us to rent on the Ile Saint-Louis almost three years earlier, on a day just as irresistibly lovely. If so, our subconscious must have been in league with the weather bureau.

I STARTED THIS autobiography with an important memory and I'm ending it with another, that happiness-filled, post-wedding party almost fourteen years ago. Everything that followed that moment has been fairly routine, without the ups and downs of our earlier struggles, Steve and I have settled into normal life, as it's expected to be if you're very, very, very lucky. Knock on wood!

We left Paris a few months after the wedding party in a bitter, blowing rain; we reintegrated ourselves into life in Los Angeles and soon many new friends, friends with whom I feel entirely able to speak my mind, friends of every kind, friends I'm totally at home with, yes, even a surprisingly large number of perfectly adorable, dearly loved *Republicans* (with whom I don't talk politics), entered our life. They've more than made up for the friends and the giddy social whirl we left behind in Paris. And every last one of them is a person who knows my nursery rhymes.

I've written six more novels, including *Till We Meet Again,* which is my favorite after *Mistral* and was the first to put me at the number-one spot in the London *Times.* Each one took more or less the average nine months, and each was written with the normal amount of sheer storytelling work, work that is sometimes in the Zone and sometimes like chewing on marble mixed with occasional moments of high, unexpected pleasure at what I thought was an inspired scene or word or line of dialogue . . . that rare treat I get perhaps a dozen times in the course of writing a book, just for showing up at the computer every morning. Each novel was followed by PR and more PR.

The major difference was that I had matured as a professional novelist. *Scruples* was written with the blind courage and bravura of a neophyte. *Daisy* was written with an overwhelming desire to improve on *Scruples* in every way. *Mistral,* by far the most difficult challenge and my personal favorite, was written as a somewhat professional writer venturing deep into unknown territory and finally, in *I'll Take Manhattan,* I'd become confident enough in my ability to endure constant interruptions and let my main characters swing and have fun the way only my minor characters had been permitted to do earlier. The six novels that followed are those of a seasoned writer. I'm proud of them all.

Steve has made innumerable miniseries and movies of the week and fully regained his good humor. Nick and Tony grew up and became men, as sons inevitably will. Nick married Lynn Blocker and they have two children, eleven-year-old Michael, a fine young man, and seven-year-old Kate, who is my only female grandchild. Kate decidedly has the potential of a heroine-to-be, but a happy one at last. In fact, to my adoring eyes, she may well be a diva in the bud. I bet she'll never say, "If only . . ." Two months ago Tony married Kristin Dornig, so their children are yet to appear.

Perhaps there will be a girl or two among them. I've been forced to invent my own female heroes on paper, but another woman will have to create the real thing.

Next year, on February 19, 1999, Steve and I will be married for forty-five years. Now, there is a number—forty-five—that I simply do *not* comprehend. It's perfectly fine for me to be seventy, as I write these words, because I can't imagine myself as seventy, *whatever* seventy is supposed to be, but such an anniversary is serious business. Forty-five years! How on earth can we have lived together for so long and be enjoying it more and more every day? And why doesn't it seem long at all?

These later years of our marriage are infinitely more honest and more treasured, minute by minute, than the first ones were. We're more than two people who love each other, we're best friends whose friendship has managed to endure through thick and thin. We *know* how lucky we've been, something young people can't fully realize, even in the never-to-be-recaptured bliss of the beginning, because the future is still shrouded. Maybe the reason I couldn't make up my mind to marry Steve is that it was already made up and I just couldn't bring myself to admit it. That must be the reason why so many characters in my books often, and convincingly, fall in love at first sight.

Writing this memoir has been far more exciting to me than any novel I've ever written because I gave myself the freedom to talk about myself publicly, in the first person, in a way I've never dared to risk before.

I've unmasked myself. I've stopped hiding any themes or persistent inner dramas in the personae of my heroines or their best friends or worst enemies. I've taken my readers behind the scenes of my own life and left out nothing of importance. (And I resisted the impulse to tell some truly fabulous and freshly scandalous information I've picked up over the years in the different worlds I've had entry into, since it would have hurt people who are very much alive.) I've faced my constant litany of "should haves" and put them behind me as far as possible, part of the dance of life and my own degree of neurosis, which I hope is now no more than average. I've admitted my compulsive needs and realized I've outlived many of them. I can live with the others because I understand their power and it's a waste of energy to fight them. Besides, they don't bother anyone but me.

Most important of all, I've investigated whatever genetic, cultural, and ethnic roots I could find and reexamined the family constellation that has explained so much to me about why I am the way I am. Everything, including the painful parts, matters to me. I've accepted them. Would a woman who'd had easygoing, average parents and a sunny, popular, normal childhood, devoid of serious problems, and then grown older, leading an uneventful, conventional life, *want* to write novels? I strongly suspect that the difficulties I lived through are the elements in my life that finally made me a storyteller.

Looked at as a stream in which one thing led to another, the events of my life, and how I coped with them, tell me who I am. And a woman should have a clear idea of who she is. For better or worse, it's a solid satisfaction.